Wightridden:

Paths of Northern-Tradition Shamanism

Raven Kaldera

Wightridden:
Paths of Northern-Tradition Shamanism

Northern-Tradition Shamanism Book IV

Raven Kaldera

Hubbardston, Massachusetts

Asphodel Press
12 Simond Hill Road
Hubbardston, MA 01452

Wightridden:
Paths of Northern-Tradition Shamanism
Northern-Tradition Shamanism Book IV
© 2007 Raven Kaldera
ISBN 978-0-6151-3915-9

Cover art © 2007 Abby Helasdottir, http://www.gydja.com
Back cover photo © 2006 Sensuous Sadie

All rights reserved.
No part of this book may be reproduced in any form
or by any means without the permission of the author.

Printed in cooperation with
Lulu Enterprises, Inc.
860 Aviation Parkway, Suite 300
Morrisville, NC 27560

DEDICATED TO ALL
MY FELLOW SPIRIT-WORKERS,
WHEREVER THEY MAY BE.

Contents

Introduction: Northern-Tradition Shamanism 1
   Loki's Lesson 21
   The Eightfold Path In The Northern Tradition 25
   Freya's Lesson 40
Utiseta and Faring Forth: The Path of Meditation 43
   Journeying Tips From A Cosmic Diplomat 53
Recaning: The Path of Ritual 61
   A Northern-Tradition Approach to Ritual Work 75
   Recaning Song for Blessing Mugwort Sticks 80
The Heartbeat Of The Worlds: The Path Of Rhythm 83
   Trance Dancing in the Northern Tradition 104
   Drums of the Spirits 114
Greenwights: The Path of Sacred Plants 124
   The Little Red Man: Fly Agaric in History and Culture 159
A Finer Focus: The Ascetic's Path 165
   Fire and Water: Sauna Purification 201
   Hela's Lesson 218
The Body And The Tree: The Path of the Flesh 221
   Making The World Tree: An NT Sex Magic Technique 236
   Ergi: The Way of the Third 241
   An Open Letter To All Transgendered Spirit-Workers 277
   Jormundgand's Lessons 283
Blood And Fire: The Ordeal Path 288
   Odin's Lesson 318
   The Ordeal Rites of Odin 320
Open To The Divine: The Path of the Horse 345
   Horsing the Gods of the Northern Tradition 382
   Fenris's Lesson 397
Afterword: Half-Life 400

Introduction: Northern-Tradition Shamanism

First, the cleansing of the body—a long bath in salt water. Then the cleansing of the space with smoke of mugwort, the first of the sacred herbs. Then the wight-claimed one sits naked on a reindeer-skin, one of his totems, and asks the stones about the client who is yet to come. There will be a crisis; they never come to him unless there is a crisis. The stones fall, and he studies their pattern, their sigils, for a long time. Then he picks up the drum and begins the beat, bringing himself into a trance. For this one, the drum, the beats circling round until his head lolls back and sound comes from his throat.

But this is only the preliminary round. When the client is before him, when the question is asked, when the stones or sticks are thrown and the pattern laid out clearer, then the work will really begin. Which tools to use? They revolve at the fringes of his mind—sitting out, cloaked, journeying to another place to search for the answers? A ritual to cleanse or heal? A time of fasting and silence to find the inner center? Dancing around the fire until the void opens? The sacred plants and their spirits—will it be one of those dire times? Or perhaps just the fire of the body, brought forth by the sexual responses, or by pain and torment carefully applied to open the paths of the soul?

Or perhaps it will bypass him entirely, and a God will enter his body, to speak straight to the client while he lies unhearing in the depths of his being?

The tools lay before him, ready to be grasped. He turns over the central stone and nods; of course, it had to be this one. He knew it all along. Bowing his head, he salutes the Gods and wights who protect him, empower him, and force him ruthlessly down this path of his Wyrd.

This book is the fourth in my series dedicated to northern-tradition shamanism. For those who haven't read the first three, this tradition of shamanism is not the religion of the Viking-age Norse or Germanic peoples that is reconstructed from bits of Christianized lore in the modern Nordic reconstructionist religions. This spiritual practice is what spirit-workers of that area did centuries, perhaps millennia, before that. It is written nowhere in the paltry existing scraps of lore, because it was an oral tradition in an age without books, mostly if not entirely lost well before the first chroniclers began to write about the already-fading Pagan beliefs. This tradition is reconstructed entirely from teachings gained directly from the Gods and wights who still speak to us, still connect with us, still teach us things that are found nowhere in books ... until now.

Many northern-tradition spirit-workers and shamans donated their words to this book, and I can only be grateful to them all, because our shared perspective is greater than that of any single one. By pooling our knowledge, we taught each other further, and I am honored to be the one to commit all this to paper and publications. As much of this information is spirit-taught, this is the first time that some of it has ever been committed to paper, or even put into words.

The first book in this series, *The Jotunbok: Working With The Giants In The Northern Tradition*, was written partly because there were so few writings about the Jotunfolk, and their Gods the Rökkr. However, there was another reason as well: When doing northern-tradition shamanism, all too often you bypass the Aesir and Vanir and run into the Jotnar holding that thread. (Exceptions are Frey, Freya, and of course Odin the shaman-king.) This lends credence to the supposition that the Jotnar are the Gods of the pre-Indo-European people, who most certainly had a shamanic culture. Therefore, it made sense to start with them.

The second book in the series, *Pathwalker's Guide To The Nine Worlds*, was written as a guide for those journeying in the Norse/Germanic cosmology. Its appearance was a little out of order, considering that journeying is a fairly advanced technique, but it grew out of a nine-day pathwalking trip that I did through the Nine Worlds, and of course being a writer I brought a journal with me and recorded my adventures. Then some friends read the journal and begged me to put it up on a website, and of course I then had to write explanatory chapters for the Nine Worlds, and what was journeying and pathwalking anyway, or no one would be able to understand it. Before I knew it, it was the length of a book and strangers were emailing me, asking when it would be available in print. So I did it, but at that point I was aware that there needed to be books describing techniques. Otherwise we were all going to be reinventing the wheel with our own wight-guides, isolated in our bedrooms across the world, and not knowing that someone else struggled with this and managed to find a way.

The third and fourth books in this series, *Wyrdwalkers: Techniques of Northern-Tradition Shamanism* and *Wightridden: Paths of Northern-Tradition Shamanism* are being published simultaneously, because they were meant to be one book but became so huge as to require two. Thus, if you've read this introduction in one of them, don't bother to read it now. Jump ahead to the meat of the information, unless you feel that you need a refresher. This is really just for the folks who are picking this up at a yard sale and saying, "What the heck is this about?"

Actually, the first thing that's likely to confuse them is the issue of northern-tradition shamanism itself. These days, at least in America where I write, shamanism is almost synonymous with Native American spirituality; even the "neo-shamanisms" that can be bought for many hundreds of dollars and that claim to be above any single tradition are basically stolen Native American flavors. The idea that "white people" might actually have their own ancestral shamanism is something that most people don't know about. However, if you go back far enough in any ancestral direction, you will hit pre-agricultural hunter/gatherer/herder tribes for whom shamanism was their daily religion. Most of those religions have been obscured by the smoke of history, but they existed, and the spirits remember. It's time for us to remember, too.

Questions About Northern-Tradition Shamanism

What do you mean by shamanism? Why do you use that word?

I use the word because it is the closest word my birth language has for what I have experienced, what I am expected to do, and what I have become. It is a word that has been borrowed from the Tungus language, but it fills an important hole in our language. For more information on how I feel about the word and its common uses, see the article *Public Horses*. (http://www.cauldronfarm.com/nts.html)

My definition of shamanism is "a spiritual and magical practice that involves working with spirits and is designed to serve a tribe". It's distinct from thaumaturgic magic, which is working magically with directed energy, or theurgic magic, which is working with divinely inspired symbol systems like runes. This is working with Entities, and that's a whole different ball game. Shamanism is also distinct from religion proper, because while it is certainly a spiritual practice, and has always traditionally been embedded in a religious cosmology, it is a practical discipline that serves the people in concrete ways—healing, divining, channeling, and generally enhancing people's lives.

"Shamanism" as a term can be compared to "monasticism"; while it is almost always found embedded in a religious context, it is not a religion per se. It could also be compared to "spiritual scholarship"; which is similar to but distinct from nonreligious scholarship, and also cannot be called "a religion".

In shamanism, it's all about the Entities with whom you have formed relationships. Some of those relationships may be akin to spiritual slavery, in that one deity (it's usually a deity) has grabbed you and made you their tool, while granting you certain powers and protections; as an example, I work for Hela, and she both protects me and forces me to do Her work. Some of these relationships may look like alliances between a superior (deity) and an inferior (mortal), where each agree to provide certain favors in an exchange; as an example, I horse Herne and Frey for the community on one day apiece each year, and in exchange they gift me with certain powers and protections. Some of these relationships may be alliances between equal powers; as an example, I work with many of the Grandparent spirits of herbs and plants for purposes of healing. Some relationships may be the (ideally) consenting use of a smaller spirit in order to borrow some power or trait; as an example, a friend of mine has bad eyesight and "borrows" the vision of her pet rats when she has to go out at night. Regardless of the level of power exchange, it's all about keeping those relationships well-greased and humming along.

Shamanism is also distinct from mysticism in that it is goal-oriented and work-focused. The mystic may share many of the same techniques, especially the altered-state techniques, but his focus is on pure experience. If you ask him, "What good is this? What's it useful for?" he will probably just smile and tell you that it has its own goodness which you have to experience to understand. For the mystic, it's between him and the Universe. For the shaman, the question "What's it useful for?" is all-important. As the servant of a tribe, rather than as a sole quester for oneness with the All, the shaman has to stop short of entirely merging with the Divine Web and instead find ways to make these experiences useful to the betterment of his people. In some ways, it's much more of a bodhisattva than a Buddha path, although the point is not getting everyone off the Wheel of Life and Death. Shamanism is set in a context that values all worlds equally, and sees body and flesh and blood and Earth as sacred; the point is to make things easier for people here and now. Therefore, shamanism is intensely practical, making use of every tool of "ecstasy", as the anthropologists like to call it, in order to make actual change in the world.

(An excellent comparison of the Path of Mystic Quest with the Path of Shamanic Mediation, as the author refers to them, can be found in the book *Six Ways Of Being Religious*, by Dale Cannon. While the book only uses Christian and Buddhist examples, the projected paths can be easily seen in modern Paganism as well.)

What do you mean by Northern-Tradition? Where do these traditions come from?

They come from many sources—Germanic (and Anglo-Saxon, which is part of that); Norse; a little bit of Saami; and a little bit of Siberian. They are from the circumpolar peoples of the western Eurasian continent. Some seem to go back as far as the Mesolithic or Neolithic pre-Indo-European people of northern Europe. Some comes from books, lore, research, but most of it comes from the Gods and spirits that are training me and others like me. Occasionally, some will come from that source and then later I discover them in books.

Is this part of the religions referred to as Asatru, Vanatru, Heathenry, etc.?

No, it is not. Those are reconstructionist religions of the beliefs of the Viking-Age Scandinavian people. They are generally based mostly or entirely on the surviving lore about that religion. While this tradition shares many of the same deities and myths, it is different in that it is a spiritual practice, not a religion (as is all shamanism), and it is not based on written records, nor is it technically reconstructionist. If it falls within any religious demographic, one could loosely say that it might be a part of northern-tradition Paganism, which is still a vague term generally referring to reconstructionist-derived northern-European Neo-Paganism, but as those borders are still being defined, we'll just say that northern-tradition shamanism is not part of reconstructionist Heathenry, by their own definition, and leave it at that.

Wait a minute. I'm a scholar, and I was under the impression that the Norse/Germanic peoples of the lore did not have shamans or a shamanic culture.

You are quite correct. The people of the "lore era" didn't even have an entirely pagan culture any more, much less a shamanic one. They had been converted to Christianity. Even if there were still a few heathens tucked away in odd corners, the writers of the books—and the dominant culture—was Christian. To minimize this is to make the mistake of absorbing a lot of Christian values along with your Heathen lore.

There was once a shamanic tribal culture in all of these areas. It was mostly gone well before the Christians converted everyone. Bits and pieces and glimpses of it can be seen and patchworked together, but we don't have a full picture of it from any written lore. That's what I mean when I say that it is lost, and why I have to be spirit-taught it. Of course, the Saami and Siberian peoples have shamans to this day, and there was a good deal of marrying back and forth.

Is this stuff like *seidhr*?

Seidhr is the term for one of the magical practices that was still in use during the late Iron Age, the time that is used by religious reconstructionists. It is likely that it has strong shamanic roots, and that many of its tools are a holdover from earlier shamanism, and/or learned from the Saami *noaidi*. There has been a lot of argument and debate over that, among academics and practitioners of *seidhr* alike, as well as argument over whether the word *seidhr* should be restricted to the sort of oracular performance that the volva does in *Eiriks saga Raude*, or whether it should extend to other sorts of magic too, and which sorts.

I choose not to enter that debate. Yes, what you'll find here has some things in common with what some *seidhr*-practitioners are doing, and in fact some of them contributed generously to this work. On the other hand, some practices written here are not found anywhere in the lore as being concretely and beyond a shadow of a doubt part of the *seidhr* complex of magic, as they likely died out centuries or millennia previously. So I do not claim the word, any more than I would claim the words *Asatru*, *Heathen*, or *reconstructionist*. This is a form of wight-taught ancient shamanism, and that's all.

Why don't you stick to information that is already written down? What's wrong with sticking to the lore?

Well, the Gods and spirits that I work with don't see it that way. If every time they told me to do something, I objected, "But wait! I can't do that unless you show me where it's written down in a book, preferably with an author who has an entire page of academic credentials," well, let's just say that it would get ugly real fast. So I use the lore as a jumping-off point, and then I keep going. In the meantime, I keep reading, because sometimes I find something that I've already been told to do. It's nice to be validated in that way, but it's not necessary. I'd do it anyway. I can't afford to be lorebound, not with Gods and wights on my tail.

Except for places where certain contributing authors have given me whole essays with references, you won't find footnotes and references throughout this book, either. That's because such things contribute to the idea that this might be an academic research work, if a poor one, and I have no desire to enable that misunderstanding. These books fall into another category entirely, and I am very clear about that. Although I may mention subjects that I ran across in research, this book is primarily material gathered through the experiences of myself and others. We *are* the primary source material.

Aren't you ripping off these ancient peoples and their cultures?

Since these are my ancestors, I would say that I have a fairly solid right to do what I'm doing, if you use the argument that one's ancestral traditions are an inheritance. Frankly, though, I'd do this even if they weren't my ancestors. I do it not because it is any kind of politically correct, but because that's what the Goddess who owns me and the Spirits who work with me say that I have to do. If I had been grabbed up by, say, Native American gods and spirits, I'd be doing that path even though I don't have a drop of that blood, and I'd just have to find a way to deal with the opprobrium that would be heaped upon me.

Besides, the Gods and wights don't give two rat's asses about what I may think that I'm ripping off. However, I can actually imagine "ripping off the past" in a way that would be disrespectful, and it is already practiced by some groups. It consists of doing reconstructionist religion without actually believing wholly in the Gods of our ancestors; one does their practices, but merely pretends to believe in their Gods. It's a twisted, blasphemous kind of ancestor worship. But anyone who wholeheartedly believes in our Gods, and worships them with sincerity, isn't ripping off anyone. They are giving back.

What do you mean, "spirit-taught"?

The Buryat Mongols have a word for shamans who are spirit-taught—it's *bagshagui*. Usually this happens when the shaman's lineage or clan dies out and the spirits who have worked with them all move over to another line or clan, and pick some poor slob that they have decided would make a great shaman. A *bagshagui* doesn't have the benefit of the old guy in the hut to teach them. Everything has to be learned from the spirits themselves, who are wonderfully effective but extremely frustrating teachers.

Since this tradition is largely lost, I as a white American don't have the old-guy-in-the-hut benefit either. I am in the service of the Norse death goddess Hela, and she sends me to various other gods and spirits for training. It's often spotty and confusing, but sometimes it is amazing. As I learn, I write it down. I am aware that I may have to teach someone else someday.

I've studied a different shamanic tradition from elsewhere in the world, and while there may be some things in common with this tradition, there are a lot of things that you say are true which that tradition doesn't find to be true at all.

That's very much the case, and at no time do I mean to speak for any tradition other than my own. If nothing else, I don't know enough about them. I haven't seen them from the inside, and known them intimately, and lived their patterns. So from here on in, anywhere you see me talk about any sort of shamanism, you may assume that I am referring to *the way it is in this tradition*, regardless of how it is in any other one. There just doesn't seem to be any point in disclaiming every instance of that.

While I like the tales of the Gods and spirits of your tradition, I'm not sure that I believe in them. Can I still practice this tradition if I believe that they are archetypes, or energy forms created by human attention?

No. You cannot. Sorry, I'm going to have to be hardline on this one.

This is a polytheistic spiritual tradition. No way to get around that one. Not only do you have to believe fully and thoroughly in these Gods and wights in order to really practice it, if you come at them with any less than complete faith in their existence, they may be offended and refuse to deal with you ... and for this tradition, it's all about dealing with the spirits. No spirits, no luck. Not only are they all real, they are all distinct from each other as well.

If you are not comfortable with polytheistic belief, perhaps you might prefer working with a more ceremonial-magic system, such as Thelema or the Golden Dawn. If you are drawn to Norse stuff, there is a sect of Norse-style ceremonial magic that combines the two. However, it is not shamanism. I realize that some neo-shamanistic workshops downplay the literal existence of spirits and allow people to reserve their disbelief. That's fine for them, but not for us. If you can't fully embrace the religious and devotional aspects of this tradition of shamanism, don't practice it. Find something that fits better with your world view; there are plenty of them out there.

Why should I believe you about any of this? Isn't it possible that you are delusional?

There's no reason at all for you to believe me. In fact, it would be unreasonable of me to expect it, considering that you haven't experienced what I have experienced. It's as unreasonable as expecting you to believe in any god that hasn't talked to you personally. If you'd like to decide that I am full of it, it's no skin off my nose. The only reason I'm laying it out for total strangers anyway is because Hela wants me to make this information available.

Can I learn this tradition even if these aren't my ancestors?

Sure, knock yourself out. I'm not sensitive about it. If the spirits are calling you, who am I to argue? If it's just that you're drawn to it, it won't hurt anything. After all, the more people who know it, the better. I'm not one of those who believes that the Gods and wights choose people only from these bloodlines—I've seen them pick out too many who weren't even white to believe that one. They take who They take, and who am I to criticize?

What is different about northern-tradition shamanism compared to other cultural forms of shamanism? Or, for that matter, modern northern-tradition religious faiths?

Well, for one thing, we have no rattles. Seriously, the first big difference in the former category is that it deals largely with the Gods and wights of Norse/Germanic pantheons rather than the spirits of various aboriginal religions. Occasionally you might get referred to a deity outside of this tradition, because a few of our Gods are like that, but mostly it's working with the three pantheons of this tradition. There are a myriad of other little cultural differences as well, which are too many to list here.

Where this tradition peels away from modern reconstructionist Norse religion is in the matter of timing. Much of modern Heathenry is reconstructed from a particular era in the early medieval Iron Age. Even before the onslaught of Christianity, it was not a shamanic culture, although a few bits and pieces survived in myth and seidhwork. The shamanic culture and practices had largely died out centuries before, although they were still going strong next door in Finland among the

Saami people and further east among the Siberians. Long ago, however, there was once a circumpolar set of shamanic traditions that shared much in common, more even than the shamanic cultures of other parts of the world. If we go back to the Mesolithic or Neolithic era, we find the Indo-Europeans overrunning an indigenous Scandinavian people, and it seems to those of us who are spirit-workers that the original deities of those people were the wights now referred to as Jotun, or Giantkind.

The various waves of Indo-European people brought the agricultural Vanir, and later the warrior sky-god Aesir, and the early gods were relegated to the villainous position, much like the Greek Titans. Yet if you study them, you find that they are extremely Neolithic and shamanic in nature—elemental, shapeshifting, animal-like, multitudinous, partaking of fire and ice and trees and ocean and sacred mountain, wielding stone blades and dark, bloody powers. In the myths, whenever there is an underworld journey, there is a giantess or a Rökkr god involved. When you come to the Northern Tradition and start pulling the string labeled "shamanism", four times out of five you'll get the Jotnar, or the Rökkr Gods (Hela, Loki, Surt, Fenris, Jormundgand, Angrboda, etc.) at the other end. That's why so many of the "deity-lessons" in the third book, *Wyrdwalkers*, are from the Jotun point of view, rather than mostly the Aesir. These are the Gods and wights that my ancestors worshiped and worked with when they lived in a shamanic culture, and they know more than anyone about this kind of work.

However, they are not the only deities who take an interest in such things. When someone gets pulled into this tradition and their patron is one of the Vanir, it's most likely to be Freya, with Frey as a close second. Freya is the mistress of seidhr, the magical tradition that survived into the Iron Age and which had many shamanic elements, perhaps left over from the early days. She is not only sex goddess and sacred whore, fertility maiden and warrior-woman, she is also the witchy-woman with the magic comb and net who knows how to sing her way into a journeying-trance. Freya and Frey are the repository of that shamanic knowledge which combined with the early sacrificial agricultural religion, creating its own flavor of shamanism which survived piecemeal into the

Viking Age. It should be noted that when golden sacrificial-king Frey is the patron of a shaman, the individual is likely to be a gay or bisexual man. There are at least two "cults" of Frey, and one is the faithful husbandman and farmer with a wife and children who has no need of this book. The other path of Frey is that of the (slightly to very) effeminate shaman/priest with his skirt hemmed with tinkling bells, and this is the Freysman who is most likely to go down this road.

When the patron is Aesir, there is only one deity for the shaman to look to: Odin. The All-Father of Asgard is the archetypal shaman-king, warrior and wanderer, magician and ruler, who learned his shamanic magic on a long nine-year ordeal from Freya, Mimir, the Norns, and other older wights. While he comes by it third-generation, so to speak, his talents in this area are nothing to sneeze at. If you're an Asatru and you get dragged down this path, it is Odin who will take you there—ravens, wolves, ordeals, and all.

What sorts of things did northern-tradition spirit-workers do in ancient times? How is it different from what they do now?

In ancient times, spirit-workers—be they shamans, volvas, seidhr-workers, noaidi, etc.—did a variety of things to help their people survive. They called the wild animals for hunting and the reindeer for herding. They called fish into rivers and close to seacoasts. They made sacrifices to make sure the crops grew. They did healing of various sorts—magical and herbal together—for the sick. They did divination for individuals and the tribe, especially when things went wrong, and figured out who had to be propitiated in order to set things right. They named children. They put people through ordeals of passage. They altered the weather. They made women and men fertile. They blessed those who needed blessings. They cleansed evil places. They protected the tribe from destructive spirits and the shamans of other tribes. They talked to the Dead, and to the Gods and spirits, and mediated for the community between these worlds.

They also did a lot of things that were destructive themselves. They fought in battles, charming weapons and calling in spirits to aid their side. They helped warriors to shapeshift into fierce animals. They magically attacked the other side's warriors, and sometimes the members of neighboring tribes who were encroaching on territory. They left their bodies in order to do reconaissance for their chieftains. They drove people mad. They made vengeance magic and curses for people who paid them, and this, too, was accepted and considered right and loyal. In fact, they probably did as much of the latter as of the former types of magic.

Today, many of these things are no longer useful, which is why I don't have a hunting drum. However, there are still many things that my ancestral spirit-workers did that I also do, including divination of all sorts, untangling people's bad luck and fate, healing, doing ordeals of passage, cleansing spoiled places, and talking to the Dead. I still fare forth on errands to Otherworlds like them, and I still mediate between the inhabitants of those worlds and of this one.

Why did you name this book Wightridden?

The terms "riding" and "ridden" have a number of interesting correlations in northern magic, as well as other areas in the world. On the one hand, some modern northern-tradition practitioners have borrowed the terms "horse" for someone who opens their body to spirit-possession and God-possession (and "rider" for the God or wight involved) from the Afro-Caribbean religions, because it's useful, and because many of us independently went to them for teaching when we discovered that the modern Pagan community had few resources for people to whom this was already happening. That's one facet of the word.

On the other hand, the term "rider" was also associated with some forms of magic-working in Old Norse. A *volva* or *vitki* was said to "ride" someone as a kind of magical attack, causing damage ranging from bad dreams to injury and death. Sometimes they would temporarily possess their victims and make them run headlong into danger in the middle of the night, sometimes the attack would just make them sleepwalk in a panic into a ditch or thornbush. It wasn't unusual for someone who was "ridden" in this way to be found the next morning scratched and cut up, naked outside their homes. Terms for the magic-workers who did such things were *kveldrida* (evening-rider), *myrkrida* (darkness-rider), *kaldrida* (cold-rider), *trollridur* (giant-rider, suggesting that such powers were learned from the giants, or perhaps that they were possessed by giants), and *munnrida* (mouth-rider, referring to someone who could only do this verbally).

Another meaning of the term refers to the volva or vitki riding about on a magical spirit-steed to do such things, usually a wolf or boar. Terms for this are *kveldriduhestr* (evening-rider's steed), and *leiknar hestr* (giant's steed). Yet another refers directly to the "rider" being an aspect of the sender's own soul, sent to do something to someone else's soul—thus the term *thradrida* (thread-rider) and *tunridur* (fence-rider, suggesting the same sort of liminal space as evening-rider) mentioned in the Havamal. There are even ancient law codes against sorcery that forbid practitioners from "riding on a farm-gate with your hair let down and in troll shape, when it is between day and night."

On of the first things that a spirit-worker learns upon becoming such is that their life slowly becomes, by degrees, no longer their own. Various otherworldly beings constantly interfere with you, telling you how this job is to be done, and for some folk it is expected to be their main work. For some of us, the wights do come into our bodies and ride us to one extent or another; for all of us, they ride our Threads, and we are expected to deal with the Threads of our clients in turn. We walk in the liminal spaces between worlds—riding that which is neither night nor day. Some of us send out parts of our souls to do work; others bond with external beings. We ride the fence, constantly. To be Wightridden is both to be a steed and to be a rider, depending on who you are dealing with at the moment. It is also about being Open to either, and this book explores the ways in which we learn to be so Open.

Can I learn to be a shaman from reading and practicing your stuff?

No. You cannot. Only the Gods and wights can make a shaman. You can, however, learn to be a shamanic practitioner. If you are already being harassed by the Gods and spirits, then you'll be a shaman if and when They say you're one, and you have all my sympathy for what has happened or will probably happen to you.

On the other hand, there's nothing wrong with being a perfectly good shamanic practitioner, and you may well find some useful points in this book.

What's the difference between a shaman and a shamanic practitioner?

Keeping in mind that the answer *is true only for this tradition* (i.e. other shamanic traditions may draw the line in other places), a shaman is someone who is seized up by the spirits and forced through a long and tortuous phase of illness that brings them close to physical death, or complete insanity, or both. During this time, the Gods and wights modify their astral body in ways that you'd have to be close to death in order to manage. Most tribal cultures acknowledge that there is an attrition rate—i.e. there's a definite risk of death, which is worse the more the beginning shaman fights the process. Once through, they must do their job of public tribal spirit-worker for the rest of their life, or the shaman sickness will occur and cause insanity and/or death. Their lives are bounded by taboos, and they work closely with spirits of many different types, sometimes as a slave, sometimes as a partner.

On the other hand, a shamanic practitioner is someone who learns shamanic techniques, and perhaps has some voluntary dealings with spirits, and does what they do because they want to, not because they have to. It's much easier, and safer, to be a shamanic practitioner, although there are a small number of people who start out in the latter category and end up in the former one. A classic shaman, however, will be able to channel heavier "voltage" and do more intense spirit-work, and have a closer connection with the spirits. They just had to give up their entire life for that ability.

Can I force or coax the Gods and wights into making me a shaman?

Force? Not likely. Coax? That depends. It has been done, in the past; some people have deliberately brought themselves repeatedly very close to death in a ritual context in order to get the attention of the spirits. Some died. Some survived, but insane. Some got the attention that they desired and became shamans, but were so mentally scarred that the ensuing shaman sickness killed them. A few made it. Generally, though, most people wouldn't want to be classic shamans if they really understand what that meant. These books will tell of what it's like in this tradition, this harsh and bloody subarctic tradition that bore so many of my ancestors. They were chosen so that their people might survive. If you are chosen, you will serve some form of a tribe—possibly not of your choosing—for the rest of your life, and that work will come before everything else. Not your parents, your children, your partners, or any other career will take anything but a back seat to this Work. If you slack off, you'll become ill. If you quit, you'll die. We don't joke about this; we've seen too many go down.

If this is you, welcome to the Boot Camp of the Northern Gods. We hope that you survive, but that will depend on your relationship with Them. In the meantime, here's a textbook for you, perhaps the only written one you'll ever get. Don't mistake it for the important information. That, only They will give you. This is only the syllabus, the course outline, the notes scribbled down in the back of the class. But here, take my shaman's notebook. At the end of the day, it might just give you the keys to get through a few thorns.

Shamanism and Service
by Lydia Helasdottir

If you look at the wandering Volva in Erik The Red's Saga, the concept is quite an interesting one—she's welcomed in, but there's all this "When is she leaving?" They go to a lot of trouble for her, ritual trouble, with feeding her the hearts of every animal on the property, in part because they want to propitiate her because she's scary, and in part because they want her to be on her way as quickly as possible. So I think spirit-workers end up feeling used, a lot, but that's part of the deal. We are set apart and used, and it's part of the power. I think that's hard for people to understand; they think that in the perfect tribal world the shaman would be just like the smith or the potmaker, just another job, but they have to be set apart.

There's a story about a young girl in a Native American Plains community who got hit by lightning. People who got hit by lightning were supposed to be blessed and taken by the spirits, but they were also supposed to die, taken by Sky Father or what-have-you. But she didn't die, so the people didn't know quite what to make of her, because here was this being that Sky Father had touched, but she wasn't dead, so was she now bad luck or good luck? So she ended up living in this tent outside the village with her door open away from the village, but they would still bring her food, because they didn't dare not to. She told about how she then began to get bitten by poisonous animals and not die.

It really is part of the deal, though—we are equally respected, and feared, and loathed, and admired ... and admired is the least on the list, occasionally. Some tribes had no compunctions about killing off their shamans if the things they were doing weren't working. So however bad it is now, one is glad to not have to deal with that. There is also the modern issue that people who are outsiders for other reasons decide that they like the shaman job because it's at least about being a powerful outsider, whether or not it's really for them. (I'm quite comfortable with people doing shamanic practices, but this does not make them a shaman.) Most of them don't really understand that you're still tied to the tribe, to the service position, even though they fear you and don't appreciate you. You can't just up and leave, unless the spirits are sending you to another tribe. You have to keep offering your help again and again, even though you will never really be one of them. It's a painful, awful, thankless place to be in, and that's the way of it. Do you really want that job? Most people wouldn't, if they understood that.

But it's absolutely necessary, because the power that you're gaining is so large that if you were not constrained to use it in a service situation, you'd just turn into a power-greedy maniac. There are stories of shamans who go bad, and they tend not to live too long, but they can get up to some bad stuff in the meantime. There are medieval stories about how the shamans and the casters of magic darts were in collusion, because as long as the casters of magic darts were there, the shamans could be called to fix whatever damage the casters had done. This was pretty convoluted, but since the writer was writing in the 1400's it was kind of understandable.

But you can't escape from the service job. No matter how arrogant shaman-people may appear, in the end, you're just humping a sack for a group of people who need the service ... most of whom are ungrateful wankers, who you can't turn down. (Although you can sometimes get some choice as to priority. "OK, I've got fifteen wankers here, which one of them is the least annoying? Maybe the day will be done by the time I have to get to the most annoying and he'll go away, because his problem will be miraculously resolved.") It's similar to the bodhisattva oath, and to the ceremonial magic idea of sacrificing everything into the cup. It's not about you. You look at the shaman role from the outside, and you think "Wow, there's all this power, and this ability to cause awe and do cool shit—heal shit and blow shit up and what-have-you." And the shaman says, "Well, yeah, but..."

I sometimes talk about it like being in the army. Yeah, you get to drive a big tank and carry a gun and look tough, but most of the time it involves eating bad food and not getting enough sleep and crawling through the mud, and you can only blow up what they tell you to blow up, and if you blow up the stuff that you want to blow up, you get court-martialed and shot, and you have to account for every round of ammo, and they might send you into wars you don't agree with, and that's too bad. While it's cool to walk into the bar in your fatigues and camo with your gun over your shoulder, in reality you're just a grunt. And if you walk into the bar with all that stuff, you're a wanker grunt as well! For me, my patron deity just says, "Make sure you carry the ID, but don't be walking around in all that stuff." Of course, it also depends on what the uniform for your job is. Some of us have to wear the crazy uniform and be the community model for what a shaman looks like. Others of us get to be stealth and look normal, except when we need to do our work. It takes both kinds, working from the outside and the inside as well. But we're all outsiders, in the end. It's part of our power. It's lonely, and dark, and absolutely necessary. We are the sacrifice made that humanity might live on.

Loki's Lesson

To Thine Own Self Be True

transcribed by Elizabeth Vongvisith

 I made a journey to Helheim, and when I had come to Hela's realm, she told me that a test awaited me which Loki had asked her to give me while I was in the Land of the Dead. This brief and simple trial and its true meaning lay at the center of many of my subsequent experiences with Loki and my work, journeying at his or Hela's behest into one or another of the Nine Worlds.

 I was shown a table upon which rested many hearts of birds, beasts, fish, insects and other beings, all alive and beating. When I held my hand out over any one of them, I could see what kind of creature the heart belonged to. Hela told me that I was to choose one of these. I would then become that creature in a sense, and take on its attributes as my own. I stood there for a long time examining the hearts on the table until I found one which showed me my own face. There were many others that I was drawn to—a crow's heart, the heart of a luna moth, a fox's heart—all of which would have given me some tie to an animal that I felt kinship with, or so I believed. But again and again I kept coming back to the one which showed me myself. "I choose this," I said at last, picking up the heart.

 "Are you certain?" Hela asked, and I nodded, waiting for something magical and dramatic to happen, but there was nothing. I didn't even feel different. All the hearts on the table simply vanished, and Hela began to speak of other things. Later, when I came out of Helheim, Loki was waiting for me, pleased as punch. "You made the right choice, my dear," he said. "You chose your own heart, and therefore you chose to remain exactly what you are, which is what I wish you to be.

 I could not have passed this trial had I not already gained a certain amount of self-knowledge. That understanding of my own inner motives, psyche, and personality were what had allowed me to accept the Gods' active presence in my life in the first place, instead of telling myself it was all wishful thinking or that I needed to check myself into the local psychiatric ward. Loki, of course, is never satisfied with doing things halfway, and in the years since this incident, he has forced me to understand and accept every little bit of myself, sometimes quite painfully. One of the many valuable lessons I've learned from him is that no matter what else you may try to pass yourself off as, you should always remember who you really are.

Some may find this an odd lesson, coming from a god who is not exactly celebrated for his honest dealings with others, but as he is faithful to his contrary trickster nature, Loki demands of all of those who would learn from him that no matter what else we might do, we do not lie to ourselves, and furthermore, we do not apologize for being true to ourselves, even if we haven't been true to much else. Sometimes that may even mean doing things that upset, alarm, or anger other people, but it is up to your own conscience how you choose to treat those around you. Loki won't tell you not to lie or refrain from using other people's assumptions against them; that would be hypocritical, and if there is one thing that Flame-Hair is not, it is a hypocrite. But he expects nothing less from his folk than total self-knowledge and the ability to trust your own judgment against all other outside evidence, so-called common sense, and well-meaning advice, when necessary. And after all, how can you hope to use the truth to your own advantage when you're operating under a load of self-delusion?

Loki's Lesson:

I am called the Lie-Smith, and I will play with your devotion to mere appearances and your own misguided assumptions as if they were my toys, until you can remove them beyond my reach or destroy them entirely. I will teach you that truth is entirely a matter of perspective, and that there is neither fiction nor falsehood that is worth compromising yourself for. I will make you understand the real nature of the world, beginning with your own heart, mind, and soul. Otherwise, nothing else I have to say to you, false or not, will have any meaning at all.

I expect nothing less than that you understand yourself utterly, whatever else you may choose to show or tell others. If you cannot see your real nature clearly, you cannot lie without binding yourself in your own snares, nor will your honesty have any worth when the times comes to be honest. Without self-knowledge, you will not be able to wear the form or appearance of another without dimming the flame at your own center, and you will never realize that these things are only masks to be put on or taken off at will or whim, rather than out of habit or weakness. If there is only one person in all the Nine Worlds to whom you never lie, let that one be yourself.

I can teach you to cover your tracks and conceal your destination, but I cannot show you how unless you first come to me stripped bare of all the flattery, abuse, illusion, and fantasy with which you have shielded your real self from yourself. There is no way to teach you how to stretch the truth if your whole existence is already a lie. You will not learn how to blur the line between falsehood and reality if you are not certain on which side of the line you already stand ... and I will not be gentle when the time comes for you to discover all this.

I will rip the veils of deception from before your eyes and make you look upon those parts of your innermost self of which you are most fearful or ashamed. I will hold up a mirror that will show you, in every minute detail, the real shape of your weaknesses as well as your strengths. I will say to you all the things you have never dared to say to yourself, and make you repeat them after me. I will burn away every ounce of self-indulgence or denial from your soul, no matter how much it hurts. You may curse me, you may even hate me, but you will not be allowed to say no to me ... and I will wait patiently—oh yes, I can be patient—for you to understand, too, that you must accept yourself as you are before you can change yourself, or other people's minds, or the world. I have done all three, and I speak from experience.

I may even show you your unwelcome reality, whether you're making an effort or not. I have done it when it cost me that which I held most dear, when those I counted as friends and kinsmen turned against me and cried that I was forsworn because they would not see what had to be done. I have done it knowing all the while that to act otherwise would be to really become the liar I was accused of being. I have been more than honest in my deceit than many have in what they consider complete truthfulness, because no matter how much I may lie to others, I do not lie to myself, and I will not allow you to continue lying to yourself, as long as we are acquainted.

I have been other than what I seemed, and seemed other than what I am. I have told the truth as if it were a lie, and lied so convincingly that it was taken for the truth. I may dazzle and conceal, flatter and omit, but there are no blinders around my own eyes, no pretty insubstantial words in my own ears. I know why I have acted as I have acted and spoken what I have spoken, even when I have taken pains never to let those reasons become known. In doing this, I have accepted the punishments as well as the rewards, the pain as well as the satisfaction, and I will demand nothing more of you than I have been willing to endure myself. Otherwise, you will not get very far, and I will laugh when the curtain comes up and your costume is still only half on.

The Eightfold Path
In The Northern Tradition

One of the differences between shamanic work and other sorts of energy work is that sooner of later, altered states of consciousness are required. This is partly because shamanic work is not only working with energy (like thaumaturgic magic) or with universal paths (like theurgic magic) but working with entities. In order to properly perceive and deal with the wights, you need to go into a state of consciousness that brings you closer to them. The more dramatic and serious the work, the more extreme the altered state needs to be. Even people who are good at going into mild altered states—the sort who trance out easily—will sooner or later find that they need to go further and deeper if they take up shamanic work.

A large part of the "basic" shamanic training is learning how to control one's state of consciousness at will, whatever that takes. Fortunately, our ancestors spent thousands of years working out a wide and varied array of altered-state technologies; much of the research work has already been done for us. These techniques have been sorted into a system referred to as the "Eightfold Path", or eight groups of similar techniques. (This is not to be confused with the Buddhist Eightfold Path, which is entirely a different thing.) To be fair, this terminology is not at all northern-tradition; it comes out of various ceremonial magic systems. I use it because it is excellent for talking about these paths to altered states, in spite of its origins.

There is also good deal of debate over what the "real", authentic, correct Eightfold Path contains. You'll find several versions of it in books about altered states; it seems that the most radically different versions seem to be those where the authors disapprove of some of the paths and conveniently eliminate them, splitting up others to fill in the gaps. The version that I explicate here is the one that is the most relevant and accurate for northern-tradition shamanism. All eight of these techniques were used somewhere at some point by my ancestors; I will be discussing all of them regardless of how controversial they are in today's modern society.

I should also say up front that no one "spoke" of this wheel is better or worse than any others. Some are admittedly somewhat less safe, but the truth is that none of them are perfectly safe. There is no way to make shamanic work safe, and anyone who says otherwise is either lying or not teaching actual shamanic techniques. Given that, the Ordeal Path and the Path of Sacred Plants are currently on the most-unwanted-bogeymen list in our modern commercial American culture. Part of this is because too many people ignorantly abused the tools of these paths and messed themselves up. Part of it is because they are simply the scariest-looking, externally, and the most likely to put you in the emergency room if you're careless and stupid. I don't claim that there is an easy way to travel down any of the eight paths, but these two require special care. They are dangerous, and every step must be taken with alertness, mindfulness, and mental discipline. You're not supposed to master them in one hundred-dollar afternoon workshop. There are people who train for years to be able to use these paths regularly. Approach them with the respect they deserve, or you'll end up injuring or killing yourself.

To say that these are all legitimate shamanic paths does not mean that every shaman or shamanic practitioner can or ought to practice all of these. I've only very rarely met people who had done all eight, and no one who used all of them with any sort of regularity. The reason that there are so many is because most people—and that includes most shamans and shamanic practitioners—will not be able to access all of these paths. Most use only one to three of them in their work. Some use as many as four or five, but usually a couple of those will be reserved for occasions when extra power is needed. Don't feel that you have to be good at them all; I'm certainly not. There are some that I seem to be "wired" for and some that simply don't work for me. I think that's the way of it with everyone ... but most people with any knack for it at all can find at least one that works for them reasonably well.

Also, there is the issue that most people don't end up using just one path at a time. The eight roads can intertwine, cross, and join for periods of time. Their boundaries blur. One can sing and drum, using both the Path of Breath and the Path of Rhythm. One can fast before meditating, using both the Ascetic's Path and the Path of Meditation. One can create a ritual of painful obstacles to build courage, using both the Path of Ritual and the Ordeal Path. All these roads are at your disposal, if you're willing to practice and learn how to use them properly.

Each of the paths has a specific set of skills and tools that the journeyer needs to become proficient in, or it just won't work—or worse, it will work badly and screw you up. These tools and skills are for your own safety and protection as well as for the efficacy of the working. Don't skimp on safety, including your own psychological as well as physical safety, when doing these journeys. Machismo is the worst possible attitude to don when facing the wights. They aren't impressed, and they may feel that you are better off stripped of that attitude, by force if necessary.

All eight of these paths have been used, to one extent or another, by ancient and/or tribal cultures of the circumpolar western Eurasian area. We have better records of some than of others, but echoes of all of them persist.

The first path—and it is first because most people start with it—is the Path of Meditation. This is also sometimes called the Path of Breath, because altering consciousness through specific forms of breathing is one of the classic techniques of meditation. However, not all parts of this path require breathing techniques; it can include any technique where one goes into an altered state while sitting or lying quietly, using only the tools of one's mind. This path includes techniques of trancework such as *utiseta*, "faring forth", and so on.

The second path is the Path of Ritual. Creating sacred space and doing deliberate (and often repetitive), mindful activities that are heavily laden with meaning in that space can create an altered state by itself. With carefully designed ritual, the mind can be coaxed into a state of openness. This path is one of the most gentle, and the best for doing any kind of consciousness work with a group of people. However, it is much less likely to take people very deep unless it is practiced on a regular basis.

The third path is the Path of Rhythm. This includes drumming, dancing, or any repetitive rhythmic motions. Drums and rhythm are an important part of northern-tradition shamanism; while there is little reference to them in the "lore-era" medieval writings, their neighbors the Saami use drums to this day. Dancing—wildly or just repetitively—has been used by shamans all over the world as a way to achieve altered states, and some believe that if the origin of the word "seidhr" actually means "seething", then it might refer to a form of deliberate rhythmic shaking used for the same purpose.

The fourth path is the Ascetic's Path. This includes fasting, sensory deprivation, and purification ordeals, all of which have various precedents in the North. While the sweat lodge has been associated only with Native Americans, the northern Eurasian equivalent—the sauna—is still very much in existence, and its rituals need only to be reconstructed.

The fifth path is the Path of Sacred Plants. From Thor's henbane beer to the infamous Little Red Man mushroom, hallucinogenic plants have been used with surprising frequency in the ancient North. The main difficulty with this path—leaving aside the issues of legality—is that it can be physically dangerous. On the other hand, for those who have trouble opening up in other ways, nothing blows the doors off like drugs. While no shaman's work is entirely safe, the folk who work with these plant substances stress that the first part of making them safer is to establish a good relationship with the plant spirit in question, which most people don't think (or even know how) to do.

The sixth path is the Path of the Flesh. This path involves using sexual energy as a way of opening one's self to the spirits. While sexual energy—alone or with a partner—has been used for raising power to do magic in traditions all over the world, using it as an altered-state mechanism is a specific subset of sex-magic technique. Since little or no references to sex magic (except for highly negative ones) survive in the "lore", much of this material has had to be rediscovered by folk who work with those Gods and wights whose specialty this is. It also seems that there are different styles of sex magic, depending on whether one works with Aesir, Vanir, or Jotun allies.

The seventh path is the Ordeal Path. This path revolves around intentional and careful use of pain in order to put the body into an altered state. Pain and endurance ordeals are found in many places in the Northern path, from Odin's suffering on the Tree to blood-runes carved into the flesh of warriors for building courage and conferring safety in battle.

The eighth path is the Path of the Horse, which involves direct spirit-possession, bringing the Gods or wights into the body for a short period of time. If there is one path that is both rarer and more direct than any of the others, it is this one. Most people are not wired for it, and it is very difficult to take if you don't have the wiring. It is also the path that is the most directly tied into the religious side of shamanism; once you've had the Gods and wights inside you, it takes a ridiculous amount of denial to disbelieve in them again.

I will be discussing the pros, cons, and techniques of all eight of these Paths as they relate to the northern tradition over the next several chapters. The important thing to remember, again, is that no path is safe and no path works for everyone. If you try something and it doesn't work out for you, don't feel as if you are damaged. Some spirit-workers that I know do wonders on the Path of Meditation alone. More importantly, in each case, consult the Gods and wights that you work with as to which Paths they think would be right and wrong for you; sometimes they can see more clearly into the situation than you can. If you've never managed to get any Gods or wights on the phone, maybe that's a message right there. Be careful. Be cautious. Don't think that this is a game.

First Step: Purpose

So why are you doing this, anyway?

Before you use any of these tools, you need to ask yourself that question. What's the purpose behind this? Be honest with yourself. Is the reason you're pushing to the forefront of your consciousness the real reason, or is it something you've come up with in order to justify the other lousy reasons behind it? If there are any of the reasons in the first list lurking in your head, you might want to rethink things. Not for reasons of vague morals, but because the experiences created by some of the more drastic tools tend to go awfully wrong if your purposes aren't clear and worthy. In fact, they may bring you face to face with your murkier reasons as part of the trip, so it's in your own best interest to think things through several times beforehand. We suggest doing divination for the efficacy of a particular Path before you begin it.

Lousy Reasons For Wanting To Do Any Of This Stuff:

1. Because it sounds exciting, and my life needs excitement right now.
2. Because it's a cool thing to do.
3. Because it's what the books say that shamans do.
4. Because maybe if I do these enough times, I'll become a shaman and the spirits will talk to me.
5. Because I want a justification for doing drugs or having lots of sex or doing SM or even spending my time drumming. (Not that there's anything wrong with any of these things, but they need no shamanistic justification.)

6. Because I find the idea romantic.
7. Because a human mentor, or the author of a book, or another spirit-worker is telling me that I ought to do them.
8. Because they sound like a way to gain power and importance and coolness points and did I mention power?

Acceptable Reasons For Wanting To Do Any Of This Stuff:

1. Because I got told by my People that I had to learn this technique.
2. Because this is a part of my tradition, and I need to learn how to do it so that I can pass it on to someone whose tool it might be, and sensibly guide them. (That's actually a good reason for doing a method that's simpler and more time-consuming than one you're already good at, when you can get there better using other methods and might find this path annoying.)
3. Because I was doing this for non-spirit-work reasons before all this started, and I independently began to discover its use as a spirit-work tool.
4. Because I need more tools for my Work, and everything keeps leading me back to one or more of these paths. (Again, this is a good time for divination.)

Whichever path catches your eye, it is our strong suggestion that you start with the Path of Breath. Simple meditation—utiseta—may seem unromantic and boring, but it is the First Path for a reason. It's on the Path of Breath that you learn all the safety techniques that will stand you in good stead when trying the other seven. In fact, we might even suggest that you wait to try any of the other seven until you've gone as far as you can go on the Utiseta Path, although we acknowledge that some people may just have a natural affinity for certain paths from the very beginning. The dancer shouldn't be prevented from trance dancing, nor the musician from drumming, if it calls out to them and is already linked to their skillset.

Second Step: Uses

Then there's the second set of reasons—not the ones for wanting to try these, but the ones for actually doing them. What do you expect to gain from going into an altered state? What sort of work are you doing that requires it, or at least does better with it? Do the spirits that you work with like and respond to this method? Can they guide you in learning to use it?

Playing with altered states of consciousness has been popular since the 1960s, but most people don't actually use them for their original purposes. There's a lot of talk in neo-shamanistic circles about the "SSC", or "shamanic state of consciousness", which seems to be a light trance that one can put oneself into by drumming or shaking rattles or chanting or breathing. Granted, those are all valid tools of trancework that fit into these eight paths (and they will all be covered later in this book), but sometimes real shamanic work requires a level of trance far deeper than the Harner-style "SSC". For instance, allowing a deity or wight to move through your body physically is something that can't be taught in a weekend workshop … because it requires the cooperation of the Gods and wights, which can't be reliably summoned for commercial or even community-bonding purposes.

So what can you do while in an altered state of consciousness? Well, first, you can hear your guides/allies/patrons better. Signal clarity is a crucial part of any spirit-worker's job. We're all human, and it's dismally easy to confuse the messages that you're getting from the Gods and wights with the desires of the puppets in your head. During times of physical or mental stress, the signal can become completely obfuscated. Don't think that this doesn't happen to experienced spirit-workers, either; it does. All the time. We constantly struggle to sift out the real touch of the divine from our own stuff. That's why layers of divination, preferably with someone besides yourself who doesn't have an agenda about your work, are so important.

But sometimes you need to do a Job, and that Job requires the signal to be as clear as possible, at least for a short period of time. You can't afford to screw it up, so you resort to serious consciousness-change. Part of what these paths do, especially the more extreme ones, is to push your everyday concerns, issues, emotions, and desires aside. The mundane "you" is shoved backwards and out of the way, and there's more room for the part of you that can cleanly hear and see and do the work. During that time, you are also reminded of who you are when all that stuff isn't in the way, which is always a good thing.

Uses for altered states of consciousness:

1. Divination that is more than just figuring out the meanings to a bunch of cards or runes. For shamanistic divination, although you may use any method you like (runes, cards, random rocks, whatever) you are simply using them as a theurgic key to open the Akashic Record of the querent. (Yes, I know that the word Akashic Record may annoy people, but it's a label that people may actually have heard, so I'm using it this once. For myself, I mostly use the term "accessing someone's file in the Big Library".) To do this, you need to have Clearance to get in—which comes from the wights that you work with—and you need to be Open, to let the information come in over your psychic wires, as it were. This is especially crucial when doing advanced work, such as Wyrdworking or Bloodwalking or Luckworking.

2. Seeing into people in order to evaluate their physical and/or psychic health. While some folks can just do this without much of an altered state, if you're actually going to be getting in there and moving stuff around, it helps to be Open enough to see what's really there, rather than what your unconscious would like to be there.

3. Hearing the messages that the Gods and wights have for the client sitting in front of you. If you have the "wiring" to be able to horse them, you may have to do that as part of a session. If not, you need to at least be Open enough to hear them, and accurately transmit their words. If the person in front of you is asking what their patron deity wants of them, it's because their own "phone lines" are blocked, or they don't have

much more than the metaphorical tin can on a string. You, the spirit-worker, are the one with the phone (or perhaps the broadband modem that you can't shut off), and it is your job to relay the message accurately, with as little residue from the inside of your head as possible. Turning divine messages into a human game of Telephone can have disastrous consequences for people's lives.

4. Learning the skills that you need to get from the Gods and wights who are agreeing to train you. Some might come to you in dreamtime, which is already an altered state, and some might come during conscious daylight, but many of them will prefer you to be in a state where you can more easily see and hear them. They may want to take you places, or do things with your astral body, or show you things that you'd miss with the distraction of the outside world.

The single biggest difficulty with being a spirit-worker in this tradition is that nearly all of the information has been lost. The lore that exists was written during an era when shamanic practices had all but died out in Scandinavia and Germany, and were not written down in Saamiland or Siberia. There's really not much to find in reading Christian writing about Pagans who had largely moved away from a shamanic culture and practices. There's barely enough for a religion, much less a spiritual practice of the complexity of the original shamanic culture of a thousand years before.

I've always resonated to the Buryat word *bagshagui*, which means a spirit-taught shaman, because that's what we spirit-workers of the Northern Tradition actually are. We have no old guy or old woman in the hut. Everything we learn, we will get from the Gods and wights who work with us. Even those of you reading this book will find that it's really only a general overview of the territory, and most of the actual on-site guidance is meant to be given by the Gods and wights who may offer to aid you. Which means, in the end, that it's going to depend on your relationships with Them, and these techniques can be useful in working with Them to Their satisfaction.

Third Step: Teachers

Human teachers or spirit teachers? That's the question, but it's strongly affected by the fact that there are damn few human teachers of this tradition. The few of us who are being harassed—er, excuse me, given *attention*—by the Gods and wights are struggling to learn enough to form a critical mass of information. We are benefited by the modern luxury of mass communication, which allows me to publish books with articles written by authors living in Massachusetts, New York, Colorado, Belgium, New Zealand, Ontario, and Spain. This allows us to compare and contrast our experiences, and it gives us a bit of an edge when it comes to putting the pieces together. However, we are still working under a great handicap when faced with thousands of years of lost tradition.

Spirit teachers are wonderful in some ways, and terrible in others. They can teach us things that no human being can teach, in ways that can't be passed on by humans. They have an uncanny ability to see into us and figure out what makes us tick, thus honing the lesson to our needs. On the other hand, they may not understand our mundane lives and the needs pertaining to them—"What do you mean, car insurance?"—and may interfere in inconvenient and often debilitating ways. The Gods, especially, may have a tendency to see us as the best we could possibly be—seeing our Higher Selves—and then expect us to act from that place all the time. This can be difficult even if we're actually trying to act from that place, and a source of constant disappointment if we have no conscious clue what that place looks like.

On the other hand, human teachers (assuming that you can find ones who can teach what you need to know) have their own foibles. They have biases, prejudices, lives that interfere, and assumptions about you that the Gods may see past. They may miss important things or teach incorrect data. However, no deity can teach you how to psychologically survive being a spirit-worker, a human being with one foot in the world of the spirits and one foot in the world of rent, electric bills, gas prices, and TV commercials. And no matter how much you try to separate yourself from that world, your clients will live in it ... and you'll need to be able to connect with it enough to help them. (For more discussion as to why all shamans get stuck with a community to aid, whether they like it or not, see the preceding book, *Wyrdwalkers: Techniques of Northern-Tradition Shamanism*.)

In essence, without teachings from the spirits, you won't be able to do the Job. The work of a human teacher is to give you the symbols, stories, and signposts that create the cultural context, because without the cultural context certain spirits won't connect with you, and those that do ... well, you may have no way to verify who and what they are. It's also their responsibility to give you human support in order to survive the Job. But the meat of the learning is going to come from the Gods and wights.

Fourth Step: Always Cross-Check The Signal

No matter how good you are at altered states, in the end you only have a puny mortal meat-brain like all the rest of us, and it comes cluttered with emotions, stresses, blind spots, biases, distractions, and random memories from this life and from possible others. You will never have perfect signal clarity, and the Gods don't expect that of you. No matter how many techniques you use to be clear and Open to their words and directions, you're going to miss some things. Some communications will come through garbled, and some may come through a filter of all the above clutter which will obscure it.

That's why continual cross-checking is such a good thing. My first suggestion for the beginning spirit-worker is to learn a few forms of divination. Notice I said a few forms, not just one—sometimes one form will clog on you, and you need to switch methods for a fresh start. Even if you never do divination as a client service, it's worth it to have it for the times when you're not sure what just came through. It's all right to do 20 Questions with the Gods—the worst that will happen is that you'll get nothing, and be back to where you started. If you can't do divination, make friends with someone who can, and who isn't heavily involved in your work or your life. Lydia Helasdottir recommends a four-step process of information verification: First, write it down and wait a day for further understanding. Second, do divination on the matter and ask whether it was real, whether it was misunderstood, if there's anything that wasn't grasped. Third, have someone uninvolved do a divination. Fourth, ask the Gods to provide an obvious omen in the everyday world, and go out of the house, but don't look too hard for it—if they care, they'll hit you in the face with it.

We spirit-workers walk the razor's edge with regard to faith: If we can't believe in ourselves, and our ability to see and hear and know what we see and hear and know, then we might as well check ourselves into the bin right now ... which wouldn't work anyway, because the spirits can find you there, too, and you'll just get sicker or crazier until you die or give up and believe it. On the other hand, we have to be continually skeptical of our ability to get all the details of each "transmission" right, or we risk overconfidently getting important messages all wrong, and havoc will ensue. Either extreme leads to wrecked lives and divine ass-kicking. We need to walk a middle ground—believing in ourselves and our Gods and our Job, yet second-guessing our imperfect brains with follow-ups. Never be ashamed to say, "I'm not entirely sure that I've got that absolutely clear ... can I get another pass at it?"

Fifth Step: Care For Your Mind

Trance states, especially extreme trance states, are hard on the brain and the mind. If you do them often enough, or severely enough, you will fry some of your circuits. To use altered states as regular tools, you need to keep your body, your mind, your *hame* (astral body), and your *ond* (chi) in good order. You need to ground and center regularly, or something similar that works for you. Have some kind of physical discipline that moves the *ond* through your body in regular and balanced patterns. Eat reasonably well and keep down the chemical load. Don't get so caught up in Otherworlds that you neglect this one, especially when it comes to your body.

There's also that this work does not have to be done alone. Shamans in many circumpolar traditions had assistants to help them, of varying sorts. Some were their sexual partners (although this is something that needs to be freely taken on by a partner who understands and appreciates the work, not forced on someone who didn't sign up for this), some were apprentices, and some were just well-trained assistants of various sorts. Their jobs seem to have been as varied as coming ahead to make sure that everything was ready for the shaman, arranging for their food, warming up the drums, making the right noises during audience call-and-response, doing their aftercare, and singing or chanting during the performance in order to create a psychic "anchor" to lead their masters and mistresses back to their bodies. Some traveling volvas often had entourages to sing the right songs to call guardian spirits, and to aid with preparatory rites during the night before the "seeing".

All told, the assistants acted as monitors for the spirit-work, and facilitators for the health of the spirit-worker in question. It may be worth it for your own physical, mental, and spiritual health to train up some trusted volunteers for heavy workings. Sometimes doing it all alone isn't the wisest idea. Some tasks do require a certain amount of talent, such as being the monitor for faring forth; other tasks require only a pair of good hands. One needn't be terribly psychic to remind a spirit-worker to eat, to bring them tea, and to make sure that they have all their equipment in good order. My own assistant is trained in runes, a certain amount of lore, making small magical items, Reiki and other small energy-workings for healing, cooking charged food, caring for my tools, massage, caring for my body, and explaining what is expected to clients in a calming and matter-of-fact way. Full-time spirit-workers are especially in need of assistance, and if you're one of those and don't have one, apply to the Gods that you work with and ask. If the need is there, they'll find someone for you.

And most important, do not allow this Work to entirely prevent you from having a life in this world, which can include hobbies unrelated to your Work, people you love and who love you, groups with whom you can accomplish great things, tasty food, gorgeous sunsets, and cheap entertainment. When you begin to scorn this world, you begin to lose your motivation for helping the people who live in it, and that way lies failure. Keep one foot here, Walker Between Worlds. Balance is the key. For every hour you spend Somewhere Else, spend one here, actually being here fully awake to Life and enjoying it. It's a privilege to be here, whether you believe that or not. Act as though you believe it. It's worth it.

Freya's Lesson

Being The Cup

transcribed by Ember Cooke of the Vanic Conspiracy

I finally got up the guts to be the one to ask Freya for this lesson at the end of a wonderful evening celebrating Yule with the Vanir. I'd had my mind set on having our eldest Freyaswoman do it, only she was not feeling well enough to join us for the evening. Indeed, all of the elders of our group were unable to join us, leaving me with no one to defer to.

Nevertheless, everyone seemed to enjoy participating in the ritual I had planned. I set the space, and we passed a horn of mead in honor of each of the Vanir, and then a horn of honey apple cider in honor of their kith and kin, and finally a horn of mulled wine in honor of the Yulefather. We invited them to join us in body or in spirit, as they pleased. We exchanged gifts, and feasted, enjoying the company of family and friends. Finally, we gathered wealth for charity, to spread outward the plenty that was given to us.

The energy was warm, and comforting. Freya came to me before we even finished passing the first horn, and stayed for much of the evening. She left after the gifts were exchanged, and brought Idunna to me briefly, though I had never worked with her before directly. (Freya is capable of handing me off to those I have not met in a way I can not achieve on my own.) Over the course of the evening, Frey, Njord, Heimdall, and Skadi each came to others. All told, the evening went quite well even without the elders there. As the evening wound down, many people thanked me for my service before departing.

I came to realize once again that I cannot wait until I am certain I am worthy of the work the Vanir put before me. I must allow my faith in them to inspire trust of their faith in me. So I asked the few who remained to help bring Freya back to me as completely as possible. It's not that I need help calling her; Freya promised me the first time I met her that she would always come when I called, and I have never had reason to doubt her word. But the more I doubt my own skills, the harder it is to simply let her settle into me. Help from others makes it easier to relax into the work. It also helps to know that others are there to take care of any problems that may arise, so I don't need to be the one in control.

I gave them a song to sing that would invoke Freya as Seidhkona, who would know best of all what skills are a spirit-worker's business. We set aside mulled wine and honey pork for her to eat, the taste of which would also help me relinquish control to her even further once she arrived. They sang and I called to her inside myself, and listened for her response. Often when I call, she responds with laughter. Not a tinkling bell-like giggle, but a soft alto chuckle. This time she was amused that I had ever thought she was very far away. I felt her warmth spread across my limbs, and a sudden, intense need to feel the touch of a soft veil against my cheek. I was reminded again that tactile sensation is often what I need most to block out the distractions of the mundane world, and allow the spirit to fill my senses. None of these lessons are unfamiliar to me, but I must repeat the discovery of small mysteries until they become fully internalized habits.

For a brief moment, I felt the surge of tears that overwhelms me during intense trance, and then she opened my eyes. Her mood was serious. The color filling my mind was not the glowing gold of the goddess of love and beauty, nor the vivid green of a fertility goddess. It was not the crimson of the gatherer of the slain. My mind was filled with the soft, deep brown-grey of the greatest Seidhkona. "Drums would have worked better for your purposes than the song," she commented. Her voice was firm, but not harsh. "Sit down. I have a lesson for you."

She took up a heartbeat on the drum, and guided the few there through her lesson.

Freya's Lesson:

Spirit workers are often much involved with the outside world, other worlds, many worlds. A myriad of beings clamor for attention. Even the most experienced Spirit worker can be in danger of forgetting to know themselves.

What happens when you are totally alone with yourself? What happens when the last of us has quieted from your mind and ear? What happens when there is no one left for you to interact with, no books to read, no tasks to perform—no distractions left to hide behind?

Close your eyes. Do not go to a place outside. Do not go to the Great Tree. Go inside yourself. Listen to yourself breathe. Listen to your heart beating. Sit alone with yourself, and look inside. At your center, there is a place of light or darkness—it doesn't matter which. It is a place that should be clear and empty. It is a place that is often filled with anxieties and hopes, thorns and treasures. It is a place often used to hold away thoughts and feelings you cannot bear to experience. Those who are depressed or lonely often say they feel empty inside. But feeling always full may well be worse for you.

It is the nature of a cup to have open space. The cup is not flawed for lack of contents. A cup by itself is a cup whole unto itself, and yet it is empty.

Look around your center, and empty out the distractions. Discard the thorns. Find better places for the treasures, or recognize that you simply don't need them here. Let the drips and drops drain away, until you are empty of them. They are not you. You are the cup, whole unto yourself without them.

When you feel clear and empty, then there is space for us. Now you have the power to choose to invite us into that space and sacrifice that emptiness. But do not invite us in for the purpose of filling the space with another distraction. If we are there merely to distract you from facing yourself, then we too should be cleared away for a while.

When you wander the worlds, you will have enough to distract you, and you will need again to go into yourself and clear out the collection of dust and thorns and golden nuggets. Do not forget to care for yourself in this way, or soon you will find we have been crowded out by the clutter, and you can barely hear our guidance, barely feel our presence anymore.

You will be distressed if we have to clear it out for you, and yet quite a few of you would find that easier by far than having to choose for yourselves. Perhaps I will abide that once or twice, but I am not terribly interested in those who cannot learn to take care of themselves. I have children enough. Those who do my work must be able to stand without my constant aid.

Utiseta and Faring Forth: The Path of Meditation

> On the chair of the Nornir
> I sat nine days,
> Then I was raised up on a horse.
> The giantesses' sun
> Shone grimly
> From the cloud-dripper's clouds.
> —Solarljod, "Song of the Sun"

The night is quiet, and the woods are full of the smell of leaf-mold and pine as she makes her way to her favorite tree. It's the great-grandfather oak a good way off of the path—empty at this time of night, all travelers sleeping—with a trunk so huge that she can't fit her arms halfway around it. Her staff leans up against the tree; cut from one of its branches, it is like coming home. On one side, she leaves an offering for the landvaettir; on the other side, she seats herself. She settles down in the hollow between its two largest roots, composes herself, pulls the hood of her cloak down over her head, says a prayer to her patron under her breath, and then begins to Breathe.

First, the Breath, in and out, no more than that. With each in-breath, notice the sounds and scents of the forest—the leaves, the pines surrounding this old oak, the stillness and rustling, the rough bark at her back—and breathe them in. Then hold them for the same count, savor them. Then with each out-breath, let them go. Let them all go, breathe out all the way to the bottom, to nothing. Let go of the senses, the day's work, the buzzing thoughts that swarm in her mind. All gone. Empty. Well, not quite empty, not on the first out-breath, but with each breathing cycle she grows emptier. Sense the outside, then no-sensing. Eventually all that she breathes in is the forest; her ordinary life is fallen away entirely. This forest is all that is, and beyond that, nothingness. She does not know how long it takes to get to that point, how many breaths. It doesn't matter. What matters is that she knows the way, and her breaths are the footprints on that now-familiar road.

Next, the Landvaettir. As her awareness of herself fades and only the surroundings matter, and even they only matter on the in-breath, she slowly becomes aware of its presence, there to greet her. It knows her; they do this dance of touch-and-greeting, of offering and hospitality, at least once a week. Its touch is friendly, but somewhat impersonal; she is not bonded to this land, but it is her old friend. It is pleased with the offering, and with her unfailing courtesy towards it. The bargain—you feed me, you hold my Thread, I feed you, I hold your memory—is reaffirmed with that swift touch, and it is enough.

Then she sinks deeper into darkness, and begins to shut off the outside stimuli. Her breathing slows, and the in-breaths no longer breathe in the forest, but only the night—and then not even that, simply darkness. She floats in darkness, in trance, and then extends herself Beyond. It is a slow process for her, and perhaps it always will be. Some can tear themselves Out with only a few minutes of breathing, but she needs to walk all the way there and back, one Breath at a time. And, perhaps, the slowest way might also be the surest. There is no need to hurry. She has all night. Sometimes the breathing alone is not enough, and then she sings or chants for a time, giving her breath-steps power of voice and ond, pushing them further, holding the notes until there is nothing left in her but vibration.

There is green light above and to the west, or to the direction that she thinks of as West. That is her destination. It is springtime in Vanaheim, and the Lady that she serves will be there, flowers uncurling in Her footsteps. During the day she is clad in pale green, awakening the fields to their springtime glory, coaxing the shoots from the ground. At night, she will hold court in a hall with no name save Hers, where the women gather to sing and chant magic. It is there that her breath-steps will take her, to Freya's secret *hall of seidhr, where the golden Lady wears her witchiest face. There is a question that must be asked, people with worried faces wondering what will be ... and there is training that she must have, teachings she has oathed herself to go through. The green light grows stronger as she moves forward, staff in hand ... for the staff too has a soul that fares forth with her. Springtime in Vanaheim, and the grass feels soft beneath her feet, the torchlight of the hall ahead of her. They know her there, and will welcome her in yet again.*

The first road of the Eightfold Path, and the one that is the simplest, the most popular, and the mainstay of nearly every spirit-worker is the Path of Meditation. It is traditionally also called the Path of Breath, as breathing and oxygen control are important elements in mastering this path. In the northern tradition, we call it Utiseta, which literally means "sitting-out". This gives us the traditional image of the spirit-worker going to a quiet and lonely place, usually far from habitation, and meditating in order to commune with Gods and wights, or do magical work on a nonphysical plane.

Utiseta can, in some cases, become "faring forth", or "journeying", which are both northern-tradition terms for what is modernly referred to as "astral projection". This occurs when a specific part of the soul leaves the body and travels to Otherworlds (or to other places in this world) while still being connected to the physical form. Journeying, and how to do it, is covered fairly thoroughly in *Pathwalker's Guide To The Nine Worlds*, the second book in the Northern-Tradition Shamanism series, so it's wise for the would-be journeyer to pick that one up. First, though, we will concentrate on how to do utiseta itself, and its manifold uses, in the words of various spirit-workers.

Utiseta, Breath, and Mound-Sitting
by Lydia Helasdottir

The best beginner's technique is the basic four-fold breath: you breathe in for a count of four, you hold for four, you breathe out for four, you wait for four, and you just do that. It helps your body not to freak out when your consciousness leaves, because it's used to doing this automatic breathing. Just sit and do that for a while. If you are working on ascending, going up through the Tree, then it's better not to lie down while doing this. It works better for your energy body anyway, if you want to be moving Kundalini, for your spine to be in a vertical position, so you should sit upright in a chair. But in terms of actually getting out and traveling, it doesn't make any difference whether I'm curled up in a ball or lying down or sitting against a tree or in the train or whatever.

The trick of doing the four-fold breathing thing is to actually extend yourself at the times when you're holding the breath out. You breathe out for four counts, and then you slip further out during the counts before you breathe in again. I've done that so long that sometimes even now, if I do it, I lose all feeling of the body; the body just doesn't exist. It's a really simple thing that I learned so many years ago, and it still does the right stuff for me. It works. I also meditate and travel when I'm running, but that's a slightly different deal. That's about 80% in the body and 20% out. Particularly if I'm having a hard time, I'll just go away and talk to whatever wights or boggarts are in the forest that I'm running through, and whine at them about how hard it is, and they kind of commiserate, and after about ten minutes it feels better.

The first couple of times that I did that for work, it was very much "Oh, I don't know if I can really do this!" And you just have to use your mind to say, "Well, what if it is all in my imagination? If I were to be able to do this, what might it look like?" It does work. Then, eventually you'll feel a sensation that there's really something there.

We do moundsitting, ordinary utiseta, and going under the cloak, and sensory deprivation stuff like cat's cradle and such things. Ordinary utiseta we like to do overnight, not just for a couple of hours. You go through the stage of "What the fuck am I doing here? This is really silly." It seems to be needful sometimes to just go through that. We start with the following exercise: Start with experiencing yourself, and that which is around you. Place your attention on the trees and the rocks, the root that I'm sitting on, the wind in the trees, the smells. We do this whole thing of "I can see one thing, I can hear one thing, I can smell one thing, I can taste one thing, I can feel one thing." Then you go to two things, then to five things. Getting to the point of smelling five different things is quite difficult, especially if you haven't moved your position, but it's a good thing. So the first point is to be really aware of you and the things around you. Do that with your deep breathing.

Then you contract your attention inside yourself. If you're wearing a cloak, at this point you put the hood over yourself. Contract your attention so that you're not noticing anything from the outside, and you're just trying to find the core of the center of your being, all the way down. Really compress it so that it's just you. It might take ten or fifteen minutes for you to even get there, and then you do that for an hour or so. Then you expand your attention outwards, but you go past the boundary of your body, so now you're experiencing all that stuff that's around you, but not as separate from you any more. And at that point, often it's easier to commune with the wights and the dead people and whatever else. And you do five or six or twelve or so cycles of that during the night. That's pretty potent stuff. You can get people who are relative brickheads—thick people who can't see things or hear things—to at least have an unusual experience in doing that ... if only because when you pull your cloak over your head it changes the oxygen content of your breathing, It's the "holotropic breath" of Stanislav Grof, this particular hallucinogenic ratio between carbon dioxide and oxygen. You can get it by hyperventilating, too, and it's just as potent as LSD. It's quite remarkable stuff.

So if you do this thing on a mound, or inside of a faery hill, then you're likely to talk to them. If you don't have mounds around, ancestor graves might work. We live in Europe, where there are plenty of mounds and faery hills, but it's different in the New World. But you have to have a reason to actually talk to them, anyway. Not just to have them show up because it's cool; they'll ask, "What are you going to do for me?"

How Faery-mounds work: You just go for a doze on some welcome-looking rock on some wild and green hill, and if you're near a faery place they'll suck you in. Of course, whether or not that's good rather depends on the situation. If you have a particular reason for dealing with them, then you can put your "I am here and would like to talk to you" hat on; you can sort of put that flag up and then go to sleep, and they'll come and talk to you if they want you. If on the other hand you don't want to talk to the Fey, but you need to have a sleep somewhere on the mountain which is Fey-haunted, I would just advocate drinking some fucking coffee and moving on. If you feel the strange desire to go lie down and sleep somewhere in the hills of Ireland, better be sure that you know what you're getting into. "But it's so nice and warm there, and everywhere else is cold and rainy…" They don't like cold iron, either, so you can do a certain amount of protective stuff with wearing cast-iron jewelry or horseshoe nails.

The deal with sitting out is that you actually need to have a purpose. "Why am I doing this?" Just to see what's out there and talk to something cool is not a purpose. "I have a question that I can't get an answer to, and I need to talk to my ancestors." Or "There's a part of me that I don't understand, and I need to get some clarity." Or "Someone has come to me with a problem that they need help on and I don't get it." Or "The land is really sick and I need to understand what to do about it." These are all good reasons, but not "Hey, maybe something cool is out there and I can talk to it." No. You might even get fed on, so be careful.

Breath is the source of life. In Old Norse, the word *ond*, meaning breath, stood for a concept that we can recognize in the eastern terms of ki, ch'i, prana, etc. In myth, Odin breathed the life into Ask and Embla, the first people of Midgard, and thus gave them the gift of *ond*. When there is no more breath, there is no more life force. When you control the breath, you affect the life force. Controlling your breathing can change your mood, reduce anxieties, clear your mind of annoying spinning thoughts, and make you more aware or less aware of your body, depending on how you do it.

The Northern Tradition does not have specific breathing exercises, such as the Yoga practices of India, or even Buddhist chanting meditation. In my youth, I did learn Pranayama breathing (the basic technique of which is simply a rather intense and lengthened version of the four-fold breath in Lydia's piece above) largely from living in a houseful of hippie roommates, but I didn't relate it to my magical or spiritual practices until I found myself combining controlled breathing with another skill I'd been trained in—singing. Somewhere along the line I discovered that the breathing techniques learned for voice training and the breathing techniques taught by yogic practitioners were not all that different, and could be combined with a form of magic that I later learned was a form of *galdr*—singing your intent out with your breath. While simple breathing is the tool of the mystic, singing is the breath-tool of the shaman. Remember again the difference between the shaman and the mystic? If you've ever heard any recordings of shamans around the world singing, you'll know that it's not that their voices are so wonderful. It's that something about their singing is so very powerful ... and that is a technique well-known in the northern tradition. (*Galdr* itself is covered in the chapter on the Path of Rhythm.)

Even if your voice is as croaky as a frog, it might be worth it to take lessons in voice training, if only to get the breathing part right. The usefulness of the four-fold breath, as described by the yogis, is to put someone into a state of mild trance, largely from the extra-long periods between the inhalations and exhalations. In general, when people breathe, they don't spend a very long time with the lungs full or the lungs completely empty, and it's this concentration on the "liminal states" of breathing, expanding them to the same length as the inhalation and exhalation, that creates the trance state. If you look at singing-breath in this way, the first thing to do would be to find—or create—a song that allowed the breathing to proceed in a way that mimicked the four-fold breath, or perhaps some other pattern of breathing that you figure out on your own. Putting yourself in that state with song makes it easier to gather, aim, and fire the energy of the song/spell. The power song is one fork in the Path of Breath, the controlling of *ond* in order to create something and move it out of you. Life force rides on the breath; remember that. If you need help loosening that up, drawing Ansuz on your throat chakra may help with that.

In both Old Norse accounts of the volvas, and century-old accounts of Siberian shamanism, the spirit-workers are referred to as "yawning" periodically throughout their public performances. According to the Yukaghirs, it is a way of "breathing in" the spirits and their messages, which would make sense considering that in *Hrofs saga kraka* the volva Heid yawns at the beginning of her rite, and then again when asked each question. While it might seem odd at first, remember that breath carries *ond*, and that includes the *ond* of the spirits. Magic-workers who employ the shamanic trick of pulling life force out of people at close range (which can be used as a healing technique to remove fear, pain, or other problems) usually agree that the technique is easiest when the "sucking-out" is combined with deep in-breaths. This is also used by healers who use "sucking-out" techniques to draw out disease, something that will be covered in the upcoming book in this series on shamanic healing.

In the meantime, it's something to be tried. Ground, center, and open your mouth wide; breathe in deeply—and it's all right if you yawn—and then do it again. The extra oxygen that comes to your brain will help to alter your perceptions, just as a lack of oxygen does the same thing in a different way. Try "breathing in" the answers when you're doing a reading and see what happens.

Another fork in the path is journeying, which is usually done silently. Here we're back to utiseta again. Once you've managed to put yourself into trance through breath and concentration, it's a matter of knowing where to go. My first suggestion to the beginning spirit-worker is to go inside yourself, because knowing yourself and all your secrets, and not having anything hiding in there that you've denied or locked in a mental oubliette to forget about, will be one of the most important ongoing jobs that you can do. Everything in your psyche that you're not aware of is a weakness when it comes to journeying. Every part of yourself that you deny is a potential saboteur to your spirit-work, an Achilles heel to leap out when you least expect it, a possible back door for nasty entities to get in. Besides, if you're frightened by the dark alleys and passageways in your own head, you're never going to make it through the worlds outside of this one. So start with You, your Self, and your Breath.

One possible meditation is simply to visualize a series of doors in a hallway, in your inner house. Some open onto rooms, some stairways. Every night, open one door and see what's in it. Don't try to control the meditation; let it flow. If there are stairs upward or downward, follow them and see what doors you come upon, but stick to one door a night unless you've put aside a whole day just to wander through your inner self. If you get a feeling of apprehension or straight-out fear, or even a feeling of "Oh, this isn't a good idea, I think I'll go back now," or keep getting distracted or popping out of trance while approaching a particular door, you've hit something important that your mind is trying to keep from you. Don't let it happen; pursue it. Even horrid memories that you hate to look at should be dealt with; better you deal with them now in safety than deal with them when they sabotage you during future work.

The other part, which is discussed in detail in *Pathwalker's Guide*, is that you need to be able to ground, center, and shield. You should be able to create shields that will go with your *hame* when it leaves your body. You should also have a good relationship with a land-wight, if possible, because they're useful for holding your thread when you go out. While spirits that go with you and guide you are great, there's nothing like a spirit that will bring you back home safely.

Once you've spent enough time working on your inner mind—and "enough" is a variable time that can only be guessed at—you will want to attempt to move outward instead of inward, and journey out of the body to another place. Some folks create an astral safe spot, sort of your own personal equivalent of the "Disney ride", to use as a starting point in beginning work. There is also a general agreement that the first ride out of the body should ideally be done with another spirit-worker present, monitoring you, and able to step in should there be an emergency. The problem is that for most beginning spirit-workers, especially in this tradition—there are still so few of us—there isn't anyone around to help when you begin this. I started alone, as did most of the northern-tradition shamans and spirit-workers that I know.

So I will say up front that you are taking your life and sanity into your own hands, and the best thing to do is to wait until A) your patron deity tells you to do it, or B) you can get a deity or major wight to motor you through it, or C) you can get another spirit-worker to come out and help you do it. Start out with the spirits that will come to you, and graduate (with their help) to the ones that will guide you outward. If no spirits are coming to you, pray to the Gods to send you some, or to come themselves. If no one comes at all, perhaps you're not meant to do this work. (We'll assume in that case that you haven't actually been chosen by any Gods or wights, but are just hoping that you will be.) In that case, you have my sympathies, but there's not much that you can do. Try again in a few years and see if the situation has changed.

In a breath-trance, you can be better aware of the voices of the wights, and your signal clarity is stronger. If you practice enough, you should eventually be able to achieve a light trance with only a few breaths … and then you should be able to go deeper. While journeying is a tricky and dangerous thing, the simpler forms of the Path of Breath are the easiest parts of the Eightfold Path, and are much more difficult to harm one's self with. You only need your body, your mind, your breath, and your will, and you have the first three in abundance and the fourth can be honed and trained. That's why this path is also called the Path of Will.

Journeying Tips From A Cosmic Diplomat

by Lydia Helasdottir

Leaving my body started with a strange experience I had during a progressive body relaxation thing. I was doing the classic Monroe Institute thing—"The toes, the toes are relaxed, I relax the toes. The feet, the feet are relaxed, I relax the feet." I got up to the throat and suddenly I couldn't breathe any more, and I got this really weird sensation, so I stopped doing it. I went back to it, and it happened again. This was very early on—age 15 or 16 or so. So what I actually learned to do was to travel out of the body. I think people misunderstand this part of it; they think that they have to feel their vehicle literally leaving their body, seeing themselves under themselves and floating through the room and all that stuff. Well, that's handy and all, but it isn't actually necessary for doing it. And it's really unhelpful if you're traveling in a car and trying to do that at the same time.

For me, I have a variety of levels, from 90% here and 10% journeying, to 10% here and 90% journeying. I sit down, I punch in the coordinates of where I want to go on my intergalactic navigating machine, and press "Go!" That's something that many of us do, making the interface look like technology we're familiar with. I started traveling a lot with the twelve directional kings. I had to figure out how to go and meet them; my teachers were saying, "You have to go see this King and talk to him." Well, how do I do that, then? She said, "Well, just intend to meet him, and go, and the rest will get taken care of." So I closed my eyes and intended to meet him, and suddenly I was face to face with this ebony-skinned man on a blasted desert landscape.

Some people can speak or communicate while they're away; their mouth will move and words will come out and describe what's going on, to whoever is there or onto a tape. That works for me sometimes, and sometimes I have to go through the whole experience and remember it all when I come back. Or I might pop in and out and back and forth. How do you know if it's real? If it's really important stuff, we have a three-level verification. First you test them. You say, "Who are you?" and they'll say something or other, and then you can test them further. Working in the northern tradition, I would tend to do an Os at them, or Isa, or Ken. You can do that with Ogham as well.

The second level is to check with divination. Is this what I really thought it was? Do the divvy. Did we get all the information we needed to get? Did we ask all the questions that we were supposed to ask? Is there anything that we need to be worried about? Is it all right? We always do a divination session after being sent to talk to things, just to be sure. If it's something really important, then we want two confirmations. We call on somebody else in our network to confirm it without us telling them what we were doing, and then we also ask for some sort of physical manifestation. For instance, let's say we got some information from some bogey about something or other. Then your mother-in-law starts telling you about some sort of strange dream that she had and this stuff comes up, and you go to the store and some truck drives past you that says "Welcome to Bogeyville" or whatever. You ask for a physical, non-journeying, non-suggestion thing to show up in the physical world. Like an omen. We always ask for that if it's something really serious, like "You should sell the house and move to Kamchatka," or some such thing of great import.

The other thing that you need to take into account is speed. Sometimes you have to really slow yourself down a lot to talk to certain entities. Things like boggarts and tree spirits don't have the same time cycles. I expect that our speech sounds to them something like "blblbllbl", and we have to really slow down to communicate with them.

We can do full-on 90% out-of-the-body journeying, but I don't find that it's all that necessary. It's a lot more dangerous and tiring. Once you get used to traveling places, you can travel with more and more of you here.

How not to get in trouble while journeying: Research beforehand. Always know exactly where you're going. What is the person that you're meeting supposed to look like? Have we met them before? And if you can't find it in the lore anywhere, or in faery tales, do divinations. You can ask people who have been there or done that—"So what does this look like, then?"—but if you can't even find that, then knowing that you have some reason for being there, you can ask the source of the information that said you had to be there—what are they supposed to look like, and how to get there safely.

When it comes to someone who's read in a book that So-and-so helps with something, and might be a good person to ask about a question ... Do 20 questions with your divination method—if I knew more about him, what would he look like? When you're more experienced, you can move fairly smoothly from meditation to journeying. Meditate on his being and presence, and why exactly you think that he might have a good answer for you. But the next question is why he would bother, though. There has to be something in it for him. Go bearing gifts. The best gift is to be willing to pick up tasks that they can't do down here.

Afterwards, do a divination to see if it was really them, if you got there. We like to be sure that we know what the space is like, and is it near something that we already know. Are there landmarks? We'll ask divination beforehand to find out if there are particular dangers in going to meet this entity; if so, what is the nature of that; can we do anything to allay those dangers; if so, what; and so forth. But it's invariably worth it to not go in like a complete idiot. The entity will be pleased to know that you've taken the time to read the guidebook and learn a few phrases and see the map. Even though it's obvious that you're a tourist, you're not a complete schmuck. You've at least tried a little bit.

There's also that people can mimic deities on the subtle plane if they're powerful enough. You can test them all you like, and it won't help. That's why the divinations afterwards are important. Of course, if you've worked with a particular deity enough, you can just sort of know if it's not them. Acting in uncharacteristic ways is a tipoff.

There are certain spaces that are time-sensitive, and if you go into them, going back into your body can be a bit weird. Most of the time when one journeys out, when you come back your subtle body juts fits right back into your physical vehicle, but if you visit places that are quite close to the manifested plane, then the movement of the earth affects your subtle body still, because you're quite close to it and its influence, so when you come back after 20 minutes or whatever, your body is slightly rotated from where your subtle body was, and you can come in feeling funky. In the beginning, I would come in and feel like "Eew! Something feels really gross and wrong and out of place and twitchy." I would have to go out of the body again and realign and come back in again. You can definitely have a bad landing.

Then I was taught to immediately write down everything, and make sure you're thoroughly back in your body—especially before you have to go and drive or something. Make sure to close the door after you, because things will want to come in after you, into the material plane. Things can attach themselves to you, or wander in after you—just little bottom feeders, usually, but occasionally something bigger. I imagine the biofilter that they use in Star Trek when they teleport people, to make sure that nothing comes in that shouldn't be there. Remember that Chi follows Zi—energy follows intentions, so you can use that to make a little magical tool. You put it around your physical body when you leave, like a little glowing mesh, and it filters out anything that wasn't supposed to be there. And if you end up feeling kind of flu-like for a couple of days after traveling it could be that you've caught something. That's something that they don't talk about—the bugs. You can burn them off doing a chi exercise of something pantheon-appropriate. Some kind of "light from the Source burning out stupid beasties that came through the portal with me and shouldn't be here." Or you can ask one of the deities to burn them off for you. Just being alert that it can happen at all is more than most people ever do. Most people don't contemplate such things.

You can come back from these things very much out of sorts, and then you have to spend a lot of time doing elemental rebalancing stuff, or purifying baths or whatever exercise it is that you do to have a physical or mental or emotional reboot. If I have to go places that are really harsh, I just don't put as much of me there. I only send maybe ten or fifteen percent. I don't generally pathwalk, because it's harder on the body, but sometimes you have to go fully there. Also, it's a lot harder to get fooled when you're fully there. And it's harder to get lost.

Getting lost: I got lost in the space between here and the directional kings. How did I get back? "Mommeee! Help!" Which is very embarrassing. You can take a rock in your hand, or something else that you can home back in on. This sort of "GPS thinking" goes like this: Here's the waypoint, the blinking beacon, the homing beacon. There seems to be a kind of "idiot's autopilot" that brings you back safely, but also limits where you can go, and it's like a locking collar, and until you've logged a certain number of hours of journeying successfully without getting lost, and without having to use the blinking light or the return button or what-have-you, you have to wear the collar. And it also tells boogies to "hands-off". So people start thinking that they are invulnerable, because nothing bad ever happens to them and they can always find their way back … until you pass certain ring-pass-nots in your magical attainment, and then that doesn't work any more, and you really can get lost or burnt to a crisp by the radiation.

But when I get lost I tend to just cry for Mommy, meaning Hela, and She'll drag me back and berate me, and I feel really ill and get a migraine for five or six days. That's so humiliating. And even if you don't have a patron deity, there's always a Mom there, a Mother Goddess of some sort who will help you when you yell. The Universal Distress Beacon, like the toddler in the supermarket. If not your Mom, some nice Lady will come by and help you out.

But to avoid getting lost in the first place, really good knowledge of where you're going is important, and don't be going into places where you're not planning to go, and don't travel to places you don't know yet. Get a tour guide, or stick to places that do have a lot of lore written about them while you learn your navigational skills. It's like mountaineering—you first go to mountains that have marked trails, and then you go to the mountains that might not have marked trails but there's written guidebooks and maps, and then you go to the mountains that have no guidebooks but you go with a local guide, and then—and only then—do you go exploring into remote aspects of the Urals that nobody's ever been to before, that aren't even on the map. To go there by helicopter and decide to walk around is just dumb.

The Disney ride—the archetypal veil—is a good way to get an idea of what the place you're going looks like. The only unsafe thing about the Disney ride is that you can believe that the real thing is that safe. On the Disney ride, you can throw popcorn at the video Gods and all that happens is that you get ejected. In real life, one of 'em will tear your liver out. "Mommee! He tore my liver out!" And She says, "Uh-huh. That's because you pestered him. Don't do that, then."

First, before you even think about traveling in Otherworlds, I would try to build up your astral stamina. Our people take six to nine months of building up their astral vehicles with breathing and meditative exercises to the point where they are actually quite strong. In the northern tradition, such exercises might be sitting with the trees and breathing up and down them and generating a heartwood and really firm bark, if you're a tree kind of person, or meditating upon and working with Thorn and Nyth ... but especially breathing and guiding energy around your system so that it becomes strong, so that you subtle body is full and strong and powerful and solid, and that you can move around without leaking everywhere. Then we test them—we feed on them, and batter them around, and see if they're still set up. So spend a good couple of months doing really basic grounding and purification exercises.

Then, when traveling, making sure that you have got some armor, or at least protective clothing before you go. But make sure that any armor and weapons are hidden, so that you look harmless. Armor does not necessarily mean "armed"; it means appropriately dressed for the conditions. So if you're going into a high-radiation environment, you need to wear a rad suit. If you're going to go into a very cold place, you need to wear something, or else go in a bubble, or a magicked-up robe that you always wear when you're doing something like this. It could be just a lightly-flowing-outward expression of energy all the time, a slight positive pressure from your being floating outwards, so that the little sucking bottom-feeding things won't latch onto you so easily.

And if you're traveling to places where you're likely to get hit heavily, wear armor, even if you wear it under your T-shirt so that it doesn't show. You can wear armor that doesn't show up. It doesn't have to be big aggressive "I Am Looking For A Fight" armor. You should not overdo the heroic knight-valiant thing. Even in "Lord of the Rings", consider Aragorn in his traveling gear versus Aragorn in his battle gear. It's very different, being a Ranger versus being a Paladin.

But being wounded ... mostly for beginners it's just bottom feeders that have suckered onto them. "Boogies", as we call them; undifferentiated beings sort of swooping around. They will come and feed on your energy. If those things attach themselves to you ... well, whenever you come back, just check. We refer to it as putting the scanning goggles on and scanning your body for parasites. Then take them off, or burn them up, and put some energy into your hand and just patch the hole, or take some healing herbs, or go talk to a tree, or whatever it is you do. You can also travel in other forms—something that's less likely to get damaged. So for example, maybe you decide to travel as a tortoise or something.

Sometimes I've been damaged by other people who were territorial about the fact that I was there, or just didn't like me. You don't always know that you've been hit when you're still traveling, assuming that you didn't actually go into battle and take damage that you couldn't see, so you might come back and feel a bit weird or logy or headachy or tired inexplicably for days. You might not be able to get rid of a cold, or whatever. In this case, it's quite likely that you did take some damage out there. You can either do some divination to find out if that's the case, and if so what to do about it; or you can go to your local friendly neighborhood shaman and ask them to have a look at you. You can go to standard energy healers with a great deal of care, and say, "I'm feeling a bit tired and ill; maybe you can just rebalance everything and make sure that it's OK." They'll do a standard cleansing reboot program, which may interfere with modifications, but if you're just a beginner you won't have too many mods anyway. Go to an acupuncturist or something and just get fixed. Eat lots of really healthy food, and take cleansing baths, and such. It'll fix itself, generally. If you've gotten into a fight with something that's gotten you and it doesn't heal, you need to talk to somebody who handles serious spirit-work and have them fix you up.

Recaning:
The Path of Ritual

He enters the labyrinth just before dawn, the same time every time he does it. It's worth getting up early for, in the summer. Years ago, when he first moved to this land, he carried the stones to the place nine at a time, over and over. Each day he honored a different deity, speaking nine epithets for them. When the labyrinth was built and that rite ended, he began the walking.

His feet know the way; there is no thought involved after so many years. This time, he is moving up the Tree, not down. The first ring is Svartalfheim, or Nidavellir—he likes being able to start with the Duergar, who are his friends. They aid him in his creative work; they have taught him about excellence in Making. He places his feet carefully here. Second ring, further out, is Niflheim; he can almost feel the cold as he makes his way around. It is a place of desolation, and his body grows colder. Next, the largest ring of all, and this is Helheim, the Land of the Dead. Now his body grows not only cold but numb, his consciousness moving away from the feet that continue to walk.

The next ring comes in smaller again, and there is a sense of relief. Jotunheim now, and the wind picks up. The land feels steeper under his feet, like climbing a mountain. Then a swing into the second smaller ring, and it is Muspellheim. Not long here—it is too hot, but the cold of Niflheim gives way to warmth as he passes through. Then back out to a longer ring—Vanaheim. Green and sweet under his bare toes. He feels fed just walking through. Then the smaller ring of Alfheim, and here he visualizes sound and beauty, singing and dancing colors. Then he is facing the short cross-path that will take him into the center, and Asgard.

A pause, a breath, two breaths, three. Then he lifts his arms, by now in trance from the winding and the walking, and steps forth into the world where he will seek the Norns at their Well eternal.

The Path of Ritual is the art of changing consciousness through repetitive devotional activities. While the Path of Ritual can be done alone, it is the only path that actually works better when done with a large group of people, because of the power inherent in the group of focused will and energy. In fact, if you need to bring some kind of liminal altered state to a mass of human beings, this is the path to use.

Lydia Helasdottir defines ritual as "...an action or series of actions carried out in order to bring an intention to bear on the world through the focusing of attention, mind, emotion, energy, and power onto that action. So for me, even running can be a ritual. The classic use of ritual is much more formal than that, of course."

Doing it alone, without the reinforcement of all those minds, requires a good deal of personal focus and repetition. One's deep mind may or may not recognize it as ritual on the first go. It may take a few rounds of it before it has the desired effect. One can speed up the "acceptance process" by using elements that are already familiar as ritual, especially in the beginning of the rite. This could be creating sacred space, declaring intent, or just a song or invocation that you decide to use regularly to begin any personal ritual. Once you've begun, though, you should go on with that opening whenever possible, because the Path of Ritual depends on repetition to begin the process of taking to you another state. It's a cue to your deep mind—"OK, we're going there again." The rest of the ritual may be entirely different each time, but try to have something familiar to hang that cue on.

If you decide that you want more than one ritual opening cue, get one implanted thoroughly before you being on another, even if you're bored with the first one. Boredom can even be a plus in this situation, as it means that you can go through it without too much physical concentration and your mind can be freed up to concentrate on other things. Each time you do it the same way, it becomes more powerful. In a way, one could consider it very scientific-method—is it a repeatable experiment which can be carried out with the same or better result? Not everything in the ritual is going to turn out that way, of course—especially the things that are new each time—but the core parts that get included every time need to be repeatable experiences that can be taught with reliable effect.

Keeping a journal of your personal rituals can be a useful tool. It's part of the scientific method, really—some things that are happening now only make sense in the context of things that are happening in the future. When you look back and read your journal entries later, patterns may emerge that you wouldn't have put together when looking at only the most recent rituals. It also helps to record things that may come to you spontaneously in the midst of a rite, such as a song or chant, that you don't want to vanish again into the Akashic mists.

Creating Sacred Space

While many might find the term "creating sacred space" to reek of New Age practices, I find it a useful umbrella term to describe what it is that we do when we delineate some space as more sacred than the rest of the space. Spirit-workers all vary when it comes to their favorite methods of creating sacred space for their own personal rites. When asked, a varying group of northern-tradition spirit-workers had rituals as different as "…go sit in front of my Harrow, light a candle, and perhaps read some lore about the deity I'm calling," in the case of a more traditional reconstructionist; or a more intuitive type who needed to put both a lit candle and ice cubes on the altar when asking for guidance; or yet another who proclaimed that after so many years of spirit-work she *was* sacred space, and didn't need to do anything to create it.

My own preference is to light a recaning stick of mugwort and purify the space, because I function in a small crowded house with a lot of people's energy and very little privacy. Then I sing the last verse of the Song of the Nine Herbs, which wards the directions (that ritual is at the end of this section), sit, and ground and center. If I am feeling particularly unfocused, I will sing my personal power song. (That last bit sounds like a load of New Age bunk, and indeed I thought that such things were just that, until I ended up with one. Never name that well from which you will not drink.)

Some folk prefer to actually go to a space—usually a natural one—that has a strong spiritual feel to it, rather than attempting to create their own in the living room. Mordant Carnival points out that: "Since I like to work out-of-doors as much as possible, I don't so much need to establish sacred spaces as identify them and form a relationship. Some places are so imbued with power and holiness that my coming along and saying, 'Hello, Space, I'm going to make you sacred now!' would be pure egotism and an invitation for a cosmic smackdown."

> I think the relative simplicity of NT group ritual influences the simplicity of my own ritual work; I don't do anything for theatrics since I don't need to impress myself or my Gods, and fuss is kept to a minimum except in certain cases. This isn't because I don't care, but to me the intimacy of simple routine is much more potent than the fuss of something out of the ordinary; these Gods are part of my normal life, and incorporating my devotional work into what I do normally seems very fitting for me.
>
> I use candles a lot; lighting them marks the beginning and closing of the time that is set aside just for myself and the Gods. Touching on that bond regularly is so important, even more so perhaps than regularly contacting the humans in our lives. Our focus determines our reality, after all; if we focus on the Gods, we find them in our lives more readily. A candle is lit (Loki likes lighters, Hel uses matches) and I just sit. Meditation is done as my devotional, and I spend a few minutes talking with the Gods.
>
> Doing this regularly (I do a little something each day) changes the feel of the physical space; it's transformed into sacred space, a temple space, and should be treated as such in mundane ways as well. This is where my Gods live, so I try to keep it clean (or at least tidy). The offerings I give aren't left longer than They desire, and are refreshed at the right times. Even living by yourself, you still have roommates (which is how I often refer to Them) and the routine by which your run your

household affects Them, even if you're all crammed into a single bedroom. A certain amount of cleanliness from all parties is necessary. I'll often incorporate cleaning into my devotional time, and consider the act itself to be a devotional activity.

Contrasting with group activities ... I think that it's largely the same. It's still taking the time to reaffirm the bonds between the human community and the divine one. Approaching that time with the correct mindset is important; these are our friends and family and, while They accept us at our worst, we like to give Them our best. The idea of cleanliness is not just limited to the physical space, but also to the emotional one; being free of emotional "clutter" allows us to allow the Gods more fully into our hearts and into our lives. A little more pomp is often called for; where you may use simple napkins for yourself, maybe you'd bring out the nicer linen if you had people over for dinner. That extra effort is not just for the Gods, but is a gesture of respect for the other people you're working with.

–Jessica Maestas

If I'm doing a big serious indoor blót to Someone I do like to set aside an area and designate it as reserved for (insert name of spirit/deity) and any guests He or She sees fit to bring. I increasingly have an issue with confused interlopers, especially when working with my Dead, so setting limits is a necessity at times. It's less about defining the space as more sacred than that other bit of space over there, and more about reminding anyone who's hanging around the area that I'm not running a bleedin' soup kitchen.

I cordon off the area (usually my workroom) and start by cleansing it, usually by smudging with white sage and lighting a plain white candle or two. After that I set up the altar. I have permanent harrows to some People, but the altar gives me more space to play around with. I put down a cloth of an appropriate colour, light candles—I like the ones in coloured tubes so the light itself is coloured and not just the wax. I get some incense going (if appropriate—of course, not Everyone likes it; some prefer woodsmoke, or cooking smells). I might put on some music or beat a drum, or chant suitable verses. I fill the area with light, colour, fragrance and sound. The idea is to fill the room with an atmosphere that's as welcoming as possible for the esteemed guest, and also to get my own head in the game so I'll be prepped and focused.

After everything is done and I've said good-bye, I open the window and tidy everything away, sweep up, wipe down, and generally re-set the space. A neutral flavour of incense and another white candle can help if things have been especially sticky. (Having said all that of course I've just been reminded of the times where I've carefully created my Sacred Space™ only to be told to pack everything up and move into another room because Somebody wanted more space to dance with me. Hey ho.)

–Mordant Carnival

Mindfulness Exercises

The smallest and most humble—though by no means the least important—use of ritual is to create mindfulness through regular repetitive devotions. It can be around any meaningful thing—giving one's gratitude to the Gods, celebrating the sun coming up, doing a string of prayer beads. For many people, this seems overly simple and trivial, but it's not trivial at all. Just try to do one three-minute practice every day, and you'll find that it will be difficult to keep up. You might do other things every day—going to the bathroom in the morning, eating breakfast, brushing your teeth before bed—but because these things are exercises requiring mindfulness, and that's partially their purpose, it becomes difficult. Even if you're well practiced and you do these things regularly, you may still end up slacking off during some periods of your life (and perhaps berating yourself for that).

Ari's Reasons Why Spirit-Workers Should Do Personal Daily Devotions:

1. It feeds your soul. Most people don't even know that their soul is hungry and ought to be fed, until you see a beautiful sunset or waterfall and something in you gives a big sigh and says "Yes!" While that sort of thing does feed the soul, it can't live on occasional banana splits alone. It needs daily nourishment. Personal devotions give this kind of daily nourishment. If you're a spirit-worker, you need that much more than the average person, because your soul is constantly under stress, being used in ways that most people's souls never imagine. Just like a professional athlete can't feed their body like a couch potato, a spirit-worker can't put all that pressure on their *hame* and their *ve* and their *maegen* and their *hamingja* while starving the soul-complex of regular nutrition. Daily devotions are the morning oatmeal of soul-food, but if you might be called out suddenly at any moment to run a spirit-work marathon, you'll be damn glad of that daily morning oatmeal.

2. It creates mindfulness. The more you do it, the more you start to notice the other daily rituals that you do regularly. Is there a particular way that you sit down, or look in the mirror, or eat certain foods? When did you begin to do things this way, and what force does it honor? Then you start to add little things to your devotions, like a silent prayer of thanks every time you put food in your mouth, or a special acknowledgment every time you see the Moon.

3. It gives you an anchor in hard times. That includes those times that the Gods seem to have left you in the lurch, the silent times that come to all of us, when our signal clarity is down and we feel alone in the Cosmos. Sometimes that's harder for us, the ones who have the Gods and wights jabbering into our ears; harder for us to endure that sudden silence than it is for those who only get the occasional divine whisper. During these times, the daily devotions give you something to hang onto, so that when They come back into focus again—as They always will—you have not lost your path to wandering and despair.

4. It gives you a tiny island of spiritual connection, no matter how crazy and materialistic the rest of your life may be.

5. It strengthens your connection to the Gods and wights, and there can't be too much of that. Daily devotions keep the connections clean and working and well-used, so that you can find them again when you're screwed up and your clarity is crappy.

–Ari, seidhmadhr

The Body Of The Rite

The two underlying premises of the Path of Ritual are that A: Repetition builds power, and B: Emotion carries power. It doesn't matter which emotion you invoke—fear, ecstasy, yearning, all are useful. This is especially true for group ritual. In order to generate and harness power, you generate and harness one or more emotions. Then you give that energy a particular flavor and send it to do a particular job. The most common job in group rite is opening the door to the Gods and their energies, but it might go toward something else—group bonding, for example, or teaching something, or reaching into one's self for something buried.

So those are the two tools, to be used in turn, over and over. Stimulate some emotion—through what is said, through some visual effect of what is seen, through music, through scent, through strongly evocative action. Then create some repetition—maybe what is done can be done again, with small changes, or perhaps each event is separated by a repeating pattern of some other action or words. Then evoke emotion again, and then invoke repetition again, and so forth. Ideally, this should be done so smoothly that the people involved do not feel manipulated by either the emotions or the repetition. Subtlety may be required; one of the biggest mistakes of new writers who try to write emotional scenes is being too heavy-handed with it. When people see it coming, they get out of the way. Good ritual is manipulative, in that it should pull things out of people that would not be released in everyday life at the supermarket; what makes it ethical is that everyone consented to be there, and people can (ideally) leave at any time if they choose to do so. No one comes to a ritual hoping to be bored and unmoved; the first motivation in entering sacred space is to experience something other than the "ordinary".

One example of a personal ritual might be: First, state your intent. "My life has become cluttered. I don't know where to put my priorities any more. I feel like I'm wasting days spinning in circles. This is not what I'm supposed to be doing." From that, you could work up a ritual with Nyth, the Rune of Need, and find out what is the Absolute Necessity. The point of the ritual would be to focus your entire being on that. You would study Nyth, and study all the correspondences that go with it, meditate on it a lot, and make sure that the words are really well phrased. Then—and this is another key aspect of ritual, it happens within a defined space—you would open a ritual space by whatever means, whether it's done with a Thor's hammer or the banishing ritual of the pentagram or just calling the quarters. Your intent should be "This is now the space in which this thing is going to happen." Which is, as much as anything else, just getting the Monkey Brain to pay attention to what's going on.

Then you infuse yourself with all your collected Nyth-related inputs. You might draw it several times. You might dance it, or sing it, or drum it. You might have it cut into your back. You might breathe its smells or chant its name five zillion times. You might make a list of all the things that you think you need, and throw them in a fire—which should be a needfire, by the way, started with the firebow, as that's the Nyth pictogram. You would design the ritual with those activities that relate to Nyth and most speak to you, and then in that ritual space you would do them, and generate some energized enthusiasm about them, some attention and focus and emotion and engagement with it. You build that and build that, until it gets to a point where it can't get any bigger, or in some cases, that you can't go any lower.

There was a ritual that I did with Skulda that was about looking at everything that was horrible and grotesque in the world, starting with me, and accepting full blame for it. Even though it's not reasonable or true, it was about just being responsible for all of it, until it became the bottom of the pit—and from there I was able to envelop the whole thing. Yes, it's irrational, but you have to overwhelm your monkey-mind. At some point you will know that it's sufficient, and it's important at that point to have some kind of birthing or grounding thing that takes all of this energy and stamps it into the manifest world, or into your own energy system. So at the climax of the ritual, you might do the carving of the Rune on yourself, or you might cast the list of confusing things into the fire, or whatever it is that is the climactic psychodramatic end. Then it's done, finished. All the power that's generated you just cast into that moment, and then you walk away and let it cook.

That, for us, is the generic basic ritual on which huge variations can be done. Sometimes the casting of the space is really subtle, so that somebody who was watching you wouldn't know that you were doing it. Sometimes I even do ritual in corporate meetings, and I use everyone sitting down and getting a cup of tea as the casting of the space, and then I close the door. The door is closed, now the ritual is started, and we're doing a round of "What is this meeting for?" So we're stating the intent. Then we're doing a round of brainstorming, which gets the energy moving, with a very nonjudgmental set of solutions to whatever it is that we're doing. Then we start to debate them—now you really get the emotion going, letting it get really fiery, and it can be quite confrontational if you're confident with it. You can be invoking deities at this point as well, saying "Come witness this, come help us." In a corporate environment that can be "What would the Board like us to do?" while silently I'm invoking whoever I need to get the deal done.

This is actually very northern-tradition, in that they had a very ritualized public debate system. That's something that isn't seen much in the modern Pagan community, which tends to prefer to suppress confrontation. There is the whole talking stick thing, but even that is used more to suppress conflict than to give it a space, even though conflict is absolutely necessary. I'd like to see it drawn out into ritualistic combat of some sort. A well-run meeting is ritualistic combat. The Thing could take days of people hailing their ancestors and then speaking, then hailing the Gods and then speaking. The ritual part of it did keep people from coming to blows, or becoming useless conversation. What I particularly like about that is to recite the deeds of your ancestors, and then to invoke worthiness before you speak, to make sure that you speak well and thoughtfully and honorably. Putting your mind on the deeds of your ancestors tends to help you to remember to act worthily. Invoking deity is very much part of it for me as well. To me that's all part of making space for divine help.

So one-time ritual is very different from doing a ritual for all time, and the only way I can generate a fully focused intent and apply myself is by doing a ritual. Eventually it gets to the point where everything that you're doing is ritualized to some extent all the time, and you have to make special efforts to make big ritual stuff on special occasions when you need to raise more power.

-Lydia Helasdottir

Shaman and Priest: Group Rites

In the time of ancient hunter-gatherers, humans banded together in tiny groups to survive. Most had only one spirit-worker among them, if any; sometimes there might be two, with different specialties. As intermediary with the Gods and spirits, the shaman was both priest and magician, healer and counselor, and anything else that was needed. There could be no such thing as regular weekly services—nomadic life was too irregular, and most time and effort was spent on simple survival. Religious rituals were held as needed, or at specific times of the year. As we can see from accounts of public rites of the Inuit *angakok*, or Siberian spirit-workers, the shaman's rites were dramatic and intense, and sometimes cathartic for the small number of onlookers attending.

Later, after widespread agriculture and the rise of cities, ritual specialists evolved who served specific deities and kept their temples and groves. (In some rural areas with small numbers, the shamans still ruled for a time even after the onset of agriculture, such as the Siberian "white" and "black" shamans, where the former presided over the spring sowing and the latter over the fall harvesting.) While they might do some of the jobs of the shaman, most priest/esses concentrated on a small number of tasks ... for an increasingly larger number of congregants. The physical dynamics alone of running a rite for thirty people in a tent compared to one for three hundred people in a temple square are sharply divergent, and required very different style and techniques. When religion became a regularized event for a sizeable population, it became toned down. It's not necessarily in anyone's best interest to have a cathartic experience every week, especially in the company of hundreds of strangers also being similarly triggered. (Certainly it can be done; rock concerts prove that if nothing else. But it is hit-or-miss, and results are more likely to be mixed and cannot be guaranteed.)

While it is still important to create moving ritual that gives space for the presence of deities, the priest with a congregation can only bring the group so far and no further. A skilled ritualist with a good team and a well-planned rite can go a long way towards opening people to feeling, but the best results will always be done shaman-style, in small groups in a small place. That's why the Eleusinian Mysteries, which drew hundreds every year in ancient Greece, took place in a cave for selected numbers of individuals to go through a few dozen at a time. The larger the group mind, the harder it is to get people past their boundaries—and rightly so. Larger groups cannot necessarily be guaranteed to be entirely safe. However, when there is not enough emotional evocation, the rite becomes empty, boring, and stale.

Today, Neo-Pagan ritual specialists are caught in a difficult and shifting space. Most of us grew up on congregational rituals of varying degrees of evocative, from occasionally transcendent to interminably boring. As a religion largely of converts, we probably started practicing Paganism in small groups simply due to lack of numbers. Again, the rituals we were exposed to may have been as reserved as those we grew up with, or they may have surprised us with the potential of small-group cathartic rite to create an intense experience. Some priest/esses went on to attempt to recreate this in larger groups, as the numbers grew, and became frustrated with their inability to do so. Some didn't even notice that their group rituals were less than satisfying, having never experienced anything else in their lives.

The job of the modern-day shaman as a ritual specialist is different from that of a priest/ess. That doesn't mean that one person can't do both, but that's a matter of donning different "hats" and being very clear under which hat you are working. Today's spirit-workers need to continue—and in some cases rediscover altogether—the art of cathartic ritual for small groups. As discussed above, group ritual is the safest and most effective of all these Paths for group workings in altered states, and applied altered states are the venue of the shaman, not the priest/ess. It's not just a single person who needs drastic healing; sometimes several people need it in a way that can only be accomplished by bringing them together into the same intense rite. The community rituals run by the Inuit *angakok* were psychodramas used for community confession and bonding as well as the more esoteric task of figuring out what the spirits wanted and what to do about it. This is more in the shamanic ritualist's bailiwick than creating regular, sustainable events for large numbers of people where the fewest possible are offended and the greatest possible number manage to feel some vague presence of the divine.

As Galina Krasskova writes in her essay below, the majority of Pagan rituals—and perhaps the majority of common religious rites throughout the world—are focused more closely on the people than on the Gods. How much of the shaman's art should find its way into temple rites is an ongoing debate—but certainly spirit-workers should be encouraged to create smaller shamanic rituals. Ari points out:

> We spirit-workers have a gift for channeling wight-energies, and that's not just about letting them speak through us. If I'm on my game, I can become an open door for the energy of the spirits to come into this world. When that happens, it doesn't matter if the audience doesn't believe a damn thing—they will experience something heavy, even if they can't identify it. They'll walk out of there saying, "Whoa. I don't know what that was, but whoa." Of course, with a whole audience of nonbelievers, you just piss off the wights who show up. It's best to have mostly people who are there for exactly what they're getting, and limit the number of thrill-seekers or those who trail along dubiously after their significant others.
>
> Because this is what we do when we run public ritual. It's what those who came before us did. That why you should warn everyone who comes that this is for those who want to be in the presence of that which can make you pretty uncomfortable, if you're not ready for it. It should never be used for entertainment—shamans in Siberia who were seduced by money to perform their traditional chants and

dances on the stage for skeptical Russian and American audiences have found that the spirits take vengeance on them for that insult. It should never be used to enhance the spirit-worker's reputation—that motivation is just begging for the Gods and wights to do something completely overkill that will ruin said reputation. The only reason to do it is to allow consenting people to connect with wights that they otherwise would never touch—and that's an excellent reason, so stick to that and it won't matter how crazy the mainstream thinks you are. Those who need what you have to give will show up for it, and those who don't—well, their disdain is a weeding mechanism, after all.

–Ari, seidhmadhr

A Northern-Tradition Approach to Ritual Work

by Galina Krasskova

When I first came into northern-tradition religion, I was absolutely appalled by what passed for ritual in the general Heathen community. I had, thankfully, received excellent training in ritual dynamics and construction during my years with the Fellowship of Isis. I knew that a good ritual was a powerful means of connecting to Deity, and that the tools of constructing such a rite belonged to all religious traditions. I'd been constructing and leading rituals for years and I'd seen the dramatic effects it could have on people seeking to develop their spirituality. For a very long time, it was my primary means—along with the Ascetic's Path—of connecting to the Gods. It was also one of two ways (the other being pastoral counseling) that I, misanthropic as I am, served as a priest. It was one of several disciplines that taught me to keep the Gods first in my thoughts, life and heart. It also helped me learn to carry my spiritual awareness into my mundane life and to keep those doors ever more widely open. (Of course, take this as something of a caveat, because it all led to my becoming a spirit-worker!) Walking the path of Ritual has the potential to lead to a well-balanced, integrated, holistic life in which spiritual and mundane flow freely into each other with little dichotomy between the two.

I think there's an aversion in Heathenry against adapting various techniques into Heathen ritual, such as chanting, meditation, altar work, etc. Those objections tend to fall into two categories: A) it's too Wiccan, and B) we can't prove that our ancestors did it, also known as "it's not in lore." And to be fair, most Heathens claim to be completely satisfied with faining and blot as it's currently practiced. It apparently fulfills them. I have to wonder, though, whether this isn't partly because they've nothing to compare it with, and partly because they are uncomfortable with a ritual that will open them more fully to the realm of the sacred, and to direct experience of the Gods. All I know is that for me, trained as I was in a tradition that has a thorough and well-rounded ritual basis, I found the typical Heathen ritual interminably boring and almost never evocative of the presence of the Gods. People rarely moved out of mundane consciousness and into that state that evoked awareness of the sacred. For all its formal structure (and I appreciate the discipline inherent in structure; I was a ballet dancer for thirteen years and I'm all for discipline and continuity with the past), most Heathen rites as practiced in the mainstream community rarely reached a point where people's attention was more on the Gods than on anything else. Rarely if ever were the attendees carried away into mystical consciousness, and I suppose when all's said and done, the average Heathen was glad of it. I, however, always felt that something vital and both very sacred and very precious was missing.

A good ritual is like a well-written paper: it has a beginning, middle and an end and everything that connects those three parts refers in some way to the purpose of the rite. The ritual worker must learn not only to create sacred space palpably, but also to move the assembled folk into and out of liminal space safely. Indeed, that's the key aspect of ritual: liminality. A ritual, when well constructed, creates a dramatic shift in the consciousness of the attendees, one that renders them far more open to the Gods and to direct experience or participation in the sacred than they otherwise would have. Ritual is a magical thing, a path that connects and links disparate worlds for however brief a time it's being properly experienced. To this end, an experienced ritual worker has numerous tools at his or her disposal: incense, altars, candles, chanting/singing, dancing, ecstatic prayer and invocation, storytelling, sacred drama, guided meditation, music, ordeal, etc. These things are found in all religious traditions (even the Norse to one degree or another) and can all be effective in establishing ritual space and flow. While not everyone will respond to the same tools, usually some combination of techniques will prove effective for most people. None of these things is restricted to any one spiritual tradition. Chanting, for instance, isn't especially Wiccan. Nor is dancing. Christian mystics chant, Buddhists chant, Sufi dervishes dance, so did the ancient Egyptians. Every single tool utilized in ritual has cross-cultural implications. They aren't in any way restrictive. Emphasis might change from one religion to another, but the same techniques cross all religious boundaries sooner or later.

However, there are a few things that one should learn to lead rituals well. The most important thing about becoming a ritual worker is this: leave your ego at the door. While a well-worked ritual may evoke intense emotions in all attendees, the ritual worker does not have the luxury of indulging in his or her own drama during the rite. The ritual is not about the ritual facilitator. It is about the Gods. The facilitator is only preparing the room and opening the door. He or she is a technician and should never forget it. A ritual facilitator or priest/ess who cannot put their own drama aside for the duration of the ritual shouldn't be leading one. Furthermore, the facilitator needs to be prepared (and hopefully trained) to deal with any emotional effects, trauma, or spiritual crises that might occur as a result of the ritual. These things are normal in the aftermath of intense rituals. What is not normal—what is, in fact, a gross mishandling of sacred tools—is the facilitator turning the aftermath of a ritual into a drama for the gratification of their own ego and unmet emotional needs. Save it for your therapist, or for your own personal rituals.

Other than that, proper ritual work takes an intense focus combined with an awareness of the flow of energy. Ideally, the ritual worker is aware of where every person present is emotionally, psychologically, and energetically. Working a ritual is like opening a floodgate and then closing it off again. The one leading the rite has to be fully focused on the proper flow of energy, but also needs to be aware that a good ritual may in fact open the possibility of a God or Goddess showing up, usually via a horse. The utilization of sound, song, dancing, incense, etc. is twofold: it not only serves as a gift to the Deities being honored, but also helps create the proper psychological state in the attendees. In my own personal rites, I prefer to use sacred chanting and *galdr* to open myself up. When I led rituals within Fellowship of Isis, I'd often incorporate guided meditations. The tools may vary but the goal is the same.

It can be helpful for the priest/ess or ritual worker to have a good grounding in counseling basics, psychology but also concentration techniques. This was never a problem for me. Having been both a dancer and martial artist for a number of years, I'd been schooled in disciplines that required an intense focus, and I was able to carry this over into my spiritual and magical work. For those without this background, studying a martial art can be helpful (it can also assist in learning to move energy) and there are numerous books on meditation and concentration techniques on the market. Learning how to focus is a skill that can help one in daily working life, not just ritual! Moreover, it is the first fundamental skill necessary for any ritual worker. Ideally, the facilitator will have spent some time attending rituals and learning to construct them. They have their own flow and pattern, and it takes a certain sensitivity to these things, which can be developed through experience, to know how to manage and lead a rite well.

Despite the connotation of its name, ritual is a very flexible thing. It may be as simple or complex as the person constructing it wishes to make it. It may be constructed and utilized by and for a group, or for one person. I find that the continuity of having daily or at least regular personal rituals very helpful in the development of spiritual discipline. In fact, experiencing rituals regularly tends to pattern the psyche to a certain receptiveness for spiritual encounters. It's almost as if the repeated, regular experience of ritual work opens the psyche to greater awareness of the Gods much like a dancer's daily routine at the barre prepares the muscles for performing classical variations. While ritual work doesn't take the place of daily devotions or prayer, it is a nice complement to both.

My daily rituals are fairly simple, though they vary depending on what the Gods are having me do at any given time. For instance, if I am expected to master a certain skill by a given Deity, then I set time aside every day (or as close to it as possible) to practice that skill. I ground and center daily and spend some time in working my altar. I also have a regular cleansing ritual that I do for myself. I pray with my Norse prayer beads almost daily and spend some length of time talking with Odin, Loki, Sigyn et al. I also chant *galdr* nearly every day. My ritual work is generally split between what I do as a devotee of the Gods and what I do as a spirit-worker. Years ago, I used to run a group devotional ritual once a week with special rites on the new and full moons plus seasonal rituals. It was the mainstay of my spiritual practice, and while I don't feel the need to maintain that intense ritual schedule anymore, I cannot deny that it was both nourishing and one of the things that came to define my spiritual development more than any other. It was an excellent training ground, and certainly it was the way I first met Odin! Years spent in regular ritual work also developed a strong sensitivity to the flow of energy and Deity presence that I have found invaluable in my work as a spirit worker. I credit this with my later ability to see Wyrd.

Rituals are passionate expressions of devotion, carefully crafted moments of concentrated power. At its core, ritual is about experience. One can write all one wants about rituals, but the best way to learn about this particular path is to experience it for oneself.

Recaning Song for Blessing Mugwort Sticks

Gemyne ðu, mugwyrt, hwæt þu ameldodest,
Hwæt þu renadest æt Regenmelde.
Una þu hattest, yldost wyrta,
ðu miht wið þre and wið þritig,
þu miht wiþ attre and wið onflyge,
þu miht wiþ þam laþan ðe geond lond færð.

Keep in mind, Mugwort, what thou promised,
What thou laid down at the great Reckoning.
First you are called, oldest herb,
Thou hast might against three and against thirty.
Thou hast might again poison and flying disease,
Though hast might against the evil that fares over the land.

This is the first verse of the Song of the Nine Sacred Herbs, a power song of my ancestors from the Lacnunga, an early medieval Anglo-Saxon herbal. I sing it over my mugwort plants when I ask permission to cut them for recaning sticks (*recaning* is an Anglo-Saxon term that roughly covers the same ground as the common American term "smudging", or the Celtic term "saining", and yes, it is cognate to *reek*) and then I sing it again when I bind them into sticks about an inch thick and six inches long. It calls the spirit of Grandmother Mugwort and reminds her of her job, which among other things is to clear the air of negative energies and cleanse the space, making it ready for sacred energy to arrive.

When I want to recan the space later, I light the Mugwort stick and sing the last verse of the same Song, which wards the directions. Since I do have a long history of practice in the modern Pagan community, the path of warding the directions is deep and strong to me, and it was with joy that I found an authentic equivalent—not because I must do everything authentically, but because it showed a connection between what I do and what was done by those before me. This final verse of the Song (along with a homemade Mugwort stick) has become my general-purpose fast creator of sacred space. I do it before each reading, before each personal ritual for clients and for myself, and whenever I feel that a space is cluttered and needs clearing.

>Gif ænig attor cume eastan fleogan
>Oððe ænig norðan cume, oððe ænig suðan cume,
>Oððe ænig westan ofer werðeode.
>Ic ana wat ea rinnende
>þær þa nygon nædran nean behealdað,
>Motan ealle weoda nu wyrtum aspringan,
>Sæs toslupan, eal sealt wæter,
>ðonne ic þis attor of ðe geblawe.

>*If any poison comes flying from the east,*
>*Or any comes from the north, or any comes from the south,*
>*Or any from the west over the people.*
>*I know a running stream,*
>*There the nine poisons you may behold,*
>*From the weeds new herbs spring up,*
>*The seas part, all salt water,*
>*Then this poison from you I blow.*

Start by waving the stick in the four directions, as you call each one on the first three lines. Then circle it around you. End after you finish singing the last line by actually blowing on the smoking recaning stick, directing the smoke where it seems more appropriate.

Pronunciation of Old English is a matter of much debate. The truth is that we are not completely certain how many of the vowels were pronounced, and different experts have slightly differing opinions. At any rate, I have reconstructed the pronunciations as best I can.

For a simple recording of the entire song (not just the first and last verses), in order that you might hear them, my CD of this and all the songs in this book, *Nine Sea-Songs*, can be ordered online at: http://www.cauldronfarm.com/music/ or can be mail-ordered by sending $9 to Raven Kaldera, 12 Simond Hill Rd., Hubbardston MA 01452. Shipping is included in the price. This is in no way a professional CD, just me and a guitar and drum, but it will give you an idea of the song tune and pronunciation.

The Heartbeat Of The Worlds: The Path Of Rhythm

He drums. The drum is a horse, a ship, a beating heart. Each beat a falling hoof on the air, a rocking wave of the sea, a step down a path. His voice, singing the chants, is the wind filling the sails of the ship, but even so it can only move with the rocking waves and not against them. Carry me, carry me. Carry me out, carry me home.

He drums. The wonder of getting there by drumming is that you don't fly, you walk every step of the road. Each beat is a step, walking at first, then running. Like going anywhere on foot—or even on a horse—it takes a while. It is not like flying on wings, like pain or drugs or sex or even breath. It is taken step by step, hour after hour. Also unlike flying, you never crash-land, and you never find yourself in a strange place without knowing how to come back. When you walk the Path of Rhythm, you learn the lay of the land. You learn every weary step, and every weary step back.

Sometimes another drums, and then he is the dancer, caught by the rhythm and whirled again and again around the fire. This is closer to flying, but not the sort of flying you experience in dreams, powered only by your own will and your own body. This is flying on the back of the wind, on great birds, on whatever spirits you can summon and convince to take you there. Your feet may be striking the ground, but your spirit flies, each thump of foot on earth the heavy beating of great wings in the air.

Mighty bull of the earth!
Horse of the steppes!
I, the mighty bull, bellow!
I, the horse of the steppes, neigh!
I, the man set above all other beings!
I, the man most gifted of all!
I, the man created by the master all-powerful!
Horse of the steppes, appear! Teach me!
Enchanted bull of the earth, appear! speak to me!
Powerful master, command me!
All of you, who will go with me, give heed with your ears!
Those whom I command, follow me not!
Approach not nearer than is permitted!
Thou of the left side, O lady with thy staff,
If anything be done amiss, if I take not the right way,
I entreat you—correct me!
My errors and my path show to me, O mother of mine!
Wing thy free flight! Pave my wide roadway!
Souls of the sun, mothers of the sun,
Living in the south, in the nine wooded hills,
I adjure you all—let your three shadows stand high!
In the East, on your mountain, lord, grandsire of mine,
Great of power and thick of neck, be thou with me!
And thou, grey-bearded wizard Fire, I ask thee
With all my dreams, comply! To all my desires consent! All fulfill!

–Yakut shaman's song, from Czaplicka's
writings on Siberian shamanism

In the words of Hazrat Inyat Khan: "A keen observation shows that the whole universe is a single mechanism working by the law of rhythm ... There is no movement which has no sound, and there is no sound which has no rhythm." Rhythm is everywhere in the animist view: it is footsteps, hoofbeats, the beating of bird's wings, the ebb and flow of the tides. It is the vibration of each note, making it distinct from each other; likewise it is the light-wavelength vibration of every color. It is sunrise and sunset, rain and wind, sleeping and waking, hunger and satiety, the four-count back-beat of the seasons, the return again and again to each solstice and equinox. It is the stroking of a lover's hand, the patting of a mother on her baby's back, the in and out of the sexual act that made every one of us. It is the beating of our hearts, the pulsing of our blood, the flashes of electrical activity across our neurons. It is birth and death and rebirth and death. When we are aware of and one with our environment, we realize that we live buried in onion-layers of rhythm within rhythm within rhythm.

Knowing this, it could be said that all the rhythms that we make with our hands are simply reflections of these experiential rhythms. It is becoming aware of this (am I drumming wings? Hoofbeats? Tides? Seasons? Traffic?) and enhancing it, opening to the specific energy that is trying to filter through us and letting it pour forth, that allows the Path of Rhythm to be a real conduit for magic. This is the real power in it, not just the mild trance that science has shown to be an easily-recreatable side effect of rhythm. However, most people are going to want to begin with that mild trance, and it's a good beginner's space.

The Path of Rhythm is one of the most popular of the Eightfold Path among modern neo-shamanistic practitioners today. It does not have the scariness of sex magic or ordeal work, or the intimidating hard work of the ascetic's path, or the illegality and danger of sacred plants. It's easy to obtain a drum, or at least a rattle (the current no-musical-talent mainstay of modern shamanistic workshops) and learn to move it in a vaguely rhythmic way. And, truly, for all my tongue-in-cheek sarcasm, it works with less effort and more regularity than many of those harder paths, at least to the point of getting into a mild altered state.

This is not news, at least to most fans of modern music. Since the 1950s when African-derived rhythms began to be incorporated into pop music, wildly dancing teenagers discovered that moving to driving, repetitive rhythms could put them into a state where nothing mattered except the ecstasy of the moment. Even today, some spiritual leaders and writers warn about the hypnotic rhythms of so much modern music, viewing them with suspicion because they don't trust the altered states that it can induce. The ancient shamans were well aware of the fact that rhythm can create a mildly open and suggestive state for anyone who listens, even if they're barely aware of it. That's why we have mood-inducing music for movie soundtracks, and why people use their favorite CD as a way to change their mood.

Music, in all its forms that strive to alter someone's mood to a greater or lesser extent, comes under the aegis of the Path of Rhythm. Even without a strong backbeat, one has to remember that the pitch and purity of every note is determined by the rhythm of its soundwaves; sing or play an instrument into an oscilloscope and see it for yourself. Rhythm is the basis of all sound. Even arrhythmically-sounding music still contains rhythms; it's just that they change rapidly from moment to moment. Every piece of music is the interweaving of dozens, hundreds, or thousands of different rhythms of sound. Given that, it could easily be said that this path is the most common of all of the Eight, available to anyone in some form or another.

Shamans and Drums

It is probably also true that what we consider "rhythm instruments" were the first musical tools, probably starting with whacking sticks against each other, or against some surface. One of the oldest known drums is the slit drum, merely a horizontal log with a deep slit carved in it which is played by being beaten with sticks; by adjusting where the blows fall, the players can create a number of different and interesting tones. The ringing of wood against wood was one of the first musical tones that human beings sought to deliberately reproduce into musical tools. Another was the sound of slapping skin (including hand-clapping), which probably predates even wooden sticks. The sound of slapping skin is the direct ancestor of the stretched skin-over-a-frame that is the classic drum of a million shamanic ancestors.

As I touch on in the (entirely spirit-taught) section following this chapter on drums in the ancient northern tradition, we have only one reference to drumming in the "lore", and that is Loki's accusation of Odin in the *Lokasenna* that he "tapped on a *vett*" during his time learning seidhr with Freyja while dressing as a woman and doing "socially unacceptable" sexual activities, all of which sounds entirely like certain kinds of shamanic training were it happening in another culture. The meaning of the word *vett* is lost to us; it could mean drum, or some other thing—a pot lid?—for all we know. However, I would point out that the oldest forms of the word "drum" in most cultures is almost always a single-syllable onomotopoeic word that mimics the sound of the single drumbeat. Drum, dob, bom, tam … vett?

Not all shamans (and shamanlike figures in various cultures, whatever their names might be) use drums, but so many of them do that the drum has become synonymous with the shaman, even more than the sacred plants. According to some of the Siberian shamans, the drum is the horse that the shaman rides while in trance, taking him from one world to another. For others, like the Evenk, it might be a reindeer that bears him, or a boat or ferry riding the waves. Shaman drums were made carefully, with the animal whose skin it bore ritually killed, and the frame cut from a tree that had offered its life up. The frame was bent over a steaming cauldron—bringing together the elements of fire, water, earth, and air—and sanctified in water, as described in more detail in the chapter on drums later in this book. In the Eurasian arctic and subarctic traditions, jingles of metal and bone were often attached around the rim, perhaps made into magical charms. Making the drum in this way called the proper spirit into it, and it was—and is, to modern shamanic practitioners—considered a living being from then on. If the head had to be replaced, it was replaced over the old broken head, for to have an empty hoop would kill the drum-spirit. If the frame broke, the drum was dead and should be burned with honors.

Circumpolar Eurasian shaman drums—especially the *runebom* of the Saami *noiade*—were drawn with a map of the worlds on them, including various spirit helpers. Divination was done by placing a small personal item of the asker—perhaps a ring—or possibly a special metal pointer made for the purpose onto the drum head. The drum was struck from underneath, and the symbol onto which the object moved was interpreted. This is a simple form of divination that I do myself; it is quick and travels well to places where one might not have the ability to sit down and spread out runes or other sortilege divinatory methods. So the drum is an altered-state tool, opener of doors to other worlds, caller of wights, energy-transmitter, and divination method.

Drummers who use rhythm in healing have found that the drum can be a good divinatory instrument for both diagnosis and repair. Ideally, the way that this works is to beat a drum held just above the body of the (usually reclining) client, moving it up and down from point to point, and listen to how the drum resonates with the energy points of the astral and physical body. If some points are sluggish or too fast, drumming for a period of time just over that point at a more correct rhythm (determined by experimenting) can slow them down or speed them up, or generally set them more right with the rhythm of the body itself. Of course, such a practitioner would have to be very humble about figuring out the rhythm of each client's body; all people are different and the range of "personal" rhythms can be amazingly variable. The drum can tell you this, but only if you go at it with no assumptions to begin with.

Some research being done at the moment claims to have discovered that regular drumming has a wide range of interesting long-term effects on the body, including raising endorphin levels for chronic pain, aiding the immune system, lowering blood pressure, reducing stress, and temporarily harmonizing the hemispheres of the brain. Each hemisphere has a different task to concentrate on while drumming—the left brain keeps track of polyrhythms and sees how they fit together, and the right brain does the work of entraining the body to the rhythm and doling out any ecstatic chemistry. Drumming—or any kind of music, but especially drumming—brings them together into one act.

The Law of Entrainment

This brings us to the Law of Entrainment, also known as Huygens' Law. In 1665, the Dutch scientist Christian Huygens noted that if you took two clocks that were ticking out of rhythm and set them next to each other, they would slowly come into rhythm with each other. This could be repeated again and again; there was no way to keep them permanently ticking off-beat. The law that he wrote stated that two or more rhythms in proximity will always fall into synchrony with each other. In other words, any things that oscillate in the same field will line up together. This doesn't just refer to mechanical objects. Birds who fly in formation know that flapping in rhythm with each other saves energy, so as not to fight against this natural law. We, as human beings, have specific rhythms in our blood and our brain, but the external rhythm will automatically override our internal rhythms, synchronizing us to whatever it may be, whether we realize it or not.

The Law of Entrainment is one of those irritating scientific truths that make most scientists—unless they're the few who are able to use science to see greater truths—squirm with annoyance. We don't know why it works, only that it does—and any theorizing about why it works tends to lead researchers into a place of seeing all things as part of a huge cosmic system instead of as separate mechanical parts, which is a frightening place to be for many secular-minded individuals. The current theory is that it takes less energy for more forms of energy to perform the same task at the same time than to go against each other ... but even that isn't much of an explanation as to "why". The "why" of it, to me in my worldview, is obvious: rhythm attracts rhythm, because everything is a dance.

However, once you realize the implications of Huygens' Law, you begin to look around you and think about what, exactly, you are entrained to on a daily basis. Are there ticking clocks by your head while you sleep, or humming appliances? In his excellent book *Drumming On The Edge Of Magic* (which I highly recommend to anyone who works with the Rhythm Path) Mickey Hart notes that all of us in technological societies grow up surrounded by a particular rhythm. That is the rhythm of electricity, which hums at a specific rate. In America, that's usually 60 hertz, or cycles per second, but in much of Europe and parts of the rest of the world, it's 50 hertz. What does being constantly surrounded from birth by a rhythm of 50 or 60 cycles per second—probably not a rhythm selected for its benign effect on the human body and mind—do to our brains and the flesh that surrounds them? Can those of us who grew up ensconced in this inhuman rhythm ever really figure that out from the inside? It's worrisome, but worth thinking about for those of us who don't respond well to modern technology.

Gods In The Beat

The point to keep in mind with all of this entrainment is that everything has its own rhythm, including the Earth itself. There is, ironically, nothing mysterious about this; all these rhythms can be measured electrically in cycles. Drumming along a cycle of 4.5 to 7 beats per minute mimics the brain's own theta rhythms, and has been shown to put people in trance states. The Earth's own rhythm is about 8 cycles per minute. When you drum along that rhythm while sitting on the ground, after a while you entrain your brain and your body to that cycle for a time ... and this is a way to connect into the land-wight in a way that is fully experiential on some level, rather than just a handshake between radically differing beings.

Not only is there a rhythm for all beings in this world, there is also one for all the beings in every other world, and for the Otherworlds themselves. These can be used to invite those beings and that energy into a person or a space in a gentle and organic way; we are not the only creatures in the Universe who are tempted and seduced by rhythm. In the Afro-Caribbean traditions, each *lwa* or *orisha* has their own special drumbeat which is used to honor them, and also to use as a vehicle for spirit-possession, should they choose to enter the bodies of any of their dancing worshipers. Those drumbeats are a high secret of the initiated drummers, and they do not teach them to outsiders due to the possibility of misuse.

At some point, it occurred to me that there would also be a rhythm for every one of my own beloved Gods and wights as well, although I might not be a skilled enough drummer to figure them out ... and although I got acknowledgment on that point, I also got a bit of an attitude that I would have to figure them out for myself; it wasn't just going to be easily downloaded into my head. Loki, especially, seemed to grin and let me know that his rhythm was hidden, and he liked it that way. Odin intimated that each of his *heiti* was a slight variation on one part of his base rhythm, but did not tell me that it would be impossible to figure out. So perhaps what the Northern Tradition needs is a bunch of drummers who can work on the problem, separately and together.

On the other hand, after a short while I was able to come up with the rhythm of the Midgard Serpent, Jormundgand, who graciously danced for me until I got it right and was able to repeat it. It is surprisingly simple, based on counts of eleven, a number which the Serpent, alone and prime, seems to like. There are five repeats of eleven beats, and then six repeats of five beats, and then the entire figure repeats indefinitely, a big circle, until one gets tired. The two parts are, according to what I could make out of the Snake's language, Me/Sea-and-Sky. The Big Snake seemed quite sanguine about letting me publish this rhythm as well; perhaps It feels that anyone who calls It up deserves whatever they get.

The Serpent's Rhythm (for those not rhythm-trained, 1 is the harder beat and 2 is the softer, "following" beat):

11211211212/11211211212/11211211212/11211211212/11211211212/ 11212/11212/11212/11212/11212/11212/—repeat and keep going

This is an example of how sacred drumming is also mathematical, and brings into it the issues of numerology and the sacredness of numbers. All rhythm is reducible to numbers (although some of my mystical-math friends would argue with the connotation of that word *reducible*) and numbers have their own powers. Nine, for example, is the highest and most sacred number in the Northern Tradition, the way that Taoism is bounded by fives, Ayurveda by sixes, and Babylonian (and their Greco-Roman inheritors) by twelves. The lunar cycle spins automatically to the number thirteen. Each of these has a specific meaning, which varies and is argued differently depending on which culture you happen to be dealing with. I am still trying to work out the numerology of the Northern Tradition—aside from its ubiquitous nines—and if I ever figure it out properly, it will show up in a future book. In the meantime, certain intuitive things can be divined by the simple properties of numbers, such as the unique Serpent's rhythm being mostly made up of prime numbers—mostly eleven, but also five and six which add up to eleven. Six (which is non-prime) has long been associated with water in other cultures, so that may be another clue. Perhaps in rediscovering the secrets of this tradition, things will work backwards and we will learn our numerology from first learning the rhythms of the Gods, and studying them.

Galdr and Song

Magical song among the Norse mostly comes under the tradition of *galdr*. This has been an umbrella term for many sorts of magic, but its main tool was sung magic. Song *galdr* is a type of spellsinging, where the intent comes out through the voice and the music; in this way, it is rather a crossover between the Path of Rhythm and the Path of Breath. Saga descriptions of *galdr* all say that it was pleasing to the ear, so perhaps the *galdr*-worker might want to get a bit of actual voice training, or at least regular practice, before performing it in public.

Galdr is closely associated with runes; one form of rune-*galdr* is just singing the names of the runes over and over again, in a kind of long, drawn-out chant that turns the rune-name largely into a string of wordless notes. (Galina Krasskova explicates on this below.) If one has a relationship with the runes, it's quite effective. If you don't know the runes intimately, it's more like singing Fee-Fi-Fo-Fum. *Galdr* was often used to curse, and many associations were made in Norse poetry about the sharpness of the tongue as a weapon. Modernly, it is generally used for more benevolent purposes.

In ancient Norse poetry, there was a particular poetic verse-form that was called *galdralag*, or magic spell meter. It is a form of *fornyrðislag* (old-ways-speech), the oldest of the poetic forms. To write a verse in *fornyrðislag*, the poem is made up of heavily alliterative half-lines, each of which was four or five syllables with two to three "lifts" or accents in the line. Each held a complete phrase, which is what gave Norse poetry its terse feel. The lines were organized in stanzas of two to eight apiece. In addition, *galdralag* is made up of four lines to a stanza, and the fourth line echoes and varies the third line. One example is from the Eggjum grave stone, Sogn, Norway ca. 700 C.E.:

> Hverr of kom Heráss á
> hí á land gotna?
> Fiskr ór fjanda vim svimandi,
> fogl á fjanda lið galandi.

> *As whom came War-god*
> *hither to the land of men?*
> *A fish from the torrent of enemies swimming,*
> *A bird against troop of enemies screaming.*

Or, as an example that I wrote, this charm to work with the plant-spirit of the Garlic plant, a common and very useful healing herb:

> *Garlic, grant my grief*
> *Rest and right relief,*
> *Strike this sickness true,*
> *Spear this sickness through.*

Another song-form mentioned in the famous volva-story that inspires so many modern seidhr-workers is the *varthlokkur*, or "guardian-spirit-enticer". This song-form seems to have been used to call spirits before a public working, ostensibly to guard the space while the volva or vitki was open and vulnerable. Most interestingly, it seems that this song was not any sort of secret lore, but that "ordinary" people were routinely taught such things in order to assist with creating and protecting the space when the itinerant spirit-workers came through. This might be something to keep in mind for northern-tradition religious communities: if various forms of the *varthlokkur* can be rediscovered, perhaps through spirit-connection, groups can routinely be taught them as common religious song, and thus be more useful to spirit-workers who perform publicly (of which, it must be said, few do).

Among the Saami, the young women of the family were routinely taught such songs in order to make them useful "ground crew" and assistants to the traveling *noaide;* the songs included reminding the *noaide* of his task, and giving him a sound-link to come back to his body. Siberian tribes such as the Chukchi, Yakut, and Yukaghir have a long tradition of "shaman-songs", some of which were only sung by shamans, and some which were sung by assistants or the community in order to help the shaman make contact with the Otherworlds.

Seidhr-workers also had specific songs that carried their magic power, called *seidhlaeti*, and like the *galdr* songs, they were said to be sweet-sounding to the ear—some so much so that they were used to lure victims to their deaths. None of the aforementioned songs have survived, of course, although some researchers speculate that they might live on in the Scandinavian custom of *lockrop*, or singing special high-pitched chants in order to summon cattle and other livestock. Others have compared them to the Finnish *tietaja* songs, and the Saami *joik*, both of which are still used today.

Joik—a traditional song of the Saami people, and special to the Saami *noaide*—is similar to *galdr* in some ways, in that it is largely improvised on the spot, letting the subject sing through you, rather than composing words about the subject. *Joik* can include words and poetic lines, wordless chanting, and even noises of animal and wind. There are random repetitions and very little structural form, and no *joik* is ever done the same way twice. Because of their unique nature, they are generally accompanied only by the drumming of the *noaide*, or nothing at all, as no accompanist could keep up with the meanderings. The *galdr*-songs that I sing are in many ways much more similar to *joik* than rune-*galdr*, in that they are not necessarily rune-centered, and they entail me opening my mouth and singing what comes through me from the wights.

In contrast, the Balto-Finnish *tietaja* had many traditional songs which were more or less concrete. Echoes of some of them can be found in the Kalevala, such as the songs sung by the shamanic hero Vainamoinen, or at least the many references to them. Actually, as far as we can tell, shamans in nearly all cultures worked with both sorts of songs—traditional songs that were passed down through generations and had their own power, and the improvised songs that were channeled on the spot for whatever purpose might be needed. In the Northern Tradition, our big problem with regard to shamanic songs is that nearly all of the first category is lost to us. Some of us are slowly creating—or perhaps recreating, with the help of the Gods and wights—that fund, but it will take generations to build it up. In the meantime, most of us work with the second sort of songs—*galdr*-type ephemeral creations that come through us, do their work, and pass on. One sort is not any better per se than the other; it's that they are both useful for different situations. A skilled shaman will be able to figure which is most appropriate at each time, and make proper use of them.

The Art and Practice of Rune-Galdr
by Galina Krasskova

Galdr, from the Old Norse verb *gala* (to crow, to cry, to scream) and related to the noun *gal* (screaming, howling) is a form of magical song or chant common to Northern Tradition magic. It is an incredibly potent form of magical practice, one in which the voice itself becomes the conduit for the power the *vitki* is raising. *Galdr* most often goes hand in hand with runes and the twinning of these two things is tremendously potent.

When a person sings *galdr*, it isn't a matter of just stringing notes together. There is form, pattern, rhythm and intent. The rune is expressing itself, telling a story, taking both the singer and the listeners someplace. It is revealing part and parcel of its essence. When someone really does it right, the listeners don't just hear *galdr*, but rather should experience it through all the senses: images, tastes, sensations…all should flow through both singer and listener. The sound is just the most immediate medium that the rune uses to open everyone up to the totality of what it is, what it wants you to experience, what it wishes to reveal. The voice becomes the key to opening up the world of the runes, the doorway to the web and the creative and destructive power of Ginnungagap.

Runes themselves are composed of sacred power. On a purely mundane level, we know the power of sound, the power of the voice (think of Ella Fitzgerald shattering glass with a single note or the fact that many governments today are utilizing sonic technologies as anti-riot weapons). When that degree of sonic power is combined with the sacred power and intelligence of the runes, its tonal energies and vibrations open points on the web, points of connection to the multiverse. It impacts the web and the listener on a sub-atomic level. It moves into and through its intended target in a way that is not easily blocked or deflected.

An acquaintance of mine believes that we all have an inborn template, part of our psyche that responds quite viscerally to certain musical phrases and notes. While not knowing where this comes from, he believes this underscores the primal power of music, noting its deep impact on cultures the world over. No culture, after all, is without its musical tradition. This inborn affinity for music might be an expression of natural algorithms, the musical equivalent of mathematical formulae that are found in nature. This makes *galdr*-work an incredibly powerful bridge between the world of temporal manifestation and the world of the web. It also makes it a potent tool when utilized for either healing or harm on the psycho-emotional level.

In fact, it is almost as though in uniting the runes with the rhythm, power and vibrations of the voice that a separate living state of being is created. The *galdr* singer, therefore, must learn to flow and navigate within this new energy. The voice inhabits the personality of whoever is *galdring* it. All worlds have beings within them that *galdr*, but Jotun *galdr* sounds nothing like human *galdr*, and Alfar *galdr* sounds nothing like Jotun *galdr*. When we *galdr*, we infuse the rune with the energies of the world we are from and form a link from our world to the web. The runes lack that connective ability on their own. The energy of our *galdr*, combined with the energy of the runes, creates a bridge and becomes an experience of the rune defined through Midgard's being/essence/experience. The runes can travel through all realms, but cannot create the bridges and doorways themselves. For that, they need the *galdr*.

The best way I have found to learn *galdr* is to practice it with the runes. The runes will teach and test the singer, but there is no better way to learn this particular practice. Select a rune (and always expect the rune to wish blood for its aid—it may not always want that, but there's a 50/50 chance that it will be hungry) and sit or stand comfortably. Visualize the rune in your mind's eye. Then feel it filling you, coming to life within you, surging through your blood, taking over your heartbeat, whispering its rhythm in your ear. Let it surge upward until it bubbles up in your throat and then allow its power to exit via the voice. See where it wants to go. Take note of any sounds, images, even smells that may come to mind as you are chanting. What should one actually chant? Well, starting with the name of the rune is good. From there, work the images or sounds that come to mind while focusing on the rune into the actual *galdr*. I never plan *galdr* out beforehand. It is a living, changing, fluid thing. Eventually, you'll get to the point where even the actual name of the rune is too constraining. At that point, the *galdr* becomes comprised of pure, raw, primal sound.

If you have never sung before (and *galdr* can come out halfway between chanting and singing with a healthy dose of screeching) the exercise above can seem very difficult, awkward, even embarrassing. If this is the case, work on building up a comfort level with making your voice heard. Practice basic singing exercises like singing the vowels, maintaining a single note for each vowel. Sing scales, sing your prayers. I don't necessarily advocate taking singing lessons because too much focus on making the *galdr* pretty will destroy it. It is, what it is: harsh, beautiful, frightening, cruel, intense, raw and pure. It's important to allow it to be what it wants to be and to not project our own sense of aesthetics onto it. All in all though, *galdr* is best learned by doing.

There are several other important factors to keep in mind with this art. Firstly, as noted above, *galdr* does not have to sound pretty; in fact, it generally doesn't. There is a reason its etymology comes from a verb meaning "to crow." *Galdr* can be incredibly dissonant. One need not have a nice, pleasing, or pretty voice to be an accomplished *galdr* master. Overemphasis on making the melody pretty can detract from the power of the magic itself. The sound heard during *galdr* is the sound of the runes flowing over and into the web of Wyrd itself. It reflects the vibrations of those threads. Therefore, what we are hearing is at best distorted.

Secondly, the *galdr* will guide the singer. Once a person begins to *galdr* with the intent of infusing a rune and a specific purpose into the web, a pattern will emerge on the threads which will become visible to the singer. The *galdr* will want to hit specific openings, fill specific gaps, creating its own warp and weft against the weave of the web itself. This may put extreme strain on the vocal abilities of the singer, but in time, the voice will strengthen and gain in flexibility (though not necessarily in any euphonic sense).

Thirdly, *galdr* may be practiced alone or in a group of *galdr* singers. In the latter case, one person should lead, controlling the beginning, the distribution of energy into the threads, and the ending of the common chant. Some people may find that they have a unique ability to harmonize and balance energies out in a group's *galdr*-working. They may or may not have the same abilities when doing it by themselves. In this case, it's not so much about vocal harmonizing in a way a singer would, but harmonizing the energy.

The uses of *galdr*-work are manifold. I have used *galdr* as an offering to feed specific Deities, and to work both woe and weal. I've used it to stop bleeding, to heal wounds, to hallow a particular place/space, to induce shape-shifting in a berserker, to induce trance and journeywork, and to connect to Odin on the Tree at the moment of His greatest anguish. *Galdr* is also one of the single most effective ways of accessing and developing a relationship with the runes. And because it provides fairly direct access to the web, it can create tremendous paradigm shifts with very little effort. It is one of the most effective tools for luckworkings; and because of its nature, one need not even be near one's intended target for *galdr* to strike home quickly and efficiently.

At its best, *galdr* is a full-body experience. The body itself, not just the voice becomes a conduit for the rune and its power. The power expressed does not just flow outward into the web; it first flows through the body of the singer, through each and every molecule. It leaves its mark and will pattern the singer to both the runes and a greater awareness of the flow and patterning of Wyrd. I don't believe this patterning can be undone. Due to its raw power, should a *galdr* singer lose control of the *galdr*, or break off before the *galdr* is complete, the backlash can be rather severe. It is one of the more dangerous of the runic arts and not something a beginner should attempt. Because the body itself becomes a tool, the singer should take care to keep him or herself in as healthy a condition as possible.

Galdr work goes hand in hand with blood magic and rune work. This powerful combination forms the foundations for northern tradition runic magic. Its efficacy is attested to not only by Odin's ordeal on the Tree but in the sagas as well. In the end, it will bring one to Odin as few other things will.

Dancing on the Earth

We know very little about the dances—and especially the religious dances—of the ancient peoples of northern Europe. Although there is a long tradition of folk dancing in that area, most of those dances were imported from more Christianized areas (and were more formal and proper and less conducive to trancework) and slowly took over the original dances. These later dances seem to have been used primarily as a courtship mechanism for culturally repressed young people, and while there's nothing wrong with that, it makes the original spiritual dance traditions harder to find. Hints of older dances can be found in such traditions as the ubiquitous chain dance—a group celebration dance where all join hands and do a simple sideways step such as the one described below in Lyn Skadidottir's article—which was reputed to "suck in" every member of a village, including random travelers pulled from their coaches, and wind across miles of countryside in their fervor. Other tantalizing hints come in the form of formal dances that mimic specific things that may have once been spiritually symbolic, such as "harvest" dances done with scythes (perhaps with the energy of Frey) or dances that mimic all the steps of fiber-making from spindle to cloth—perhaps originally done in honor of the Norns? We may never know.

There is also the fact that solitary dances, done by shamans and their ilk, were from their descriptions interpretive and improvisational, created on the spot for whatever purpose was staring them in the face. Shamans in anthropological literature do not dance quite as often as they drum or sing, but there is a good body of references to their dancing, often reported as "wild" or even "crazed". These types of dances are likely used for the purposes of altered states, as the repetitive, rhythmic motions encourage such a headspace. If a shaman does dance, their ability to keep it up tirelessly for hours (even if they are old and lame most of the time) is seen as proof of their spirit-powers. As a spirit-worker who has had the wights use my body for things that would be physically impossible for me to do, and as someone with a chronic illness who has still found that an on-duty light for my job gives me sudden reserves of energy and strength that I wouldn't have had otherwise, I can believe that this is so.

Other accounts have the shaman dancing, drumming, singing, and possibly keeping up a running commentary for his audience at the same time, describing where he is going and what he is doing. This is a spiritual performance-art masterpiece of a level that requires a huge amount of skill (and probably a few well-trained assistants) in order to put together. Altered states are not often conducive to the kind of performance that most modern audiences are used to. An altered state which invites the spirits often requires the spirit-worker to do things that are strange, weird, or embarrassing, and as Lyn Skadidottir describes below, one has to do them anyway. The kind of paying-attention-to-the-audience that is part and parcel of a polished theatrical performance may have to be put aside in order to achieve the proper headspace. In a tribal society where the people were used to such things, audiences would be used to shamanic performances that concentrated more on spiritual content and less on impressing the onlookers, but in today's societies such things are sharply separated. This means that the spirit-worker who is called to dance (and do any other kind of performance) in front of a group needs to be particularly courageous, and not let their connection with the spirits be altered by their worries about what the people staring at them might think. It is only thus that we slowly reacclimate modern people to the realities of watching real spirit-work rather than Hollywood fakery.

One small piece of information about the spiritual uses of dance in ancient northern Europe comes to us as the small pendants and carvings that show what we have come to refer to as the weapon-dancer. This figure decorates many charms, helms, and other pieces of metal. It is a man, sometimes naked except for a weaponbelt and sometimes in a short tunic sewn with metal circles, carrying a spear in each hand, or a spear in one hand and two arrows in the other. On his head he wears a helm with a noseguard and two upward-sweeping bird shapes, ravens or eagles, whose heads face and meet above his. He is clearly shown dancing on many of the charms, and often followed by other armed figures wearing animal skins. While some cautious scholars prefer to refer to the weapon-dancer as merely Odin's messenger, it seems clear to others that this is Odin himself. One interesting fact about these little metal figures is that they are not only one-eyed, in each case the "missing" eye was put in and literally hammered out again, or deliberately punched through with an awl, perhaps as a way of recreating and honoring Odin's loss of his eye in return for wisdom anew with each charm.

The weapon-dancer is a war-dancer, Odin leading his totem-warriors into battle. It is likely that their dancing was at least as frenzied as any Apache war dance, with no real steps per se—although it was probably rife with simulated battle moves, and/or simulated motions of the animal whose skin and spirit protected that warrior. It may be that those motions were more than simulated, if the ritual was designed as a mass shapeshifting (see the chapter on Shapeshifting) in order to familiarize the warriors with fighting in the style of their patron animal spirit, and bond them to both the spirit and the battle that was to come.

It may be that with the medieval Norse emphasis on warfare as the most honorable activity of all, the weapon-dances were the last of the shamanic holdouts to be phased out of their culture as it turned from a shamanic one to an anti-shamanic one. Rather than looking to any lore, the spirit-worker who would use dance as a tool has to look within, as the next article discusses.

Trance Dancing in the Northern Tradition

by Lyn Skadidottir

The autumn air was quite cool. I thought it lucky that it wasn't raining as I stripped off my shirt and began dancing. It was a demonstration, and I hadn't planned on entering a full trance state. I opened up, and asked Erda and Hela to guide me. I thanked Erda for her firm standing beneath my feet. I had asked that no one drum, but I did ask a friend to sing galdr while I danced.

I began to spin. As I turned in circles I noticed the land beneath my feet resounded with every step. It became the non-present drummer that dictated those steps. I began to play the earth-drum with my entire body – leaping, rolling, exploring the contours of my body against the earthen-skin drum beneath me.

Soon I was fully entranced. The world disappeared around me. The only things that were left were the earth below me, the air around me, the gaping chasm of the sky above. Occasionally I would notice my handler behind me, there to make sure that I didn't lose my way, did not get hurt. I continued on and did not stop the dance until the final song emerged, a mournful song that escaped my vocal chords about my own death. I was spent, and I did not remember much of the event.

(In this article, I will be using the term *trance* liberally, though I find the term exceedingly inaccurate. In most cases, I will be using the term *trance* to imply the intentional induction of an altered state of awareness.)

One of the most important things to understand before engaging in any form of physical trance work, be it dancing, swaying, seething, or any other, is that it is not in any way a "beginner" technique. It is not recommended for unseasoned trance-workers, and it is not easy to harness or utilize until you have reached a certain skill and mastery of your own Self to effectively use the tool.

My first introduction to physical trance, or "trance dancing", was through Jan Fries' book *Seidways*. I remember seeing the warning, similar to the one I just gave, against this being a beginner technique. Of course I didn't really pay attention to that, and leaped into the techniques he listed with everything I had. Much to my disappointment, it took years to understand and develop my own set of practices that work for me. I did achieve some nominal results in the beginning, but they were not without their disillusionment. I didn't get the miraculous transformation I sought—I didn't find other worlds, didn't see glorious things on the other side. As a form of Draconian/serpent magick, it left me with the invisible pot of gold, and a fictional dragon at the end. I walked away from the practice for a couple of years, and returned to it later with a better understanding. This is not to say that Fries' techniques were flawed; in fact, quite the contrary. It was simply that my abilities did not yet match my enthusiasm.

Part of that understanding was that I actually "got it" before I tried it under strict ritual conditions. My first big lesson: I'd been doing this since I was a kid, did it whenever I "walked" to the other worlds in labyrinth patterns, and did it almost every day that I played a musical instrument. But once I imposed the ritual on it, once I tried to make it more "real" in a concept for magical process and understanding, it didn't work. Oh, the lesson of letting things be what they will be is such a very hard one. That is, of course, the first lesson in any type of trancework. Don't force it, let it be what it is going to be, or you just might cramp up. I will attest to many long nights of cramping up.

This is the hardest part of the whole affair: You have to learn to become comfortable in your body. This is a very hard thing for any magically-trained person, particularly in a Western tradition, to do. We spend days, months and sometimes even years trying to learn how to leave our bodies, to escape into other worlds by astral projection, journeywork, trance work, worldwalking—the types and terms are endless. The point is that once we figure that out, we have to learn how to live in our bodies again. Sometimes that is very difficult. Actually, almost all of the time that is difficult.

For most people, the only time they really pay attention to their bodies is when something is seriously wrong with it or when they are engaged in a sexual activity. This is why, for many people, ordeal and sex magick is used as a way to engage with the body. Even athletes, who spend day in and day out training, are not always engaged with the body, though they tend to be a little better at it than your average human. The best way to start becoming engaged with the body is by practicing a physical art that requires perfect attention to the body. Martial arts, dance, tai chi, yoga, mountain climbing, swimming—these are all things that are easy for most people to access in order to find access to the body. It can be anything as long as it requires coordinated motion of body parts and concentration to execute. I find that even exercises like running and walking can be effective, but they require a lot more intention than other forms of physical activity to create body awareness. My personal favorite is rock climbing, or any other activity where if you go even one moment without being aware of what is happening you run a risk of getting hurt. The same can be said for martial arts, especially if you are sparring. If your body is not able to participate in some of the more extreme activities I have listed, conscious convulsing or motion of your body on a regular basis is a good place to start. It doesn't need to be pretty or graceful—just get the parts of your body that have motion to move.

So here we find ourselves at the crux of "why this isn't for everybody", and why this isn't a beginner technique. It requires awareness not only of advanced trance states, but also requires you to spend as much time learning how to reach and control a trance state as it does learning how to live in and use your body. Of course, the hardest thing to understand is that no book or teacher can give you that; they can only tell you that you need to do it. The how is up to you—you are the only one who can judge what type of exercise and physical activity is right for you. As for how to learn and adapt to non-physical trance states, I suggest beginning with simple meditations and go from there. For my own practices, I began becoming a lot more serious when I had the opportunity to learn Zen Buddhist meditation techniques. If you listen to your mind and body, you will learn which technique works best for you.

Anyone who has a nominal Wiccan background has most likely read about dancing around a cauldron, fire or other sacred object to raise energy. Books are filled with these techniques, and it almost seems mandatory in that tradition. We find ourselves mimicking behaviors we've seen on television, in books, and other forms of ethnographic research on tribal cultures. Costuming is often involved, and there is a notion that you will dance around the fire in a sidestep motion, sometimes spinning and leaping to raise energy to cast out the intention of the group or individual. This is a form of trance dancing, and the purpose of this motion is to create an altered state wherein energy is raised to affect a specific end. For some groups, the specific steps matter a great deal, for some, it does not matter. How do you know where to begin? Should it be a scripted event, or should it be free, with the dancers allowed to do whatever they choose?

For a new group that does not have a set tradition, this is a very difficult choice to make. However, if you work with a scripted motion or ritual dance, you can easily create a group consciousness within the dancers where they must be aware not only of their bodies, but of the bodies around them, and work together to create the desired end and result. It is up to peripheral members—either a high priestess or some other person who is able to harness and send energy forth—to utilize the energy raised for specific ends. It is too much to ask the dancer to harness and send the energy continuously unless they have years of practice in order to learn to do so. The dancers' entire focal point must be on the immediate, and it cannot waver from the immediate in order to create an actual energy/entity that can function in that time and location. An additional beauty to ritual dance is that the dances will begin to carry their own weight, their own history. The ritual becomes a mnemonic device for the entire group, allowing a vessel for storage of psychic and sacred history for a community, tribe or coven.

If you find that you have very competent dancers with years of experience and a direct connection to their bodies, it is likely okay to go with a free and improvisatory set of dance. This is much more difficult to do for a group, as it asks the dancer to incorporate another skillset—the skill of listening to energy patterns and entities to find the niche where they can fit in and alter things within a group. This is an extremely high-functioning space to be in, as different types of energy require different types of motion. Particularly in a group situation, this must be handled only by those who can execute not only the dance or physical movement but can also direct the energies as they move. (This is a topic best left for an entire book, and cannot be fully discussed properly in a short article.) This practice is one that takes years to develop, as it goes beyond a basic technique to induce trance and energy creation into an entire spiritual practice.

Sample Ritual for Pagan Group Dancing

This is a basic simple step that can be used to start physical energies flowing.

Have the dancers stand in a circle facing inward. This works particularly well in front of a bonfire or some other fire type source. The dancers should move clockwise, doing a "line dance" type of step, stepping sideways while facing into the center of the circle, first with the left foot crossing in front of the right foot, then move the right foot over, then move the left foot behind the right foot. Do this motion until each person has stepped 7 times, and then reverse directions. I realize this is simplistic, but that's the point—it is best to begin with simple intentional moves by the participants that all can follow and keep in time. As they do this, the energy will slowly begin to build. You may even want to play with the amount of steps or how many circles are done. Include tempo changes and experiment. Eventually, you will find a combination that is suitable for the group and intention behind the motion. With enough practice, the dancers will be able to reach a trance state—perhaps easily, if they care to pay attention to only themselves and the other dancers as they move. It is often effective to have a point where the dancers are allowed to "break free" of the group, and then rejoin the group motion. These moments of fluidity and then chaos are great for elevating both the energy of the group as well as the notion of dance and manipulation into trance states. It may help the group if there are drums accompanying this practice.

If you've been to any Pagan festivals or gatherings, you've seen similar acts to the ones listed above. Chances are, you're most familiar (even as a new practitioner) with the Maypole. This is another entry-level way to get into group trance dancing.

There is already a good deal written on the intention and proper way to manage a large group or even a small group in dancing for magickal and trance purposes. I encourage you to research as much as you can on the subject. Do not limit yourself only to the bookshelves of your local pagan shop for these concepts! Your public library will have books on tribal dancing from many traditions, and you may find that in your research a particular form of dance works particularly well for you and your purposes.

For The Solitary Dancer

For the solitary practitioner (and for anyone, really), the first step is to become comfortable in your own body. You most likely do not have a teacher or a real tradition to learn from in this situation, so the following will hopefully give some decent pointers for how to do this alone.

The most important thing is to be outside. (Oh, the horrors!) This too, is something that is difficult for your average Pagan, confined to an apartment or other group-housing situation. We find that all of a sudden we are ashamed to do things outside, in public places. What would the neighbors think, or the strangers passing by? What will you think of yourself if questioned? So the first step in this is to go outside anyway. Start walking, riding your bike, anything you can think of, but start doing physical activities outside. Not in a gym—though that is a good idea too for physical training—you must be outdoors for learning physical trance states. This is an absolute must! When we dance or use physical motion to execute altered states, it actually changes your perceived physical presence. Practicing inside will seem confining and limit you to walls. Outside, that need not be the case. Besides, what better way to find your body than dancing or moving outside in the rain, snow, sun, shadow, night, and any other condition that occurs in a natural environment? (This was my first mistake when trying to learn this practice—I didn't go outside! Much to my dismay, I was not able to access what I needed inside, and eventually learned better.) Once you are outdoors, your body becomes more real. This shell that houses your spirit is actually forced to deal with the discomforts of nature rather than the climate-controlled world we live in from day to day.

Once you get used walking or doing any other normal, mundane activity outdoors, begin to explore other types of physical motion. Something wild and raucous is best—something that you find slightly embarrassing that isn't illegal but may seem downright silly. Do this often. My favorite is to walk and then incorporate different motions at random intervals—waving an arm or kicking. Yes, you will look like you aren't quite right to others, and that's the point. You must get over your inhibitions for doing things in public, especially if you live in a city as I do. You have to learn how to interact outside—be it leaving offerings to land spirits, gods, giants and other entities, or dancing in a park alone without music. There is also power in the outlandish—do not forget that, no matter how contrary it may seem, no matter how Tricksterish it comes across—there is power and energy in the absurd.

Once you are freed from the constraint of fear of humiliation, you can move onto the next step, which is dancing outside. Go to a space you find sacred and stand there. Listen to your body and see if it wants to move about. It might only want to sway, it might want to kick, walk, roll... let your body guide you, not your head! Of course, be careful not to hurt yourself or do something that would end with a permanent injury, but by all means move around. If you are comfortable moving and can learn to listen to your body, you can start letting music guide you to motion. Music is powerful, but it is not mandatory to physical trance states. This is something that is not known by many, but it is true: We do not need music to dance.

One thing that I hope you've gathered from me so far: dancing alone isn't about specific steps or specific motions. This is something that only matters when you have to work with a group to specific ends. Of course, like many people, you may find that you are only comfortable with set motions. This is fine, but I do encourage you to begin to explore your full range of motions and begin to put them together without instructions from others. Let your body, the spirits around you, the land, your gods, or your deep mind be the force that chooses what you are to do. Once you embrace this type of movement, you will find that you can slip quite easily into trance states, both controlled and uncontrolled.

Should the dancer use drums for accompaniment? This is actually a very important question. It is my personal belief that music should only be considered much later in the evolving practice of the dancer, rather than early on. My reasoning behind this is quite simple. In my own practice, I believe that it is imperative to listen to the spirits talking to me before I let someone else guide me. This is a fine line, as a highly trained and skilled drummer can create beats and sounds that would guide even the most unskilled into a trance state that may or may not contain motion. But more often than not, a highly skilled drummer is not present, and an unskilled one may be worse than none at all.

More importantly, it is the external, the unknown that I am dancing to connect with. I dance to connect with the spirit world. I find that they are more than "noisy" enough to guide me to the correct moves. When I did finally begin to work with external sound, I found that I would enter trance easier, but the messages and the learning experiences were not as enriching. It took a long time to learn to do that differently. When sound is used, the drum or voice or whatever is the catalyst sound, the sound that guides the dancer along their journey. For this reason alone, a new dancer should only work with drummers and musicians that they trust. If you learn without the music and drumming, and you find yourself in the presence of a less than skilled guide/musician, you will be ready to face any of the places or challenges that the musicians' journey will present to you.

I would like to take this moment to break away from dance to talk about sound and music. Within the past century, the face of music has changed immensely. As our world evolves, so does our soundscape. Globally, "noise" has become a part of our vernacular music. The music of everyday life is filled with the sound of electricity, of air vents, of traffic, of key clicks. Those of us who live immersed in these sounds can find them quite powerful. Drum and Voice are not the only instruments that are adequate for trance and spiritual music. While drums awaken a primal memory in us, I wager that for many, there are everyday sounds that hold as much power as drumming—the sound of our lover's footsteps, the shuffling of papers, the whirr of the computer heartbeat, the sound of our coffee maker. These sounds may be for us like the rustling of leaves and rain was to our ancestors, and we can utilize these newer sounds of power in our work, in our music, and in our art. This is one of the many ways to harness a "modern primitivism" stance. We are at the beginning of a new aeon, and as such we create the vocabulary of our own evolution. I am not necessarily advocating trance dancing to your media playback device, but rather I am suggesting that you learn to work with the tools at hand to make the sound world you need in order to effect the correct results.

Many Helish folk that I know are digital media artists, both in the visual and audio arts. I doubt very much that Hela (or many other Gods for that matter) is unaware of the power of these tools and sounds. If you find that your best drum, your best music for trance is made with your computer, your coffeepot, or any other sound-creating device at your disposal, than it is more than appropriate to use it. The Dada art movement, as well as the Futurists, understood this in their art, but it is only now that society is in a place to accept these notions of the present as a force of power. I doubt very seriously that these subtle sounds were lost on our ancestors. In fact, it was these subtle sounds that enabled hunting and survival—the ability to listen and distinguish the forces that would enable us to continue living.

You may have noticed that my focus in this article has been towards innovation and listening to your own self. This notion comes from my own practice. It is not from the external world that we learn truth. In the worlds of music, drumming and trance, although skills to obtain their truths can be taught and written about, the fact of the matter is that they cannot be wholly quantified into distillable drops. I cannot tell you that Step X or Sound Y will give you a specific result. I can tell you that in my own personal experience Step X did effect some kind of result, but in the end, that result is based entirely off of my own worldview. What I do here is to usher in the notion that you must be in charge of your own development, be it by audio or by physical motion. You are the only entity that can tell you what is true for you. The rest can only hint at it and give you a notion; you must determine it yourself.

Drums of the Spirits

> You practiced seidr on Samsey,
> And you beat on a *vett* as volvas do.
> —Lokasenna 24

This article starts with a controversy, which I will describe and then sidestep. In many of the Norse/Germanic reconstructionist religious sects, there is debate over whether the early-medieval Nordic folk ever used drums as part of their religious ceremonies. (It's part and parcel of the argument over whether their religion was shamanic in nature.) There are a few vague references to things that could be seen as drumming, but nothing definitively conclusive. The above reference is frequently argued over, with scholars disagreeing on whether the mysterious *vett* is a drum, or some sort of ordinary object like a shield or a pot-lid. (I would, however, point out that if beating on *something* is the mark of a volva or an *ergi seidberendr* in this poem, it doesn't matter much whether it was a special drum or something seized for the purposes of creating a trance rhythm. It was still drumming, and clearly important to the practice.) Even in places like Sapmi and Siberia where the local shamans routinely used ritual drums, sometimes such objects were pressed into service for drumming when a drum wasn't available.

As I've said before, I accept the fact that the Nordic religion of the "lore-period", which was mostly Christianized at that point anyway, does not have enough remnants of shamanic practice to accurately call it a shamanic religion. However, at one point far back in the pre-written-records past, it was. Some of those traditions and beliefs lingered, disguised in the later practices which were more suited to a society that found itself to be less about tribe and clan and more about city-states and agricultural nations. There was also the ambient knowledge that if anyone wished to learn shamanic religion or technique, all one had to do was to ask their Saami neighbors, who (not infrequently, according to historical sources) intermarried with the Norse people. The Saami did have a tradition of shamanism and drumming, and do to this day among their *noiadi*.

All that aside—and here's that sidestep that I warned you about—when I began my training in earnest, I was told that I needed to have drums, and not just one, either. Two are currently in my possession; others are still to be made. I am still very much a novice in this study, and having noncorporeal teachers doesn't make it any easier.

There seem to be three kinds of drums in the shamanic tradition I am being taught that are useful to the modern-day shaman. The first type is a Worldwalker. These are generally flat frame drums, and are used both for moving between worlds and for doing divination. Its energy is a combination of Fire and Air. The second type is a healing drum, for healing rituals, and it is sometimes cylindrical, made of fired clay like the earth, although wood is a secondarily acceptable medium. (In some cases, this could also be a very large frame drum for resonating over people.) Its energy is a combination of Earth and Water. The third is a large drum carved out of a single log, probably stationary, with a whole animal skin as a top. It is used for public ceremonies, and for calling the Dead. Its energy is Earth and Air.

I've been told that there were other sorts of drums long ago, but I have not been introduced to their energy. One was the hunting drum, which the shaman uses to call the herds and the prey animals close to human habitation, so that the tribe would not starve. Its energy was Earth and Fire. Another was a weather drum, which could be used for calling or turning storms, but the spirits that it was associated with were dangerous and capricious, and playing it sometimes invited disaster. Its energy was Air and Water. Yet another drum was played for sexual fertility rites by the community; its energy was Fire and Water. In this article, I'll share my experiences with finding and using my own drums, as I was instructed by the Gods and spirits who I am apprenticed to.

The first drum I used had to be a frame drum. Size didn't seem to be important, but it had to be round or oval, broad and shallow and flat. It also had to be a gift. Fortunately my wife took the initiative and bought me a Pakistani frame drum from a shop for my birthday. I sat with that blank white surface and drummed it, experimenting with different beats, until I got my next instruction. I was supposed to hang things all around it, things that jingled and rattled. I experimented with different jangles over the next several months, trying them out and seeing if they brought the spirits' approval. (Generally I get a yes or a no pretty quickly, like within minutes.)

I ended up drilling tiny holes all around the exterior of the drum, and I attached tambourine jingles from another, broken drum. Each of the jingles conveniently had a dangling ring attached, and from then I hung more things—metal cone bells, a jangly metal earring given to me by a friend, an anklet of Indian bells from another friend, rattly beads. My friend Tannin of Bones and Flowers, who specializes in magical items made of bone and animal parts, cleaned and dried the hooves from some of the goat kids that we slaughtered to be drilled out and hung them on the drum as rattles. When my buck goat Phil died, she cleaned three of his shinbones for me, and I drilled the tops and hung them on the inside. I found that with this modification, I could hang the drum from one hand and walk, swinging it rhythmically, and Phil's bones would beat it for me. I had the distinct feeling that there was a little of Phil left in them, and that he very much liked being able to kick the drumhead. I jokingly called it "the drum that beats herself".

I was finally told what was to go on her head. I drew the World Tree, with the Nine Worlds around it. I drew it looking from the top down, and in its branches I drew dozens of tiny figures which came to me while half in trance. I wasn't sure what these were for, although I had the strong feeling that they were more than symbolically useful. This decoration, and all the jangles and hooves and bones, made me feel like my drum was some sort of bizarre mutant, especially when compared to the drums I saw in the hands of others. Most of the people that I met at

Pagan gatherings, drum-and-dance groups, and the occasional powwow had drums that were Native American or African in style, or they had Celtic bodhrans. These were generally plain and streamlined and elegant. If there were designs on the top, they were spare and simple, and didn't cover the whole drumhead in a jumble of lines. Jingles or rattly decoration were considered tacky, unaesthetic. I had never seen anything like what I had been told to make, and it worried me a little, especially when I would take my mutant drum out at drum circles and people would raise their eyebrows.

Much later, I read some anthropology and stumbled across the drum of the Saami shamans, which is called a *runebom*. While it can come in many sizes and levels of decoration, it is a frame drum, often hung with metal jangles and rattly bits. The pictures I saw had drumheads completely cluttered with seemingly random symbols, including usually drawings of a World Tree and at least three levels of worlds. I immediately recognized my bastard drum-child, and realized that I was far from the first person to create a drum like this. I read that the tiny symbols drawn on the top were for a form of divination—a ring or tiny personal object was placed on the drumhead, and the shaman would beat the drum from underneath and do a reading from where the ring lands. "You're supposed to do that," said the spirit-voices in my ear.

The drum was vital to the Saami *noaidevuohta*, or shamanic work. It was also important to many Siberian tribes, but others preferred to use a staff, or hammer on something else, similar to the Norse. Saami drums were either the classic frame-drums or bowl-drums carved out of tree burls. They were beaten with an antler handle, and covered with symbols of the various Otherworlds, as well as other symbols for prediction and divination. Some said that the spirits spoke through the voice of the drum, having been called into it at the beginning of each shamanic performance. A small frog-shaped flat-bottomed pointer of brass, horn, or bone called an *arpa* was sometimes used as a divinatory "seeker" on the top of the drum. They were festooned with rings, jingles, coils of wire, charms, figurines, claws, hooves, teeth, ribbons, and sometimes even the penis bones of bears.

The spirit of the drum was very feminine—both of my drums have been like that—and I did a ritual to ask her name, and formally name her. She had two names, Yggdrasil Moonsong. Yggdrasil for her first job, which is to be used to walk between the worlds, Moonsong for her divinatory abilities. The jingles were Air, and her beat was Fire. Although I have a piece of stag antler for a beater, I tend to play her with my hand anyway.

My second drum had to be made of wood or clay, and preferably clay. It didn't necessarily have to be a frame drum, so I used a clay doumbek from Greece—not northern, but then Yggdrasil Moonsong had originally hailed from Pakistan, so I suppose we first-re-generation shamans have to do the best we can with what we can get. She was also very feminine, even more so than my first drum, and was painted blue-green. My assistant Joshua spent hours hanging strings of shells on her (mostly culled from trashpicked macrame plant-hangers) until she had a gentle, delicate rattle whenever I played her. She's a healing drum, to be used for trances whereby one moves through the body of the client. I dipped her base into the ocean, fully awakening her and finding her name.

I am not going to describe how to use a drum for the purposes I mention here, because there is no way to describe it in writing. If you are apprenticed to the spirits, they'll help you out, but generally the best way to learn is just to make and awaken the drum, and then work with it. Each drum, when awakened, has a spirit. It's alive. It can teach you things, but you have to put in the time and the attention. Don't worry about how to do it. Just do it. Learn what rhythms put you into what kind of trance by working with these creatures.

It should go without saying that you should treat your drums with respect. That means not ever neglecting them—it is said that a drum left alone without attention for a year and a day goes to sleep again and must be reawakened. It means taking care of them, and making sure that if for whatever reason you decide to no longer work with a drum, you must ask the spirits to find someone to give it to, someone who will value and use it. These are very much like your children, and you should give it as much thought as you would in giving up a child for adoption, if you got to pick the parents.

While we're talking about drums, I have to bring up the sticky point of rattles. I was told by the spirits that I am apprenticed to—flat out—that rattles are not part of our tradition. It wasn't that I couldn't own or use one, but they would not come for one, nor have anything to do with it. No rattles. Is there something wrong with a rattle, I asked? After all, it seems to have been adopted as the beginning shamanic practitioner's tool of choice, although perhaps that's because they are cheaper and easier to use than drums. The answer seemed to be that there was nothing particularly wrong with them, but that they were simply not part of our tradition. Period. "You won't need one," I was assured.

So, all right, no rattles. I concentrated on learning my drum, inside and out. And then, one night when I was very tired—hours of drumming will do that to you—I ended up exhausted enough that all I could do was to lay on my bed and rest the edge of the drum on my belly and shake it ... and I discovered why I didn't need any rattles. The *runebom*-style drum is, in itself, a rattle as well. When I made my second drum and discovered that I was supposed to hang rattling shells all around her, I wasn't surprised. In this tradition, the drums are multipurpose instruments, and the different soundmakers call different things. And for some reason, the spirits are picky about that.

Ideally the northern shaman builds their own drum as part of a week-long retreat. A similar process is described as part of traditional Saami shamanism by Jaana Kouri in his presentation "The Other Side Of The Drum". I expect that it's possible that eventually I'll have to do this. Although it's acceptable to start out with an already-made drum, this is a good way for any would-be NT shamanic practitioners to start dealing with spirit drums, especially if they aren't sure what this drumming thing is all about. Sometimes going about things the long, hard, ritual way can help you to form a better understanding of what you're supposed to be doing.

1. The would-be drum-maker spends time in a piece of land, ideally one where s/he has a good relationship with the land-wight. In fact, I would suggest that this be the first order of business, because a cooperative land-wight can help you find the right tree. Saami folk make their drums out of pine, mostly due to its availability. Ash wood is good as well, as it recalls the World Tree, and oak will do, although it is harder to bend. The best wood was chosen from trees which are grown in a swamp beside a rock, with the caveat that there may not be any spruces nearby. Offerings are made to the spirit of the tree, who must be willing to sacrifice themselves. They should be sung to, and asked that their spirit will pass into the drum.

2. The tree is cut down, split, and the long narrow board that will be the drum's frame is sawed out of it along the heart. Each end should be cut with a bevel at least 2" long, facing in opposite directions so that when the board is bent in a circle, the two beveled ends will overlap and join perfectly together. The length of the board will determine the diameter of the frame; for an 18" or thereabouts frame you want at least five to six feet. Have the ideal measure ready beforehand. Smaller drum-makers might want a littler drum; there's no shame in that. As the tree is cut, a song is sung in praise of Earth, who gives us these resources. The board is placed in a stream, lake or pond overnight to soak. The drum-maker rests, meditates, and sings.

3. The next morning a fire is built, ideally a sacred fire (see chapter on Mastering Fire), and a large cauldron of water, preferably from a lake or river or stream, placed on it. A song is sung in praise of Fire. The rest of the tree is burned on the fire. The board is drawn from the water like a midwife draws a baby from the watery womb, and with the same attitude. A song of birth should be sung while it is drawn out, and a song in praise of Water.

4. Then the wet wood is laid across the cauldron—or if you can do it, several cauldrons—and steamed until it can be bent by the hands. The drum-maker has to keep moving it around so that all parts can

catch the steam, removing it, bending it, and then putting it back to steam again. When it can be bent like a bow, a very long strap (about 12' long) with a buckle and holes along its whole length is placed down its length on the outer curve, and buckled where a bowstring would be. At this point, a song is sung for the Hunter. At any point in the steaming, a song can be sung in praise of Air. The four elements must be present and active for any birthing, including the drum, but Air is last, of course—it is the first breath drawn.

5. The drum-maker keeps steaming the wood and cranking down the strap. This should be done quickly—don't delay. Strike while the iron is hot; bend while the wood is wet. No part of it can be allowed to dry out. If any part looks as if it is drying out too fast, dunk it in the boiling water. Songs are sung to the fire to keep it going, and to the drum to keep it bending. This part of the ritual symbolizes how the shaman is cut, bent, submitting to their fate to become a tool of the spirits.

6. Another tree is found. It should be a live tree of any kind, but with special energy, preferably close to the fire-site, and exactly as big around as the interior of your drum. (It should probably be found and measured beforehand.) The strap is temporarily taken off, the board bent entirely around the living tree so that its two beveled ends meet, and the strap rewrapped again to hold it in place. More straps can be added if need be. This "mother tree" will provide energy for the new drum, which is kept there for a few hours and removed while it is still flexible enough. Then it is restrapped, hung on a branch, and left overnight to set.

7. When the frame is entirely dry—which may take an overnight or a couple of days, depending on the weather and humidity—it is removed from the mother tree, and the mother tree is thanked with an offering on her roots. Two small holes are drilled in the overlapping ends of the frame, and two small wooden pegs are hammered in. If necessary, wood

epoxy can also be applied, if you're not sure that mere pegs will hold. When that is dry and firm, the frame is sanded.

8. A skin is found for the head. This can be deerskin, goatskin, or what-have-you, but ideally it is from an animal that you got to know while it was still alive, and killed yourself or saw killed. Some of the animal's blood should be saved to anoint the inside of the drum frame, giving it life. The skin should have been thoroughly scraped, stretched, and dried, and then it is soaked overnight, possibly in the water of the great cauldron. It is stretched over the frame while wet, trimmed so that it extends only to a couple of inches beyond where it wraps around the frame, and holes are punched in the edge. Rawhide (from a cow, as goat is too fragile) is laced through the edges, lacing them to a metal ring a few inches smaller than the drum diameter, which should "float" in the center of the back of the drum. As the skin is put onto the frame, the meditation is of how we ourselves are a skin stretched over a frame, how we are drums for the Gods to make music and magic upon.

(Note about lacing on a skin: When I had to rehead my frame drum, I got advice from professional drum-makers, and found that the best method for lacing was as follows: First, stretch the skin over the drum and tie it temporarily with a ring of rawhide. Then punch holes in close pairs all around the protruding edge, and lace the rawhide around it in a running stitch, up/down, up/down. Then take another piece of rawhide and use it to lace the running lacing to the floating ring. When that is dry and adjusted, more rawhide can make a handle across the ring.)

9. After much adjusting and retightening, the skin is allowed to dry. If it is too loose when dry, it is pulled off, soaked again, and retied tighter. The tightening is done to the four directions, East, South, West, North, asking for blessings from all these directions. When it is at its best tightness, and makes a good sound when struck, it is done.

10. Then the drum is awakened fully in a ritual which will vary depending on what its purpose is to be. Sometimes one might make a drum thinking of one purpose, and the drum that is made will actually

end up being for a different one, so the spirit of the drum should be asked before it is forced into a job. The drum will give you its name, and then it is alive, and your responsibility. It should be blessed with the elements that are associated with its final purpose—healing drums are generally dipped in the ocean or a lake, and then laid at the roots of a tree; worldwalkers are waved around a fire, and so forth.

Greenwights:
The Path of Sacred Plants

The man has come to her in a panic. Something is attacking him, he says. It's not the first time that someone has showed up claiming to be haunted by some evil presence, and usually they're just creating it out of their own fears, lack of responsibility, and need to feel important. This time, however, it feels real. The shudders run up and down her back as she sees his haggard face. He doesn't know what it is, can't think of anything he might have done wrong.

She knew then, at that meeting, that it was going to have to be the greenwights that would take her there. Just to make certain, she prayed at the harrow that she has built for them, with the little potted plants, the seeds, the green stones and water. The red stone for the Little Red Man. She could feel them reaching out to her, which meant that it had to be that road.

She hadn't planned to work with the plants of her ancestors, but somehow they had called to her, and reluctantly she followed. They were harsh spirits—old, wise, merciless, murderous. Dealing with them was difficult. One could die quickly, with one misstep. When they took her somewhere, they controlled everything. It was all in their hands, but they delivered the goods. And, so far, she was still alive.

Now she sits in the circle marked on the earth, a bonfire burning nearby for warmth and a beacon. Her assistant tends the fire, worriedly; journeys with the plant spirits are always walking the edge. The man sits in his camp chair, uncertain; he's been warned that this will take quite a while, but he's willing to try anything at this point. She has spread the crumbled bodies of the greenwights before her, asking for their wisdom. Will it be Henbane, the seed found by the hundreds in a volva's grave, Thor's friend that brings the rain when burned, used to smoke chickens for stealing? Will it be hemp, found in another volva's grave in the great ship burial, giving of fiber and dreams alike? Will it be poppy juice, sacred to Odin? Will it be belladonna, that seductive maiden with fangs? Will it be the Little Red Man, the amanita mushroom, growing only where the Wild Hunt has passed, who takes her on this path into the depths?

Whoever it is, she will make offerings to that wight and take its body into her. Then she will journey—for hours, perhaps—in time, in space, to wherever it is that this haunting comes from. It's not something she could find herself; that's what the greenwights are for. They are tour guides for those who do this work, but the tour is theirs to run, and she could only follow along. As her hand hesitated over the powdered plants and mushrooms before her, she prayed to the Gods who watched over her work that she would come back whole again to her lich, whole and safe. Because there was nothing safe about this road.

For most folk involved with shamanistic practices, the term "sacred plants" means, without exception, the use of natural hallucinogens. Indeed, in certain subcultures, the word "shamanic" is synonymous with "psychedelic". Using the word "shaman" as a keyword on any search engine on the Internet will draw up a significant percentage of sites devoted mostly to drug peddling and experiences. It seems that it's impossible to separate the shaman, in the mind of most people, from the use of entheogenic drugs.

Nor should they, in my opinion, be separated. The hysteria of the War on Drugs forced many spiritual practitioners who dabbled in shamanism to loudly distance themselves, their shamanistic practices, and occasionally the indigenous culture that spawned those practices, from any hint of ritual entheogen usage. The difficulties endured by the Native American Church over ritual peyote use illustrated this problem all too well. However, there is no way to wipe out the fact that the shamans and spirit-workers of many ancient cultures used the sacred plants as tools to do their work, nor that many still use these tools today.

To ignore that, or to skim over it, is to do a disservice to the technology of millennia of our ancestors.

The Path of Sacred Plants has been, as one spirit-worker put it, "horribly partified and desacralized, which is blasphemous; the plants are wasted and cheapened and misused to party with. Most people really don't want to seek ultimate consciousness. Although ironically, I do think that for many people it's the first door that opens to them." Yes, it can be dangerous; so can driving a car in bad weather, or wielding a chain saw. It's not the method, it's the lack of skill, care, and thoughtfulness on the part of the wielder that can make the difference. Of course, these days it is difficult to find a mentor who will train people on this path. Lacking a human mentor, the spirit-worker is reliant on the spirits of the plants themselves, and if you don't have a clear channel and the willingness to proceed with caution and reverence, you probably shouldn't be doing it.

> Many European and North American authors have done extensive work researching the chemical makeup and the historical uses of these plants, tempting minds towards experimentation and spiritual exploration via this medium. Many serious practitioners take issue with this undisciplined exploration, saying that yes, there are spiritual traditions that make use of these herbs, and each culture has prescribed ways to handle them; exploration for its own sake takes the use outside of a very particular context, which negates much of the value that could be gained since the substance is not being used in the same way or for the same reasons. Others say that the effects these plants have are unnecessary, a crutch, and that they aren't needed to reach enlightenment or be a spiritual practitioner (even going so far as to dismiss the use of these plants in a modern context altogether); traditional practitioners who administer these plants to those they are treating do so only to fool gullible uneducated savages. Yet others tout sacred plants as the ultimate spiritual experience, the means by which the human mind is opened fully to the reality of the life and the Universe.
>
> I fall somewhere in the middle of this debate. I neither see these plants as the ultimate means to an end, nor do I see them as unnecessary or irrelevant. To me they are independent entities, not resources to be tapped, and must be approached

with a great deal of respect (as well as a measure of humility) before any work is to be done with them. They are not suited to every job, or to every person.

Of course, some people dismiss the use of sacred plants in a spiritual context altogether, preferring to reach an altered state through less invasive means, like drumming, breathwork, dance, or meditation. While these techniques certainly have their place and valuable uses, they will not always be the correct tool for every job. Not everyone's nature is suited to those techniques, either; the Mysteries that animate those techniques are no more "equal-opportunity" than the Mysteries of the knowledge of sacred plants. While I make use of many ways to alter my awareness (including, but not limited to, ritual, drumming, sex, meditation, seclusion, trance-possession, and chanting), the mental state I arrive at by using the sacred plants gives me access to a particular set of Mysteries that is best suited to what I wish to achieve.

–Jessica Maestas

To that end, this chapter in this book will not cover all of the various entheogenic plants that one might want to take, or even solely the ones native to northern-tradition usage. While I do include descriptions of the spirits of various plants, given anecdotally by the spirit-workers interviewed here, there isn't room in this book to go into depth with every plant, or even every historically accurate entheogen. That depth will be covered by an entheogen-plant-spirit chapter in the next book in this series, *The Northern-Tradition Herbal*. Similarly, you won't find information here on where to obtain plants, or how to grow them. That's not terribly difficult to find elsewhere, if you look.

You also won't find long political discussions on the issue of legality versus illegality. That's something that every plant-worker must decide for themselves. I will say this, though: If you are called to work with a plant that is not legal, and you feel that the work justifies the risk, remember that this plant now has a very, very strong hold over you, and not just on the spirit plane. If you misuse, exploit, or are otherwise disrespectful to that plant spirit, it may not simply withdraw its aid, or even strike you spiritually. Having police show up on your doorstep might not be unrelated to the vengeance of an angry plant-spirit, just as having a good relationship with an illegal plant-spirit might well keep you safe from prying eyes. It is critical not to mess up your dealings with an illegal plant, or it could reverberate through the rest of your life ... and then you'll have a lot of long, lonely nights in prison to think about how you screwed up with them.

However, as one plant-shaman points out: "Having a working relationship with any plant spirit is no guarantee of safety. They will show you the ropes, but aren't ultimately responsible for your well-being. Mistakes on this path show up fast and can be particularly unforgiving; there's little safety net here except what you prepare for yourself through study and careful exploration. Plant spirits aren't all cute and sweet; the spirits of entheogenic plants can be downright vicious and will rip through a human psyche with pleasure. Some traditions refer to spirit allies in terms of servitude; the practitioner is said to 'command' or 'compel' the spirits of forest and field, and true to their subordinate nature, the spirits mutely obey. In my experience, and the experience of other spirit-workers I've spoken with, the idea of commanding one of these spirits to do anything it wasn't already planning on doing anyway is laughable (and is likely to be something you'll never try a second time). We aren't summoning demons or winged monkeys to do our bidding; these spirits are our equals and should be approached with the same courtesy you would give any stranger."

Like all the paths on this wheel, the Path of Sacred Plants is not something that will be required of every shaman, or even most of them. Some may be banned from it by the wights that they work with, for a period of time or permanently, if those wights feel that they cannot properly work with the greenwights for some reason. Like all the other paths, this path is also a tool ... and more than any of the rest of them, that point needs to be driven home. The altered state is not a goal in and of itself; if it has no useful purpose to serve the community, then one shouldn't be bothering. (For myself, this is not one of my current paths, and I am grateful for the contributions of Ari, Lydia Helasdottir, and Jessica Maestas for their coherent advice on dealing with entheogenic plants.)

The most important thing about working with plants is that the experience is not the same as the attainment. When you take a plant, they will take you on a journey in a particular realm, and then you go back. That does not mean that you have mastered that realm. If a mountain guide short-ropes you up a particularly difficult mountain, and you get to the summit, and you come back down in one piece, that does not make you a qualified and competent mountaineer. You're someone who has been there with a guide. You do have to have the fortitude to stand some of the places that the plants take you; you are actually on the mountain doing climbing. The dangers are still real; the storm can still come, you can still fall off, but it's a different thing. You can't claim to be doing it yourself. This is controversial, because with some of the people who take plants, they say, "Well, that's all we need to do, and that gives us all the attainment we need," and I disagree with that. Certainly for the insight it's good—when you've got the message you can put the phone down—but you must remember that what you're really doing is practicing working with that mountain-climbing guide, so that you can get some things done.

–Lydia Helasdottir

How To Court A Sacred Plant

I actually took half a year to court the Salvia spirit. I chewed the salvia leaves and had tincture. She became very present. I had what we would call an altered state, but not a visionary state, not a breakthrough experience. But Salvia as a presence showed up immediately, and she was just overwhelming greenness. Green as green can be, and she was there as a leafy presence. The same with Datura. I courted Datura for years.

–Lydia Helasdottir

So how do you know if you should touch this path at all, or which plant is best to approach as an ally? One of the ways in which plant allies are different is that they rarely do the approaching. Occasionally a plant will follow you around, trying to get your attention. For years, everywhere I moved there was either an elder tree or a great belladonna plant in the yard. I even began taking their presence as a sign that I should live in this or that apartment, but as I was young and ignorant, it never occurred to me that the message could be deeper. When I found the farm where I would eventually settle down permanently, both were present the first time that the realtor walked us through the property. Eventually, I got around to talking to the (by now very impatient) plant spirits, and realized that I'd been stalked, so to speak.

However, most of the time plant spirits need to be courted, and this must be done in a patient and thorough way. Plant spirits don't owe you anything. Remember that. You need to convince them that they ought to help you, and sometimes that just isn't going to happen, no matter what you say. Some plants need to be courted for half a year at a time. It's worth doing, in order to show your respect.

> Everyone is different. We have unique biochemistries and the plant that works wonders for one person will fall flat for another. Some people have the wrong personalities for this work; those with addictive tendencies must naturally steer clear, as well as those who can't tell when enough is enough. It can be very easy to become dependent on the effects of these plants for their assistance in more than just spiritual practice; they are useful in pain management and stress relief, but if relaxing becomes impossible without the aid of the chosen plant, there's a problem. Cultivating the skills necessary on this path involves a lot more than just knowing how much mushroom to eat; research in subjects like history, biology, and botany will need to be done, and it's important to have a working knowledge of magical work and spirit contact. Studying this path takes a lot of time and dedication, so no matter how well-meaning a person's intentions, they just may not have space in their life for this path.
>
> Plants and plant spirits are wild, anarchic beings. They will find their way through cracks in pavement, rock, or consciousness and have as much power to destroy as they do to nurture and uplift. The powers of the Green World affirm every part of life from emergence and birth to rotting decay; these powers speak to humanity in each stage of life and remind us to face each transition with pure wild joy. How then can we bring this wild lifeforce into a context we can use?

Giving the ecstatic experience boundaries does not limit its potential potency; rather, structure gives ecstasy a focus in order to concentrate the experience and achieve the most use from it as possible. Carefully structuring the environment of these spirit-inspired ecstasies will allow you to immerse yourself deeper into the experience and emerge with a greater chance of safety.

–Jessica Maestas

Step One: Read The Books.

First read everything about that plant—the botany, the history of use, reports from people who have used it. If there are chemical alkaloids that have been studied, read about them. Ari writes, "I usually make a little mobile, with beads and wire and other little things, of the molecules of the plant's active ingredient, and dangle it from my ceiling. When I do the first ingestion, I focus on that mobile. They become power objects through which I can call that plant spirit." Most of all, read up on how to grow the plant. Find out if it is possible to grow it in your area, if only inside in a container. Jessica points out that "...not everyone's climate will be conducive to growing every substance you utilize. It may just be plain impractical; not everyone has the space for a Brugmansia to grow to full height, or the ability to care for plants sensitive to climate conditions like tobacco." She also emphasizes the need to learn about plant-lore that is not directly related to the altered-state experience of the plant—its traditional magical uses, for example, and its medicinal and household uses.

> Since we work to know a plant on all its levels, it's important to study the magical, spiritual, and medicinal properties of any plant you work with. Many entheogens have a lengthy history of being used for medicine and are the origin of some of our most valuable modern medicinal drugs. Knowing these uses will help you get a feel for the physical effects of an herb, as well as how much is too much; be sure to pay attention to any known antidotes and treatments, too. A plant's medical uses are sometimes reflected in its magical applications, and vice versa, but this equation is far from consistent. Knowing the magical uses is a clue to a spirit's personality and may be the first step in getting to know a spirit. What cultures have made

use of a particular entheogen, and how was it used? What taboos surrounded it and what did people think of it? A plant's spiritual use is not limited to any culture or single understanding, but knowing what those who have used the plant traditionally had to say about it is very helpful.

While I feel that using a plant's physical parts by means of eating, smoking, drinking herbal teas, or bathing in infusions is an essential part of this path, limiting ourselves to only the physical act of ingestion ignores the holistic approach that we strive to foster. Our knowledge should not be limited only to knowing how much herb to dose ourselves with, but should also include knowing how to work with the spiritual power that exists outside of creating an altered mental state. For example, I have found Valerian to have unique protective properties that have nothing to do with the tea made from her roots. Brugmansia and Datura are known to induce trance states just from their presence alone; this is something I have personally experienced and in the right circumstances could be very useful. Having a plant around taps into their subtle effects; they brighten our day with flowers and soothe stress with their quiet green energy.

Be aware of any potential drug interactions. Mixing chemicals can be very dangerous and can aggravate conditions that may normally be under control. Unfortunately, not all plants found on this path have been scientifically scrutinized. Even with ample research, you may still find yourself unsure about interactions. Always remember that just because something is "natural" doesn't mean that it's safe to use. Research *thoroughly*.

An herb may have several given associations (love, luck, wealth, etc.) that it shares with many others; this doesn't guarantee that one may be cleanly substituted for another. Skilled herbal magic involves being able to get a sense of the spirit of an herb, what it feels like and how it fits into the other plants being used in a magical blend. Both Mandrake and Vanilla have associations with powers of love and lust, but they are not interchangeable. Crafting your blend around the spirit of the ingredients to augment the power you most specifically want to manifest is skilled work and takes a lot of time getting to know a variety of plants, both in their dried and fresh form (if possible). Introducing entheogenic plants into these blends is sure to open a new dimension of possibility in herbal magic endeavors. Sprinkling an herbal mixture while preparing a space for rituals involving high spirit activity could be useful for warding and to begin to "open" the pathways between Worlds. If a good working rapport is established with the spirits related to the herbs you are working with, they may be willing to assist in your magical goal.

–Jessica Maestas

Step Two: Grow The Plant.

Grow the plant yourself, even if you can only do it in a pot on the windowsill. If you're not comfortable growing something, you probably shouldn't consume it. The absolutely least-level engagement with the plant is to just grow it. You may say "Well, growing something is going to be a huge commitment, and I don't know if I'll like it or if it will suit me." Well, that's just too bad. It's the price you pay. Others would disagree, but I'm very respectful of the plants. So grow it, then start to enter into communication with the plant, and see if you can get in touch with the plant entity, the plant spirit. Maybe you stroke the plant. If it's something possibly poisonous, you don't want to be eating any of it straightaway. Commune with the plant, sit in front of it and meditate, and seek it out and poke it, as it were, invite it. Hold your hands over the leaves and breathe that in, and see how your hands tingle and pulse and feel weird, without even touching the plant. That's just experiencing the energy of it. Proceed with extreme caution with these plants. When I courted Datura, I went first to the local nursery and went to the angel-trumpet section, and held my hands over it there, and asked if I should bring her home.

–Lydia Helasdottir

I talk to my plants all the time. I don't feel that I can rightly partake of a plant that does not grow naturally in my climate unless I have cared for it myself. It's different with wild plants that have their own homes in the woods around me—then I'm partaking of their hospitality and generosity, not the other way around—but for the ones that wouldn't normally grow here, I gain the right to even begin to approach them for their wisdom by sharing my home with them, feeding them, watering them, and generally treating them like an honored guest.

–Ari, spamadhr

Step Three: Divine The Next Move

Do divination on how to approach it. Ask when the right time might be. If it says "not yet", respect that. For some people, this just isn't what they're supposed to be doing. Be ready to be told No. Clear signs for a No would be: the divinations say no, the plant spirit doesn't show up, or she says, "Don't do it." People are greedy, and they want the experiences, but if you really respect the plant and you want to use it for the right purpose, then if she says that it isn't the right time, or it isn't for you, then just don't do it. Whenever I ask about taking a particular plant, I always expect that possibility, I don't assume. Because sometimes you grow out of things. For a while it was not OK for me to do any entheogens at all. These days it seems to be OK again.

–Lydia Helasdottir

Step Four: Propitiate The Grandparent Spirit

A plant, like any being, is made up of more than one body. It has a physical body that is rooted in the earth, grows as a parasite on other organisms, floats on water, or creeps across the surface of stones. This body generally stays in one place throughout its life, barring outside interference. Its spirit is tied to its body by the same mechanics that attaches our own spiritual counterparts to our bodies; the spiritual body of a plant is generally local to the physical body, though like us it has the option of moving some part of their spiritual force around (we call this astral projecting or other names meaning approximately the same thing) or appearing in remote locations. This mobile spirit body can take any number of forms depending on the plant's desire and (to a lesser extent) what part of their nature we are best able to perceive. This form may be a copy of the physical body, a human shape of some description, another kind of creature, or something abstract like fields of color.

Aside from individual spirits local to their bodies, entire species of plants have what I refer to as "Grandparent" spirits; Grandmother Valerian, Grandmother Marijuana, Grandfather Wormwood, Grandparent Skullcap, and so forth. These spirits rule over all the plant-children in their care, and the

Grandparent keeps track of each one; it is these spirits that you will likely be communicating with them most in your work with entheogens. The small spirit in an individual plant may not have as refined a level of communication; the Grandparent may speak to you through that small spirit, or communicate with you directly. In my experience, the Grandparent spirits have always appeared in more or less human (bipedal) forms. It has been my experience that while the small spirits may be very friendly, the Grandparent spirits are generally more reserved and care should be taken against allowing too much familiarity to form; even if they have agreed to work with you, some have little concern for human life and I have found that it is best to think of them as business partners: trusted, but not close friends.

The Grandparents are teachers and give their permission to use their plants in your work. Working without their permission and blessing is inadvisable. People who don't know better may get away with abusing these plant children for a while, but there may be extreme consequences as well. There are numerous accounts from people experimenting with Datura, often describing horrific experiences that sometimes culminate in severe illness and even hospitalization (fatalities due to Datura's chemistry or injury from the actions of those under that influence are also well-documented). Queen Toloache, Datura's ruling spirit, has no patience for those who trespass on her spiritual territory and shoots intruders on sight, so to speak. The Queen behind Salvia divinorum is particular, revealing herself to some people while ignoring others altogether. Other spirits, like Grandmother Marijuana, have more tolerant attitudes towards abusers or even a measure of twisted affection. However, this affection results only in a growing addiction, which is a form of spiritual (and physical) punishment and debt.

Part of why being experienced in trance states is so important on this path is that you aren't in direct control of the altered state you enter with the help of a plant. You control when you take the dose, but past that, you're largely at the whim of the spirit (or whatever assistance medical science can deliver). Some of these plants naturally create emotional states that have to be dealt with as they arise without allowing them to take over; fear, anxiety, or lassitude are just part of a plant's powers. Those feelings need to be accepted and set aside as they arise, or they may become overwhelming and halt your progress. Many herbs have the ability to call forward hidden emotions that have been tucked behind the front we use to face the world. A person's attitude and emotional state are important factors when engaging in entheogenic work, and it's no wonder that many cultures have prescribed routines that need followed before engaging in a plant-induced trance. Practices such as fasting, abstaining from sex, periods of meditation and seclusion, and withdrawing from normal activities help create a mind that is clear from distraction and a body that is open to the full biological effects of an herb. How necessary these practices are will vary from person to person and will depend on the plant they're working with.

Plants are connected throughout almost all the Worlds; wherever plants are found, they have some power. This far-reaching perspective is useful in several ways if you are allowed to become familiar with the plant network; the spirits are often very close to the Threads as well, and being familiar with one will help bring about an understanding of the other. This network communicates behind-the-scenes (so to speak) of the Worlds accessible when Journeying. Some plants have recognizable counterparts on other Worlds, some only outwardly resemble familiar Midgard plants. The plant Grandparents are more universal and having their attention through your work with them often gives you an in when you encounter plants and plant spirits in other Worlds. As on Midgard, the small local spirits of plants will be looked after by larger spirits of place—mountain spirits, valley spirits, patrolling land spirits, and others. When you seek to get to know these Otherworld plant spirits, be sure to introduce yourself to the spirit of the place you will be in and ask their permission. Courtesy is a universal language.

–Jessica Maestas

Dealing with wild sacred plants, the ones that you can't grow yourself in a garden or a pot, is a whole different ball game. The rules for harvesting wild entheogens are these: First, talk to the land-wight. Make sure that you have its permission to pick these powerful creatures from its surface. Make an offering to it, and if you don't get permission, don't go any further. If the land-wight accepts your offering, the next offering should be made to the overarching plant spirit, asking it also for permission to use its child. Treat them the way you would treat a tribal elder, which is what they are. Tell them who you are, and what you intend to do with the plants that you pick. When you pick, be gentle and don't uproot other surrounding plants by mistake. Some people are against cutting as being disrespectful and suggest taking the whole plant, but if you only need the flower and the rest of the plant will grow back, cut and apologize. Never take more than a tenth of the plants of any species on any given acre of land—it's not sustainable. Don't go telling people where the wild plants are, either; not all who hear will harvest respectfully.

I'm very much for learning the plants in your own region, even if they aren't "northern-tradition" plants. For those of us with transplanted (pun not intended but appropriate) ancestors, we have been forced to learn the ways of the land and the denizens where we were born and grew up. When it comes to the plants I work with, I use about two-thirds northern European plants (the plants of my ancestors) and one-third local plants (the spirits of the land of my birth and my home). It's important to me to be able to talk to the wild flora around my home, many of whom are useful and wonderful entities. If the Kinnikinnick-wight, or the Queen of the Meadow wight, is willing to work with me, I'd be a fool to turn them down.

–Ari, spamadhr

Step Five: First Dose

Then take a very small dose. Find out how it's best prepared. That might be tea, or smoke, or making a tincture and taking a drop, or putting a drop on rolling papers and smoking that wrapped around safer herbs. For instance, I made an oil-based tincture of the plant—boiled up the plant matter in oil to extract it—and then I started with one drop of oil on my wrist, and then three drops. There are those who would tell you to just jump straight into eating a leaf, or have a couple of the seeds, and there are some people who get away with that, but that's incredibly dangerous, and for me it isn't worth it. You may be one of those people who has a really potent reaction, and if it's a hallucinogen, you don't necessarily recognize that what's happening is because of the plant. There might be no swirly colors, just weird shit happening. But you can get very, very sick from it. People die, every year, lots of them. You can't be too careful. Besides, a strong reaction to a small amount may be another way of the plant spirit saying "No". Always have a sitter when doing this; you don't know what kind of reaction you might get."

There are many ways to take them—you can smoke them, you can make tea of them, you can make them into an oil that you rub on your body. There are also ways to use entheogens that don't involve ingesting them. You can burn them as incense, although you're still going to be breathing them in somewhat. Simply sitting with the plant and breathing with it, or putting your hands near it, exchanging energy with it; that can be quite effective, especially if you do it with a big strong plant, like an enormous Angel's Trumpet. Even their leaves are kind of hand-shaped, and that's a wild thing; you can just sit under it and be intoxicated by the perfume and it will work with you. Same thing with sleeping under a Yew tree. The oils will send you somewhere; it'll do it for you. If you grow them yourself, you can commune with them. Offering the plant matter as an offering to a particular deity is another method.

There are differences between natural and chemical forms of plants. I personally always prefer to take the plant, because the plant has been engendered with this particular mix of apparently inactive chemicals for a reason. Certainly, in terms of talking to plant spirits, it's happier if you're ingesting the real thing. You can get to the plant spirit through man-made copies of the alkaloids—for example, Valerian and Valium—because the plant spirit is out there anyway, but its primary interface is through the plant material. However, just as you can journey without having ingested any plants at all, and go and talk to a particular plant spirit, I think you can achieve its attention by using a substance that mimics it. It's much more difficult, and they may or may not decide to show. Your chances of talking to the plant spirit with the actual plant are much, much higher.

–Lydia Helasdottir

The first time you use an entheogen will be the most formative and will set the tone for rest of your relationship together. This first time has the potential to be a complex dance between your will and the power of the spirit; the spirit may have conditions for you to agree to if you wish to continue using its plant children and you will have to decide if those conditions are reasonable. While the spirits will hold back a measure of the plant's poison once an understanding has been reached, this allowance should not be mistaken for anything except permission for you to enter their territory and work with their power. *In no way* does this make a plant "safer" to use; you're still playing with poison. The poison is there to remind us that we are not the one in control of the trance that we worked together with the spirit to create. The first time I drank Datura tea, Queen Toloache let me enjoy a fever that took all night to break; it wasn't life-threatening by a long shot, but it was enough to drive home just how much I was at her mercy and won an even greater degree of respect from me forever afterwards. Entheogens also aren't the tastiest plants around; the bitterness is another reminder that this work has the potential to take us far outside our personal comfort zone, and the willingness to accept the bitterness of the herb is a form of sacrifice for the knowledge gained.

I won't tell you how much of any herb to take to achieve an altered state. That's for you to learn from study and working with the plant spirit in question. The dose needed to create the altered state may be surprisingly small; this is because, as I have said, we are working with more than just the physical components. Having spent time getting to know the spirit and its power now pays off and the entheogenic power of an herb works on more than just your physical body.

Practices such as fasting or a restricted diet also help physically prepare the body. Your body is the vehicle for your mind and awareness, so your body is the natural starting point. Body and spirit are affected by each other; problems with one will often translate to problems with the other. A healthy body (or at the very least a not unhealthy body) helps support a healthy spirit and vice versa. Pay attention to your body's energy flow as well. Are there blockages, seeps, or snags anywhere? Do you have any hitchhikers or indwellers? Are your energy centers balanced and clear? Basic grounding, centering, and focus techniques are the first step in maintaining energetic health. From there, look to your energy centers and make sure none are closed off, dark, or over-compensating for centers that are closed off. A closer look at internal flow can show you weak spots and any troublemaking hangers-on. If you have trouble getting your flow to circulate out garbage or if you need help ridding yourself of a troublemaker, someone skilled in energy healing techniques can assist. Another thing you can do on your own is exercise.

For someone not on this path full time, long term regular dietary and activity requirements may not be necessary, but you should keep the techniques in mind when preparing for entheogen work because they help begin to structure your session with a sacred plant and its spirit. Give yourself more than a few days to incorporate these considerations into your life; drastically changing your diet and activity levels stresses the body, which could make you less receptive to the entheogen. Work slowly and steadily over a period of weeks or months, if possible. Paying attention to physical and energetic health never hurt anyone, and the longer these considerations are made, the more responsive to the ecstatic experience you will be.

Look at your environment next. Where will you be using this entheogen? Who will be with you? The challenges presented inside a house will be different than the challenges of an entheogen session in the forest, so prepare accordingly. If you are in a house, take time to clean and organize everything; there is nothing more distracting to a growing trance state than the mental reminder that you haven't washed your dishes yet. Clear away clutter that would distract the mind; make your space comfortable but not overwhelming. Turn off the TV and unplug the phone – these intrusions have no place in the work you'll be doing. Be mindful of the condition your body will be in. Will you need blankets, water, or a place to lay down? Keep these close at hand so you won't have to hunt them down.

Having another person keep an eye on things can be invaluable; these spotters can pay attention to your body while your mind is elsewhere and handle any potential disturbances. This is an important job and ideally shouldn't be filled by your friend who just happens to have a free afternoon. They may have preparations of their own to address before the session, and they ought to figure into your planning. While we sincerely hope that this is never a need, having a person who knows some basic first aid or who can call emergency services with the names of the chemicals you're dosed with could make a great deal of difference should something very bad happen. Spiritual emergencies such as losing bits of yourself or having trouble coming fully back to your body can also arise during entheogen work. Someone who knows you well and is experienced in this sort of care is also very helpful.

Personally, I like setting aside the first session with a new plant to just get to know it; how my body will react, how my mind will react, and exactly how the spiritual powers work after the chemical effects have taken hold are important considerations that I don't want to be unprepared for when the time comes to use a plant for a particular task. Needless to say, this experimentation is vastly different than the experimentation done by casual users; it would be more accurate to call this education rather than experimentation. These purely educational sessions don't end after the first time – I think I've spent more plant trance sessions learning from them then I have spent doing anything else. Again, this will vary from person to person and herb to herb; some plant spirits have a great deal to say and desire your undivided attention while they speak, others give you some basic information and then step back.

–Jessica Maestas

Step Six: Recovery

Finally, consider what will happen after you're finished with your session. The effects of an entheogen will vary a great deal, not just from plant to plant, but from session to session with the same plant. One session may leave you exhausted and emotionally shot, while another leaves feelings of renewal and joy in the wake of chemicals dancing through your brain. Minimizing your responsibilities after a session will give you time to recover in body, mind, and spirit. Even when you feel fine, keep in mind that a great deal has happened, and it will take time to come completely back to yourself. You're likely to be more emotionally sensitive and may react strongly to situations normally handled with ease. This is where another person again comes in handy; the simple physical proximity of another person helps you come back to yourself, and a skilled spotter will help comfort and counsel raw emotions.

Working with entheogenic plant spirits should not be something that you do on too regular a basis. How irregular it should be will vary from person to person, but you should give your body plenty of time to not only come down, but fully recover and have several days of rest period before going there again. Traces of the plant's alkaloids can remain in your system for a surprisingly long time, and if any of it got locked into your fat supply, that can release again when that fat supply gets used. Traces of the greenwight's energy can remain throughout your body for a long time as well, affecting you in subtle (or not-so-subtle) ways. These need to be noticed and catalogued, and possibly integrated, before you jump back in to collect more of that energy.

Keep in mind that ingesting something is letting it permeate your whole body, via the living waters of your blood.

It is more penetrative and more violating than any sex act, and your body needs time to take itself back, as it were. Constant ingestion of some of the more dangerous herbs can also place a strain on the kidneys and liver, so it's good to spend the period between plant workings doing some gentle support of those organs, perhaps with herbs such as Milk Thistle, Burdock, Yellow Dock, and Dandelion. That's another reason why some people prefer to fast or eat very cleanly for a day or so before taking this path; it puts the lightest possible load on the body's detoxification systems.

Knowing how to recover from an entheogenic trance is just as important as knowing how to go into one. This is often very draining work; the body must assimilate unfamiliar material and the mind has been stretched in new ways. It takes me about 24-48 hours before I begin to feel like myself again, and until then I'm usually drained and may be a little addle-brained, though some herbs have little lasting effect after the trance has ended. When done correctly and in accordance with Right Action, the after-effects of an entheogenic trance are healing and peaceful, even considering physical and mental fatigue. What can kill can also cure; the trance state induced by several plants are similar to deep healing sleep and will leave a person feeling renewed. Ideally, you will be able to take the time to enjoy the recovery. It's a very sacred time and deserves to be savored.

–Jessica Maestas

Step Seven: Set The Intent

Then, if all has gone well, you can do a slightly larger dosage under ritual circumstances. Set your intent first. We feel that the intent with those plants is crucial. It's important to have an intent with any plant trip, and do your purifications beforehand, bathe or whatever, have your set and settings worked out, but with the very visionary plants it's particularly important, because it influences the nature of what you're going to get.

–Lydia Helasdottir

Step Eight: Accept The Taboos

Shamans who work with plant spirits, whether they be the spirits of entheogens, healing herbs, or just food plants, usually find that they develop taboos on the recreational use of plant matter for mind-alteration. Addictions are right out, and even play may not be allowed any longer. Those who work with the spirits of medicinal herbs may find that they can no longer use a herb to heal themselves unless they have developed a hands-on relationship with the "grandparent spirit" of that herb. Those who work with food plants may find that every bit of plant matter that they consume must be eaten with awareness of and offerings to the spirit that died that they might live. Plants may be sessile, but plant allies are not passive. They are every bit as demanding as animal allies. Perhaps they may even be more so, as on the whole they do not trust most humans to properly respect them ... and they have good reason for that attitude.

> Even if you use a plant only once, you will carry that relationship with you. It may be necessary to continue to observe certain taboos; most often, a person is forbidden future recreational use of that herb. Other action may be required, such as assisting others to know that particular spirit and herb, or giving ritualized attention at some time. Whether or not a plant is physically in your life seems to be unimportant (unless they have required it of you); they are still part of your extended spiritual network.
>
> These plants are not benign vegetables or simple mosses. They are powerful, potent beings. Misuse can lead to illness, injury, and even death. One must be highly disciplined in order to resist addictive tendencies. Many of these plants are very seductive, and they specialize in "catching" people. The required discipline exists past the teacup of brewed psychedelics and extends into the way one lives. For those on this path full-time, many forms of indulgence are discouraged, even outright denied. Some of the reasons I adhere to a near-vegan diet and take care to avoid artificial food ingredients are related to the physical side of this path. My long-time indulgence in coffee and caffeine was also challenged, so I have to be careful that my sometime use does not turn into habit. The path of sacred

plants stresses the connection that we have to our surroundings, what we allow into our bodies and how that affects us, though the level of commitment and taboo will vary depending on why you're exploring this path and what you need to get out of it.

Some of you may have experimented with psychotropics before starting on the path of sacred plants, or used them recreationally. I was a casual pot smoker for a few years, and was then told to quit cold turkey when I started working with my patron God; once my relationship with plant spirits began to develop, the reason for this became clear. (I'll admit to missing it a little bit every so often, but what I've gained is greater than the temptation to toke; besides, the risk I'd run by giving into temptation far outweighs momentary pleasure.) It can be tempting to use that recreational experience as a basis from which to create your practice with a certain plant, but as you are no longer a casual user, you are no longer able to rely on that knowledge. Indeed, having a recreational past with a plant necessitates starting over from the beginning after a period of abstinence. Any addiction will have to be broken, and it may be that you will not ever use the substance you were addicted to in your work; addiction has connotations of spiritual debt, and staying away from that substance and its derivatives may be required. Once you begin a working relationship with any entheogen, you will not be able to use that entheogen for recreational purposes. For those like myself who are on the path of sacred plants for the long term, recreational use of any entheogenic plant is taboo, whether or not it has a specific place in my practice. Medicinal use seems to be the only exception to these conditions, though even this should be carefully considered.

Even if you only have need of an entheogen for a single task, you still carry that relationship with you. The same attention to building a relationship with the spirit will need to be given each time, though each plant will have different needs and will likely expect different things from you. Violating the trust of that relationship through misuse incurs a spiritual debt. These debts won't function exactly like a monetary debt, for example, with balance being restored by making recompense. Instead, other spirits will be reluctant to work with you after the violation occurs and, if enough debt is incurred, this will negatively affect your spiritual health.

–Jessica Maestas

Using The Green Trance

So what is this path good for, anyway, if it's so dangerous? What does it lend itself to especially? As Lydia points out below:

> This comes down to uses. Why would you do this? I can think of several uses for which they are excellent, where the plant way is quick and very potent. One is just to show you what can be, or what could be. They are brilliant for that, all of them. Of course, if one were to do one's meditation and Ch'i Gong and energy work exercises, one really could see the world more this way all the time. People joke about smoking marijuana that after a certain attainment as a magician or a shaman, you're stoned constantly. I'm now in a state where how I see physically with my eyes is sort of an extra 3-D; the trails and all the rest of it. When someone who doesn't have that attainment describes that, they're describing being stoned. But I'm like that all the time. It's now permanent. That's why I stayed away from taking plants for ten years, to be certain that it wasn't because I'd smoked a lot. Now, though, when that plant is being taken, it's a completely different experience.
>
> So, showing what could be; giving you a glimpse into the dimension or another world that you couldn't get into otherwise. Finding answers to questions, particularly divine ones; mushrooms are good for that. You go into it with an attitude of "I need to find out about XYZ." Something that often spontaneously happens is to get shown the workings of the world, the mechanisms behind how the whole big picture works. On an emotional level, the visionary plants can give you new insights into questions you're struggling with. But then you need to figure out what the question is, meditate on it, and really be intent on seeking an answer to that. And sometimes you'll get it and sometimes you won't. It depends on the plant.
>
> But the price is high. There's always a danger; there's always attrition on your physical or mental or emotional or energetic body. That's something that people don't always believe. The price varies with the plant. In marijuana, the price is your short-term memory, and there's a certain blunting of your abilities, your psychic talent, when you're not smoking, if you use it a lot. That's noticeable. And since Marijuana is a Disney ride guide, you kind of get chained to the

Disney ride, so when you're trying to travel for real, it makes it much harder, and the temptation is just to enjoy the smoke. So while what you're seeing is real, it's limited, and you're going to turn left now and go back to the station. With acid and Mescaline, you can get Kundalini-style damage from plugging in with too much voltage in your system. The Poppy damage is known, of course; it's pretty straightforward. And with plants like Datura, Aconite, Monkshood, you can get killed.

–Lydia Helasdottir

Applying Plants To Others

While we've so far been talking largely about applying the sacred plants to the shamanic practitioner themselves, one can also apply the plants to a client, or an assistant, or someone else, and utilize them in this way. As someone who is currently forbidden by my patron deity to put these plants into my body, this is an alternative method that has been useful to me. If you as the practitioner are intending to do this, you still need to go through steps one through four yourself. In fact, you need to have an especially solid relationship with that greenwight if you aren't going to have the conduit of your own flesh in which to temporarily contain its spirit. You'll then do steps five and six with your assistant (I recommend practicing with an assistant first, rather than jumping into using it on a hapless client), and step seven together, with both of you working on setting intent. Step eight is also done together, because the greenwight may demand that both you the spirit-worker and whoever is ingesting the plant both accept whatever taboos it insists on. This is, of course, something to warn the other party about before trying this method.

> Another method is giving it to other people. This works well for people who can't take the plants themselves because their guides or patrons won't let them, or because it's a bad idea physically for them for some reason. Some tribal spirit-workers will take the plant; others will give it to their patient, because some of them really open up people's energy. I have also had the experience of having another

person take marijuana, and then it's much easier to install energy mods into them, because it opens them right up. It helps to get them into that state, this kind of enhanced energy-empathy between people. Somebody who's really a brickhead and very difficult to work with, you might have them smoke some Marijuana. If someone smokes in the presence of someone who's really a high-potency energy being, they'll have a different experience than what they're used to. And that's quite weird for people, because they'll have this hugely more hallucinogenic trip, because you're catalyzing their experience, and you're amping up the power level. So I would use this to reduce their filters; to take some of their filters away and increase the gain on their microphones, as it were. What normally comes into them is just their ordinary environment. Now you're in their environment, like a ten-thousand-volt-charge, and the experience will get heavier, especially if you play the energy-exchange game.

We've experienced giving the patient a rather large dose, and the healer taking a small sympathetic amount to stay connected, but not necessarily off their heads themselves. An experienced shaman who isn't even ingesting the plant matter can work with the presence of the spirit when they show up. To use it this way, you might feed it to your assistant, and the plant spirit would show up and you could ask them questions, and the assistant would speak the answers as a medium. Or you can ingest the tiniest amount as a tea, or chewing on a few of the little leaves, but give the assistant quite a bit, so their experience is very full-on, but the plant's got enough molecules inside you to do the work, without you needing to go and have a visionary experience as such. That's a nice way of doing it. It's not an entheogenic dose as such, because you're not out there in the 96th dimension having a reality-shattering experience, but she is here and she's working on you. It appears that just a few molecules are enough.

–Lydia Helasdottir

One of the most dramatic ways that entheogens are useful in the way that other techniques aren't is the fact that entheogens can alter the awareness of ritual participants, or the person who the spirit worker is assisting. Several other consciousness-altering techniques are very insular, affecting only the practitioner (such as meditation); other techniques can potentially involve others, but only someone with a certain level of experience or training will be likely to get the full effect (such as drumming). Ritual and ritualized drama have the potential to change the awareness of everyone in one way or another. Entheogens can be used by the practitioner alone, by the practitioner and participants, or by the participants alone.

Giving entheogens to ritual participants or to someone being healed is well attested to in traditional use. Entheogens often play a part in initiation rituals and coming-of-age ceremonies, and help mark the transition from one stage of life to another; the chemical and spiritual effects of these plants can create a forgetfulness of the body and even identity, leaving the sensation of having died or changed in some way. The shaman who facilitates this experience takes on a role of guide. Their job is often that of sacred performer, someone who embodies the themes and images important to their culture in order to play on that importance in the minds of the person in a trance; this work is often criticized in outsider's accounts of traditional shamanism, the theatrical element being dismissed as nothing more than slight-of-hand conjuring to fool an aboriginal audience whose lack of "real" education leaves them open to exploitation. The concrete reality of the ethnographers and the intangible world of the shaman have been generally seen as incompatible, though when it comes to dreams, drama, and visions, reality is much more fluid than many people expect. One person may have a dream that changes their life, thus altering their reality; how that importance is accepted by others depends on the value they place on the validity of the intangible and personal. In the case of the shamans poo-pooed by ethnographers, the importance of an individual's intangible world was emphasized and accepted as valuable.

Under the influence of an entheogen, the mind is very soft and open to influence; normal thought process is suspended and what amounts to hypnotic suggestion can be used to reinforce the idea of healing, of transition, or of whatever else the trance is being used to achieve. Giving a dose to the person who is being cured or assisted is well known, and sometimes is the way a particular entheogen is typically used. When properly applied, the right dose has the potential to put a person into the correct space to allow you to perform deep healing or other work that would involve the altered awareness of a client. Giving an entheogen, however mild, to another person is very risky business. You can have no idea of their body chemistry, allergic reactions, physical or mental tolerance, or emotional stability when under chemical influence. It doesn't matter how well you know them; there will be things that they themselves are unaware of and won't be able to tell you. The only exception to this would be if they could tell you what and how much of a substance they use, but even in these cases I would caution against it unless you are very sure what you're doing. Though several entheogens have little or no toxic chemistry, you will still be dealing with someone in a very vulnerable state; even with the best intentions, trouble can arise any time we are dealing with the internal landscape of another person.

–Jessica Maestas

Healing With Plant Spirits

Greenwights have been a source of healing since humans have figured out that plants have medicinal value. In fact, that's usually the first use of their energies: adding to their medicinal properties. Those wights taught Stone-Age spirit-workers how to call upon them for healing, and not just in terms of prayers said over a patient. When a spirit-worker has a relationship with a herb and its Grandparent, they can ask the greenwight to aim and concentrate the effects of that plant so as to facilitate better healing. This is something that will be covered in more depth in the next two books of this series, *The Northern-Tradition Herbal* and *Mapping The Hollow World: Northern-Tradition Shamanic Healing*.

Entheogenic plants, on the other hand, have a different role in healing. The Yanomamo Indians of South America have little left of a tradition of medicinal herbs; their "healing plant" shamanic tradition consists entirely of doing healing work while under the influence of entheogenic trances. Most tribal cultures, including those of northern Eurasia, utilize techniques from many places along that spectrum. It is that far end, however, that we will cover here.

> We do think there's a healing aspect available with all entheogens. With some of them, you have to go looking for it more. For instance, with marijuana, it just expands your consciousness so that you can move chi around your body in ways that are healing. With mushrooms it's about finding out what you need to do to heal, and with Salvia divinorum the plant itself does the healing. The

actual effects of the plant on you is noticeably more caring. It's cellular healing—improved immune system, better liver function. We've certainly seen physical improvements with skin diseases and liver ailments and migraines and various kinds of pain caused by fibromyalgia. You could actually say that those things are Ch'i-Gong-like effects that are even more improved by your ability to direct the energy—with the exception of the Salvia, which fixes things itself.

They are good for healing—first diagnosing what's wrong, which is a species of asking questions, but also for doing healing work. So, for example, if you are doing Ch'i-Gong-style healing, you can accentuate its effect with marijuana, for instance. You can visit creatures who can help you with your healing, who might eat out a particular section of your energy system that isn't working properly; to fix it, or to tinker with it and not fix it. Not everybody's nice. Some people use drugs for combat stuff, use it to see what's incoming, which is a species of question. Or you can shapeshift and travel and then counsel people; it's an aid for that. It can be used simply to enhance traveling; whatever reason you have for traveling is your reason for taking the plant. And finally, of course, there are the plants that are for hastening the end of a life, because you're tired of living, or you're too wounded to live, or you want to pass on. There are plants that help with that, which make that transition easier, and I'm for that. I'm in favor of that. It's generally not legal, although in Holland it's legal under certain circumstances.

–Lydia Helasdottir

General Warnings

While we've scattered warnings throughout this chapter, and it may seem redundant to go back to them again, we feel that one cannot overstress how easy it is to screw yourself up on this path. If you don't go into it with tiny steps, with incremental moves, checking all the way—at least in the beginning—you can end up in the hospital or dead. The wrath of these spirits is nothing to be flip about. Ari comments: "I sometimes wonder if the escalating number of deaths—to say nothing of wrecked lives due to addictions—has something to do with the fact that we have synthesized the sacred plants into chemicals, and thus changed the spirit of those plants (or at least the manifestation of the spirit that you get from those substances), made them harder, sharper, less compassionate, less caring, more mechanical. While the spirit of the Coca plant may manifest through crack, it's not the same face that it wears when you chew the leaf. It's been ... well, if we were talking about humans we'd say 'dehumanized'; I don't know what one would call it with a plant spirit. Made less natural, certainly, and thus much more deadly, more interested in simply using you while giving less back."

It's important to have a ground crew for using these plants, especially the first few times that you try them. It's also important to remember that the twentieth time may be different from the fifth time. Make offerings to those spirits regularly, if they are your allies in spirit-work. Don't neglect them, or they'll take offense, and get you in trouble. Also, the more that you work with plant spirits of all sorts, the more you'll have to change your relationship to plants in general, including the ones that you eat. Hydrogenated soybean oil, or the soy "protein" dregs that are its byproduct, is to the Bean Spirit what crack is to the Coca spirit. It's something to think about.

> There's a whole mystique about fighting to master the plant spirits and make them your allies which was perpetuated by Castaneda, much of whose stuff has been debunked, some of whose stuff is definitely crap, and some of whose stuff is definitely true. I do think that they test integrity and they test your intentions, though.
>
> There's a whole story about Datura where if she comes toward you with the black side of her face, you'll be fighting for your life, and if she comes toward you with her white face, you'll have an OK experience but you won't remember much of it. But you'll live, she won't try to take you. And if she comes toward you with both sides of her face, straight on, then you'll be in for a challenge to try to master her. But that's one person's view. I don't think that you master the plant spirits. That's like the idea that you can conquer Everest. You just don't. It's still there after you finish flinging yourself against it, and nothing's changed. Nobody masters the spirits. You master yourself vis-a-vis them. With Salvia divinorum, some people experience themselves as "Eek! I'm a walking plant!" and there is a trace of chlorophyll in your mitochondria, of course, so in that sense you carry your life through plants, because plants are the only things

that can absorb the sunlight, and from there all life on earth proceeds. So to say that you're mastering it, that's just daft.

People have to understand that they aren't this all-powerful being just because they can smoke heroic loads of weed. That doesn't make you a magician. That makes you vulnerable. However, doing heroic doses of weed and learning, during that, how to manage and control your chi, and keep doing that after you stop smoking, that might make you a magician. But just sitting there on the Disney ride staring off into space doesn't do shit.

–Lydia Helasdottir

Entheogens aren't a shortcut. Chewing some peyote buttons or smoking a lot of marijuana won't make you a magician, shaman, or prophet; the chemistry of these plants make visionary experiences possible for many people, but those experiences in themselves don't necessarily mean very much. You may speak to spirits or see the world from a fantastic new perspective, or maybe you'll have profound spiritual experiences, but what you see does not automatically exempt you from plodding towards enlightenment the hard way. Entheogens can give you a clear picture of what it is you are working towards, but should not be mistaken for the goal itself. Sacred plants augment personal practice, they are not in themselves the practice

And this is a highly subjective practice. On different occasions, factors such as setting and dose may be the same, but very different experiences might result. The ecstasy of one session may be lacking in the next for no apparent reason. A person's unique cultural and subcultural symbolic language will shape their visions. Emotional state has a huge impact on the effects of a plant; fear and anxiety quickly halt progress by creating unpleasant sensations. If the necessary preparations haven't been completed, the outcome can be less than desirable. Anticipation and expectation also play a role; the power of suggestion has particular potency on this path. Creating special entheogen rituals can be very useful in giving structure to the ecstatic experience, but again—what works for one person won't work for another. Rituals aren't exactly mathematical formulae anyway, and adding the unpredictability of sacred plants can create a lot of unknowns. Maybe the expected result will be achieved. Maybe something wholly unexpected will happen. Maybe nothing will happen at all.

Setting a controlled surrounding allows our awareness to be released into the strength of the spirit and the plant we work with. We can cultivate the willpower needed to turn ourselves over to another being by self-knowledge and by creating structure in our lives that supports the ecstasy of this path. It is entirely possible for someone suitably skilled to resist the mind-altering effects of these plants, but what is proved by this resistance? Some could argue that the strength to revive from radically altered states, to resist addiction, and to gracefully surrender control is a truer indication of self-mastery. There is a more esoteric level to this ingestion of poison; the spirit worker who goes forward on this path with knowledge and willingness helps transmute the poison of a culture into a new substance. This is done in small increments, maybe in measures barely discernable, but poison can be battled with poison. This is unusual work found in several parts of spirit work and shamanism, accomplished through several different means. It is, so to speak, homeopathy for the world.

As humans, we try to impose systematic order on a world that we perceive to be chaotic. We try to apply our understanding of order onto systems that have their own ideas of how they should be ordered; little concern is given to the self-image of the beings we seek to define. The search for patterns in what would otherwise be complete chaos doesn't have to be so one-sided. Working with the spirits of this path helps a person create structure that supports and enhances their work and gives the spirits useful tools to communicate with us. We each have to learn to speak the other's language. Naturally, some give and take will have to happen; the plants willingly give up their bounty, the spirits give their assistance, and we respond with care, attention, and adherence to the rules that help keep all parties safe. Our willingness to cultivate discipline on the path of sacred plants creates a launchpad for ecstatic experience and gives a safe place to which we can return. Beginning and continuing to live in a disciplined manner is the first step towards the self-mastery needed to work on this or any path and will give you skills that will affect and enhance every other part of your life.

–Jessica Maestas

Lydia's Musings On Plant Spirits

Entheogens that I have known and loved ... well, of course you can't advocate doing anything illegal, but should people want to, it is known that there is a history of using the following plants for beneficial associations with the Divine. First, the classic plants that I would consider energy-awareness-expanding. Marijuana, which isn't strong enough to be that visionary, unless you live in Holland; it tends to take a lot of the filters off, depending on how much radiation you are receiving. Having lived in Holland where things are legal, we find that up to a certain point you have automatic safeties. You can only go so high, and you don't really get any radiation damage from being there. You do get a guided tour a little closer to the Source, and some of the natural radiation-dampening effects that you get from living quite close to the material plane are diminished. You get increased awareness of energy and such—for us it's pretty real. You can experience this state in a variety of ways, but we consider it valid.

When you've passed certain ring-pass-nots in your development, that safety isn't there any more, so you really can get burnt. It can certainly trigger a Kundalini-like experience with all the disadvantages and pains that go with that. You really can get burned by the radiation up there, and it can really crisp your organs. So if you read the literature about the things that can happen if you get an uncontrolled Kundalini experience, all that damage can happen to you. It's as if suddenly your 110-volt system is running on 220, or 440, even. We have seen a lot of cases of wires burnt out in people's energy bodies from smoking.

Other plants may be slightly more visionary in information content. Instead of simply being an enhancement of the existing dimension, you're going into a completely different dimension with overlays. You can take the various mushrooms, which give access to what to our minds are quite different realms, with different creatures in them. Are those creatures false or real? The DMT elves and the Psilocibe guide and the rest of it; for us these are real entities that you should check just like anything else. There's a big debate about whether that's real or a figment of your imagination, but we are objectivists, in that we feel that it's just as real as you and me.

DMT-type plants—Ayahuasca and Iboga and Syrian Rue—those are ordeal plants, really deep rides, long and often uncomfortable. Iboga definitely gives access to whole other dimensions, ones that people are not usually ready for. But interestingly, the DMT chemicals are in your brain already. The DMT class of plants are the classical snuff-plants; a lot of the Amazonian forest peoples are using DMT-type plants. It's full-on visionary, it's gives access to animal spirits and spirits of ancestors. If you take those within a ritual setting with a specific intent, then those are the types of things that you will see. If you take them as a party drug then you might see the Machine of the Universe. But they tend to reveal the fabric of the nature of things.

True hallucinogens such as Mescaline and LSD—LSD being a synthetic of ergot—they are still plants in some way. I definitely had a breakthrough on acid. I was shown what it's like to come through Paraketh, through the Veil there, and had a little death and all the rest of it. The trip itself is a fairly boring story, but in fact it was significant because it involved condensing onto a single point, expecting to just plop out of existence, and not have a body to come back to, and the dawning of the light and all that stuff. But then again, it's not the attainment of that space—you are being shown a movie of it, basically, even if it's an immersive 3-D movie—the attainment itself didn't come until seven years later. But having experience with what it looked like, I was able to recognize it when it came. I think that's an important part of taking plants. It left me with enough markers to know the real thing when it came along.

It was the same with Mescaline—it was similar to acid but more organic. And, more recently, with Salvia divinorum. A remarkable plant, used by the Mazatecs in the Amazonian rain forest. With Salvia, there's an odd type of reverse tolerance. It takes several times using it to make a breakthrough. There's sort of six levels of using it, from a subtle experience of something having changed to a meditative enhancement state where you're aware of the Salvia entity, and more aware of how things fit together; through to light and visionary states through to fully identifying with a different environment where you don't even know that you've taken the plant; you're just moving in a different place. Maybe you're the side of a house, or merging with objects. Then comes a fully amnesiac overload, usually only experienced by people who are smoking pure salvanorum A crystal that's been extracted. That's an experience so overwhelming that even experienced psychonauts can't process it and they just come back amnesiac.

As to the reverse tolerance—obviously it's different for different people. It also depends on how you do it. If you take it in extract form, make an acetone tincture and then evaporate the tincture onto leaves, so that you have a 5X or 10X extract, you can get a pretty full-on experience with first-time use. If you use the extract and take a few really deep lungfuls, it can happen. The next time you use it, you might only need the one lungful, and the time after that you can switch onto one or two ordinary leaves, unextracted, and have massive experiences. The reason that a lot of people have train wrecks with Salvia is that they'll have the 10X the first time, or even the first couple of times, and think that more is better, and have a bigger dose of 10X, or 20X, even, and just have this grossly overwhelming experience that just scares the shit out of them. And it is scary, because Salvia is very invasive. It's frequent to have the experience of vines coming in through your body. You can feel yourself pulled away from—or ripped out of, if you try to resist it—your physical body. It's short, it takes only 15 minutes if you smoke it, but it is heavy. But it's a healing plant; you can feel it.

Salvia spirit is an ultra-green lady who is often seen tending a garden. Sometimes one experiences oneself as a plant in her garden. She's also got two sides of her face, like Hela, and like the Belladonnas. Actually, it appears that with Salvia, she can work through the chlorophyll that's in your body. I think that's why it's easy for people to recognize her presence when she shows up. It's a pretty unusual plant. It's legal for now, too. It has a marked antidepressant effect; there have been clinical studies on that—people taking subclinical doses two or three times a week as a tea. Salvia plays well with others as well—Kava Kava, Mugwort, etc. She doesn't play well with DMT or mushrooms; she renders Marijuana unnecessary, overwhelms it. She's very expressive in what she wants you to do.

Another sort of drug might be Canna. That's a hunter's drug. It potentiates marijuana like … well, I've never seen anything like it. It makes the experience far more intense, but at the same time it prevents it from being too painful. Really weird stuff, Canna. It can give you a bit of a headache afterwards. It's a sort of a euphoriant for the first couple of hours and then it puts you to sleep, which is great if you're taking it with weed. So you've got the energy-awareness enhancers, you've got the visionary hallucinogens, you've got the deleriants—Wolfsbane, Henbane, they're dangerous, but still a little less dangerous than Datura in the body-safe doses. And there's Amanita, the Little Red Man.

Henbane used to be used in beer, in Pilsner. It's dangerous, but you can get quite a bit of scopolamine out of travel-sickness tablets, because the active ingredients are atropine, hyoscine, and scopolamine. People have gotten into taking larger quantities of travel-sickness tablets, because it's the same active ingredient. But we feel that if you're going to take the plant, take the plant. That whole plant is like that for a reason. There are protective elements to the plant that aren't there in pills and extracts.

Datura, and Brugmansia in particular, was for me this tall, haughty, achingly beautiful female who was ... well, you just knew that you weren't going to mess with her. As for the mushrooms ... Psilocibe was a more male presence for me, quite jokey-trickstery, but definitely quite serious as well. The spirit of Canna was more elusive; it was dusty, male, kind of runs away from you, like he wants to lead you places. The Marijuana spirit ... she seems to be very diffuse, because so many people are smoking without knowing that she's there, or caring, which is a shame, so she seems to be very shy. But I've experienced her as a kind of late-teenage, early-twenties, beautiful flitting fey-like entity that could wear a thousand different dresses, she's always different. She's aloof, and vexed with the way it's being used these days. So sometimes she just drops a really bad one on someone, just for the sake of it, who wasn't expecting it.

The Poppy entity ... I've seen both male and female in the Poppy. The Poppy entity almost always has this corona of tendrils growing out around its head, but they're not green tendrils; they're more energy that you can see streaming off it, and they reach out to wrap you in this comfortable place. Very embracing, but a bit too easy to get embraced by. Monkshood I have experienced as a very male figure, stern and upright, with chiseled features.

There are other plants that go alongside, like Kava Kava, Passion Flower, Valerian, Mugwort, other traditional medicinals. But they do have visionary features to them, they just aren't quite as overwhelming. And I think you can classify them into uses. Mugwort—I don't know anything better for clearing a space than Mugwort—it's unbelievable. Actually, I think even using the more extreme plants as an incense is useful. It's another way to go. You can reasonably safely burn a little bit of Datura as an incense, if you're outside, as opposed to sucking it down your lungs in a big toke. That's been done with some success. Then after that you take microdoses of the stuff, in tea, or tiny little amounts once you've got to know the plant, just to make the connection. You don't have to have a heroic epic every time that you just want to commune.

–Lydia Helasdottir

For more in-depth information on the nature of different plant-spirits, including those specifically of Northern Europe (and with the exception of the Little Red Man, who is mentioned in the following segment), please check out the next book in this series: *The Northern-Tradition Herbal*.

The Little Red Man:
Fly Agaric in History and Culture

by Jessica Maestas

Recognizable by sight if not by name, the red and white fly agaric mushroom (*Amanita muscaria*) has a long association with elves, fairies, and the Otherworld. It was the entheogen used by Siberian shamans and, until recently, was thought to be how berserker rage was inspired. Compared to poppy, the use of fly agaric was spread over a relatively small geography although its imagery is still used in folk art today. In modern-day Europe, it is still associated with luck and good fortune; one can't help but wonder at the power this mushroom has had over the minds of so many people.

Around 10,000 BCE, birch and pine forests appeared as glaciers melted to reveal what is now Canada and Siberia. The people living there were not long in discovering the power of fly agaric, which appeared in brilliant red at the base of its symbiotic partner, the birch tree. In the New World, the only firm evidence of fly agaric use is found in the Ojibway tribe who lived in the Great Lakes region of North America. Although some people have linked artifacts found as far south as Mexico with fly agaric, little has come to light to scholastically suggest that it had nearly the hold on New World cultures that it did elsewhere. The bulk of traditional information comes to us from Siberia and sub-arctic and continental Europe.

The eastern Siberian Koryak people credited the deity Vahiyinin with creating the wa'paq spirits who appeared as the fly agaric mushroom; the trickster Big Raven found the wa'paq so useful that he allowed them to remain on earth to teach the people what they needed to know. Many images connected to the fly agaric come from Siberia, depicting human figures crowned by and surrounded by mushrooms. Though each tribe had different ideas about who used fly agaric, and how, and why, everyone agreed that the mushrooms brought gifts of divination, healing, vitality, and communication with the Otherworld to those who used them. There is the consistent, almost universal, understanding that the shaman and the mushroom were partners in spirit work. It should be noted that in some tribes fly agaric use was recreational as well as religious and there was no stigma against it; fly agaric was the intoxicant of choice until Russian culture introduced alcohol. Even into the 20th century, fly agaric was still used religiously in Siberia and northern Finland.

It is generally supposed that Europe was introduced to fly agaric by the Laplanders, who originally came from northern Asia. There is some evidence that the Saami shared culture with those people who would later be known as Vikings; the Saami were famed for their "sorcerers" and children from other Scandinavia cultures were sometimes sent to them to gain power that could then be brought back home.

Long after Christianity took hold in Europe, the mystique of the fly agaric mushroom persisted. In Yugoslavia, the peasants said that the god Votan was out riding one day when demons appeared and began chasing him. Votan's horse galloped faster and faster until bloody foam fell from his mouth to scatter in all directions; from the foam grew the red and white mushrooms. Modern German nursery rhymes name him *Glückspilz*, the "happiness mushroom." Mushroom imagery, sometimes suspiciously reminiscent of fly agaric, is found in French and German churches. In 1784, Swedish professor and doctor of theology Samual Ödman put forth the idea that fly agaric was the source of the berserker warrior's inspired fury; this idea was accepted until R. Gordon Wasson, the man who coined the word "entheogen," challenged the idea with his work in the 1950's and 1970's. It is now believed that fly agaric was not used by berserkers; a number of other substances, including alcohol, are currently believed to have influenced them. If those writing the accounts had tried the mushroom themselves, they would have found that it often induces a stupor rather than motivation towards legendary feats of strength. Gaiety and increased activity levels are mentioned in many traditional accounts, but these hardly approach the described strength of the berserkers.

Some researchers have spent their entire career chasing the fly agaric spirit across the globe; Wasson believed it to be the legendary soma of the Vedic scriptures and wrote extensively about his ideas. The Little Red Man's footsteps have been traced through India and Afghanistan, and to secret Buddhist sects. Fly agaric has even been connected to secular Christmas symbolism; the red cap trimmed by white gills is the red and white hat of Santa Claus, and the reindeer that ate the mushrooms on the Siberian steppes are his flying reindeer (it is interesting to note that the Latin root of *muscaria* is *musca*, "to fly"). Fly agaric grows at the base of pine trees, giving us a Christmas tree where German-made ornaments in the shape of mushrooms can then be hung; wax shaped like mushrooms were sometimes used to decorate the traditional Yule log. Some scholars and European folk tales even connect fly agaric to the Christian tradition. Did a single mushroom really shape so much of our present Western culture? How can a single half-remembered spirit lead respected scholars across the globe in pursuit of his secrets? As usual, the most important voice has been mysteriously silent.

Fly Agaric in Spirit Work

I first became aware of the fly agaric spirit, the Little Red Man who I call Father Redcap, in a vision I had of my plant allies; they were all shown to me, the tall ones and small ones, the ones who were green or brown or rainbow colored, and the ones who sang, smiled, or beckoned with addictive seduction. He was there too, distinctive in his red cap, his eyes very bright even when screwed up in a grin. He was diminutive, but I knew better than to let apparent size fool me. Later he flitted in and out of my attention, nudging at the edge of awareness when I read something I needed to remember and slowly guiding me towards being ready to eat the mushroom itself. The experience was extraordinary. While that first time was far less "altering" than marijuana or alcohol, the power of the spirit made the experience one to remember.

My dear Red Man has never left. He teases sometimes, wanting me to leave my home and run through the Colorado Rocky Mountains with him in pursuit of his earthly counterparts; he may race on ahead to entice me, dizzy, further into his trance. I think this one of his great mysteries: he never leaves. If he gets into you, whether you eat the mushrooms or are intoxicated by the spirit, you just may up and chase him. You may run together, not even knowing it, surrounded by images that remind you of him. If he gets in you, you may see him everywhere—in the Coca-Cola sign, in polka-dot fabric, in the Santa Claus at the mall. Sometimes you don't even consciously recognize his touch, but something odd in a peculiar shape or color combination rings a very distant bell. I have looked at the sky and, seeing only clear blue, known it to be the inside of an eggshell that was actually speckled red and white. He gets into your mind and changes it forever, leaving his footprints on your soul. He never leaves.

Mushrooms occupy a slightly different place in sacred plant cosmology than do vascular plants. They are very connected to the power of the roots of the World Tree, for instance. Growing on or at the base of trees gives this clear association (attested to in various Siberian traditions) although something about the energetic dynamic of fly agaric ties in with the sensation of architecture and of solid support; the energies of plants are often more "in-between" and will disregard the barriers they flow through. Fly agaric also goes through barriers but in the way that a supporting wall passes through each floor of a tall building. The power of the mushroom can be thought of as the parts of Yggdrasil that support the Nine Worlds, and the power of vascular plants is the space that surrounds the Tree and Worlds.

While vascular plants are, to my mind, most clearly connected to the powers found in the part of the lifecycle that moves from emergence to rot—from birth to death—mushrooms are the part of the cycle concerned with the movement from death to rebirth. Things are turned on their head, mirrored, or presented inside out relative to this familiar cycle. Whether things are really mirrored depends largely on perspective and where an individual draws their power from; slight semantic differences can present a person with the understanding that life comes from death or that death itself contains a life cycle. Seeing the life cycle from Death's point of view gives an interesting counterpoint to more traditional interpretations. As those who work closely with Hela and Her dead folk can tell you, death is not a frozen state and a lot may happen to a person, or a soul, while in that state. Death has its own pattern to follow before cycling towards life again.

Depending on the specific tradition you refer to, fly agaric was used by only shamans and magicians, or by everyone; sometimes the use was restricted to special occasions, sometimes not. For someone working on the path of sacred plants, a personal choice about use must be made; some people feel that the traditional recreational use of a substance is enough to justify recreational use nowadays. This choice must be left up to you and the spirit. Fly agaric sometimes has toxic effects on a person, including vomiting, gastrointestinal distress, and convulsions; no deaths have been irrefutably linked to fly agaric. It is my feeling that these unpleasant side effects have as much to do with the revenge of the spirit as with any misidentification by amateur mycologists. Father Redcap can be very easy going and generous with his gifts, but it is only polite to ask him before attempting any work, even when a working relationship has been established. Fly agaric doesn't occupy the same place in modern Western culture that it did in some historical cultures, so using tradition to justify current choices may be misguided. Instead, I feel that working to know the spirit on his terms is the best way to learn how to use this mushroom in a modern context.

I have found Father Redcap working closely with Odin. Both have similar personalities, beneficent or terrifying as the situation warrants; knowing one may be a good way to begin an acquaintance with the other, and they may be willing to arrange introductions. Red Man is tricky, and his warm, funny nature hides a calculating mind that is well acquainted with humanity and our quirks. He charms a person away from their comfort zone and into the deeper architecture of the Nine Worlds. Like other plant spirits who work closely with a deity, Redcap and Odin are allies and partners and consider themselves to be equal in their relationship.

Working with Father Redcap has been a wonderful thing. He has been key in helping me compose spirit songs for the sacred plants I work with and has given me healing and feelings of wholeness when I work for him. He is certainly one of the oldest plant spirits to associate with humans, and he may even be fond of us in a distant, plant-like way; there are certainly those who he is individually fond of although, as with any plant ally, that fondness holds no guarantee of safety or affection in the way we might think of it. It is my feeling that the Little Red Man belongs in the northern-tradition pantheon along with the other wights who, while not strictly divine, play an important spiritual role. It is certain that he is asserting himself in the tradition as more and more spirit-workers are being moved to work with him. After all, he never left.

Sources

A.J. Ahlber-Venezia; "Raven's Bread" (appeared in Idunna volume 58)
Lars Levi Laestadius; *Fragments of Lappish Mythology* (2002)
Dale Pendell; *Pharmako Gnosis* (2006)
Solomon H. Snyder, M.D.; *The Encyclopedia of Psychoactive Drugs: Mushrooms—Psychedelic Fungi* (1986)

A Finer Focus:
The Ascetic's Path

First the fasting—three days with only water to drink, until he feels clean and clear all the way through. Then the rest of the purifications, inside and out. Then, when he is entirely clean, he goes naked into the woods, with only the great mantle of black wool, lined with linen. He lays the cloak on a bed of soft pine needles and sits on it for a while, centering himself and sending out his senses, connecting with the wights of the place, preparing himself. He chants each of the nine long prayers to his patron deity, nine times each. Over and over. It is his discipline, and he welcomes it.

Then, as night falls, he lays down and wraps himself in the cloak. Head, eyes, body, all covered like a fetus going back to the womb. He will be here, under the cloak, all night and perhaps into the next day. Perhaps longer. A small bottle of water is his only companion; he will make its sips draw out slowly, so that he will not have to relieve himself for a long time. Eventually, in the dark and the closeness and the emptiness, the wights will speak to him and the answer will come.

The Ascetic's Path has three important points to it: discipline, purification, and paring down. It has been practiced by hermits and anchorites all over the world for as long as human beings have sought out the transcendent. Also called the Path of Silence, its purpose is not to work the soul up into a state of high vibration in order to blast it open, but to work it downwards into a place of utter stillness and silence, so that it may open gently and slowly.

It's a slow path, and probably the least likely to give any form of immediate gratification. In fact, it's the opposite of everything to do with immediate gratification. However, doing it with a martyred attitude is not going to get you the results that you want. As with all these paths, headspace counts for a lot. Going into it with a semiconscious mental rumble of "This is boring. When can I quit? When am I going to get to where I want to go so I can stop this?" is a sure route to self-sabotage. It's all right to acknowledge emotional and spiritual struggling, but your attitude should be one of being determined to engage in that struggle, not merely flailing passively and resentfully. If you absolutely cannot do an Ascetic's Path activity with a decent attitude, don't do it. Try something else instead.

On the other hand, if you begin an Ascetic's Path activity and you find it difficult, but you're not so sure that you want to give up just because of difficulty, ask the Gods and wights for help in deciding. They may have a better idea than you as to whether this will be useful. Some people do just give up too easily, and it may be good for you to stick it out. If you've been ordered to do one by a deity, you'd best do it even if you hate it. Your task will then be twofold: making it through the activity, and working on having a decent attitude about it while you're doing it.

The Ascetic's Path is one of coming to terms with limitations and restrictions. It's not about overcoming them, it's about using them as tools. Most people think of limitations and restrictions as entirely negative, but you can't focus on something fully without limiting your peripheral attention in some way. Some restrictions are good, like a rope anchor while mountain-climbing, or a safety helmet, or not living on chocolate fudge and soda for fourteen days in a row. In fact, spirit-workers throughout time have deliberately taken on restrictions and limitations in order to gain more power, or been ordered to take them on by the spirits that they work with. We call these taboos, and the further you go down this path, the more taboos you will gather. They are the structure that will hold you up when you need it, which you will.

I. Discipline

The first point is one that many modern folk have a hard time with, especially those on Pagan paths. Spiritual discipline is seen as something that other, more uptight, less hedonistic religions do—Catholic or Buddhist monks, for instance, or Hindu beggar-priests. It's not ecstatic like the Path of Sacred Plants or the Path of Rhythm, and it's not impressive like the Path of Ritual or the Ordeal Path. At the same time, it's daunting. As one teacher of spirit-workers points out elsewhere in the book, getting someone to do even one small devotional thing every single day is nearly impossible, especially in today's hyperactive sound-bite fast-food society. We are, as a culture, very poorly equipped for any work on this path. That's a good reason why we need it all the more. Remember that part of getting into an altered state has to do with doing things that are not part of your outside-world routine, things that jar you into a different state of being. For those who lead irregular lives, a disciplined routine for even a few minutes per day can create that non-everyday space.

Spiritual discipline has been likened to the soul-equivalent of developing body memory. As any martial artist knows, if you do the same movement over and over in a ritualized manner, eventually your body will pick up the memory of how to do it, and be able to replay it without conscious direction from your mind, thus freeing you up to do other things while the body runs on automatic. Similarly, the psychic acts of grounding and centering and other techniques, if done often enough, can create a psychic astral-body memory that will run on automatic while your mind is freed up to notice other things. Spiritual disciplines do this same thing for the soul. Eventually, after a time, your soul will learn to fall into a groove and reach a certain preliminary state of openness and clarity, triggered by the discipline.

Conversely, body memory—especially when done mindfully and accompanied by the proper moving of chi through the body—is a common and accessible route to spiritual discipline. Certain types of martial arts are good for this, especially meditative ones such as tai ch'i, or the ones with repetitive solo katas. Getting up and doing the same series of body-and-chi-moving exercises over and over can be a good tool for quieting the mind and creating spiritual silence. Other useful body-path vehicles might be yoga, repetitive physical labor, or running.

> I get a lot of clarity from running. In my case, running very long distances is a good thing for me. I consciously run; I'm not just some idiot jogging. I'm purposeful and I'm scouting or I'm being an envoy, listening and looking around to see what's happening in the woods or with the animals, being aware of my breathing, not shirking from the negative emotions that are coming up. If I do ten or fifteen miles, I can pretty much push everything aside for that time. Fifty miles? It comes and gets you. You can't ignore, it, because you don't feel good all the way through a fifty-mile run. So when it comes and gets me, I continue to breathe, and do my various mind-tricks for it. If I really can't just ignore whatever it is that's bugging me at the time … if it's physical pain and discomfort, I'll say, "OK, I'll run for a thousand paces and then I'll see what it feels like." And then if it still feels bad, I'll take a ten-minute walk or something, and then I'll stop altogether if it really still feels that lousy, but generally it doesn't.
>
> But in terms of personality crises—you kind of wear them down. After three hours or so of running, you've thought of all the obvious stuff to think about, and it's all gotten a bit boring. Now you're starting to think about things you've done; maybe they were worthy and maybe they weren't, and invariably your mind comes to rest on things you've done that weren't so worthy. But you can look at them from the point that you're running a fifty-mile run, and that's a very worthy thing to do. So it's an antidote to wallowing.
>
> –Lydia Helasdottir

Other disciplines might be daily meditation, or devotions, or repetitive physical activity, or using repetitive breathing as a daily cleanse, or specific prayers that are done routinely at certain times every day, or during certain specific activities. If you want to do some kind of daily discipline and can't seem to remember to do it every day, lining it up with other things that you do every day can help that. Some people have lined up their daily prayers with the first meal of the day, or brushing their teeth or hair, or even taking daily medication.

One young woman I knew had a schedule so amazingly erratic that there seemed to be nothing that she could count on doing every day, including remembering to eat food until late in the afternoon. She felt that there was nothing that she could use as a trigger. I asked her if she had to go to the toilet every morning when she awoke to urinate; she responded, "Of course!" I suggested that she do her prayer every morning while on the toilet. At first she felt that this seemed somehow wrong or sacrilegious, but I pointed out that if this was the only guaranteed routine moment of privacy and stillness that she had every day, it was better to do her prayers on the can than not to do them at all.

Mental disciplines can also be used as a form of mindfulness. One example of this would be spending a period of time speaking only absolutely truthful things, or speaking only absolutely necessary things, or not using specific words that trigger patterns that aren't good for you. One person that I know spent a good deal of time not using the "I" pronoun, either referring to himself in third person or (more generally) mindfully restructuring sentences so as not to refer directly to himself. This was done as a way of hammering home the personally needful message of "It isn't all about you." The idea isn't that one is doing this for the heck of it, but that the restrictions are part of building a healthy spiritual structure that discourages all those things we use as excuses for not doing what we're supposed to do.

II. Purification

Purification is about removing blockages from the body, and cleansing both the body and the spirit. While there are many ways that one can do small amounts of physical and psychic purification—healing baths, herbal teas, energy work, etc.—the Ascetic's Path takes it further. Indian yogis, for example, have come up with some truly extreme levels of bodily cleansing, from cleaning out your sinuses with string to severe enemas. In the Northern Tradition, we don't necessarily go that far, although if you're drawn to that, do what thou wilt. On the other hand, techniques such as fasting, herbal detoxing, and ritual sweats are often used in this tradition.

Heat Purification

The northern-tradition ritual uses of the sauna (or *banya*, as it is called in Russia) are outlined at the end of the Path of Ritual section, so here we will only touch on the cleansing and purifying effects of using sauna as a solitary Ascetic's Path preparation. Sauna meditation is not only a strong physical detoxification, it also (ideally) has the added benefits of being done in a small, isolated, consecrated space with spirits already present and watching. If sweat-work is something that works for you, embrace the fire-etin path and go with it. Combining it with the Path of Breath and a personal ritual can be highly effective. This is the path of Muspellheim, and if you have spiritual questions about it that can't be answered by human beings, ask the dwellers in the Land of Fire.

The sauna can be a gentle purification, or it can cross over into the ordeal path, depending on how hot it is versus the heat tolerance of the individual utilizing it. Which way any particular worker leans will depend on what paths they work with; some like to push their limits as part of their purification, and some don't. Saunas have proven health benefits, including raising one's heart rate in the same way that exercise does, expanding blood vessels and improving circulation, relief from arthritis stiffness, calming respiratory problems, reducing tension, stimulating endorphins, and of course a good detoxing through the skin. (Remember not to lick the sweat off of your own or another's body during a sauna; it's loaded with your toxins and can make you nauseous. Shower off afterwards and get all that off of your skin.)

Because it's similar in many ways to inducing a fever, saunas can give your immune system a boost as well. Saunas have little effect of people with normal blood pressure, but they will temporarily lower high blood pressure. Those with naturally low blood pressure should be careful about high temperatures; calibrate your sauna tolerances slowly. The steam released from splashing water onto hot rocks also releases negative ions, as the positive ions are heavier and ground out on the rocks. This can cause a feeling of well-being and even euphoria—ever stood outside during or after a storm and breathed the air, and wondered why you were grinning like a fool? Sauna heat also increases the need for oxygen, so you breathe more deeply. Both changes in breathing and ion situation can create subtle changes of consciousness.

The tradition of going outside after a winter sauna naked and standing in the cold, or even rolling in the snow, has its own effects as well. One gets massive goose bumps, the heart continues to beat rapidly, and sometimes one can get psychedelic flashes bouncing across the retina from increased adrenal activity. A fast hot-cold transition stimulates the kidneys, causing a need to urinate. Going from hot to cold like that can be symbolically seen as stepping from Muspellheim to Niflheim, and can be ritually used in that way. In terms of ritual, the group sauna ritual later in this segment can be used solo as an opening to personal purification. However, the House of the Ancestors is usually a place where silence feels more appropriate, so don't plan loud, verbose rituals, unless you and the sauna spirits have discussed it and it feels right.

Remember to remove all of your metal jewelry when going into a sauna. If it's a very hot sauna rather than a mild one, that may include the jewelry embedded in your flesh. It can heat to skin-burning temperature in the hot steam, and it's bad to be interrupted in the middle of a ritual purification in order to run outside screaming and stick your ear, nipple or other tender place into a snowbank. If you have piercings that shouldn't come out because they will close, replace them with heat-resistant organic materials such as bone or horn, perhaps even special ones made for the occasion that can be charged with intent. Stone and glass will heat up like metal, and unfortunately amber isn't a good idea either, as it is sensitive to high temperatures and can crack, melt, or break down, and fossilized mammoth ivory can sometimes do that as well. Organic piercings of bone or horn can be wonderful ritual things, partaking of the energy of the Dead and/or horned animal, but they should be put into well-healed piercings, not stuck into fresh ones, so if you've got a fresh hole, heal it up first before going into a really hot sauna or else use plastic, lucite, or some other non-heating but sadly synthetic material. Glasses, too, may need to come off if they've got metal frames.

Water Purification

Moving from the technique of Muspellheim to the technique of Niflheim, we go from fire to water. Water is thought of as a gentler purifier than fire; this depends on how it is used. The simplest and most ancient water purification is bathing, generally a soak in a salt water bath, using about a cup of sea salt to the average tub of bathwater. Bathing regularly in the ocean is even better, but may not be possible for reasons of location or climate. Water purification is also associated with Aegir and his family, especially if you're using sea salt or the ocean itself. Herbs can also be used in the bath to produce certain magical effects; any nonpoisonous herb can be crumbled into the water, or made into a tea that is then poured in. Rather than making a giant list here of all the sorts of herbs one might use for specific things, it would be better to choose the herbs on the basis of their magical meanings or deity affiliations. For instance, one might suggest yarrow, rue, and elder for a purificatory bath prior to working with the Dead.

The areas of Niflheim that are water rather than ice include many lakes, but also the great Well of All Rivers, Hvergelmir the Boiling Cauldron. The purification technique associated with Hvergelmir is the enema, which goes back thousands of years all over the ancient world. Flushing out the bowels can be done as part of a ritual preparation of cleanliness; depending on how your body reacts to it, an enema can also verge over into the Ordeal Path, or even the Path of the Flesh. It is an intense physical experience, and the feeling of cleanliness afterwards is unmistakable.

It is also very humbling, and forces one to deal with the eliminative parts of the anatomy, which most people would rather pretend they didn't have. It forces one to be aware of the root-chakra powers of feces and rot and burial; it is important to remember that Niflheim and Hvergelmir are the haunts of Nidhogg, the Dragon who devours the corpses, the power of the Bottom of the Tree where compost is created that new life may grow. To deal ritually with one's colon and anus is to see the sacredness in the part of the cycle of life that includes death, rotting down, and letting go. It is about facing the depths rather than the heights, and learning that there is no shame or disgust in being a whole person who eats, shits, and partakes of the entirety of the natural world.

For a ritual enema, we strongly suggest either pure water only or water with the addition of some strained herbal tea made from very mild herbs, heated to just above body temperature. Don't add soap, alcohol, drugs, or any of the other things that people have put in for purposes of "cleanness" or intoxication. Yes, the lining of the rectum is more permeable than that of the stomach, and substances put in there are quicker to get through the mucous membranes and into the bloodstream ... but that also means that it's much harder to calibrate the right dose. Also, those mucous membranes are much more prone to irritation, and chemically-induced colitis is no fun. There are plenty of medical and nursing books on how to properly administer enemas, so there's little point in taking up space detailing it here. Contraindications for this method include being in the third trimester of pregnancy, having active and severe hemorrhoids, intestinal obstructions, and an actively bleeding colon. One of the problems with too-frequent enemas (and what's too frequent will depend on the individual in question) is depleting the friendly flora in the bowels. You might also want to follow up an enema by eating some form of acidophilus for the next few days, either in active-culture yogurt or in capsule form if you can't do dairy. Another piece of advice to remember is that this is not something to be approached with a macho attitude; several small doses are just as good as something large and painful. The point is purification, not warrior-ego, which has no place on the humbling Ascetic's Path.

Fasting

When people think of fasting, the first thing that they usually think of is simply ceasing to eat all food, existing only on water. Certainly that is something that many spirit-workers use, and we'll get to that in a moment, but first I want to make the point that fasting can simply mean refraining from doing any one of one's usual activities. It doesn't even have to be food; one could fast from any substance that comes in contact with one's body, or any particular activity. One example of this could be fasting from contact with polluted air, or overly-chemical cleaning agents.

In terms of food fasts, the place of beginning is fasting from specific foods for spiritual reasons. Many people already avoid certain foods for reasons of health, or allergies, or dissatisfaction with the way those foods are harvested. To fast from a specific food(s) for spiritual reasons is a mindfulness activity. One example is our Ancestor Fast. For this, we simply spend three days each season (usually the three days leading up to a solstice, equinox, or cross-quarter day, because they're convenient markers) abstaining from foods that our ancestors would not have had at that time of year. This sounds simple, but try abstaining from anything made from grain, beans or seeds for three days leading up to Lammas! It simply reminds you, by way of limitation, of your place in the Universe. (The full description of the Ancestor Fast is on our website at http://www.cauldronfarm.com/asphodel/articles/feast_and_fast.html .)

Fasting for purification moves from simple mindfulness to actually having an effect on the body and mind. If you can't do a nothing-but-water fast due to health issues, you can still cut down to very simple foods for a few days. I'm hypoglycemic, and can't go without a certain amount of protein for more than about 12 hours, so my version of fasting is raw fruit and vegetables, and raw dairy for protein. (I keep my own milk goats, so that's probably easier for me than for others, although some people will use raw fish.) If I am fasting for more than a few days, I will add in soaked grains, but the idea is to put in just enough protein to maintain blood sugar and the rest lightweight foods. It goes without saying that any food eaten on a fast should be organic. In fact, one of the things that spirit-workers should fast from frequently (and possibly permanently, if you can manage it, which not everyone can) is chemical-laden foods. It really helps with signal clarity and sharpness; your extra "senses" will have less interference.

If you're trying a fast for the first time, you don't necessarily have to go all the way down to water-only. For inexperienced fasters with no blood-sugar disorders, it's probably best to go down to a juice fast, just drinking raw fruit and vegetable juices. For most people who are used to the average Western diet, that alone will be quite a shock to the system. Regardless of whether you're drinking water or juices for your fast, don't cut down on liquids. In fact, you should be drinking more liquid than usual, especially extra water. This will keep your kidneys going, which is imperative during any detoxification process. Keep the internal rivers flowing for your own safety.

Doing a nothing-but-water fast is what most people think of when they imagine fasting. The health benefits of water fasts have been documented in many places; it is a strong detoxification method that burns up waste elements in the body. Its mental effects are both short-term and long-term. The initial short-term effects are a side effect of low protein, including light-headedness and mental fuzziness that is the body's alarm system for lack of fuel. While this phase can be mistaken by some people for enlightenment, it's more a matter of low blood sugar. In a reasonably normal body, this will pass after a while, although a general feeling of lightheadedness may continue, including times of euphoria as the body attempts to release endorphins to deal with the discomfort associated with not eating.

Ideally, this phase of consciousness moves into another phase, where the body goes into "hunting mode". Senses become sharper, and the brain wants to focus strongly on specific things. (If your mind continues to be fuzzy, and you never move into this phase, that's a serious sign that fasting isn't for you.) While the atavistic purpose of this phase is to hunt food, it can be used for focusing on other things, including psychic work and spirit-work, religious devotion, meditating, writing, studying, crafting, or other focused activities. The emotions, on the other hand, may not be nearly as focused. Fasting can bring up all sorts of issues, and it's fairly classic for the presence of other people to seem irritating, and to be irritable towards them. There's a reason why ascetics of old went off into the wilderness in order to fast. It's an art best done in solitude, where there are no other people to break your focus or for you to snap at. It combines well with isolation, silence, low-stimulation environments, and repetitive discipline, the other ascetic-path tools.

Fasting, as a tool of consciousness, is associated with Vanaheim and the Vanir. This seems at odds with their rulership of food-growing and abundance, but few in the Nine Worlds know better about nourishment and the effect of food on the body than the Vanir, and that includes the effect of lack of food. If you have spiritual questions about fasting that cannot be answered by other humans, speak to the Vanir about them, especially Nerthus.

There are a few cautions when dealing with fasting. First, your body needs to be built up enough to be able to maintain a fast. Most modern people have a terrible diet, with enough serious holes in their nutrition that they may be subtly malnourished in certain ways. The best prelude to a fast is eating simple, healthy, nourishing, organic foods for a month beforehand to build up your nutrition. I'm not one to say that this or that food group is bad; every body and metabolism is different and there is no one diet that is best for everyone, but I'm personally in favor of food that is entirely made of food, meaning that it has not been processed into inertness. The ideal is to reduce the number of steps between harvesting the vegetable or animal product, and putting it into your mouth. Simple food, made from recognizable ingredients, is best in my opinion. Build up the nutrients in the body before depleting it.

Also, continual off-and-on fasting, just like dieting by the same method, can convince your still-living-in-the-Paleolithic body that there is a famine on, and decrease your metabolism drastically. The likelihood of this will vary depending on your natural genetic metabolism, your gender and hormone levels, your level of muscle mass, whether or not you have ever been pregnant, and how much serious exercise you are getting between fasts. If you notice your metabolism slowing, discontinue fasting and do a period of healthy eating and exercise instead. Some people just have slow metabolisms that are easily triggered into famine mode, and fasting should be used only occasionally and with care by these folks. Full fasting can also be contraindicated for people with blood-sugar disorders such as diabetes or hypoglycemia, or who have liver or kidney problems. It's also contraindicated for those with a propensity to gastric ulcers, or any condition where leaving the stomach empty can lead to internal corrosion. These folks should probably just try an extremely correct, extremely organic, partly or entirely raw version of the best diet for their health problems in lieu of fasting. If that's what they're doing anyway as a matter of course, well, there are plenty of other methods of consciousness-change listed in this book and others.

Another caution is for the medically managed, individuals who are taking daily medication of some sort for health problems. On a fast, medication (especially oral meds) may act differently, becoming stronger or weaker. It may cause gastric distress; your stomach may be able to handle getting nothing better than it can handle getting nothing but pharmaceutical chemicals. If your digestion shuts down temporarily, as it will for an extended fast that is more than two days, the medication may pass through you unabsorbed. This includes such things as oral contraceptives, antibiotics, etc. If you are on regular medication that you can't stop for a few days without serious side effects, see your doctor about getting it in injections rather than oral methods for the duration of your fast. Even if you can afford to be off of it for a few days during fasting, remember that the toxin-clearing effects of fasting can eliminate its residual effects entirely from your system, which means that after an extended fast you may need to start over as if you'd been off of it for a much longer time. This is something to keep in mind for people who take psychiatric medications which must build up in the body in order to be fully effective. If the medication is habit-forming, you may end up dealing with those effects during your fast, which can be distracting.

I fast at least one month a year. Fasting is good for a lot of things. First, it's just good for your body, because your body's got two settings, like a self-cleaning oven—the "I'm cooking food" setting, and the self-cleaning setting. The self-cleaning part comes on after about two days of not being able to digest food. Your body then will scour everything that isn't needful, and use it as fuel. This makes you feel really cranky, because it's running your car on the dregs of the diesel to get the tank cleaned; it's running on dirty fuel, so it hunts up fat cells to use them. Some people have done very long periods of fasting; for example, people with cancer who have fasted on water for 90 days or more have found that their body has actually consumed their cancer, because the body recognizes that the cancer cells aren't actually something that it needs to survive and it eats them. There have been a number of studies that have been done on this ... but when all else fails, why not try fasting for 90 or 120 days? There have been some quite miraculous cures from that.

But I don't do it like that. I'll fast on juice or something for two to three weeks. I like the MasterCleanse system, which is drinking fresh lemon juice with maple syrup and cayenne pepper to just give your body enough energy to keep doing everything. Then the last week is pure water. It's good for your body. Mentally and emotionally, food is such a comfort thing that it distracts us, so fasting gives you more time, because you're not spending any time cooking or preparing food or eating it or cleaning up after it. You have much fuller days, and the days seem to last a long, long time. So you come face to face with your karmic accounting; you can quite dispassionately look at your issues. When you're fasting your body seems to give signals that say, "We might be dying. This might be a starvation that won't stop until we're dead, so now would be a good time to get the accounts in order." So it tends to bring up those issues.

Mentally, the first couple of days are "Fucking hell, why am I doing this? I want to eat!" I have that for two days, and then from the third day on there's a great amount of clarity and it's very easy to meditate and travel and see things in a new light. You feel good about yourself, because you're purifying. I tend to incorporate the sauna and Epsom salt baths and salt-water flushes as well. You're detoxing, and it's just a good thing in general. I do it because I know that I'm a lazy coward, and if I can prove to myself by doing such disciplined things that I'm not one, then this helps me to do my job better. I definitely have to energy-feed a lot more when I'm fasting, and I'm a lot more interested in it. Everything gets very sharp, because when you're hungry you hunt better. When you're sated you don't hunt as well.

–Lydia Helasdottir

Fasting in the Northern Tradition
by Galina Krasskova

Years ago, when I was first easing into journey work, I was very drawn to the discipline of fasting. In fact, for a couple of years, fasting was one of the primary training practices that Odin (perhaps having realized my affinity for the practice) laid out for me. Part of this natural affinity may have stemmed from my earlier profession as a ballet dancer (a career I left when I was 22), where such discipline with food was essential. More likely, it was Odin's way of tempering me, and starting my feet down the road of the ordeal, something I only recently realized He began very early on in our relationship. It is my belief that because fasting opens a person up psychically, it enables the Gods to quicken the pace of Their teaching. It may have been for this reason alone that I was drawn (or pushed) toward it.

I seriously have a love/hate relationship with fasting. It is an incredibly useful technique. I've used it for cleansing both physically and spiritually, for shaking loose my hold on the physical body, as a form of extended utiseta, and for the sheer useful discipline alone. At the same time, emotionally, psychologically and of course physically, it can be grueling. In a culture of material abundance and spiritual dearth, food – the most fundamental of nourishers—carries an enormous amount of psychological and emotional weight. The extended absence of food has the ability to unleash an emotional torrent. The very process of being emptied brings with it an immense vulnerability. Emotional (and energy) wards, blocks and shields just crumble and the body's energy pathways are opened by virtue of the act of consciously stripping away. One's ability to physically defend oneself grows less and less the longer the body is denied physical nourishment. On every level, extended fasting is not only an exercise in spiritual discipline, but an exercise in utter and complete vulnerability as well.

If one is doing an extended fast, after the fourth or fifth day all the senses become exquisitely heightened, particularly smell and touch. Something as simple as curling up in a blanket or pulling on a sweater becomes almost erotic. The constraints of Midgard slowly begin to lose their hold on the flesh, and herein lies one of the dangers of this practice. The process of driving one's body to the breaking point can be remarkably addictive. It's important to remember that this is not the purpose of a fast. A very wise man recently told me that if you battle the flesh, sooner or later the flesh will win. This is a painful truism that eventually is brought home to all of us warrior types, so I'll state it clearly: The purpose of fasting is not to break the body, but to break down the emotional and psychological fetters that we all too often place on ourselves.

Fasting is a process of opening on every level. It is to enter willingly into a state of utter vulnerability and to consciously commit to opening one's energy channels. Fasting is a particularly effective means of purification, as it works from the inside out. The major battle is with one's will and desires. It tempers the mind, because one must learn to ignore the mental harangue of the body for food. It tempers the body, because it provides a means of exploring hunger not only in the abstract but in an intensely physical, personal, minute way. It tempers the spirit because it causes opening of the energy channels and carries the fasting person into a state where one's internal energy is uniquely and exquisitely at the forefront of one's consciousness. It makes one intimately aware of the flow of one's energy and any existent blockages. It also highlights the myriad ways in which we utilize food over and above simple sustenance. And, sometimes, it can be a means whereby one's God demonstrates dominance, control and ownership.

Now I suppose I should be clear about what I mean when I speak of fasting. The times that I have fasted in the past, it has been a complete fast: nothing but water has passed my lips for the duration. Not everyone should do that from the beginning. We each rely on food in different ways and in the beginning, fasting can be a very painful discipline. I always found it difficult to go out or interact with people (let alone work) during serious extended fasts. The entire process simply left me far too open and undefended. That's why I believe it is best to work up to long periods of fasting gradually. Initially, I began by fasting one day a month, a complete fast, allowing myself only water. Then I'd fast one day a week, then three consecutive days once a month, and then finally I managed to do nine-day fasts. It took me a good six months to work up to my first extended nine-day fast. I believe it's important to pace oneself and to accustom oneself and one's body to what is, after all, a very ascetic practice.

I found it very helpful to work up to the fast itself: three or four days prior to the fast, start limiting food intake. Cut down on sugars, processed foods and meat. Drink more water. Eat lightly: bread, soup, fruits, vegetables. Gradually decrease until the day you begin the total fast. Most importantly, when you break the fast, DO NOT break it by eating a full meal! (Trust me on this, you'll regret it.) Rather, gradually work up to solid food again over a period of three or four days, starting with soup and bread. This way the process of fasting is not a complete shock to the body's systems.

If one cannot fast completely due to medical reasons, modified fasting can also be beneficial. Restrict meals to one small meal a day. Cut out processed foods, sugars, meats—meat is particularly grounding, hence why it is often counter-inductive to the whole purpose of the fast. Or allow yourself milk during the fast. People with blood-sugar issues should consult their physicians before attempting a fast of any sort—or at least use common sense!

As spirit-workers, our bodies are our tools, the conduit through which we do the work that is required of us. It's important to keep one's tool in the best condition possible. We experience enough wear and tear in this line of work that if a bit of fasting can help rebalance and maintain one's energy channels, it is worth any temporary discomfort. As an aside, it certainly teaches one respect for food.

On a more personal note, I find it interesting now that as Woden releases some of the hold he has on my sexuality (while not exactly demanding that I be celibate, He has demanded the choice of my lovers—which has amounted to celibacy for me), at the same time, He's beginning to demand greater physical discipline in other ways ... ways that involve the self-same tempering of the will. While I have not fasted in quite a while due to hypoglycemia, I suspect that it won't be too much longer before I'm required to do it again, even if only in modified form. In fact, He's already told me as much. It's something of a trade-off, and He seems to favor such physically trying disciplines – perhaps on the theory that if we can govern our desires, our hungers, the chaotic crying out of our undisciplined wills, we will prove to be better tools and open ourselves up to the acquisition of greater wisdom.

There aren't many references to fasting in the lore. Perhaps the only existent example is Odin's sacrifice on Yggdrasil, where He hung for nine nights and nine days in agony sans food or drink before seizing up the runes. But then Woden is all about testing one's strength, discipline, endurance, desires ... on every level He is about sacrifice, ordeal and the challenge, so perhaps it is not so strange that he would find a tool that so challenges body, mind and spirit to His liking.

Herbal Detoxification

The northern-tradition deities who are called upon for dealings with herbs are Iduna (for domestically-grown "crop" garden herbs), Gerda (for both herbs grown in the walled garden and those grown outside of it), Eir (for healing herbs), and Mengloth (ditto). For those looking into herbal detoxification, it would be wise to have some kind of relationship with, or a least do some serious propitiation of, at least two out of four of those ladies. One of the gardener goddesses and one of the healer goddesses is advised. Those who work more with the Aesir will likely prefer Iduna and Eir; those who are Rokkatru can work with Gerda and Mengloth. The Vanatru types can take their pick, although they may prefer Gerda as she is after all married to Frey.

Herbal detoxification is less short-term and drastic than fasting or heat purification; it requires taking the herbs for a long time and is less about immediate gratification. That means that it works better as part of a long-term spiritual discipline than a quick "I need to purify myself in less than three days for this upcoming ritual". While herbs can be taken during fasting, drink them in tea or in a tincture made of nutritive organic apple cider vinegar. Don't take gelatin or cellulose capsules; they don't break down well in an empty stomach.

The first sort of detoxifying herbs are the sweating-promoters; in essence, they mimic the effects of the sauna on a very low level. They include cayenne, ginger, and peppermint. The second sort includes bloodstream detoxifiers, which vary depending on whether you're aiming at the liver, the kidneys, or the respiratory system. If you go researching modern herbal detox methods—on the Internet, for example—you'll find about a million combinations, most of them from sites claiming miracle cures and selling products. Instead of doing that, I'm going to list here some herbs that were actually grown by the ancient northern Europeans and that can be used for a gentle detoxification. Make them up into a tea or a vinegar tincture (there's no point in attempting to nourish the liver with an alcohol solution that irritates it) and drink it once or twice a day.

Northern-Tradition Detoxification Herbs

Milk Thistle: sacred to Sigyn, good liver support during times of physical extremity

Burdock: sacred to Farbauti, blood cleanser par excellence

Yellow Dock: stimulates bile, cleanses liver and bowels, detoxifies skin

Dandelion: sacred to Sunna, increases bile flow and detoxifies the liver

Mugwort: the first of the Nine Sacred Herbs, stimulates bile flow and detoxifies the liver

Nettles: another of the Sacred Nine, clears uric acid and other waste from the body

Cleavers: sacred to Gerda, cleanses the lymphatic system

Parsley: one of Odin's herbs, reduces free radicals and tones the kidneys

Marshmallow: sacred to Eir the Healer of Asgard, soothes mucous membranes

Slippery Elm: reminds us of Embla the first woman, also soothing to membranes

Mullein: Loki's plant, clears out the respiratory system, stimulates fluid production

Agrimony: Angrboda's herb, clears the urinary, respiratory tracts and helps diarrhea

Garlic: Thor's plant, blood cleanser and detoxifier

Juniper Berries: the classic recaning herb of the Siberians, beloved of the Dwarves of the Four Directions, clears acids from the system and cleanses the urinary tract

As with all things herbal that are being used for ritual or spiritual purposes, one should ideally have some kind of relationship with the actual plant spirits (see the chapter on the Path of Sacred Plants for more information on that) and have asked for their blessing when harvesting the herbs (if you did that yourself) and preparing the tea or tincture. Having the plant spirits as allies means that they can direct the energies of the plant matter in a more focused way than you can, and increase its ability to act. If you aren't a plant-shaman type, have another spirit-worker who does that sort of thing make up your tea or tincture, propitiate the spirits on your behalf, and bless it for you. Information on the medicinal uses of the old northern-tradition herbs will be in our next forthcoming book, *The Northern-Tradition Herbal*.

Another easy and quite ancient purification is to soak in a salt water bath, using about a cup of sea salt to the average tub of bathwater. Bathing regularly in the ocean is even better, but may not be possible for reasons of location or climate.

III. Paring Down

Paring down is about reducing distractions. That's why isolation and sensory deprivation are important techniques of this path. Our lives are inundated with thousands of bits of data and stimulation, all begging for our attention. Some of us may live in a constant state of multitasking in order to simply cope with it all. No matter how hard we try to work on getting into another state of mind, those outside things clamor for our meager focus and distract us. If getting into that other state is of absolute importance to your work, you may need to forcibly remove those distractions.

Isolation

Isolation is the first technique. Just being alone with no one to interact with for a period of days can be amazingly challenging for some people. To really do it right, one should remove all the modern *faux* interactions of television, radio, the phone … and yes, the Internet. To go one step further in terms of isolation from the minds of others, one could cut out all reading of written material and/or playing of music with lyrics. Yet another step might be a vow of silence for the duration, effectively removing one's own voice from the mix. Especially for those of us who are serious talkers, the impact of going for days without seeing or hearing words, or hearing a human voice—including our own—can create intense changes in consciousness.

Set and setting become crucial when it comes to using isolation as a technique. The idea is to cut down on stimulation, and that includes clutter, loud noise, lots of random objects, and other people. This means that such activities as cleaning, throwing out clutter, and giving away unused physical possessions can be a good soul-practice leading up to or during a period of isolation. It not only creates a lower-stimulation environment, it can also be turned into a ritual paring-down of parts of your life that are no longer needed.

Of course, using this technique may find you forced to be alone with your own thoughts, fears, anxieties, neuroses, and other things that you've been avoiding. It may be that you find it necessary to spend some time—days, even—plowing through that muck in order to get beyond it. It may also be that you need to utilize other techniques to push even that aside, especially if you have a job to do, but you can be guaranteed that when you get back, they will no longer be willing to sit quietly in the basement. The price for facing them while in a non-ordinary state and temporarily going beyond them is that they will be the first things to greet you at the gate when you get back. When you go into an isolated space for this sort of thing, remember that consequence before you leave and decide how you will handle it.

Most human beings have an absolute horror of isolation, being social animals. Much has been written about how forced isolation drives people mad, which it certainly can. On the other hand, I was struck by the words of a Western man who was in prison for years in a Third World country, and who told Western newcomers to that prison that it could be a torment, or it could be a monastic experience ... it was all in how one approached it.

Sensory Deprivation

We depend on our senses day-to-day in a way that we generally only notice when they're muffled or cut off in some way. When this happens, our first reaction is usually annoyance—we're not getting the full spectrum of information that we're expecting—and then, if it doesn't resolve itself, we may progress to mild panic. To be cut off from information about our surroundings can make our survival-brain feel helpless, and we have to move past those feelings in order to cope with any kind of sensory deprivation. After a while, though, our bodies adjust. As anyone knows who's done the experiment of blindfolding one's self for a whole day or more, our other senses extend themselves to compensate. That's why sensory deprivation is used for psychic work; if you close off enough of the senses, the nonphysical ones may start to pick up the slack, and it's a way of forcing them to do that. While for some people this may simply recall the *Star Wars* scene where Obi-Wan Kenobi puts a blinding helmet over Luke Skywalker's head and tells him to "use the Force, Luke" to hit the ball with his light-saber, there is solid magical practice behind that concept.

Severe sensory deprivation techniques have included the so-called "witches' cradle" or "cat's cradle". This term refers modernly to a variety of techniques which either suspend a person in a frame or specially-built harness and subject them to pendulum-type movement, or fasten them securely to inversion devices that immobilize them in an inverted position. The former technique is the more popular of the two. Researcher Jean Houston is credited with inventing the "witches' cradle" in its modern form. The modern technique is named for a medieval torture method of binding suspected witches in a sack, suspending them from a gantry, and spinning the sack around until disorientation produced hallucinations and confessions. As far as we know, there are no references to this particular technique prior to the late medieval era, and then only as a torture technique. Using it as an altered-state method was developed in the explorative 1960s and 1970s, where the "witches' cradle" term was fancifully applied to it, and eventually that got the attention of modern witches.

The classic witches' cradle consists of mummifying the body tightly in cloth wrappings (or these days a full-body suit harness), stopping the ears and eyes, and suspending the person from a gantry to swing. After a time, unable to see or hear or touch anything, and unable to move or even find where one is in space, with the inner ear constantly disoriented from light swinging, the individual "goes within" and then goes out of themselves.

The low-tech traditional equivalent to this was the practice of "going under the cloak", for both Celts and Norse/Germanic peoples. As illustrated in the first section of this chapter, this was simply about wrapping one's self in a cloak and staying there, in the closeness and dark, until visions came. The most famous recorded incident of this practice was in the year 1000 in Iceland when Thorgeirr the Lawspeaker, a pagan elder, went under the cloak for a day and a night to ask as to whether the religiously divided Iceland should accept Christianity as its sole faith. When he emerged, he sadly told the waiting masses that the Christian conversion was the only way to avoid widespread war and slaughter over the entire Icelandic colony. (One also wonders if he sensed the drawing apart of the worlds, and the fading of the doors to the Tree, which had begun by then.)

Going under the cloak is a combination of the Path of Meditation and the Ascetic's Path, in that it can be used as an adjunct to utiseta. The most common places to go under the cloak were barrows, or burial mounds, where one could commune with the Dead, but it was also used to commune with the Gods and seek out knowledge of the future, as Thorgeirr's example shows.

Going Under The Cloak
by Lydia Helasdottir

Going under the cloak can be done for a short while or a long while, and it means basically that you literally get a blanket or a cloak and lie underneath it, and then depending on how extreme you want to make the thing, you put rocks on your chest, as the Druids used to do, to depress your breathing, and that alters your state. Or you can have your helpers cover you up with earth, all but just a small area on your face so you can still breathe, but you're going to be carbon-dioxide-stressed, because it isn't the same amount of oxygen.

You want to have ground crew for this, so you can stay alive. They need to be able to very unobtrusively check on your physical well-being, to keep their energy to themselves, and be comfortable in the space. Warding is good if they can do it, but it's not always necessary. If you're going to go and do something like this you probably want to put up wards first anyway, however you see those things. The ground crew keeps checking that the blanket is still becoming moist from your breath. If you stay there for many hours, then you have to get used to the idea that you'll probably have to urinate, so you might want to dig a shallow grave or trench and lay there on a sheet and have it all covered over except for the breathing part of your face. You can be there for twenty hours if necessary. The Earth is quite a good insulator, and it's a weird experience.

Traditionally it's three whole days, but that's pretty severe and rarely done. You can do a whole long fast before that so you don't have any issue with solids, but you will urinate. You need water, too. If it's less than 18 hours you can do without as long as you don't have any heart, kidney or bladder problems; you won't do irrevocable damage, but for more than that you need water. We modern people have soft bodies and we aren't used to hardship. So you would set up a little tube or a camelback that you could sip from without actually getting outside interference. But three days is excessive, for the most part. Overnight is more than enough for most people. We find that usually six hours is more than enough for most people, and you can certainly do without water for six hours.

The experience of having the earth on you is weird as well. The weight of it feels strange, and you also have the earth over the third eye part of your forehead. You get cramps and twitches, huge claustrophobia, panic attacks and weird sensations, even if you're not usually prone to it. You can't move, and you definitely get sore, and that's kind of part of the deal, detaching from that. Of course, spending three days under the earth is neither safe nor basic. But using a mummy bag for a few hours ... even just spending the night sitting vigil in the woods is enough to creep most people out. And that's not a bad thing ... getting a good fear-on will put you into an altered state.

In contrast, float tanks are great, but that's very high comfort. When I do a float tank, I kind of feel like I'm cheating, because it's not hard at all. It's really nice. It's dark and weird and creepy and you can't distinguish the boundary of your body from the water. You can also make a modern witches' cradle or cat's cradle out of a good army surplus hammock and just tie it up.

We do a thing where we just stopper up the ears and the eyes and put a hood on and get in a mummy bag and be wrapped up with duct tape. If you have someone who is adequately knowledgeable about bondage, you can do it as being tied up. Make sure that there's plenty of room for circulation. Or use a big sack, a mailbag or spandex body bag, and a darkened room, and just lay there. The first hour, you'll feel silly. The second hour you'll feel silly and uncomfortable. The third hour you'll feel silly and uncomfortable and claustrophobic, but after that it starts getting interesting. It's a very labor-intensive way of doing things. But the key things are regulating and/or limiting the breath, sensory deprivation, and doing awareness exercises, and the length of time that it goes on.

On a smaller scale, mild sensory deprivation as an ascetic discipline need not be so all-encompassing or immobilizing. Simply spending a period of time limiting a single sense to ritually cut down on stimulation, or creating a very unstimulating space in which to do work, can be done in a way that can be combined with limited (or even regular) daily activities. One might wear gloves on one's hands, or keep one's face and head covered, or not raise one's arms above the heart. While some of these may seem rather silly and useless, they do create a condition of mindfulness and in some cases an altered state. Jessica Maestas's essay below shows the value of this practice, ordered by a Northern-Tradition deity. Indeed, silence and sensory deprivation are things often associated with Hela, the Goddess of Death, and the other demigods who are the staff of Helheim. It is very much a Helheim-type practice, which is why it is associated with the Dead, but at the same time it also has associations with such silent Aesir goddesses as Vor and Var.

Silence
by Jessica Maestas

At the end of October 2004, the Goddess Hela instructed me to set aside a week for some in-depth work with Her. I knew that this would be a departure from previous work I'd done with Her, and put off facing the inevitable preparations. When I couldn't avoid it any longer, I spoke with Her and She told me what was to be done. I would be observing a "sound fast" for a week, abstaining from any audio/visual media, computer time, phone conversations, and speaking to others, including any spirits, deities, and the cat. While on this fast, Hela told me to wear a special ring, keep a dark veil over my head, and to display the rune necklace I wear in honor of Her outside my clothing; I was uncomfortable wearing my necklace where others could see, but it struck me as appropriate since I was on Her duty roster for the week. She also gave me some rules regarding diet; I was to stick to the vegetarian diet I maintained, and keep my food choices simple. No Halloween treats for me.

Hela's primary instruction to me was "Rest." I'd been running at a spiritual full throttle and it was wearing me down so much that I wasn't sure how much I had left to give. I'd spent months confronting some of the worst and ugliest parts of myself, the stress of which put a huge strain on my relationship with other people and with my Gods. Hela was giving me a whole week to rest, to heal, and to prepare for whatever came next. Along with resting, a few other activities were given to me. Earlier, Hela had told me I'd be spinning so I purchased some dyed black wool for that purpose. Study, meditation and other simple devotional activities needed attention as well.

Since I didn't have the option of cloistering myself against the world, I did have to break my silence for short periods each day. At the time I was visiting my father to help him through a difficult space, so I had to run errands and spend time with him. I had also agreed to face paint at a local Witch's Ball that I couldn't back out of. Hela accepted these obligations and allowed me to have the time I needed to devote to them, so long as I didn't add to this schedule or allow other taboos to slip.

The night of October 26th began my week of silence. Of the 16 or so hours I was awake each day, around 14 of those were spent veiled and silent. The shift to a different state of awareness happened very quickly; I have a difficult time remembering any specifics about that time, except for the moments I spent with other people in routine activities and even those are a bit sketchy. The first thing that I noticed was that the veil (a translucent charcoal-blue item that had started life as a belly-dance accessory) very cleanly shut off my natural energetic shields. The veil took the place of those shields, thus allowing my whole attention to turn inward, away from the constant bombardment that we face every day without even being aware. Not having those shields up was an odd and sometimes unnerving experience, but the veil created a small world for just myself where I felt safe and protected. It's hard to describe the combined feelings of vulnerability and safety I experienced; on one side was the knowledge that it was just a bit of cloth keeping me safe from free-floating energetic garbage, but it seemed like that danger belonged to a world very far away and no longer applied to me. When I needed to remove the veil for whatever reason, I carefully "brushed" away the astral junk that had collected on it so it could be folded and put away; my personal shields slowly started up again when the veil came off.

I spent hours spinning the black wool with no real purpose in mind. The activity, not the goal, was the important part. It was Frigga who taught me to spin, first in the Otherworld and then later when I made a drop spindle for myself. I came to appreciate and understand Her patience just a little through spinning, and it's an activity that continues to yield insight to myself, to my Gods, and to magical and spiritual principles. During this week I spun enough wool to yield a few dozen yards of two-ply yarn; eventually the insight came that I would create a veil for myself out of this yarn.

The silence factor was probably the hardest to confront. I'm not a wildly verbal person, but I longed to communicate with friends and to spend the mindless hours on the internet I was accustomed to. I thought to catch up on some reading, but by the second day of silence I found that the words on the page didn't really speak to me like they normally do, and I lost interest pretty quickly. I had intended to complete some writing projects I'd been working on a little at a time; several of them had a spiritual or devotional theme, so I thought that would be an acceptable way to use my time. However, I found that when I sat down to begin I had no words at all; my vocabulary had vanished, grammar skills were barely present, and the ability to construct a coherent sentence gone. I had moved so far out of normal awareness that I couldn't switch back and forth between silence and communication at will. Though I later found out that some of what I was working on wasn't what my Gods wanted me to be writing, I think it had perhaps less to do with any interference They might have thrown at me and more that my world had stopped being ordered by words and the linear thinking that encourages composition.

Like I said above, I don't remember a whole lot from this experience. I remember the face painting event I worked at, and the Disirblot I was invited to. I remember my frustrated attempts at reading and writing, and the errands I did for my dad. Other than that, there's little definition to that whole week. Most of our memories are built by association and by an ordered chain of events; a smell or sudden sensation calls back a single moment with perfect clarity, or causes us to say, "Remember when?" There's nothing like that to help me access this experience; it was apart from time. Days passed very slowly and, for the most part, my experiences existed as a nebulous everywhen. There was no transition from one point to another, no cause and effect, just a quiet peace that was neither happy nor sad. I stopped being defined as a woman, as a human being, or as anything specific at all.

My week ended one day early, or rather, the veiled-and-silent taboos ended. On the night of November 1st I took a bath to which I added some herbs; the herbs helped bring me back to life and I spent the night speaking with my Gods about the progress I had made. I woke up on November 2nd and was allowed to enter the world again. There's no way I can describe the vibrance I encountered, or how different everything appeared; everything was drenched in life and vitality, and I felt my own living force with an impact I'd never even noticed before. It was no small coincidence that my birthday is November 2nd; I got to celebrate the simple fact that I was alive by returning to life in a very real way.

It's my understanding now that I spent that period essentially dead. I wasn't taking part in the world; instead I found a comfortable spot between the worlds of the living and dead. My mind had stopped ordering the world by means that humans do on the most basic level, but my body kept me tied to this plane; I just slipped to a space removed from discerning thought and dwelled apart from anything that contributed to it.

Being veiled and keeping silent are very simple things, but quickly and subtly changed me at levels so deep that I was barely aware of them. The shift was radical even though I hardly even noticed how far I had gone until I was suddenly back; I felt like I had wandered a very long way and had been gone for a very long time. This observance was challenging, but took me to a very unique place that I've come to find power in. Hela greatly approved of me being veiled, and hinted that She'd keep me that way. Even without Her saying so, I knew that I'll be repeating this process again next October, and probably each October after that. It's a challenge, but I look forward to the peace that comes with it.

Silent Fasting
by Galina Krasskova

I think it fairly safe to say that as children many of us heard the maxim: "Silence is golden." Well, in magical practice it actually is. I've been thinking about this quite a bit lately. I live in NYC and at the best of times, silence is not an element this city generally has to offer. There is constant noise, even in the wee hours of the morning, even in one's own home with doors and windows closed to the outside world. The noise is part of the cityscape, born of the very structures that give it vitality and keep it alive. New York, like every city, has its own unique energy and even those energy flows hum with their own particular sounds and rhythms. Even the quietest, most remote place in a city landscape is fraught with ambient noise. It can be maddening.

What's more, American culture is not a quiet one. We are a people obsessed with noise. We have our mechanical gadgets that chirp and burp and hum. We indulge in ambient noise in elevators, restaurants, cafes.

Conversations are loud and often continual. Cell phones are everywhere and the idea that consciously-sought-out silence might have extraordinary benefits is not one that I myself have seen discussed in either popular culture or media. Yet it does, and not just for the dedicated magical practitioner. Noise pollution leads to stress and stress leads to kinetic traps that block internal energy and vitality. Lack of vitality can make it almost impossible not only to effectively work magic, but simply to get through the day feeling well. Stress can lead to migraines, exhaustion, illness and pain, even depression.

So this article is about silence. This may seem like an odd topic for a magician or spirit-worker to concern him or herself with, but before one can open to the flow of power, create charms and spells that truly work, before one can learn to hear the voices of their Gods, a point of stillness within must be reached. Esoteric systems the world over, most especially in the East, have held to this for centuries. The majority of meditation systems at some point address this fact. To find one's center, one must find inner stillness. That's pretty hard to do, especially for the first time, when one has no sense of the purity of solitude and silence.

Silence has its own sound, as paradoxical as that may seem. It has pattern, texture, rhythm and to some people, even color. While it is true that in certain forms of magic the voice becomes the conduit for power, that power has to come from someplace else and that other place is one of both silence and stillness. There are dozens of exercises designed to introduce this concept to neophytes. 99% of meditations are designed, at least at first, to help the student turn off the distractions, not only of the outside world, but also of his or her own "chattering monkey of the mind." For some, achieving this goal can be a terribly difficult endeavor.

After over ten years of teaching esoteric arts, I've come to realize that most people avoid complete silence. I don't just mean silence without, but silence within too. Of all the skills that I have attempted to teach students over the years, an appreciation of silence is the one that generally proves the most difficult to instill. Silence is a powerful teacher. The embrace of silence forces a person to confront all those inner thoughts, emotions, sensations, all the inner demons that we are customarily taught to hide, even from ourselves. There's nothing to use for distraction, nothing to use as a façade when confronted solely with silence.

In the beginning, silence can be a very difficult discipline. It's not only the fact that one's inner demons will emerge, but we must then fight the initial compulsion to do something about them, which in turn distracts from the lesson of silence. We're not used to simply sitting and being with our own inner selves. It's like sitting on a beach watching a huge wave approach: the instinct is to run away. The power of silence is like that of a well-honed knife. It cuts away illusion and brings clarity. This can be a frightening thing. Also, the flip side of the discipline of silence is the discipline of speaking rightly, wisely and well. It is very easy in this culture to squander our words.

I believe that if we learn how to better utilize the power of our voice, it might become easier to then utilize the power of silence. We're often so busy that we waste the power of our voice. We aren't mindful of the words we speak. It doesn't give us enough time to hear the wisdom of silence. There is a Hausa proverb: "Even silence speaks." It is only when we ourselves stop our incessant love affair with noise and endless chatter that we are able to hear its lessons. Learning to withstand and even embrace quietude leads to a greater awareness and appreciation of the power of our words: to weave, to harm, to heal, to manifest. This is a very powerful truism in magic. We're all taught, from very early on, that to name something is to bring it into being. That axiom doesn't only hold true in spell-casting, though. It holds true in every conversation we have, every word we speak whether or good or for ill, whether carelessly or in the full flower of mindfulness.

This is perhaps the reason that mystics the world over in many different religious traditions, have sought out extended periods of both silence and solitude to deepen their spirituality and their connection to the Gods. Perhaps they instinctively grasped that silence is an active discipline. One doesn't just sit like a vegetable when engaging in this discipline. It is a process of readying oneself for opening—to the Gods, to the flow of power, to greater knowledge of oneself.

So how to begin? Well, I'll start with a caveat. Two possibilities may occur when one is first learning to work with silence: either internal (or external) distractions come up almost immediately or the person falls asleep. A period of such resistance is perfectly natural and the student shouldn't feel too badly about it. Sometimes the latter response simply indicates that the person is carrying so much tension that when he or she begins to relax, the body's natural exhaustion (because carrying tension is work!) takes over and demands rest.

I think the best place to begin is to start listening to all the sounds that permeate your day. We are bombarded on a daily basis to an amazing degree by random noise. To approach silence and to understand this discipline, it is first necessary to understand what it is not. So begin by learning to listen. On your ride to work, consciously note each and every sound. Note their quality, the timbre, how they interact in the overall fabric of sound that is being produced. Note your physiological response to them and your emotional response if any.

Take a few moments during your day to simply sit and listen to everything that is going on around you. See how many individual sounds you can pick out of the aural jumble. When you listen to music, try to follow one instrument throughout. As simple as his may seem, by doing this regularly, you're developing your awareness of silence and you are attuning your senses to its flow.

Take this a step further, when you have a quiet moment. When you're going about your day and think to steal a few moments of quiet time, really listen to the sounds around you. You might be surprised at how noisy your quietest time really is! For instance, as I write this, I'm sitting in my computer alcove in my kitchen. The TV is off, no music is playing, my neighbors are asleep and to all intents and purposes, the house is quiet. But in reality it's not. If I think about it, I can hear the almost-silent hum of my computer, the electronic hum of my refrigerator, my cat gently snoring half a room away, the far away sound of traffic, even the ticking of my kitchen clock. In city life, much of this is inevitable. Once you begin to become aware of your daily tonal palette, try wearing earplugs during those stolen quiet moments. While it may not block out all background noise, the difference can be staggering. People have been using sensory deprivation techniques in meditation to further their spirituality for centuries. It's nothing new. It can, however, be tried the first time in this (albeit modified) form.

As an aside, if you have the interest, learning to play a musical instrument can increase one's sensitivity to the interplay of sound and silence dramatically as can learning to sing. These things are beneficial to magical practice because not only are entire systems of magic (like Norse *galdr)* based on sound, but understanding rhythm and flow helps one better sense and understand natural energy flows. Everything is connected in this way. One pattern of flow mirrors another.

Best of all, begin to moderate your speech. Speaking simply to fill up natural silences, to break uncomfortable silences, or to hear oneself speak is a deeply ingrained habit in many people. It is one that it behooves the mystic, spirit-worker, magician or priest to break. Words have immense power. Begin to seriously consider the meaning and import behind the words you speak. How often do you lose your temper and speak vitriolic words out of a lack of control? Or how often do you respond to platitudes of affection with similar comments of your own out of a feeling of social obligation? How often do you tell tales or spread gossip without ever thinking about potential consequences. Do you talk just to avoid the silence?

The place where magic begins and gathers lies in silence. It takes a balanced understanding of both the discipline of silence and the discipline of speech to truly tap into it. Not to mention that it's nearly impossible to hear the Gods and deepen that relationship when in the turmoil of constant sound. So an excellent way to approach this new discipline is to work on becoming aware of the words you speak. Try going through an entire day at work speaking only when necessary. Or better yet, try going through an entire day speaking only the truth. Or try the same thing but never speak either the truth or a lie—there is an interesting verbal game to play. Observe how much verbal noise you create for your co-workers or family members and think about why. Really explore and examine how you yourself utilize the power of your words.

I've saved the best for last, of course. The silent fast is a powerful meditation and at first it can seem deceptively simple but it's more difficult than it looks. For three days, engage in a silent fast: no TV, CDs, radio, computer, books, friends, family, phone, cell phone or any other computerized gadget. For three days go off by yourself (or stay in your home but turn off all communication devices) with just a journal. Spend those days meditating, praying, and writing. Nothing else. Above all else, don't speak. I once did this for ten days, and though days three to five had me going stir crazy, in the end I found it immensely beneficial. Be aware that coming back into the world of noise can be quite jarring after the silent fast is finished. If you are able to arrange to do this for a longer period of time, that is even better. 10-14 days is ideal. Be sure to record your responses, thoughts, feelings and any other inspirations that come to you throughout this time.

Not only is this beneficial to the budding magician, but it is especially beneficial to the spiritual devotee. Spending two weeks in prayer, meditation and interaction with the Gods can be an amazingly opening experience. You may even want to try silent rituals, a ritual utilizing only gesture but no sound as part of the experience.

Of all the tools and techniques of magical practice, this is one of the most neglected in the modern community. Yet conversely it is one of the most beneficial and even necessary. The discipline of silence, like that of breath or *galdr* take nothing but what we carry with us: our awareness, our breath, our voice, our minds and our wills. It is magical practice at its most basic and its most enduring.

> "You can hear the footsteps of God when silence reigns in the mind."
> —Shri Sathya Sai Baba

Fire and Water:
Sauna Purification

"Saunassa ollaan kuin kirkossa."
–Finnish saying: You should be in the sauna as in a church.

For the northern European peoples, a hot room full of steam was the best way to get clean. When half your year is bitterly cold, enough that it would be impractical to be wet and naked for very long, being in a tub of water in your drafty longhouse isn't a good idea. Unless you live next to hot springs—which were sacred places and much revered—your best choice is to build a separate small building (or a small space within a large one) where you can heat things up and encourage your body to sweat out impurities. If you lay a supply of rocks into it, heat them, and throw water on them, you get the cleansing steam that the Finns refer to as *löyly*.

While the sauna is mostly associated with the Finnish people these days, we know from archaeological digs that ancient cultures all over the arctic and subarctic regions of Eurasia used them to one extent or another. In northern Europe, the oldest ones were small domed stone buildings with a hole in the top, rather like a permanent stone version of the Native American sweat lodge. Somewhat later ones were round or squarish stone buildings; occasionally a Norse longhouse would have a separate small room that seems to have been a bathhouse. In the *Eyrbyggja Saga*, a Norse bathhouse is described that is a room dug into the ground, or perhaps the side of a hill. A window over a stone oven, just at ground level, provided both ventilation and a place to pour water over the stones.

The word *sauna* is Saami, the language of the original inhabitants of Finland. We don't necessarily know what the various Scandinavian and Slavic cultures called a bathhouse, because the modern words are more recent in their etymology, such as the German *Aufguss* and the Russian *banya* (which was originally derived from an Italian word for bath). However, some linguists have pointed out that the Old Germanic word *stofa*, which is where we get our modern word "stove", originally meant a heated bathhouse and may have been the equivalent word for the Finnish sauna. It later evolved into the German *Stube*, which became *Badstube* or bathhouse.

During the Middle Ages, public bathhouses went from being family and tribal retreats to being busy centers of commerce and prostitution. The Catholic Church finally cracked down and banned them, and so the sauna and its various forms were lost to most places west of Finland for a long time, until those countries rediscovered the health benefits of the sauna in later centuries. This interruption via first civilization and second Christianity means that we have very little in the way of remaining lore about the religious rituals of the *stofa*. We can conjecture from the scraps left behind, especially those remaining in Finnish and Russian culture, or we can ask the wights and work them out ourselves, which is what some of us have done.

As far as we can tell, one of the primary religious functions of the sauna in Finland—and likely in the rest of northern Europe as well—was as a holy place of transition. Women were brought into the sauna to give birth, and the dying often lived out their last days there. Once dead, their bodies were washed and wrapped in the sauna before removing them to a grave. It was also used for secluding one's self for such things as casting charms and spells, and healing rituals of all sorts were performed there on various sufferers. Indeed, the ill were often brought into the sauna for the duration of their illness. Aleksa, a Russian-descended spirit-worker, points out that: "They are generally kept on the outer edges of a homestead or village—a further symbol of their position as being in-between the ordinary world and the non-ordinary one. In Russian folklore, sorcerers both good and bad were said to practice there, doing things unacceptable to normal society in that in-between space. Similarly, stillborn children were buried under the threshold to protect them and guard their spirits—like baptizing them without a baptism."

Ancestor worship was also a function of the sauna; it was thought that the Dead would return to places that they had enjoyed, including the bathhouse, and that the *löyly*, or sacred steam, held their souls. It is the Breath of the Ancestors, a word which originally meant "spirit" or "life". (One cognate is the Ostyak word *lil*, which means "soul".) The sauna is, in many ways, an ancestor altar that is also useful. Its usefulness stretched to the mundane as well; it was sometimes used for such practical purposes as curing meat or drying out malt, hemp and flax. It was a doorway between worlds; the fact that fire and water held an equal balance in sauna sanctity drives home the image of liminal space.

> The sauna is where all the transitions happen. People who are sick go there, people who are about to die go there, women who are about to give birth go there, the midwives go there to pray before they bring out the pregnant woman. Those critical times are celebrated in the House of the Ancestors. There isn't any lore on it, but I suspect very strongly that there is an order to who sits where, who sits closer or further away. The senior person sits closest to the fire, because they are deemed to be the one who can manage the heat best, and the coming of the löyly. There's also the agricultural aspect to this: when you have to do hard, hard work in the cold and dark winter in order to eat and heat yourself, a communal warmth, beyond just physical heat, is very important. In the more moderate climes, hospitality is a completely different thing. In the more northern climes, you could demand hospitality, at least three days of it, before they could kick you out. It's the idea of having ancestors, and warmth, and social cohesion, and rites of passage all in the same place.
>
> –Lydia Helasdottir

The *banya* seems to have endured in Russia as well, although it is not as famous in the West as the Finnish sauna. Herodotus wrote about the people of the Black Sea region making a felt-covered hut and throwing water onto red-hot stones inside, creating a vapor hotter than any Hellenic bath. (He also relates that hempseed was thrown onto the stones for purposes of visions and prophecy.) According to his accounts, this Slavic sweat lodge was used for ritual cleansing before marriage and after burying the dead. 2nd-century excavations of Slavic settlements in Poland show earth-sheltered houses with fireplaces in the middle, but no separate bathhouses. The concept of building an actual permanent structure seems to have been unknown in the southern Slavic areas until the people of Novgorod moved south, as mentioned in the *Lay of Igor's Campaign*. Novgorod, a northern Slavic city, had been heavily settled by the Rus tribes, and was the mercantile capital of trade between them and the Norse. (There is a good deal of evidence to suggest that the Rus people, or at least their leaders/upper classes, were Varangian/Norse-descended. There is also some evidence to support opposing conclusions; the debate still rages. However, regardless of how Norse-descended they were, they were certainly Norse-influenced.) With archaeological evidence showing that the early Russian *banya* was basically identical to the Finnish sauna and the Norse equivalent, it is likely that it is an ancient import from the Rus settlers.

As the Catholic Church never held much sway in Russia (and the Orthodox Church was not as fixed on sweat-bathing as a moral problem), the tradition of the *banya* continued unabated, complete with its folk beliefs. The *Russian Primary Chronicle* describes, in 1113, the monk Andreas' observations of the *banya* practice in Novgorod wherein he described the pagans "drenching themselves":

> Wondrous to relate, I saw the land of the Slavs, and while I was among them, I noticed their wooden bath-houses. They warm them to extreme heat, then undress, and after anointing themselves with tallow, take young reeds and lash their bodies. They actually lash themselves so violently that they barely escape alive. Then they drench themselves with cold water, and thus are revived. They think nothing of doing this every day and actually

inflict such voluntary torture upon themselves. They make of the act not a mere washing but a veritable torment.

As today, this does show the sauna as an ordeal of heat. In many ways, sauna-work is poised on the edge between the Ascetic's Path and the Ordeal Path, depending on how hot it is, and for what purpose it is used—purification, community bonding, creation of sacred space, or strength ordeal? When performed as a group rite, it partakes of the Path of Ritual as well. A multipurpose tool, the House of the Ancestors can be all of these. A community sweat is very different from using the sauna as a safe and sacred place to give birth, and even more different from using it as a solo purification and sacred-space creator for a spirit-worker.

If well tended and kept holy, it could also be a source of power to call upon. The Russian Primary Chronicle also tells of Princess Olga, the pagan widow of Prince Igor of Kiev, who punished the Derevlians for the murder of her husband in 945 A.D. Their leader had designs on her, considering her to be booty earned by the murder, and sent messengers to discuss their future marriage. Olga invited the Derevlian messengers to use her *banya*, and while they were inside, her men barred the doors and burned the *banya* to the ground with the Derevlians in it.

Aleksa stresses that: "From my own UPG, this historical tale relates to the use of the *banya* as the guardian spirit of Russia to defend her and her people from the enemy, as the tradition of no enemy ever surviving an attempt to invade or conquer Russian lands is well documented. (The only ones to do so are the Mongols, and the degree of success in this regard us subject to debate, as they left Russians in charge and didn't stay there themselves). The use of the *banya* calls forth three things: Mokosh the sacred Earth in the wood and stones, the *leshii* (forest spirits) in the birch trees, and the *rusalki* and *voidianki* (water spirits) in the water. While sometimes referred to as masculine, Mother Russia is Mokosh; steam and rain are said to be Mokosh's milk. It's the Rodina (Mother Russia) that is always honored, regardless of the use of 'fatherland'. The taiga forest defends the eastern borders, and in the early years the western forests were what prevented the Germanic tribes from penetrating too deeply into Slavic lands. The forests on the borderlands between Poland and Transylvania and Belarus are very dense, and the rivers are the key transit mechanisms of the period. The sacred rivers relevant to the *banya* tradition are the Volga, the Don and the Dneipr in the west."

Another way in which the Russian *banya* was a peripheral space was the tradition that sorcerers had to be brought there to die. (Keep in mind that many of the medieval descriptions of a "sorcerer" sound more like a shaman—they had spirit allies, they had to complete their sorcerous transition or die, and so forth.) It was said that a wizard's spirit would be unquiet if they could not pass on their knowledge, so the *banya* offered a protected space for them to teach their heirs without the "magic" leaking and accidentally conveying their gifts to the unsuspecting, and also a place where their spirit would be sent firmly on its way by the power of the *banya* in case there were no heirs. This association with wizards (and with pagan beliefs; the banya is said to be the *vtoroi mat*, or second mother, referring to its symbolism as a small temple to Mokosh the Earth Mother) caused later Russian Christians to say that the bathhouse was full of devils and unquiet ghosts. In general, Russian sorcerers (referred to as *koldun*) were said to go off to the *banya* when all the good Christians were going off to church. Besides the idea of the bathhouse being a private place to work magic, this comment reinforces the idea of the *banya* as a holdover from the pagan temple. Because of this, anyone who snuck off to the *banya* alone at odd times might be accused of sorcery, especially if they visited after midnight, which was when the spirits (evil or otherwise) took over the building.

The *banya* was also a place for prophecy and divination, as well as healing and rites of passage. According to folk belief, babies were born there because birthing women and newborns were terribly vulnerable to evil forces, and the guardian spirit of the *banya* was so strong that it kept all other spirits at bay. Bringing a child into the bathhouse would, for some reason, earn the favor of the *domovoi* and *domikha*, the male and female spirits of the house itself. One custom supposedly had the midwife stripping naked and carrying the newborn child around the *banya*, chanting an invocation to the Morning Star to keep the child from crying. As a house of both the living and the Dead, this was the place for seeing the Dead off on their way. Forty days after a funeral—during which time water, vodka and towels were left in the *banya* for the dead soul—the fire was lit and a feast prepared for them. Afterwards, the family walked out of the bathhouse and crossed the road, ceremonially sending the dead soul away.

Specific ritual dates associated with the *banya* were Mokosh's holiday—said to be in the late fall after the harvest when winter was beginning; one could possibly assume around the western-European festival of Samhain—and Yule, when pre-marriage prophecies were sought and made. (At any time of the year, brides were sent to the bathhouse to have a pre-wedding purification steam bath the night before the nuptials, and at least one source suggests that the village sorcerer or shaman was in charge of such ceremonies.) From all its associations, it is clear that the bathhouse in these cultures took the place of the sacred temple or grove once Christianity took over. Having a small building on one's property that could also be used for quite practical tasks provided the average peasant with a place to store all the reverence, memories, and suspiciously magical practices left over from a pagan past.

Building The House Of The Ancestors

It is the opinion of those of us who consider the sauna to be a spiritual tool of the Northern Tradition that if you are going to do it at all, you should do it right. Some modern "saunas" have electric heat, or infrared heat, or no steam at all, or not enough ventilation. Except for that last item, which can make people ill from oxygen deprivation, the rest aren't exactly a crime. If you want to use such a "sauna", fine. Go ahead. You can even use it as a purification ordeal, which is part of what the sauna is … but don't think that you'll get deep religious ritual out of it. Tapping into the original spirit of the sauna/stofa ritual is honoring the powers of fire and water and stone, and the steam that is the Breath of the Ancestors. Without those, the wights will not come.

A proper sauna/stofa ritual should have the following in attendance:

1) A source of wood heat, with real flame. Usually this is a woodstove, although a stone hearth or oven will do just as well.

2) Ventilation. Many modern airtight saunas make people sick because the oxygen level falls too low. Even an open window to the cold is better than nothing—just crank the fire up. The ideal is an adjustable vent near the floor, to vent the cooling, sinking air, and another higher up to vent the excess heat later on.

2) Stones to throw water on. They can be collected ceremonially and charged with intent, if you like. Do not use river stones, which have a tendency to blow apart during temperature changes. Lava rocks are best.

3) Water to throw on the stones, preferably rainwater.

4) A birch whisk. To make this, collect birch "twigs"—meaning branches less than two feet long—and tie them together. It is best made and used fresh, but of course you may not be able to get fresh leafy birch twigs for a good portion of the year. Think ahead and make a bunch of them, and let them dry. They should be spring or summer branches; fall branches tend to defoliate easier. Hang them to dry and then store them flat in paper bags. You will use each one up every time you do a sauna ritual, so be prepared. (If you have a chest freezer, you can freeze them flat in bags and then thaw them later.)

To use a fresh whisk, simply rinse it off before going into the sauna. During the second round—the Community round—dip it in warm water and turn it gently over the steam. For a dry whisk, rinse off the dry branches and then put them into a basin of warm—not hot—water. This is usually done on top of the sauna stove. As soon as it is rehydrated, it is ready for use. The birch whisks bring a beautiful scent to the hot air. It has a long history as well; among the ancient Slavic people, a certain number of birch whisks were actually paid as tributes by weaker, conquered tribes.

5) Knowledge of the proper sauna etiquette. A sauna is not for partying, rowdiness, or fondling each other. It is a solemn occasion, and a quiet, meditative ambience should be promoted. Being naked is

mandatory; one should go in as one came out of the womb. The sauna is a rebirth experience in its own way. In our modern society, some people may feel shy about being naked, but this is fairly critical. Anyone who would be so rude as to comment on someone's body, or give someone an unwanted touch, shouldn't be allowed to be present during such a ritual anyway.

Community saunas are traditionally mixed-gender and mixed-age, although there were occasional saunas specially for men or women (for example, part of a puberty rite might be held in the sauna). One saying held that of the three sauna rounds, one was for men, one for women, and one for the faeries. (One would assume that this refers to firing up the empty sauna for the Saunatonttu; see below.) However, the ancestors of men and women are the same, and we strongly encourage mixed-gender saunas, with everyone well versed in the proper behavior. If nothing else, it obviates the problem of where to put the people who are neither male nor female, some of whom may be the community shamans.

The first step is to build and consecrate your sauna. While the original ones were made of stone, by the 5th century they were being built of timber. However you make yours, be sure that it has good ventilation. Situate the hearth carefully—remember that it is the altar of the room. You will likely be using some wood, if only for the benches. Traditionally, all lumber scraps were saved and burned in the ceremonial first firing. The door to a traditional sauna should be shorter than a "normal" door; one should have to stoop to get into it, which shows reverence for the ancestors. In Russia, it was traditional to leave the *banya* backwards, bowing to the spirits. Another of their traditions was burying a sacrificed black cock under the doorstep, a custom which the modern builder may use or not, as they prefer.

The first saunas were smoke saunas, referred to by the Finns as *savusauna*. The fire was lit under stones, and the smoke went out through a hole in the wall or ceiling. When the smoke had heated the entire room, the hole was shut and the window opened to let in fresh air.

There are varying claims on the health risks of *savusauna*; some say that the smoke is bad for your lungs, others that the smoke creates a bacteria-free and oxygen-rich environment, assuming that you leave the place alone long enough for all the deadly carbon monoxide to leave it.

However you feel about it, the first ceremonial firing of your sauna should be as close to a traditional *savusauna* as possible. Afterwards, you can do it the "normal" way. To do this, remove the stovepipe from your stove (or stop up your chimney, if there's no pipe). Place containers of water out for heating. (It's also good to have it around in case of fire.) Start your fire using an older method, the sort that is appropriate for sacred fires—flint and steel at the least, or a fire-bow or fire-drill if you have mastered that art. Add pieces of birch, then harder woods as the fire gets going. It is traditional at this point to burn the scrap lumber from the building project.

Make sure that you have your vents open. It will take three to six hours to properly smoke up the sauna, so start it early in the day. Appropriate activities during this time might be to sit outside and drum and sing. What you're trying to do is to call a guardian spirit into the sauna. For some folk, the guardian spirit was an ancestor—in which case they didn't call one in when building the sauna, but merely waited until a family member died in there. Since we are unlikely to want to wait that long, start calling for a guardian spirit during the smoke-out.

Another sort of guardian spirit, popular in Finland, is the Saunatonttu, a little gnome or wizened faery. It was customary to warm up the sauna just for the gnome every now and then, or to leave some food outside for him. It is said that he warned the people if a fire was threatening the sauna, or punished people who behaved improperly while inside it. The Saunatonttu doesn't seem to be an Alfar-type so much as one of the "little people", the earthly nature sprites who live astrally in this world. If you work with them, calling a Saunatonttu might be a good idea. If not, try calling an ancestor to watch over the place, or just ask the land-wight to send the right spirit over. The song that you sing doesn't have to be brilliant, just sincere.

In Russia, the guardian spirit of the *banya* was the *Bannik*, a spindly, hairy creature described here by Aleksa: "In ancient Russian culture, the (usually male) spirits of the *banya* provided safety in bad times or against evil spirits, so if you were being chased through a field or a forest by evil beings or bad men, you may take refuge in a bathhouse and pray to the *banyanka* or the Bannik to protect you. The Bannik controlled your experience of the *banya*—the heat and steam levels—and it was heated and cleaned once a week to placate him. In Christian times the offering became the sign of the cross (although, ironically, icons were not allowed to be hung in a *banya* due to their residual pagan associations), but vestiges remained of the pagan practice of feeding the Bannik in offerings of vodka. In order to see the Bannik, you had to go alone at night, and you had to sit with part of yourself in the banya and part out—in other words, you had to be in-between. (This was why people didn't bathe alone at night, unless they wanted to meet the Bannik.) If the *banya* made a purring sound, the Bannik was at home." He was sometimes known to appear to late-night wanderers as a village elder or dead ancestor, and it was important to leave the fourth steam round for him, to propitiate him with food and vodka, and to refrain from bringing anything from the house into the *banya* and vice versa, as everything in the *banya* belonged to him (whereas the rest belonged to the *domovoi*). If properly treated, he would protect his guests; if maltreated he would become hostile and cause failures of fertility (crop, animal, and human), again showing the connections to the *banya* as a temple to Mokosh the Earth Mother.

But back to your ceremonial first smoke sauna. When the room is very hot and there is only a small blue flame left in the fire, shut the vents for a while—perhaps 20 minutes. Then open them all up and let the air in for at least an hour, to clear out all carbon monoxide. Pour water on your rocks, which will have been heating on the stove; it helps clear the air. When it's safe to be in there for more than a minute, go in with buckets of water and old rags and wipe everything down—the smoke will have blackened things. Sweep the floor, putting your intent into purifying the space. Then reconnect the stovepipe (or unstop the chimney), relight the fire, and have a regular sauna in the mellow heat from the *savusauna*. You have now honored the ancestors by doing your first firing in the way that they would have done.

A Northern-Tradition Sweat Ritual

To prepare for the sauna, first clean yourself. In the winter during older times this would have meant a scrub with snow; at least take a shower first. There will be enough toxins coming out of your pores in short order. Clearing the skin is a good idea. It can also be used as ritual pre-cleansing in order to make yourself ready for the sacred space of the sauna.

A sauna is divided into rounds, each called a *gang* in Finnish. The ritual we create here is done in three rounds, as are many traditional versions. The first *gang* is the opening of the space, done to warm up and release the pressure of the everyday, a transition from daily concerns. It is the Ancestor round, in honor of those who came before us. The Ancestors are always honored first during a proper Northern-Tradition sweat ritual. Although this ritual is written as if for a group—since it may well be the job of the spirit-worker to lead it—it can also be adapted to a personal religious ritual by one individual.

The first round is the Perth round, going into the Mystery in silence. To begin, each person is recaned with mugwort and then sent inside the sauna. Everyone comes in naked, bowing before the low lintel, and seats themselves. The one who is in charge of the rite lets everyone get settled in silence. Keep the silence going for a few minutes in order to let everyone calm down and transition away from their daily movement. If there are those who are uncomfortable, the silent warmup may help them as well. Ideally, one ought to get to the point where there is no psychological discomfort with being naked in a roomful of other naked sweating people. Physical discomfort is to be expected, at least in small amounts—in fact, if someone needs to leave during the rite for physical reasons, let them do so, and don't give them trouble about it. Having someone keel over will disrupt everything. It should go without saying that everyone in the ritual space should have been briefed on what this is about and how to properly behave.

If possible, encourage people to start by breathing together, difficult as that is in the hot room. The ideal is to get folks into a headspace where they are the tribe, all together, quietly celebrating their group bond. Don't push it, though. Overenthusiasm will not work here. Let the *löyly* do its job. As Lydia Helasdottir puts it: "One of the things that is said about sauna by the Finnish is that the everyday isn't there. Marriages are brokered and enmities healed in the sauna. It doesn't matter who you are; when you're in the sauna you're just a sauna-mate. Doesn't matter if you're a Prime Minister or a peasant."

The officiant (which is how we will hereby refer to the person in charge of the rite) kneels before the fire as one would an altar, extends their hands towards the fire, and says:

> *In the beginning, there was Darkness,*
> *The never-ending Void of Ginnungagap.*
> *Then came Surt into the world with his flaming sword,*
> *One point of light in the Darkness,*
> *And so was Muspellheim, the World of Fire, brought into existence.*
> *Before anything else, there was fire.*
> *Out of the darkness, Fire.*

All participants repeat back, "Out of the darkness, Fire."

On top of the stove, a number of stones have been arranged, ideally in a spiral pattern, or perhaps that of a rune or a pictograph. They have been heating up all this time. The officiant has held back and is carrying one stone, which they now carefully place with the others, completing the pattern. The officiant says:

> *Then came forth the world of Niflheim,*

The land of ice and snow, and cold stone.
And so came forth also Ymir, great as a mountain chain,
Suckling the nourishment of Audumbla, Mother Cow,
Giant of stone and ice, Ancestor of thousands.
At the beginning of the world, there was fire and stone.
Out of the ice, stones.

The participants all repeat: "Out of the ice, stones."

Then the officiant wipes the sweat from their forehead with a bit of (natural fiber) cloth, and tosses it into the fire, saying:

Then of the sweat of Ymir was born the first frost-giants,
As cold as the sons of Surt are hot,
Ancestors of many worlds,
The powers of air and wind,
We honor them with our very breath.
Above fire and stone, there were the cooling winds,
And out of the sweat of earth, life.

The participants all repeat: "Out of the sweat of earth, life."

There should be a bowl of water placed on one of the benches; it can have some kind of herb or essential oil if you like. For appropriate scents, I prefer pine needles for the first round (symbolizing the evergreens which are the oldest trees), birch for the second (as this is the birching round, although if you're using birch whisks, there's no need for anything but clean water), and the third should be chosen on the basis of which Gods you are honoring. The officiant holds up the bowl of water and says:

Then Muspellheim did draw near to Niflheim,
The moment of worlds colliding,
The fire melting the ice,

And the mists of water rose between the worlds.
Hot to cold to hot to cold; here we live this first cycle.
In the beginning, fire and water and stone,
Changing the Land of Ice to the Land of Mists.
From fire and water and stone, all creation.

The officiant pours water onto the hot stones, and as the steam rises the participants repeat: "From fire and water and stone, all creation."

The officiant then speaks of honoring the ancestors who came before us, and may speak of some deed done by an ancestor. Others then might speak forth with tales of their own ancestors. For those who do not know their own ancestors, or do not wish to honor them by name for whatever reason, speaking of a spiritual ancestor that inspired them will suffice. Not everyone needs to take part; if the round falls to silence, that's fine. Whatever people say, it should end with a time of meditative silence.

Meanwhile, the *löyly* is surrounding everyone slowly. As Lydia puts it, "...this presence fills the sauna area, and it's more than just the steam somehow, and it makes your skin tingle, and the hackles on your neck rise if it's really there properly. It overwhelms you; when *löyly* comes you are just quiet for that moment until it gets absorbed into the walls."

One Finnish farmer referred to there being four kinds of *löyly*: Maiden *löyly*, Lady *löyly*, Mother *löyly*, and Grandmother *löyly*. The first time that the water is thrown on the rocks is Maiden *löyly*, which surrounds you like a fiery lover; you can hardly bear her touch, but it is exciting and ecstatic. The second is the Lady *löyly*, which caresses you like a loving wife. The third, Mother *löyly*, is so gentle that it is "like sitting in your mother's lap". The fourth, Grandmother *löyly*, is said to be the sweetest of all ... it happens when you go out to the bathhouse after the sauna and toss a little water onto the still-warm coals for the sake of the Saunatonttu and the Ancestors.

When the first round has gone on long enough—and "long enough" is something that needs to be carefully gauged by the person in charge;

remember that you'll be doing two more of these—everyone takes a break. This is the time to wash in cool water, or take a cold shower, or roll in the snow, depending on how sturdy one is. If someone has high blood pressure or a heart condition, have them soak or sponge off with warm water—a sudden drastic temperature change could create problems. Then it's back in for the second *gang*.

The second *gang* is for weighty matters. It is the Mannaz round for the Community. While this is traditionally for bringing up important issues that are besetting the community, it is not for arguing or starting fights. Instead, people should frame their issues as hopes, stating what positive changes they would like to see happen in the future. "Community" could be anything as small as one's family to as large as the world. The round is formal, and people should not speak out of turn. If the group is intimate and trustworthy enough, negative matters between people can be brought up, but the officiant should keep things on track and not allow grudges to affect the energy of the rite.

This is the round where the birch whisks are brought out, steamed over the fire, and used to flagellate each other. It is done to loosen off the dead bits of skin that are peeling off of everyone's back, and also for spiritual purification. When done in community, it is important that people do it to each other as well as themselves, as an act of acknowledging the community bond. If no birch whisks are available, essence of birch can be put into the water. Birching is sometimes done in the sauna, and sometimes during the second break, depending on people's preferences. Birch is the tree of Frigga, the Queen of Asgard and the Lady of Frithkeeping. Part of Frigga's gift is to make sure that social interactions run properly, with as few people being insulted as possible. During this round, the officiant takes on Frigga's role, making sure that the atmosphere is maintained and that nothing degenerates into argument or, conversely, mere partying. An invocation to Frigga can be done, if the people involved wish to invoke her, to keep things peaceful. The UPG of one spirit-worker was that this round would be appropriate for divination done with symbols—runes or pictographs—drawn on birchbark or carved on birch twigs. After this round, the whisks are burned in the fire.

The third *gang* is done for the Gods, the Ansuz round, and it is mostly quiet. The Gods may be hailed in the beginning, by name as people choose or all together, and then silence falls again. The group meditates on how they are going to enact the vision that came during the *löyly* or the divination or the talking on the last two rounds. Then all leave in silence, shower off, and the sauna is left going for a while longer in order to propitiate the guardian spirit. Someone should be chosen to watch the fire—checking in on it periodically until it goes out—and if there is a feast afterwards, some of it should be brought out and set at the door of the sauna as an offering.

Hela's Lesson

transcribed by Lydia Helasdottir

How does Hela manifest? She's a constant presence, I look around and I see her everywhere, in leaves turning, and dead animals by the roadside, and people in waning stages of their careers, dust on the floor, all that. As a personage, she shows up in my dreams. I notice her when I start to feel cold and get a creepy sensation up the back of my neck, and there she is. And it's like, "Oh, no, I hadn't forgotten that we had an appointment at two o'clock this afternoon, and it's only three minutes past two!" And it's either to give me some job to do, or to give me feedback on some job that I'm doing, or some information that I need to do a job, or to point out something that I've missed.

Understand that when you call upon Hela for aid, what will happen is that she will take things away from you—things that were getting in the way, weighing you down, complicating your life, keeping you from moving on—even if they are things that you love and believe that you need. She knows differently. You only think that you need them, and you will be better off without them. Be careful in asking for her help, because that almost always comes in the form of taking something away. Don't ask her to have more of something—more joy, more peace, more contentment …that is not her job. More help, perhaps, but that usually presages more work. The reward for a job well done is a harder job.

Of course, you might be tempted, in the beginning, to think, "Well, what if I just don't do that ever so well, then?" That's trouble. She just looks at you and says, "Is that the best you can do?" And at that point you can either break down and say, "No, it wasn't, I'm really really sorry," or you can try to smile and say, "Oh, yeah," but I don't advocate that. Confess as soon as you physically can. Pride has no place in her temple at all. It doesn't work.

What people don't understand is that if you ask her for help, and she says, "I will help you, but…" that "but" is your last chance to say "Never mind!" Once she's spoken, and told you what you have to do to solve this, there's no way to back out. You can't call it off. You have to do it, period. And if you don't—which you might be tempted to do, you might say, "Oh, maybe she's not really real," then the consequences will quickly become very apparent. And if you still stubbornly refuse to associate those consequences with the fact that You Broke A Deal With Death, then they just become more and more severe until your stubborn dumb-ass head understands what's happening.

Hela's Lessons:

First, live like I might take you tomorrow. This means that you'd better have your life together. Get it all sorted out—your estate, the things that you need to be saying to people, not leaving a mess behind for those you love. Make sure that you say to people who need to hear it that you love them. Say it at the end of every phone call. What if they aren't there tomorrow?

This will lead to understanding what is really important. What are your priorities? Are they the same ones that you would have if you were told that you had a month to live? Think about that. If your choice for tomorrow lies between a crucial move in chasing wealth or status, or seeing a loved one and creating a fond memory together, which will you do? Which treasure will be most valuable to you when you find yourself dying?

Second, you must understand that the life side, the yang side of the equation doesn't work without the death side. You cannot be happy all the time, because you wouldn't know what it meant. The ideal state of a human being is not to be happy all the time. This is an idea that's perpetuated in the West, but it is a myth. It is a Prozac addiction. It is anti-life. It is numbing out. You are not meant to be happy all the time. It is not the purpose of life. If you look at the old texts around the world, they do not speak of "happiness", but "perfect joy". Perfect joy can also make you cry; it encompasses sorrow too, and boredom, and adversity, and despair. Despair is one of my sacred states, and it has its uses. That does not mean malcontentment, though. You can be despairing and honor me with that despair, but malcontent? No. No whining.

You can say, "Help me! I don't know what to do, this is all far too much and I can't cope with it, and I don't even know what to do next, I can barely breathe!" I might answer then, even if it is simply "Shut up, breathe, and do this next." But whining "I hate this and I don't want to do it! Do I have to?" No. Definitely not. And if you don't learn the lesson the easy way ... well, you can learn it quick, or you can learn it hard. And believe me, the quick hard is better than the slow hard.

So that is my third lesson: doing without. There are things that you need, and things that you only believe that you cannot do without. Remember, to have is riches, but to be able to do without is power. Which things in your life does it frighten you to do without? Try seeing how long you can go without them; test yourself. For I am Loss, and you fear me for it, but if you come willingly to the altar of Loss for short periods of time, then should you ever be dragged here by force and chained to its empty, echoing space, it will not be so unfamiliar to you.

The Body And The Tree: The Path of the Flesh

The firelight casts red shadows on their naked bodies as they circle the fire together. The acknowledgment of the elements for this rite are not spoken; although she hums as she moves, a soft slippery galdr; tonight the sense is touch. Her hands reach out to the east, where the fan of collected feathers lie; she brushes its silkiness down his arm, fans him and lets the soft wind touch him as well. Ansuz. *He reaches out to the south, where a pile of furs are warmed by the fire; he rubs their warmth and sensuousness down her back and across her breasts.* Wunjo. *In the west, their hands dip together into violet-scented water and anoint each other.* Laguz. *In the north, they stroke and trade the smooth round stones, the carved and polished wooden phallus shining in the light of the flames.* Mannaz. *Their hands slip from sacred objects to bodies, and they sink onto the blanket thrown down in the field, marked with chalk in a circle of runes. The stars wheel overhead as the come together.* Gebo. *Hail to the Green Ones, the Golden Ones, the Twins that bring life to the barren earth, She of springtime flowers and He of autumn harvest.*

It matters, and yet does not matter, what the bodies do, what touches what or slides through what. The part that matters is the energy that rises in them, between them. First the breath, synchronized between them as fingers slide over flesh, heart to heart. Ond. *The winds between them fan the flames and the fire rises, a small piece of the primal warmth that melted the primal ice.* Litr. *It rises up their spines, coaxed along by caresses. The winds grow fiercer, gasps and panting knocking each one out of the rhythm by turns, yet each returns again. Then there is the link, the connection of flesh as two* hamar *meld for that moment.* Lich. *Then the climax, spiraling upwards together.* Lady, let the land we share together be green this year, let the seedlings uncurl from the Earth even as this passion uncurls and springs skyward. Lord, let there be a rich harvest to bring forth and lay on your altar. This is our gift, this is the best that we have, offered to you. Wod. *The stars wheel overhead, reflecting the light of the fire.*

As they Open to each other, they also Open to the forces that watch, laugh, touch them, bless them. Sparks of green and gold burst behind their eyes, and for a moment they are one with the Earth beneath them, and understand what that means. Their hands guide the energy down into the soil beneath them—or is it divine hands that do the guiding?—and they lie spent, hands still clasped together. It is the Rite of Spring.

The Path of the Flesh is the path of sex magic, using the energy raised through sexual activity as a tool to do things. There is almost nothing written about sex magic in surviving northern-tradition historical lore, and what there is of it is generally cast in the worst possible light. Considering that most of the chroniclers were Christian, this is not surprising. For that matter, even before Christianity, the culture seemed to have been inclined to leave such things as sex magic to the professional spiritual worker or ritual priesthood. Like traditional Tantra (not the neo-Tantra circulating in America today), it was a cult tradition, and not something to be talked about generally in public. However, this means that reconstructing northern-tradition sex magic is not something that can be done through written materials.

Sex magic is a biological process; the range of bodies and physical responses is present in every human population the world over. Although different cultures have a wide variety of uses and goals regarding sex magic, the basics are the same everywhere. It is neither difficult nor inappropriate to synthesize the teachings of other cultures—at least where they all find the same biological truths—and apply that to this tradition by consulting with the appropriate Gods and wights for their teachings on the matter. Sometimes the Gods themselves will be the teachers; something isn't talked about much is that our Gods like to have sex with us, and masturbatory devotional sex magic done by a spirit-worker has a fair chance of ending up being a sexual encounter with a deity. If you put it out there as an offering, there's the chance they'll come and take it themselves, and teach us more about this Path in the process.

> That said, what is the specific "flavor", if you will, of northern-tradition sex magic? It's vigorous, it's warmth-generating, because this is a cold northern climate. That's not necessarily kid-generating, more like warmth against the ice. It is community-generating, and bond-generating. You need those community bonds brought together by bodies. It is similar in that way to the sauna custom. Consider what it's like to walk fifteen miles in a blizzard, and how you feel to see another human being then, particularly one who has an open front door and a hot room that you can go and sit in? Take that further into a sexual metaphor—the warm bed with human comfort is the ultimate in hospitality.
>
> –Lydia Helasdottir

From discussing the subject with spirit-workers who are actually doing the work, rather than merely theorizing about it, we all seem to have come up with the concept that there are three "flavors" of northern-tradition sex magic, depending on which pantheon you are working with. The most common flavor, and the one that is most achievable to the average person, is the Vanir type. Its teachers and patrons are, of course, Frey and Freya. It is the sex magic of the everyday people, used to connect to the spirit of nature and of fertility. It is immanent rather than transcendent. Regardless of who is doing it, it links very quickly into the fertility archetype of energy creation for keeping life going. It is earthy, joyous, and extremely egalitarian. It is about tapping bodily into the force that keeps the cycle going and everything running. It maintains the status quo—as long as they do the same thing every year, Life will continue.

There is definitely a side to Vanir sex magic that tends to be placatory, in the sense of "Look, look, we're making all this nice warm energy, please make sure that summer comes back!" or the reindeer breeds, or the moss keeps growing, or whatever. It is very basic, not at all like either the ritual sex magic where you want a particular result and you're going to mechanically put it together to create that result, or the sex magic of the shaman, who is using it as a tool to get into an altered state. Its egalitarian nature means that in order for the energy to come up right, both individuals have to be working together to raise it. In this way, it is the most similar to the Tantric ideal of Shiva-Shakti combining their energies as one. It is the ritual sex of the Maypole, the Green Man and the May Queen creating the pole of energy that stretches from under the earth to the faraway sky. As the magical Middle Path of northern-tradition sex magic, it carries the energy of Midgard and Vanaheim, rather than the worlds at the top and bottom of the World Tree.

It also does not have to be done with a partner, or heterosexually, although this is the easiest way to achieve results. Solo Vanir sex magic is reflected in stories where the man masturbates into a hole in the earth, giving his seed as an offering while joining to the energy of Earth as Lover. Some women that I know have done the equivalent by using corn dollies or wood from a live tree (or even a live tree itself) as ritual sexual aids. This works because the deity is coming to you, embodying themselves in the natural world, and making love to you. If you are taking the Vanir path and you want to join with the Gods in that way, wander into a secluded place in Nature and ask what form the God/dess with whom you seek to be joined wishes to embody. Using some kind of a physical, natural anchor seems to be important. For example, those who horse Frey find that the size of one's human phallus doesn't really matter, because they all pale in comparison to his, and that a consecrated phallus made of natural materials is often the most effective option. This phallus can later be lent out as a tool to those wishing to join with Frey, without even being attached to a human being for the event.

At this point, we should veer aside for the moment and refer to archaeological finds of many phallus-shaped wands, called *gondull* or *gandr*, in northern European soil. These were certainly involved in symbolic sex magic, and may have been used literally; they are most often referred to as being used to summon spirits. There are also tales of the *volsi*, a phallic wand made from a preserved severed stallion's phallus and said to be a magical object of great power and worship. Stories of the *volsi* have women commenting bluntly about using it for both masturbation and magical practice. Some scholars speculate that the short staff of the volva and vitki was a phallic symbol, and that by taking it up the seidhr-worker was proclaiming their willingness to be open and "penetrated" by the wights. Some even theorize about it being a remnant from ancient literal sex-magic performances with a phallus-like staff.

While the magic that creates Life and fertility is generally heterosexual, Vanir sex magic freely welcomes not only those who are not heterosexual but those who are not strictly male or female. Both Frey and Freya historically and modernly welcomed *ergi* types, third gender people who cross between. As some Freysmen have discovered, there are two separate cults of (or, perhaps, paths to) Frey: the heterosexual farmer, husband, and father; and the effeminate queer man with the bells on his skirt. Frey and Freya are both deities not only of sex but of love, and to them, all love is a Good Thing—the more, the better. The same goes for sex.

Nonprocreative Vanir-type sex magic is used either for bonding, regardless of who is using it, or for magic. After all, Freya is love goddess, fertility goddess, and seidhkona. As the Sacred Whore of the Northern pantheon, sex magic is one of the gifts that she teaches. Before you bridle at terming her a Sacred Whore, please understand that this title is laid with the greatest respect, and only the overlay of Christianity has made it otherwise. One of the things that Freya teaches, for example by laying with four Duergar in exchange for Brisingamen, is her way of asking the question: *What are you worth?* This is the question of the Sacred Whore throughout Western civilization. Freya is sure of her worth; she knows that four nights of her body and her skills are well worth the most beautiful necklace in the world, and she is unashamed of herself. She is hetaera, qadishtu, the one who opens her arms to all yet is still in full control of her sexuality and her choices, the one who cannot be owned by another. To be a seidhkona requires similar independence and self-confidence.

Freya's other questions, which the spirit-worker who would enter into sex magic ought to answer, include: *What is sex worth to you? Do you value it, or does part of you still believe that it is dirty, or perhaps beneath you as an intelligent, rational being, or at least something that oughtn't to be put too high on people's priorities? If so, perhaps this isn't the path for you. Or perhaps you need to learn to value it for what it is—not as a vehicle for procreation or love or duty or bonding or validating attractiveness or getting attention or enlivening a boring life, just what it is. Have you ever had sex with no ulterior motives at all, just opening up to the experience itself and letting it take you, no expectations, no goals save pleasure? If not, start there, before you go adding yet more goals and motives to clutter the mix.*

While Freya is constantly independent, Frey's path is one of willing sacrifice. Actually, it's more than willing, it's enthusiastic. To go to Death every year as a bridegroom, with a big smile and an attendant large erection, is more than most of us can comprehend. When we are asked to sacrifice, we do so with apprehension, or resentment, or grim dutifulness, or a host of other ambivalent emotions. Frey's embracing of sacrifice, every year, for the good of the crops bewilders us. Scholars try to explain it away by calling it a metaphor for the crops that fall, or the phallus that shoots and wilts, but what does it mean to us if it's more than metaphorical?

Frey's questions for the spirit-worker on this path are: *Do you understand that this energy is always ephemeral? That whatever you raise will be gone in a moment, washed away like a rune in the sand at high tide? That no matter how much you pursue the moment, trying to catch it again, it is gone? Do you understand being grateful that it was granted to you even that once? More important, do you understand how to express gratitude to the Universe with your body? Can you see that your flesh is a microcosm of the Earth, and when you use it in this sacred way, you can raise energy to heal the broken flesh beneath your feet, which shall return to you as healing tenfold?*

Frey and Freya are sexual with each other, and the fact that they are brother and sister as well may take some people aback, but they are not human beings and their ways are not ours. They perform ritual sex in order to create the energy of fertility, abundance, and growth; combining their essences creates the green growing-ness that keeps our world running. As such, they can be called upon as a couple to teach with Vanir-style sex magic. Their multiple sexual connections—Frey is married to a Jotun goddess, Freya is the lover of an Aesir god, and both reach out to folk of many races—show that their place, in the middle ground of energies, closer to Midgard than the top or bottom of the Tree, is one of connection in all directions. Their connection with each other reinforces the centerpoint.

Aesir-style sex magic has a different flavor, and can be less egalitarian in role. To be more specific, if two people are involved, one is going to be the primary magician and be focusing the intent/energy/work, and one is going to be providing stimulation, support, and a battery of sexual energy. This doesn't imply a permanent inegalitarian system outside of that single act; the two (or more) individuals can switch off at different times, and there is no gendered supremacy involved, as anyone of any sex can be in either position. But whenever you leave the middle ground, things tilt in a general direction, and here that direction is Up, towards Ascension and High Vision and Creativity and Acting From Above. Therefore, the primary magician is the person who is A) physically on top, and B) doing the majority of the actual sexual work. The other partner is receptive, or passive, or whatever works for the people involved; stimulation is given to them, but for the purpose of raising energy for the magician to use. Again, we stress that physical gender is irrelevant here; while much of society would have us believe that men are active and women are all sexually passive, that has never been the case for our cosmology, which is filled with assertive female beings who are quite capable of being sexually aggressive and taking responsibility for the encounter.

Aesir sex magic can have various goals, but the first and most important goal is to bring people closer to the Gods, and open themselves to the Light at the top of the Tree. Here, while the process may be difficult—it's hard for us to keep from getting bogged down in our own issues and make a clean offering of our sexual energy to Them—it is still fairly safe once you achieve it. It's between you and Them, and your responsibility is only to Them, and to each other. It's ethical and clean and harder to get in trouble with it. Lydia comments again: "Aesir sex magic is all about ascension. To use a Kabalistic model, the Tree of Life starts with the Veil of the Profane, which is basically 'Have you got any clue at all?' You then have the Veil of Paraketh, and it's all about seeking the divine light. In the Christian model you'd say it's about the burning heart. In Taoism it's the Greatest Kannon Li. But it's about seeking the divine light as love. That for me has always been the Aesir way. Go for the light."

The Divine Couple who can teach this best to you are, of course, Odin and Frigga, in their own version of the *hieros gamos*. We tend to forget, in our focusing on their relationship as either Chieftain/Lady Of The Hall or Wanderer/Hearthkeeper, that they carry the sacred marriage energy for Asgard. They are invoked at weddings not only because Frigga is a "goddess of domesticity", but because the two of them together create the sacred Polarity of Sky, the sacred marriage brought to great heights.

Frigga's questions to spirit-workers on this path are: *Do you understand that this work creates bonds, even between strangers? Be careful with whom you spin these threads, for they may grow stronger than you expect. Choose your partners in this wisely, perhaps even more carefully than you would choose a mate to marry, for in following someone down this path, you may yet bind them to your soul. Do you wish to feel them make love to their new lover, years after you have left each other? The world is fickle, as is Wyrd, and you may not know how things will ride in the future. It is better to practice alone a hundred times than open the soul-paths together with someone unsuitable.*

Odin's questions to spirit-workers are: *Can you breathe? Breathe in! All things start with breath, with ond, and this most of all. Sex magic starts with breathing. Learn to breathe the ond around your body, and into that of your partner. Do you understand how to link each other together with your very breath? Start by breathing together, in unison. If you do nothing else, do this; learn each others' rhythm and make it one. Can you see them as your instrument to play, your creation to bring to new heights? Can you excite them, speed their breath, build their energy, bring them to climax—then use that out-breath, that exhalation of the genitals, of the root chakra, the body's music, to galdr across the space between you and the Light? Do you understand that the song of the body is its own galdr, and that its shout can be louder than that of lungs and voice? Climb upwards on the ladder that is the body of your beloved, and then when you fly off the top, carry them with you.*

If you are finding it difficult to move away from the Vanir model of earthy sex magic, a "transitional" couple that can help might be Odin and Freya. Odin's sexual relationship with Freya is not a divine marriage; it's more of a working partnership in which they learn and teach power to each other. It lies between the earthy middle ground and the sky, the place where the trees brush the clouds with their leaves, and yet it is a place of equal respect. No part of the Tree is evil or wrong, just as no part of Life is less than any other, and Odin has no less respect for Freya just because her home is closer to Midgard; indeed, he humbly went to her to learn the mysteries of seidhr. As a sexual couple, they may be able to help with moving from I-Thou to a model that can best be described as "one looks up to the other who looks up still further".

Rökkr sex magic is also inegalitarian in role, but in an opposite way to Aesir-flavored sex magic. In this dynamic, the primary magician is the one who is being "done to", more receptively. The other partner(s) are there to do the job of getting them into a state where that work can be done. The active person is the technician; the receptive person is the shaman who is working towards the goal. Rökkr sex magic is, as Lydia explains below, more practical and task-oriented than worship/devotion oriented.

> For Jotun sex magic … well, the stuff that comes between Paraketh and the abyss is the stuff between the stars. That is Nox; that is the dark stuff. It's dark and it's nasty and it's power, and sex and death and all that stuff. Here, love is a given, and the fact that

you have your own furnace, your own star in your heart shining, is a given. You can't even work this stuff without that. It's about integrating the monster within and doing something with it. It's not about getting into bliss and shooting straight up the middle—that's the Aesir path. No, there's a job to do there down in the dark. It's like comparing the Buddha versus the bodhisattva path. It's more Vajrayana than Hinayana. The Rökkr path is coming back down out of bliss and doing the dirty work. So Rökkr magic is all about works, not enlightenment.

In order to use sex to do something, make some change in the world, or integrate some dodgy part of you, or heal somebody, or help someone heal themselves, or whatever other reasons ... well, there has to be a good reason, first thing. Suddenly you're in a world of responsibility that isn't there if you just do divine magical sex. Therefore, the controls and the safeties and all that have to be so much tighter, and the person who's actually doing the connecting with the Gods or the energy needs to be more in control of what's happening. So it's more useful if they're the operator, if they're having the stuff done to them.

And what that sex magic is like? It's saying, "We're going to have this kind of sex, to raise this kind of energy." I'll give you an example of the ritual that we did to fix the broken parts of the Wheel that is over there in Europe. Seven girls in a circle laying clockwise, with each one of them in the next one's cunt, doing that. At one part of the circle, the lightning conductor, who was standing, and who had the arms and legs of the ones in the circle winding around her legs, and she had the most senior of the girls to her left, so that this girl could take all the energy that had been winding and winding and winding, and gather it all in by changing her position, and go up and adore the conductor's whole body. The conductor was there to generate this earth-up energy. There was another one who was hanging from hooks in her back who was getting really pumped full of pain energy from Hela, but it wasn't going anywhere, because she was off the ground. She was wearing a strap-on, and two of the girls were constantly dripping honey off of that, into a bowl where there was another phallus symbol. They were drinking from that the whole time, to generate more.

When there was enough energy wound up, and there was a sufficient differential, these two kissed, and the charge earthed, and it was like—boom! And that's what needed to happen. It all happened inside of a Faraday cage too, which was pretty cool; a stainless steel cube made of scaffolding material, inside which this was going on. Very nice and transportable and good for suspensions as well. We also had two guys sitting guard, watching and making sure that there were no interruptions. And that's an example of Rökkr sex magic used for a northern-tradition purpose. I would use the same configuration if I was working a large piece of sex magic for anybody else.

It's very goal-oriented, there's work to do. The Jotun are all very elemental. It's about rock and earth and tree and fire and sea, clearly physical and primal things which you shouldn't have any control over until you have achieved a connection with the divine, because it can become a greed thing and this is where people go wrong, and end up doing things that will do damage to the world.

Being used as a tool, seen as a machine that has a particular shape, is something that we use in sex magic. "We need one of these, and one of these, and a few of these, to work with the energy wiring diagram, and we need these two to do these things to each other." And then, blammo, it's there. People who hear that are taken aback; they say, "Hey, where's the divinity in that? Where's the spontaneity?" But frankly, if you can't manifest divinity and spontaneity within a designed ritual context, you should not be doing sex magic. Your sexuality, by the way, is another way that patron deities use you as a tool. Did you think that this would be exempt? No. It's not.

–Lydia Helasdottir

Rökkr deities who work with sex magic include Angrboda, Surt, Loki, and to an extent Hela. Loki is capable of all sorts of sex magic; as *argr* as he is, he's tried it all and enjoys being a hands-on trainer of such things. He specializes in sex magic that requires versatility of role, as he has done that all over the map—being male, being female, being active, being passive, being solitary and partnered and in a large tumbled group.

Loki's questions to the spirit-worker are: *So you want to do sex magic, eh, sweetheart? Do you know that it's playing with fire? Fire and the Tree. The key to sex magic is found in the root of your body, the seat of the* litr, *and that can burn you up if you're not careful. No, really. You don't believe me, you think that it's all safe and easy? That if you lose the thread of mindfulness,* it'll just turn into a really good fuck? Well, maybe it will. And maybe something will leap up and scorch your pipes, and burn out some of the circuits in your head. Won't that be fun? Do you understand the Tree, boys and girls? Have you worked with it, moved up and down its length? Because the Tree is a good thing to link to, the Irminsul from roots to leaves, from Void to Void. The Tree's old, it understands these things, line yourself up there and you'll be safer. Not safe, just safer. Because your body is a Tree as well, or hadn't you noticed?

Angrboda is skilled in sex magic of many kinds that will extend to people of different genders, but it is all of a raw, primal variety. For her, shapeshifting is very bound up with sex magic, especially in terms of how one moves one's energy around. Whether she agrees to teach you, though, will be entirely up to her. She will probably want to test you out first in some way, sexual or otherwise, and see if you are worth bothering with. If the test is sexual, her questions will be—verbal or not—*"Who are you? Are you better than what I can get from my wolf-boys? What's in this for me?"* You had best have answers to these questions before you ask, especially the intimidating second one. The sex she likes is passionate, rough, and animalistic; the sex she teaches is more dark and mysterious. Don't go to her for that training until you are reasonably skilled at shapeshifting and can keep up with her, because she may start teaching you with a whirlwind tour of the mating instincts of many different creatures.

Her other questions are: *Do you value your body, or do you hate it? Do you value the animal in you, or do you believe that sex is more sacred the further from the animal you are? Can you understand the sacredness of animal lust?* If not, you'll never make it down this path, for the animal in you is the beginning point, your very root. It's called the root chakra for a reason, you fool. Base of the spine, base of the skull, the lizard-brain still does it best. You have to be able to do this with your animal self before you can move up the chakras to the heart, the mind, all those refined places. Do not deny or devalue the animal instinct in you! It is the part of you that loves the body, no matter what it looks like. There is no place in this path for hatred of your flesh.

Surt's sex magic is rather cataclysmic. He is definitely the active partner, no matter who you are, and your job is just to open up and take it as best you can. Surt's orgasm is like a small nuclear bomb, a wad of lava, a small drop of primal fire, a piece of pure manifestation, after which he walks away and leaves you with it inside you. If you can catch and hold it, you can use it to power some serious magic, but if you can't catch it—if you haven't done with work it takes to make yourself capable of holding a white-hot fiery piece of pure manifestation—then it can burn you up if you don't get it out of yourself. An orgasm will shoot it out of you, but if you can have your intent ready to mold something that needs making and shoot it out as a formed magical intent, that's better. Surt likes this, because he likes to see his energy used to create.

Surt's questions to the spirit-worker are: *Do you understand that sex magic uses primal fire? Yes, first it's about the breath, but then it moves to fire. Within each of you is a tiny spark of the flame of Muspellheim that warmed the ice, buried in your root place. It is your* litr, *your vitality. Without that, you would be cold and limp. All that breathing, it's just blowing on that spark, calling it into a flame that leaps upward. Then it's the fire of a forge with which you can hammer out your will. It will do that anyway, it's up to you to be mindful about it. What will you do with this? Do you realize that it will leave its track imprinted on your flesh? What do you want that imprint to say? Prepare yourself wisely before you open with fire from the bottom up.*

One doesn't really think of Hela, the Goddess of Death, as a teacher of sex magic, and it is true that she chooses to teach very few people her method of this path. That's partly because sex magic with Hela is always an intersection between the Path of the Flesh and the Ordeal Path. Sex with her is always an Ordeal, intense and terrible and a great blessing. Lydia writes: "With Hela it's very formal and ritualistic. It's all about clinically cleaning and purifying. If there was such a thing as diplomatic sex magic—not passionate, but energetically alive, it would be that. It is precise, constricted, job-oriented. When Hela is working with Fenrir, it's about realness and chaos. You see, if Hela just decomposed stuff that was already in the world, recycled it, then nothing new would ever happen. If you use the same stuff in the same pattern, it goes into a stagnant loop, which is why stuff that's really fully dead is stagnant until it's reused. When she works with Fenrir, it keeps a certain amount of chaos in the world, which is a good thing because it allows the Vanir lords to do their thing with Life. Like the Vanir twins, the Rökkr pantheon has a brother-sister pair who get it on not for reasons of love but ritually, out of obligation, to keep the cycle going."

Hela's questions to the spirit-worker on this path are: *Do you understand what this will do to you? Do you know what happens to the trauma that you endure, the anger that you repress, the responsibility that you shoulder, the helplessness that you feel, the pain that you put aside to deal with another day? It is all stored in your body somewhere, unless you have vented it out—and how many have done that with every moment of pain? Do you know that the Path of the Flesh opens you up not only to what is without, but what is within? You will understand when it happens, when flesh passes ring of flesh and suddenly you weep, you scream, your body whiplashes with feeling. That is not failure. That is purification. Until enough of that is out of the way, you will not be able to Open outwards. This traps you within yourself, and it must come out, and that will be as painful leaving as it was entering. Can you see that as pure, as cleansing, not as evil, no matter how long it takes?*

For those who are starting with the centerpoint of Vanir magic and want to spiral down towards the raw, primal, practical element of Rökkr magic, a good transitional couple to call upon are Frey and his etin-bride Gerda. Unlike Freya who reaches upwards to make the link to the Aesir and anchor their Light to the Earth, Frey reaches downwards to bring light into the darkness and depths. He does not fear Death or Pain, as he endures it yearly and is reborn, and Gerda is an excellent and comparatively gentle guide through self-examination, communing quietly with one's inner darkness, and mourning.

You'll notice that nowhere in this chapter have I described physical techniques such as would be found in many books of Tantric studies—positioning bodies, sticking tab A in slot B and for how long, etc. That's partly because one could fill a book with that sort of thing—and indeed, such books already exist out there, written by people who are better masters at this sort of thing than I am, so why reinvent the wheel?—and partly because in the end, it doesn't seem to matter what rubs what so long as the energy is raised. Working with sacred sexuality and/or sex magic in this tradition seems to be less "formal" than, say, in the cultural venue of Indian Tantra. There is less emphasis on polarity of gender unless one is following in the archetypal footsteps of an actual divine couple. In our tradition, the body is closely linked to the elements. Part of understanding sacred sexuality here is to experience the flesh as part of nature. How would you masturbate if you were a flame? A mountain? A cool lake? How would you have sex with your partner if you were a wolf, a bird, a snake, a wind, a river, a tree bending in the wind, a sheaf of wheat bending to the scythe, a wave of the sea? Learning to bring these energies into your sexual practice—or perhaps to discover that they were always there all along—is the best lesson that you can learn on this path, and it's one that lends itself well to experiment and self-discovery.

It's also something that can be taught by the wights themselves. As spirit-workers, we sometimes (or often) get into sexual relationships with Gods and wights. Most of them are ephemeral; we dance together, the energy is raised and directed, and then it's over. Occasionally people will enter into long-term love or even marital relationships with deities, becoming god-spouses, which is its own greater issue. Even a small encounter with a deity, however, is instructive. It's impossible to encounter them sexually and not learn something about the sacredness of sex. It's also true that monogamy is not the same thing for a spirit-worker that it is for a normal person, and that goes even more so for a shaman. The Gods come first, and while a vow of monogamy (or polyfidelity) to a human being may eliminate all sexual contact with other human beings, it does not mean that gods and wights are exempt, especially if the Path of the Flesh is in your future. As with all things, They are better teachers than any of us. It is an honor and a joy to touch them in this way, and be touched and Opened in return.

Making The World Tree:
A Northern-Tradition Sex Magic Technique

by Elizabeth Vongvisith

In the Northern Tradition, sex magic seems to be focused three different ways among three different races. Among the Aesir, the active partner (regardless of actual gender) is the primary magician, the one who is channeling and directing the energy—so if two males are performing Aesir sex magic, for instance, the (actively) *ergi* partner is never the primary magician. Vanir practices rely heavily on the equal interplay between partners and may include more than two people; the energy is raised and channeled by both (or all) partners. Jotun sex magic, on the other hand, requires that the receptive partner be the primary magician—so using the above example, the *ergi* male would be the main conduit and director of energy for the working. The differences may seem subtle to the untrained, but anyone with even minor experience in sex magic should understand them without much further explanation.

The technique called *Making the World Tree* can be used by anyone reasonably skilled in sex magic, regardless of whether it's Aesir, Vanir or Jotun-style. It is not something beginners ought to attempt because it requires a certain pre-existing familiarity with the way sex magic works, and for other reasons I'll get into later.

First of all, you'll want to decide what the goal of the working is—elementary to even the most rank beginner though it may be, it's even more important here because the purpose of the working determines the form that the World Tree will take when you manifest it. This is very important, so be absolutely certain that all partners involved in this working are clear on exactly what it's meant to accomplish.

When you've got the purpose nailed down, you need to figure out who is going to be the primary magician, who will decide when the moment is right to manifest the Tree, although s/he may have little control over what form it takes or how long it's there. Don't decide lightly; this is an extremely powerful technique for which the primary magician will run the risk of a complete though usually temporary drain of all their energy reserves afterward. Actually, either Aesir or Jotun-style sex magic, in which one person is the focus and carrier of energy, works better for this technique than Vanic-style sex magic where all partners share in the responsibility.

This working can *theoretically* be done by a single solo magician. Masturbation is certainly as valid a technique for successful sex magic as partnered sex. However, one person alone may not be able to raise the requisite amount of energy to accomplish this, and it may even be dangerous to try it. I would strongly suggest you consider doing this with at least one partner and only resort to solo sex magic if you have no other option, if only for the fact that it may very well leave you severely debilitated for a time. Having at least one other person present and involved will lessen the strain considerably and also provide you with someone to help you recover afterwards.

I'm not going to go into the usual how-tos about sex magic; you should already know how to raise energy by these means if you're going to attempt this working. Whatever you usually find useful, entertaining and erotic in order to stimulate the primary magician is appropriate. The one caveat is that no matter what activities you use to get things going and raise power, at some point before the energy reaches its height, the primary and at least one secondary partner need to get situated sitting up, genital areas pressed together or connected, or if you're having anal sex, connected that way—the idea is to have the base energy centers (root chakras, in Eastern thought) as close as possible. If there are any others involved, they need to be as close to the primary magician as possible and touching him/her with focused intent

The primary magician has to decide when the moment is right, but when it is, you need to visualize a tree rising from the base of the spine, its roots connecting your body to your partner's and springing more or less from both of you. Usually the moment right before climax is the time to let oneself go and allow the Tree to manifest itself as the energy of orgasm fuels its growth, so getting the primary magician off should be the focus of activity after assuming the position.

You should literally feel the power rising through your body, much as the serpent-fire (called *kundalini* in other traditions) rises up the spine, to emerge from the top of your head and reach beyond. At some point, you probably won't need to keep visualizing because you'll lose control of the vision entirely, which is what is supposed to happen. *Your body becomes that of the World Tree.* There is a delicate balance between controlling the experience, and allowing the Tree to manifest itself, and this may take practice, but when you get it right, you'll know, because you won't even have to think about it as it happens. When you've had enough experience, all you'll need is intent and at the right moment in the erotic activity, the Tree will spring forth of its own accord.

The vision may last anywhere from a few seconds to five minutes or more. No matter how ecstatic you are or how good it feels, try to note the size, shape and appearance of the Tree for future reference. A rather enjoyable side effect is that if you happen to come right as the Tree appears, your orgasm will be about twenty times more intense, and may even cause you to pass out, but do the best you can to remain conscious. If your partner or partners are at all psychically sensitive or aware, they will probably also have some idea of what form the Tree takes

Don't assume that you'll always get a mighty, aged yew or some other Yggdrasil-appropriate tree. You may get a Chinese weeping willow, a Yule tree complete with lights and baubles, or even a tree on fire. The shape and form of the Tree is as much an indicator of the success of your working as it is indicative of its purpose. Sometimes the Tree's form takes on a divinatory aspect. Sometimes the Tree itself – the real World

Tree, the one that you've just tapped into with your sex magic spell—will communicate something to you through this vision. Whatever happens, know that you have tapped into every one of the worlds that spins around the Tree through your working. *Whatever purpose your magic was meant to serve will have immediate repercussions throughout all Nine Worlds.* This is really why Making the World Tree is not a beginner's exercise—not because the actual sex magic might be beyond the expertise of a newbie, but because few are ready to handle the consequences of this sort of working. (For that matter, few experienced magicians are ready for that, either.)

Although your partner(s) may not have as intense a vision as you, they will also be able to sense when it does and doesn't work. The shared ecstasy of the manifestation is made even more intense if mutual climax is achieved among all participants, but the manifestation itself is pretty intense no matter what. The primary magician will be the one who actually manifests the Tree, but any and all secondary magicians and partners will feed their energy into that vision, and so all will be a part of the working in a way which may not necessarily be true for other types of sex magic. It can be a very emotionally intimate experience that may be best shared with your regular and/or trusted partners, rather than with those with whom you only occasionally practice sex magic.

The most intense form of this activity, which few of us get to practice that often, is of manifesting the World Tree with a god or goddess as one's partner. Whether you end up being the primary or secondary participant in that kind of interaction is almost irrelevant; having sex with a deity is so intense in and of itself that using the World Tree technique might leave you utterly dazed, drained and limp as a rag doll for hours afterward, which can be dangerous. However, if a deity is going to ask you to do this, chances are S/He will also ensure that you will not be left completely debilitated, and if said deity is being horsed by a human being, whatever support staff you may have available can help you overcome the aftereffects anyway. If you are not using a human horse to have sex with the deity, the effect may be lessened ... or it may give you a heart attack. It depends on the nature of the interaction, the purpose of the magic, and the deity Him/Herself.

You will know if and when you've "done it right" when you actually manifest the Tree—it is an amazing, overwhelming experience that cannot be faked or half-accomplished. It will blow your head open and push you to new levels of awareness that may take a long time to come down from. There's no mistaking it. If you aren't sure if you did it or not, the answer is no, you didn't. Once you have mastered this technique, it both becomes easier to accomplish and more powerful and intense; use caution if you are the addictive type, as the rush of full and total connection with all the forces of the Nine Worlds coupled with a really intense orgasm is something that's difficult for even the least driven of us to resist attempting for its own sake.

Ergi:
The Way of the Third

This particular chapter is going to cover what is probably the most controversial of issues in the entirety of northern-tradition shamanism. Many scholars, magicians, and spirit-workers have skirted the issue, or touched on it gingerly only to back off again. Discussing it angers both homophobic heterosexuals and assimilationist homosexuals, both modernized tribal peoples and researchers wary of projecting modern assumptions about sex and gender onto the ancients. However, like it or not, the constellation of power and taboo that the northern tradition calls *ergi* crops up again and again all over the world, including among fledgling modern spirit-workers.

I've chosen to use the much-debated word—*ergi* or *argr*—even though its meaning is unclear, and it may have had many meanings over the centuries as being Third became less and less acceptable. (Some of them have been conjectured as "morally useless", "perverse", "cowardly", "effeminate", "receiving of anal penetration", and, tellingly, "a sorcerer".) That's not to say that it was ever completely acceptable; even in tribal societies where it is not seen as a terrible or shameful thing—and for that matter, even in places where it is or was seen as a sacred thing—it was never exactly the sort of condition that any parent wanted for their child. Even "sacred" can mean "taboo", which can mean "kept at a respectful and/or fearful distance", a condition that any spirit-worker will recognize. What it doesn't mean, and never will mean, is "normal".

If you look at the research on shamanism worldwide—and especially that of the subarctic circumpolar shamanisms, from Siberia to the

Inuit—you find, over and over, the disturbingly frequent presence of spirit-workers who transgressed gender roles and indulged in unusual sexual practices. In some cultures, just showing evidence of these behaviors was considered a sign that a child was bound to be a spirit-worker of some sort.

This was remarked on particularly in Siberian shamanism, specifically among the Chukchi, Koryak, and Kamchadal, and across the Bering Strait with the Inuit. While Siberia may seem to be a long way in the minds of many people from Scandinavia or even Finland, there are many things that the circumpolar subarctic shamanic traditions have in common, much more so than shamanic traditions from further south. That includes northern Europe, especially during Neolithic times. (I could also discuss gender-transgressive shamans scattered throughout many other cultures around the world, but for the sake of brevity I'll stick to northern Eurasia; anyone who wants to find the other material can do so without much difficulty.)

Interviews with these "transformed shamans" report that the spirits informed the shamans in question that they were required to put on the clothing and take up the jobs of the opposite sex; in some cases, they lived their whole life in this way, including taking lovers appropriate to their role, and in some cases the male-to-female shamans would ritually mime childbirth. (Even here, however, the "special" role of these shamans as still not playing by the gender rules can be seen; a "shaman-wife" of this type did not have to observe the taboos of women, but could accompany their husband to battle, and rather than taking their husband's name, sometimes the husband took theirs instead.) Sometimes one also finds reports of male-to-female shamans who changed gender later in life, but remained husbands to their wives and fathers to their children, merely adopting female clothing and household jobs. Some merely donned women's clothing during ceremonies.

Some claimed that they picked up the traditional skills of their new role as quickly as they did due to the spirits helping them with it constantly. In some cases, the transformed shaman had a spirit-husband or spirit-wife who had transformed them to be the "right" gender for that marriage as far as the spirit-spouse was concerned. Researchers tell of the troubles of being married to such a one, as the spirit-spouse was considered the "real" head of household, and the shaman's mortal spouse had to obey the commands of the shaman's spirit-husband or be fatally punished.

Interviews also repeatedly came across the fact that while these transformed shamans were not necessarily fully accepted or much liked by their tribesfolk, nobody gave them any trouble due to their perceived power. While tribesfolk differed on whether male or female shamans were stronger, they were united in believing that the transformed shamans—*koekchuch*, *kavau*, *yirka-laul-vairgin*—were the most powerful of all. In fact, the social respect allocated to them was used by researchers as an example of the power attributed to shamans in general; if an ordinary person of the tribe decided to change their gender, they might be shunned, but if a shaman did it, it was a sacred thing done by the spirits to give them extra power.

It's also often observed that when it comes to tribal sex-roles and the tasks and taboos differentiated between them, there are really three gender roles—men, women, and shamans. Regardless of the shaman's gender presentation, they are permitted to do what is not permitted, because their position sets them apart, and because doing so gives them power—not just in public opinion, but in the web of *maegen* and *hamingja*. Male shamans could be around women in childbirth without harm to themselves; women shamans could touch sacred objects usually restricted from female contact.

Many of the Siberian tribes had third gender shamans, to the dismay and bewilderment of the "civilized" scholars who wrote about them with words like "perversion" and "sexually inverted". Chukchi shamans spoke about the terrible transformation of a man into a "soft man", which all shamans dreaded to be told to do by the spirits. Still, some received the command anyway, and had to go along with it or be killed. (To this day this is the difficult choice of some people with gender dysphoria, and when they are also spirit-workers, refusal can also eventually be fatal.) Some men apparently preferred death to going through this transformation, and received it, although not all who began it went all the way through to the end. It started with a change of hairstyle to that of the opposite sex, and then progressed to a change of clothing. The final phase had them changing their job roles in the tribe, taking on the tasks of their new gender, and marrying partners appropriate to their new role. They would in turn acquire special spirits appropriate to that role, sometimes "spirit-spouses". There were also female-to-male equivalents of the "soft men", and scholars were further horrified by tales of how they used artificial phalli for sex with their female partners.

Among the Saami, who in many places lived intertwined with the descendants of the Indo-European invaders and the invaded aboriginals, two of their many deities stand out. One is Juoksahkka, the "bow-woman", who unlike her two very feminine (and more popular) sisters and her mother, is a woman warrior-figure who carries the bow generally reserved for men. (The bow-woman figure is oddly echoed in other parts of the world, such as the Hopi woman-warrior kachina god Pohaha who carries both the male bow and the female rattle, and is the counterpart of a cross-dressing male-to-female kachina figure named He'e; and the Egyptian archer goddess Neith, whose rites supposedly made use of women wearing artificial phalli.) The other is Leabolmmai, the "alder-man" who brought game to hunters. The first element in his name, *liejp*, refers to both the red sap of the alder tree (a sacred substance that was used to paint symbols on shaman drums and protect people from danger from ritual objects) and to menstrual blood. The power of the menstrual-blood man takes on more significance when we remember that the alder, which made the best charcoal, was the tree of Loki the fiery *ergi* shapeshifter among the Norse. Juoksahkka and Leabolmmai were said to be bitter enemies, as it was their job to choose the sex of the unborn child, and they often disagreed over what that ought to be.

When it came to smaller wights among the Saami, there were again cross-gender beings in the middle. The *vuojnodime* or "invisible ones" came in three categories: male (*bassevarealmma*), female (*bassevareniejda*), and double-sexed (*gadniha*). Similarly, the three sacred animals—reindeer, bird and fish—were seen as masculine, feminine, and third-gendered respectively, any male or female members of those species notwithstanding. The assumption of "fish" as third gendered echoes the Norse hermaphroditic serpent Jormundgand, and the line in the Anglo-Saxon Rune Poem about the Big Snake's rune Ior—"Serpent is a fish, although it feeds on land."

Other parts of ancient Eurasia had traditions of third-gender spirit-people. Herodotus and Hippocrates both discuss the "enarees", or male-to-female transsexual shamans among the ancient Scythians, who "mutilated" their genitalia and took on female roles. They were said to be the most powerful shamans of their people. Ovid actually claimed that some Scythian priestesses knew how to extract "female poison" distilled from the urine of a mare in heat, with which to dose men in order to feminize them. The average person might throw this off as silliness, if they didn't know that pregnant mare's urine is the main source of Premarin, the most widely used estrogen drug today. They also ate a lot of licorice root—so popular among them that the Greeks to whom they exported it referred to it as "the Scythian root"—which is also an anti-androgen.

There has been a good deal of research done on the Norse seidhworker as *ergi*, as sexually and/or gender-deviant, most notably by Brit Solli, Ing-Marie Back Danielson, Jenny Jochens, and Neil Price. Referring to someone by one of the many colorful insults that indicated a less-than-completely-manly nature was grounds for death in medieval Scandinavian society, and this discomfort rubbed off onto the reputation of sorcerers and seidhworkers. According to the Gods and wights that I work with, it wasn't always this way; in the centuries and millennia before the medieval era, such folk had a social situation more similar to that of many other circumpolar tribes. While it wasn't exactly what a parent would necessarily choose for their child (given all possible choices), and while it did set them apart from the people (although that was the way of things for a spirit-worker anyhow), it was not a shameful offense. Instead, it connoted greater shamanic power. One wonders if an echo of that "too-powerful" nature was part of what fueled the fear and hatred of the average Viking, causing them to react in a manner so extreme that accusations of *ergi* were legally akin to attempted murder. One might also wonder if it continues to fuel it today.

For all that medieval Norse/Germanic society seemed to have been extremely sexist—at least by the Christian era when most of the lore was written—archaeologists keep turning up pre-medieval graves with cross-gender clothing and artifacts. Seven male skeletons with female clothing and jewelry have turned up in pre-Christian Anglo-Saxon burials in England, another in Holland, and more in Scandinavia. Similarly, female skeletons have turned up buried with weapons. One cremated couple were buried in connecting graves; the female skeleton had woodworking tools and the male one had female jewelry. Probably the most interesting cross-gender burial is that of what seems to be the grave of a gender-crossing Saami *noaide* in an area where Norse and Saami people lived intermixed together. The Saami skeleton is biologically male, but is dressed in Norse female clothing and jewelry and is buried with a woman's needle case.

The medieval Norse accusation-insult that a man "acted like a woman every ninth night" shows its magical roots by the sacred number nine. It may be that "shapeshifting" into a woman's form every ninth night was a way of gaining magical power, as a sort of temporary *ergi*. For those who feel called to *ergi* but are not ready to leap in all the way, this might be a way to start slowly, doing it in a magical context. Every ninth day and night, try to live as fully as you can in another sex, including shapeshifting your hame in that way. Dedicate that time to devotional, ritual, or magical work, and see what happens. Changing sex, especially temporarily, can be a powerful kind of altered state all its own, with an intense shift in perspective.

Then we have the infamous claim that some priests of Frey behaved like women and wore "the tinkle of unmanly bells" on their skirts. (The wearing of bells is something that many feminine-male ergi spirit-workers in this tradition have found themselves compelled to do, even if they have never actually heard of this claim.) There are also picture-stones in Gotland that show figures wearing the trailing skirts of women, and prominent beards as well; whether these are cross-dressing men or women with false beards is unknown, but either way we are looking at gender-crossing behavior that deviates from the conventions of depicting ordinary men and women. Some scholars have pointed out that you can't have set examples of "normal" gender activity unless you have examples of what isn't "normal", and that making that latter the province only of holy or supernaturally-ridden people with a mandate from the Powers to defy those laws is a way of keeping "normalcy" in place, without entirely banning the "wrong example" entirely.

Another interesting example is the line in *Hyndlujod*, where Hyndla comments on the ancestry of the volvas, the vitkis, and the "seidberendr" folk. The second half of this third term—*berendr*—is tantalizingly unclear; technically it means "carrier", but in practice it seemed to be an obscenity used to refer to female animals, and then to female genitalia themselves (as in the modern term *pussy* for vulva). In modern Icelandic, a related obscenity is *berandi*, meaning ass or buttocks. That would mean that this word could be considered to connote "seid-carrier cunt" or "seid-carrier ass", and while we may recoil at this term, one should remember that what seems rude in one culture is ordinary dinner-conversation in another. Certainly it makes sense if this third category refers to third-gendered spirit-workers, being as the first two refer to female and male ones respectively.

The ancestor of the *seidberendr*, Svarthofdi—Blackhead—reminds us of the fact that there seem to be more cross-gender entities among the "dark" gods, including Loki, his child Jormundgand, and possibly his extremely assertive warrior-wife Angrboda. (His daughter Hela, while she is all female, is conversely half-alive and half-dead.) As one would expect, there are greater percentages of *ergi* spirit-workers among those chosen by those dark Gods, especially Hela who seems (anecdotally, in this modern era) to be very fond of human servants who are between male and female. It fits well with the tradition to have a spiritual ancestor who was associated with darkness and the Underworld.

This also coincides with the research of the Russian scholar Troshchanski on Siberian shamans, who found that the "black" shamans (not evil per se, just those who worked with underworld rather than upperworld spirits) had significantly more gender-crossing behavior. Among the Yakut (who at the time of his interviewing had more "black" shamans than white ones, and assured him that they were just as useful, if more fearsome), most male "black" shamans wore women's clothes as daily dress, dressed their hair in female hairstyles, and had two iron circles sewn on the chest of their ceremonial aprons, symbolizing breasts. As someone who would, if these categories were applied to my tradition, be a "black" shaman, and having seen the high concentration of transsexuality, intersexuality, and other gender-crossing drives among Rökkr spirit-workers, this all falls into place rather ominously. It's not just a "back then" thing. It's a "happening now" thing.

Some people reading this will make an immediate negative connection between "dark" underworld deities and their "perverted" human servants, and find it creepily appropriate in another, less positive way. To this I can only speak from my own personal conviction, which has in turn been strongly affected by the priorities of my patron deities. I can only say that from the point of view of a northern-tradition *ergi* underworld shaman, change is a Good Thing. Rigidity of viewpoint needs to be shaken up, lest it become a false prison. Unquestioned *anything* is bad, and questioning in a spirit of openness can be a holy act. When we call Loki Breaker-Of-Worlds, we mean it as a compliment. Sometimes worlds grow old and stale and need to be broken open, and that includes people's internal worlds. Sometimes defenses grow so rigid that they inhibit all but the most squeezed and crippled growth, and they need to be torn down. Sometimes what was a survival necessity in past times becomes a social liability, and needs to go. If that weren't what the Gods wanted of us, at least periodically, then They wouldn't have made us this way. To be *argr* is to be a catalyst. To be an *argr* spirit-worker is to be a catalyst with all the power of the Gods and wights behind you.

One of the things that struck me when I was reading about seidhr—and especially on the issue of seidhr as being historically considered to be "evil magic" because it could be used to alter men's minds and thoughts—was the term "turn the world upside down". This might be a reference to an earthquake (which would be pretty serious magic) or to changing someone's perceptions so drastically via this mind-altering magic that their world might as well be turned upside down. The phrase struck me so strongly because that's exactly what third gender people do. By our very nature, we turn the world upside down. We are living, walking catalysts, and this is the first mystery of our existence. We turn everything that people think they know about gender—that supposedly safe ground beneath their feet—upside down. We change worlds.

Of course, it's not just Rökkr gods who are picking up *ergi* people. Frey and Freya have always attracted effeminate gay men and some transgendered people, especially those that are involved with explorations of sacred sexuality and sex work, and there seems to have been a spate of *argr* servants of Odin being chosen recently. Most of these are along the female-to-male spectrum, although a few are going in the other direction. They range from women warriors who are fairly "masculine" in their aggression and lack of "frithfulness" (recalling his servants the bloodthirsty Valkyries), to female-to-male transsexuals who have become fully male except for "natural" factory-equipped genitals, echoing the Old Man's most *argr* heiti, Jalkr (Gelding or Eunuch).

Of all the "bright" and "upper-worldly" Aesir gods, Odin is paradoxically the "darkest", as any survey of the rest of his heiti will show. He is a god of the Dead in his own right as leader of the Einherjar, a god of war and frenzied berserker states, a god of sorcery who cohabits with ravens and wolves, a dead man hanged on the Tree. He is also just as *ergi* in his own way as his blood-brother Loki, if less obvious about it. He has also managed to overshadow the *ergi* archetype with the King archetype in most people's eyes, and so avoid being outcast, and thus he is a God of both those in power and those cast out at the fringes, the ruling class and the homeless wanderer. He is a deity of extreme opposites, and so it is not unusual that he takes both uber-manly warriors and *argr* sprit-workers.

So what does this have to do with modern shamanism in the northern tradition? Long ago, after years of living with my intersex condition, when I was first ordered to change my gender by the Goddess who owns me body and soul, I didn't connect it to the phenomenon of shamanism. That was largely because I was ignorant of the entire thing, and wasn't connecting much of anything. When I began to read up on shamanism, the transgender issue hit me like a shock wave. These things weren't separate, they were part and parcel of the same system. Still, I thought, it could just be me. I could be an anomaly.

Then I met, for the first time, another spirit-worker who was also owned by Hela, and had gone through a death-and rebirth process ... and had an intersex condition, and considered herself to be a third-gender being. Then I met a third one of Hela's bootscrapes, who was dealing with transgender issues. On top of that, I made the acquaintance of two spirit-workers dedicated to Odin, of which one was a female-to-male transsexual and one was a very gender-transgressive woman. (And yes, there have been more since; we keep cropping up.) It was when we began to exchange knowledge that it all came together: the taboo that we, needing a word to describe it, call *ergi*. Yes, there are a lot of different possible connotations for that term, some of them extremely unflattering (which we believe came from a later and much more homophobic and sexually conservative era), but the word still rings through us. This taboo needs a name, and this is as good as any.

These words—*ergi (n), argr (adj)*—are Old Norse terms that we are using to refer to a specific constellation of shamanic-power behaviors, which include the following:

1) Gender-transgressing behavior, from partial cross-dressing to full social gender change;

2) Gender-transgressing sexual activities—for example, men receiving penetration, or women giving penetration or having nonpenetrative sex;

3) Being public about these activities and accepting the social taboos (including being outcast or marginalized) that come with them. One can see this reflected in the shaman's position as not having to accept the taboos of either men or women in their culture, but having an entirely different set all to themselves.

These three things seem to reoccur together in tribal cultures around the world, creating an international sprinkling of third-gender spirit-workers. It seems to be a taboo, or set of taboos that go together, and bring great power at the cost of being even further set apart from other people. (For more information on spirit-work taboos, see *Wyrdwalkers: Techniques of Northern-Tradition Shamanism*.)

You'll notice that I'm not using the words "gay" or "lesbian" or "homosexual" or even "sexual preference". That's because the phenomenon of *ergi* is not centered around those things, although most people confuse them terribly. An individual can be *argr* and be interested in all sorts of people sexually—male, female, in between, all of the above. Being *argr* is not about who you want to be sexual with. It's about who and what you are when you're with them, and what you're doing with them, and if it turns social gender and sexual taboos on their heads.

There's a lot of supposition and argument among intellectuals about the "true" meaning of *ergi*, but as usual none of them are actively researching it rather than just vaguely theorizing. For many of us spirit-workers, it's not just a theory. We need a word for this thing that we are and do (for it's both something we are and something we do), and we see the echo of this same power/blessing/curse/wiring/energy/sacredness in those brief glimpses of the ones called *ergi*, and whether the researchers like it or not, that word is where our paths lead us.

First, gender-transgressing behavior. When this moves from shameful pastime to hobby to identity to spiritual path, it ceases to become a private thing. For the spirit-worker with the *ergi* taboo, it isn't enough to be third-gendered internally. You have to be visibly different in that way as well, whether it's only that your ceremonial costume has strong elements of clothing that is socially acceptable only for a sex different from the one that you most appear, or that you must act in a way that is deliberately gender-inappropriate. Your gender transgressing has to be evident to everyone who comes to see you in your professional capacity, and you may never deny it when asked.

For myself, when I lived as female I went through a phase of being very butch, especially when I stopped shaving off my chin hair and lived for a time as a bearded woman. Then when I started taking testosterone and shapeshifting my body, it quickly swung to the other side of the apparent-gender pendulum. I went from being a masculine-acting woman to being a somewhat effeminate man, without actually changing my behavior. (Funny about that.) The wights for whom I work did not allow me to "complete" my gender change, insisting that my genitals stay a mixture of both. I am not allowed to be either wholly man nor wholly woman, but always somewhere in between. I also found that once I passed perfectly as male on the street, I was compelled to wear skirts (something I'd eschewed during my butch-female years) as part of my ceremonial costume, and sometimes my daily wear as well. It was as if I needed that reminder of femaleness to balance out my masculinity.

There is no one right way to do the first part of the *ergi* taboo, except that it must be visible and apparent, at least whenever you are doing anything to do with shamanic stuff. No one who knows that you are a spirit-worker should have any doubt that you are also third-gendered in some way. Whether that moves into physically changing your body or not is your own decision, and you will have to make that depending on your own bodily comfort. Further advice on this matter is contained in the "Letter to Transgendered Spirit-Workers".

Second, sex. Most of society today assumes that being transgendered is about sex, or sexual preference—that it's sort of "the far end of gay", as it were. Transgendered people, and especially transsexuals, will tell a different story; any given transperson may be attracted to men, women, and/or other transfolk, as I said above. Sex isn't part of gender identity, they will say, and I'll say it too, when I'm talking purely about transgender as a biological phenomenon. On the other hand, here I'm talking about the *ergi* taboo, which is a spiritual phenomenon, and as with all those sorts of thing it's never so simple and clear-cut. Sex is most certainly a part of this constellation of taboos, and it has to be sex that is gender-transgressive as well, whatever that means in the context of one's society and gender-role programming.

For anyone living as male in this culture, that usually does include being penetrated, if only astrally. In our culture as in Migration-era Scandinavia, there is still a cultural superiority around being penetrated; it's seen as female—and therefore automatically passive and definitely lesser, something that takes away from the "superior", active manhood. That lack of being willing to be penetrated physically easily runs over into unwillingness to be penetrated emotionally, mentally ... and spiritually. This is a problem when it comes to spirit-work, even if you're not being used as a horse. The qualities of openness, receptivity, and submission are important ones to master if you're going to go down this path, and being sexually penetrated—by another person, by a sacred object, by a deity—is a fairly sure-fire way to get there.

We've also discovered that if you are wired for it—and if you are third-gender, it's highly likely that you are wired for it—anal penetration, done correctly and ritually, can be used as a sacred-sexuality tool for psychic Opening. This seems to work equally well regardless of what kind of body you have and what direction you're going in; as many female-to-male people have reported this as male-to female, perhaps because anal penetration is gender-nonspecific and could even be used as a way to stimulate *litr* and sexual energy for people who do not use their genitals due to dysphoria, or have had them entirely removed (as some ancient historic third-gender groups did), or had too much nerve damage due to surgery. (More information on this technique can be found in the book *Dark Moon Rising*, published through Asphodel Press.) I have no reason to doubt that our ancestors figured this out as well, and indeed all the historical fuss over anal penetration and its association with *ergi* and seidhr would seem to bear that out.

On the other hand, if you're female-bodied and living in a female role, and penetration is what's for breakfast in your normal sex life, ordinary vaginal penetration is not going to do the trick when it comes to accessing the considerable power that is the *ergi* groove in the

Universal web. This was brought home to me by a conversation with a woman who was working with *argr* energies as a method of mind-altering sex magic while still in a heterosexual relationship with her male partner. During these periods of ritual sex, she would refuse penetration, but would instead have him perform oral sex on her for long periods of time. For the two of them—and the culture in which they'd both been raised—one-way oral gratification was something women did for men, not vice versa; to switch roles in this way was to cast an aspersion on the man's manhood and to put the woman in the dominant (and therefore, according to the culture in which their libidos had been programmed, masculine) role. It was very clear to her that she'd hit that groove, because it worked, and it had that certain *argr* feeling.

Other female-bodied people I've spoken with have gone further and accessed that taboo by creating a strap-on phallus and charging it ritually. The trick here is to be able to insert and embody one's astral penis into the artificial one (this technique, too, is described in *Dark Moon Rising*), and use it for masturbation or the penetration of others. If done right, this is a straight shot through to the *ergi* power, and it's something that most female-bodied folk who are naturally *argr* will be able to figure out quickly on their own. Some combine this with anal penetration, if it's seen as a "male" thing to them.

I'll now take a quick tangent, because the reader has no doubt noticed that I'm doing a lot of mentioning of social sexual taboos from different cultures. We don't live in the same culture as any of our ancestors, nor are we raised with their taboos, or those of early tribal (or in most cases, modern tribal) societies. We were likely also raised in a variety of different cultures with regard to what we were taught was sexually acceptable/unacceptable and masculine/feminine. Why does this variable social programming count? All I can say to that is: Because it does. It doesn't matter what messages you internalized around these things, it only matters that you violate them, because that releases huge amounts of archetypal power.

In this way, the *ergi* taboo strongly echoes one of the pillars of Indian Tantra, where violating sexual taboos are encouraged as part of the power of sex magic. In early Tantra, vegetarian initiates were made to eat fish and meat as part of a "love-feast" before partaking of ritual sex; the breaking of the flesh-eating taboo not only symbolized the male and female energies, but also paved the way to breaking the sexual taboos (sex with someone not one's wife, not for procreation, and not in an "ordinary" position) that were to follow. Tantric yogis were not the only ones to realize that the breaking of sexual taboos created power, although they did not (as far as we know) go so far as to break sexual gender taboos, which is an even greater "offense" and thus a greater power source. That's the job of those of us who were born wired to do it.

Doing it publicly—which can simply mean being known to do such things and not denying it when forthrightly asked—is a greater "offense" still, and thus multiplies the power. Far from making one "passive", it requires a huge amount of courage and endurance. Today, in the country and society in which I live, the numbers of transgendered people who are being violently murdered in the streets is rising to a frightening rate. To defend ourselves not from insult, but from violence and death, we who walk the *ergi* line need to band together and be proud, and watch each others' backs. We should go down neither to the blows of others, nor the blows of socially-induced self-hatred. As one such spirit-worker said to me, "I realized that this is a perfectly reasonable way for a shaman to be, as we have been this way all over the world for many thousands of years."

That brings us to the third pillar of *ergi*—being the outsider, the outcast. The idea that social extremity brings shamanic power is well known in shamanic societies, and even non-shamanic societies. Part of what we do as spirit-workers is to see the larger picture, and where our tribe sits in that framework. In today's world, that means sorting through all the cultural pressures brought to bear on men, women, and those not wholly in either camp. You can't see that clearly unless you are outside of it, and stepping outside is not something done lightly … because you can't go back. You may see things that outrage you, or at least make you profoundly uncomfortable, and after that the shoes of "normal" will never fit again. It is a "higher" perspective—not in the sense of being more morally elevated, but in the sense of being someone perched in a high place, seeing farther, looking at the people walking down the narrow road and seeing only what is in front of them, and knowing what is coming before they do.

As discussed in the very beginning of this book, and the third book in this series, it is the shaman's Wyrd to be both the outsider—an important position—and the servants of those very people who may fear and keep their distance from them. The *ergi* taboo seems to reinforce the former side of that equation, and it will take a lot of work and creativity on the part of the spirit-worker not to give up on the second part—because that way lies disaster, just as surely as refusing the call. It is our Wyrd to live both as the outcast and the spiritual center simultaneously, and it is our *orlog* to figure out how to do that in a modern society that no longer remembers this, by triggering older memories of who we are, or creating new ones. It's a challenge that has already killed many of us. We must not dishonor their memories by giving up ... and besides, the Gods believe that we can do it, and they wouldn't have chosen us, each one of us, if they believed otherwise. Their trust is our Road, and we have to walk it.

> In *Skirnirsmal*, there is mention of an *ergi*-rune, which either causes one to become ergi, or validates the existing condition. Fairly sure that this was a bind rune of some sort, I went off to find out which runes were bound up in it, using my method of asking each of the rune spirits in turn, and drawing from my bag the right ones. I was amazed at how quickly they came forth and went together ... but then again, I'm fairly *argr* myself, so I suppose it was to be expected—like coming to like. It is a bind-rune of Inguz, Mannaz, Nauthiz, and Ior, looking rather like an Inguz boundaried between two vertical lines, with another vertical line in the center.
>
> First, you draw a Mannaz—these things have a proper order, you know—which is the handfasted man and woman, the male/female pair that build all society, and the symbol for society itself. Then you draw the Inguz in over that, symbolizing sacrifice—the castration both physical (Ing-men were castrated before being killed, giving their fertility to the Gods) and social

(becoming alien, different, never quite the same).

Then two Nauthizes are drawn in, facing in different directions. Not-man, not-woman. They are the commitment, the wall that is put up, the fact that once *ergi*, you can never go back to being blindly, blissfully normal. Yes, they also acknowledge the hostility that you will get from your community, as you go about messing up their careful, safe, false categories. Finally, the Ior is drawn in the middle—the symbol of the Snake who has been our patron in many cultures—one thinks of Tiresias, Athena, Ariadne and Dionysos, Shiva, and of course the fluidly-gendered Jormundgand—and the rune of all boundaries and liminal states. It is fitting that it is in the middle, and that it is drawn last, as we accept who and what we are, and what that all entails for our work and our existence.

Can I cast it on other people? You bet I can. What will it do? Well, if there is anything in their brain-wiring that might be termed hidden gender issues, they'll come out in all their flaming glory and torment the person until they do something about it. Maybe someone close to them will come out with it, forcing them to deal with it there. If there isn't anything like that in their lives, the rune will look for some other comfortable social assumption they've based their mental existence on, and tear it down. It's a dangerous rune. It changes people ... just like we do.

–Ari, spamadhr

I should now stop and disclaimer that not all spirit-workers are *argr*, nor do they need to be. We all have our sets of taboos with which we gain power. This is simply one set that has attracted a lot of attention through the ages, and that is particularly socially difficult. However, it does predispose someone to be better than usual at certain sorts of spirit-work skills. In a very real sense, spirit-work is the only job for which being somewhere between male and female is actually an advantage. That's why there are so many of us doing it.

There is a strong link between shapeshifting and *ergi*, and with good reason. Being born with hardwired neurological gender dysphoria has a dramatic effect on the astral body. Most primary transsexuals, when asked, will admit to having intense experiences of "phantom limb syndrome" from childhood, only for them it was a matter of having phantom genitalia that were not the ones that they were born with. This dissonance caused them a great deal of psychic pain, usually leading to a significant amount of dissociation from the body.

When used to refer to a severed limb, the phenomenon of phantom limb syndrome is fairly well explained by science—the brain doesn't know that the limb isn't there any more, and the parts of the brain that would be receiving sensation from there are still giving off signals. On an astral level, it's been explained by energy-workers as the fact that the physical limb may be gone, but the astral one is still there. Some people with phantom limb syndrome have been able to continue the phenomenon indefinitely (instead of having it fade out over time) by moving their astral limb on a regular basis, so that the brain doesn't decide that the limb has finally withered or become paralyzed. It's a good example of a phenomenon that exists at the crossroads of the physical and the astral. Similarly, someone afflicted with gender dysphoria is both born with a brain that expects to be attached to a body of a different sex, and continually gives out distress signals about the situation ... and an astral form that differs jarringly from the physical body that it is attached to.

To grow up with such dissonance leads, as pointed out earlier, to mental dissociation from the physical body. Unlike dissociation due to abuse or trauma, in the case of gender dysphoria the individual is actually coping, on an energy level, with a serious difference between *lich* and *hame*, something which (especially as a child) they may have no idea how to articulate, much less work with. But when such an individual begins to experiment with separating their *hame* from their *lich* and moving it about, they'll discover that they are better at it than someone who has gone their entire life with seamless coordination between the two. "Which fish discuss water?" goes the Zen proverb, and the answer is: "The drowning ones." If the only way that you can survive mentally is to become more aware and more identified with (even if only on an unconscious level) your astral body than your physical one, that's a powerful training ground for being aware of what most people ignore.

In a very real sense, many shamanistic techniques are about using states of mind which would be dangerous and damaging when induced unwillingly and unexpectedly into the inexperienced, and learning to control them and induce them carefully as tools, thus (ideally) avoiding the ill effects. In this way, the mental and astral dissociation of gender dysphoria becomes a useful tool for journeying, pathwalking, preparing to receive spirits, and of course shapeshifting.

There is the ancient Germanic rhyme, "Call me Varg, and I'll be Arg"—call me a wolf, and I will be *argr*. As this rhyme suggests, being able to change species is closely akin to being able to change gender, to the point where if you do one, it's assumed that you can do the other. Changing your astral gender is an excellent intermediate step to changing your astral species—if you've got the kind of brain that can do it without a huge shock to your self-image. Ideally, the *ergi* shaman should be able to function while astrally male, female, or somewhere in between, regardless of where their physical form is at any given time.

There's also that an actual physical sex-change is a form of shapeshifting—in fact, it's probably closer than almost anyone in this culture ever comes to going through that process embodied. It's especially shamanistic in the sense that it is done with mind-altering substances (hormones—and anyone who claims that they aren't mind-altering hasn't ever lived through changing them from one type to the other from week to week), pain ordeals (surgeries), and involves the death of the old identity and the rebirth of a new one. For someone who isn't a spirit-worker, going through this process is the closest that most people will come to something paralleling a shamanic death-and-rebirth process. For *argr* spirit-workers who are called to this change—and not all will be—it will almost certainly be a very literal part of that process.

It's an act of magic to watch one's flesh shift from male to female or vice-versa. Spirit-workers who have taken this path have discovered, like I did, that astrally shapeshifting can speed the physical process along. Some claim that this shapeshifting, especially when it is fueled by the energy of gender-transgressive sex, can work small physical changes in that direction without the aid of hormones, by magically manipulating the body's own endocrine substances. This would be a way of harnessing the Path of the Flesh for the purposes of shapeshifting, and it is a technique that needs more experimentation by willing volunteers.

There's also a death and rebirth aspect, whether we like it or not, in the fact that we change our identities. Even for those who don't change their physical bodies or the letter on their driver's license, there will be a transition of sorts—at least, if you're a spirit-worker, a transition will be enforced by the Gods—from being a publicly gender-normative person to being a publicly non-gender-normative person, in whatever way you are required by Them to manifest that. This will lose you a lot of actual or potential friends and allies. It may lose you your entire blood family. It may lose you partners, jobs, housing, automatic respect, and community status. Since we have no social position for spirit-workers, it can leave you more or less an outsider.

However, things are different now than they used to be in ancient times. First, there are exponentially more people around, period. Second, communication is such that we may connect with hundreds of people who live nowhere near us, unlike our ancestors who probably only met a few hundred people in their entire lives, if that. An *argr* member of a tribe might go their whole lives without meeting another such individual, or might at best only know one or two. If they lived in a large city, there might be half a dozen. Today, population and communication is such that I can personally connect with three or four hundred transgendered individuals, and see twenty of them regularly. (There is also the fact that the incidence of intersexuality and transgender is increasing with every generation, largely due to endocrine-disrupting chemicals in the environment, but that's another book's subject.) There are enough of us that we are now a tribe unto ourselves, should we choose to be one. The day that we named ourselves a Tribe was a turning point in the world's Wyrd, and it reverberated through the tapestry. Several of the Gods heard it, and became interested, and got involved. There is no turning back now. We claimed every person who lives in whatever way between male and female as members of our tribe, even if they have no idea about it, and so it has begun.

Like all tribes, we have honored ancestors. Most of us are sterile or do not bear children for other reasons, and many of us are cast out from our blood kin. Right now the murder rate of transgendered people is appallingly high, going from one to two a month just on this North American continent. It may also be rising, although some attribute the escalating rate to better reporting of deaths that are already occurring. Some members of the population want to wipe out our very existence, and they attempt it in the streets and in our homes with fatal beatings, shootings, and stabbings. There are also those *ergi*-folk who go mad from the strain of constant discrimination, and take their own lives in the struggle. Some lived lives of secrecy, in and out of the military of centuries ago, with no one ever knowing that their bodies, under clothing and uniforms, were not what others expected. A few lived long and became elders, passing on their wisdom.

These are all the honored ancestors of our tribe, some fallen in battle and others living to the end of their days. Regardless of whether you have a connection to your blood ancestry, if you belong to our tribe, you can rightfully call upon them for aid, and they will answer, and claim you. However, there is a price. The Dead of our tribe are angry. They are tired of seeing their children fall young and alone in the streets, and they say that this must stop. If you call upon them, you join in the obligation to protect your tribe, by whatever means you have.

(For information on who the honored warrior-dead of our tribe might be, in order that you may call their names, I suggest checking the website at http://www.gender.org/remember/ and making a list. The holiday for the honored Dead of our tribe is November 20th.)

Being Ergi
by Lydia Helasdottir

Yes, you have to be in the middle, you can't be at one end of the gender continuum or the other, and you have to do things that are averse to societal norms. Sex is involved too, the taboo-breaking of sexual gender roles. There's a huge amount of power in breaking taboos anyway, but especially these. Ergi is something that you are, not something that you do. It's not an easy road at all. I was born with hugely excessive amounts of testosterone from my mom taking fertility drugs; testosterone poisoning from the womb onwards. I came in being genetically female, physically in-between, and mentally about 2/3 female, 1/3 male at all times, which is a kooky space to be in.

There was taboo and power in that from the very beginning. From the age of about 12 on, my mom said, "You know, not everybody's like you." I think what she meant was that we had lived all over, and we had just moved to a small village in Holland where everyone had lived five generations in the same street, so they just didn't get us. But I took it on a much deeper level, because I was just realizing that not everybody did things that I did. Does that mean I'm abnormal? I had no idea, at the time.

I struggled with it a lot. I didn't want to transition to male, because that isn't me. I'm both, and I want to be 50/50 in that third space, but I find that I can swing either way in terms of who I'm being, and what my energy system has got on any given day. We have this running joke, when I have to deal with corporate guys—that we all slapped our dicks on the table and mine was the biggest one of all, and I'm the only "woman" in the room. But it meant that I had to get used to being the outsider. I was the outsider for a number of reasons—not being from wherever we were living, having a weird sexual orientation, being masculine ... the best thing that could happen to me at that point was that someone would mistake me for a boy, because then it would validate the fact that I was both. It gave a lot of access, strangely enough, to being ambiguous about who I was—which was good, because it let me out of the social role, and once I accepted that I was ambiguous about my gender identity, then I could also be ambiguous about all the other social expectations, like being a nice person and not drinking people's blood and stuff like that.

And then I found that there's just simply a lot of power in it. I like that a lot; it's an exciting, life-affirming thing to me. It's powerful partly because it's just perverse to societal norms. If you consider that all fixed structures are potential power, then when you knock down a tower, the energy released is huge, because of all the potential power that went into building it up comes exploding out. Societal structures hold a huge amount of power, and when you break that by being unusual, or having unusual proclivities—and particularly in doing it in a ritual or magical or spiritual context—you get a huge rush of power. Also, from being able to mingle male and female energy in me, and have all of the bits working on an energetic level at once, it gives not only a different power level, but also a different flavor that you cannot achieve otherwise. Baphomet has got both, and uses all of it, and all of it is functional. It's the power contained in the double wand of power, the dual phallus. All these things are only available to people who can do both, or at least have some kind of ability to get into the space where unusual sexuality is happening.

And just to seduce otherwise really straight people, and for them to realize three-quarters of the way down the road all of a sudden that "Oh! But this is so abnormal!" but they still want to do it! It is natural for even a fully female-identified female to have a strong reaction to my maleness, but because I don't come in a form that they're used to having a physical attraction towards, they don't really realize it until it's too late. Then it's like Wile E. Coyote running off the edge of the canyon cliff, and then he looks around, and only falls when he realizes that he's run off the cliff. And there's a lot of power in that, too. There's a fear moment in that about what will the neighbors think, and or if I do you, what am I? Am I queer now? If I was entirely female and a girl did it with me, that just makes her queer. But given that I'm a bit of both, what does that make her? What part of you am I attracted to, and what part did I have sex with?

I have functional female bits, although quite larger than normal by a long way. But my astral bits, my energy bits—I have both, and funnily enough I can actually be in a female space but use the male astral bits, the phallus, even though being female. Hela taught me that trick. She can have a phallus, but it's a female phallus, a very strange thing. And similarly, I can be in a male space and use my vaginal opening. One of my favorite weird twisted things has been to imagine that I was a boy imagining that I was a girl, because then the fantasy is fulfilled by the female bits. That I find a very healing experience to have. One could do it the other way around, too, if one has the boy-bits that one doesn't really like, that aren't sufficient to cover the whole spectrum. I've found that this is beyond even being a 50/50 mix; it's something that has become something else altogether.

I was forced to learn to stay in my body, even with dysphoria. That staying in the body with a dislocated kneecap was a lesson in that as well. When it first happened, I said, "Oh, this is going to be OK, I'll just disassociate." Tink. Tink. Tink. It was like there was a bell jar around me; I couldn't get out of my body. But dissociating from gender dysphoria does have advantages; it teaches you that you don't need to stay gendered ... or human. If you can have a phallus, you can have wings, or claws. But actually, for me it went, if I can have wings I can have a phallus. If I can have claws that really, functionally do something to someone, and make them feel it ... then I can do it with a dick.

The two poles of ergi sex magic seem to be about being stone, or getting buttfucked. Being stone forces you to use the astral bits rather than the physical ones—I'm stone with everyone except Joe. Relying on the astral bits rather than the physical ones, I find that really brilliant because you just don't get involved with all the usual boy meets girl (or girl meets girl or boy meets boy) contexts, which have all the ordinary sexual decisions and roles that limit you. As soon as genitals get touched, it tends to get complicated. Anal sex opens you right up, if you're ergi and you're wired for that sort of thing. And everyone has an asshole, regardless of gender. It makes a channel that goes right up and out the top of your head, opening you up.

There's a point that is like being a species that never had two genders; they just are, and when they come together with new ones, they just are. I got a lot of that from doing sexual but non-carnal energy exchanges with people that didn't even involve astral genitals, it involved hands and exchanging energy through the hands. Because it was just not focused on the genitals at all, it was relieved of the polarity that goes with bits, and it just became a very swirling kind of energy, like a yin-yang with a million fractal yin-yangs inside of it, and all these little polarities going on, just little dynamos that didn't determine the nature of the interaction at all.

I understood at a very young age what it was to be sexually penetrative, even though it wasn't done with a penetrative organ made of flesh. In a way, you're piercing someone with the experience of sex with you. The meat may be coming in one direction, but the actual energy penetration, and the strong experience, goes the other way. For me, it's like putting a plug in the socket. All the electricity comes out of the socket into the plug, end of story. You might stick the plug physically into the socket, but everything important goes in the other direction, out of the socket and into the plug and down the wire. So that was my concept of sexuality from the beginning.

Tales of a Transsexual Norse Pagan Spirit-Worker
by Linda Demissy

I have three patron Deities: Loki, Freya, and Lofn.

Loki, God of Change, Humor, and Sex-Changing, is the one who is training me to do spirit work by putting me in situations where I have to figure out what to do, and gain the necessary skills to fix the problem. He started that with abducting my raccoon spirit-friend into another world, thus giving me the choice of learning to journey to get him back, or of using the now empty raccoon skull to make a stang for travelling to the nine worlds. Either choice is fine with him, as in both cases, I get skill in traveling to other worlds for future errands. He doesn't seem to believe in classrooms much. And as God of Change, having lots of choices is a good thing. As a hypnotherapist, creating change in people is what I do best, and so I think he's pretty happy with my day job. I seem to have an almost magical knack for helping people change.

Freya, Goddess of Desire and Women's Magic (*seidhr*), has told me that she'll have work for me to do later. I am almost sure that she is waiting for me to have my sex change surgery and be anatomically female before setting me to work for her. In my mind, Freya is a goddess of desire, and I think of *seidhr* magic as seducing the world into doing what you want, rather than imposing your will with *galdr* magic. So while her brother Frey is about the having of abundance, she's more about the desire that motivates you to get it.

My third is Lofn, Goddess of Forbidden Loves and Passions. The sum of her lore is about 3 lines in the Prose Edda, and so most Norse Pagans tend to ignore her. Arranged marriages aren't the norm anymore, so why would she be relevant? But if you think about it more carefully, aren't there forbidden loves today, of a different kind? Loves that are socially unacceptable? Passions that are called perversions? I should think the big battles raging right now for and against gay marriage should make it clear that there are still "forbidden loves" today. And what about bisexuals, who are treated as traitors by both straights and gays? And of course, there's all the BDSM relationships, kinks and fetishes. You can find them all in Lofn's realm in the Dreaming, in trance journeys, or during sleep. She's not just about forbidden relationships, you see. She's also about forbidden passions, such as crossdressing, and even simple fetishism for wearing panties, as well as the need to transition to the other sex. If it's a forbidden or socially unacceptable passion (in a given society), then it's part of Lofn's realm.

Lofn helps me directly with my day job, and I've learned quite a bit about her from how she's interacted with my clients as a guide. Lofn's name literally means "permission". A lot of what I do is really about giving people permission to be themselves, and to encourage them to do what they want to do with their lives. Permission is also the central concept for hypnosis: without consent, nothing can be done. This is also true of therapy, as you cannot change someone who does not want to be changed. Another name for this concept is "acceptance", something that many transgendered people badly need to give themselves, as they are often wracked with guilt and shame about their irresistible need to manifest gender-transgression. I think all queers wrestle with that to some degree, and Lofn is the one most capable of helping with that.

For devotions and magic, I consider the key to be her symbol, as well as her magical tool. I see it as an old-fashioned silver key with a golden glow, and I also have a old key like that among my magical tools. For statuary, what I found is a woman showing the way in through an archway or door. It's meant to hold a picture, and I got it at the Las Vegas airport (made for the Monte Carlo hotel). She has asked me to collect flower petals, and has explained they were to be put "on the path". I'm still not clear on what she meant, but I assume laying down flower petals would be good to consecrate a place to her influence, or call her to a place where her magic is needed.

And where does all that leave me? Well, my main spiritual talents are for seership, and I was told by two other seers to get in touch with my ancestor spirits. I've since started talking to one who is responsible for managing the gifts of seership for my family line. However, the situation is complicated by the fact that this bloodline talent is exclusively reserved for women of my family ... and I'm sort of in between. So I'm only getting part of the package, and she says I'll be getting more of it after my sex change surgery, which is about 2 months away for me now.

You see, I transitioned to living full time as a woman 15 years ago when I was 21, took hormones briefly and stopped because I thought they were causing problems with my health (I just had an incompetent endocrinologist), and put the surgery plans on the back burner, having no money for it anyway. In my 20's I practiced ADF Druidism with a Norse focus in a grove that I had founded, until the group closed in 1999. During that time I sought to learn mediumship and trance possession, to be able to learn directly from the gods what the scholarly sources omitted. But after the grove closed, I had about 6 years of getting the divine answering machine: "Please say your prayer at the sound of the beep, and place your offering into the designated slot." I'd occasionally get vague hints about what to do from Freya, and when I didn't carry them out because I didn't understand, she'd ignore me for 6 months to a year. After a while, I pretty much gave up on trying to talk to Them, and focussed on my work with transgendered people, getting occasional hints from Lofn when she helped clients through me. And while I didn't get direct orders during those 6 years, I suddenly found myself interested in doing things, which *seemed* to be my ideas at the time. For instance, belly dancing lessons were my idea, but the exotic dance lessons I started two years ago weren't. How is me knowing exotic dance useful to the gods? Beats me. I'm also pretty sure learning to weave on a loom wasn't my idea, either.

Many years went by, and then I had a penetrative sexual experience that blew my mind, and prompted me to start hormones again and to sign up for genital surgery. Then, suddenly, my patrons started talking to me again, and for the first time, asking me to do things! I was very excited, after so many years of silence. Were they waiting for me to resume my transitioning before guiding me to peers and teachers? Or did they decide to give me a push to get on with the next phase of my life? Either way, my transitioning and my returning to active status as a spirit-worker seem to be intimately connected with each other. In my 20's, I was trained for two years as the apprentice of the guardian of my city, who has since moved to another province. I wondered if I should take up the job again. The answer I got was basically: "We shouldn't have to tell you to do the right thing." In other words, it's my choice, but the job does need doing, and they'll approve of it if I do. Divination indicated I should wait till Beltane before officially taking on the job, and that there would be challenges in the meantime. At the very least, I'll need recovery time, and be out of commission for a while after my surgery in January.

So what does it mean to me to be a third gender spirit worker? It means being a betweener, being and understanding both sides, but never completely. It means having experienced what it feels like to ride my brain on male hormones, and then on female hormones, and realizing I make more sense to myself on female hormones. It's understanding being obsessed with sex, and able to utterly ignore emotions to focus on a goal on the boy side. It's having too many emotions at once to be able to understand them, and knowing you're being completely irrational on the girl side, but that it will pass. It's understanding how two very different types of humans feel and think, while being both and neither. Perhaps that helps in understanding how non-humans think.

Shamans are living bridges between the spirit world and human world. We who are between genders are living bridges between men and women. The only problem with this metaphor of being a bridge is ... well, people walk all over you while trying to figure out what the other side is rambling about. On the upside, I'm very good at translating boyspeak into girlspeak, and vice versa, for helping couples understand each other. I'm also lucky in that I look very female, and that I live in a city where people usually don't care what you do or what you are.

There is one more aspect that ties into my being third gender, which is being an agent of change. I've been given hints that the ancestress originally responsible for my family's talents was a Norn. There are many Norns of varying ranks and powers, drawn from all the races of the 9 worlds, ranging from the individual lesser Norn guiding a person's soul, all the way up to the big threesome at the Well of Wyrd. And I've come to believe there are two types of Norns, both of whom can see the threads, but who alter them in different ways: I call them Fates and Muses. Fates are the ones who actually decide what is for the greater good, and arrange the threads to make it happen. It's all done behind the scenes. I can see the threads, but I don't know that I can actually alter them. Muses, on the other hand, are the inspirers. They inspire people to act and think in certain ways, but this only works with the person's consent. Which doesn't mean it's necessarily informed consent.

I have found there to be three kinds of Muses: Muses of Desire are those who motivate people to do things, through what they most want to have, do, or be. Muses of Virtue are those who inspire people to act honorably. Some of them do so by promoting the code of conduct of their faith (i.e. Mother Theresa, Gandhi), and others by urging people to follow their own inner wisdom and code of honor. Then there are Muses of Fear, who motivate people with what they fear most. If you haven't guessed it already, I consider myself a Muse of Desire.

On Being A Twenty-first Century Argr Man
by Jálkr

Attaining some measure of understanding about my identity has been a convoluted journey, requiring sleuthing, research, personal introspection and just plain audacity. Any worthy explication of the process is consequently likewise. I don't think using terms of identification from an archaic culture is inappropriate, but I do think it is making a large leap, a justifiable one.

The basics, to establish my credentials: I am a middle-aged female-to-male transsexual, of Anglo-Saxon and Scandinavian ancestry. I have borne multiple children. I am also newly arrived on the Heathen spiritual path, that of my forebears. I decided to embark upon it after careful reflection on my life's purpose. At this point I can only say my Fulltrui, Óðinn, is satisfied with my current understanding, but I am fully cognizant that there is no such thing as reaching a conclusion—with no further striving required—as long as I draw breath. Valföðr tries his votaries to the breaking point, that much I know for sure. Obtaining a sex change at 39 was no easy feat.

I see Heathenry being grounded in pre-existing lore, but influenced by UPG—unverified personal gnosis. Without UPG, all we have is static soul-less artifact. Without pre-existing lore, UPG can take wild flights of fancy. Neither can function without the other.

Neil Price's exhaustively researched *The Viking Way: Religion and War in Late Iron-Age Scandinavia* has been my primary resource regarding historical reference to being *ergi* or *argr*. Of course, Price ties being *ergi* with performance of seið, and I am not a practitioner of seið (yet). What I am, though, is a being of socially stigmatized status whose sexual behavior would definitely be described by many as "deviant", and whose childbearing experiences have definitely affected both my sexuality and my perceptions of things both physical and spiritual.

Socially, I have gone through all the necessary processes to be granted legal status as a man, but they are far from ironclad, and I think most people reading this have a fair idea of just how marginally transsexuals are regarded in contemporary society. My manhood is regarded as suspect, even moreso because I still use my remaining female anatomy, my genitals, as a source of sexual gratification for myself and my partners. I am the frequent and enthusiastic recipient of penetrative sex, not merely of "tab A and slot B" variety, but extremely queer and transcendent unions. Whatever shreds of normalcy I may have once managed to hide behind are really quite irrelevant these days. If anything they underscore just how deviant I have become, in the eyes of society. Just like the *ergi* of old, not a one can meet me or know of me and think that I am "just a regular kind of guy."

I leave you with a personal journal entry from when I was first coming to knowledge:

Back in September I went down to Brown University during their week of Viking-related programming and heard Neil Price, from Uppsala University, discuss Viking Age archeology, cosmology and social structure. In particular, I wanted to find out from this amazing man about the concept of ergi *as it related to gender and sexuality. I ended up buying Price's gigantic tome* The Viking Way: Religion and War in Late Iron Age Scandinavia *and could spend hours in it, prowling around and learning. As an FtM (female-to-male) mother of northern ancestry, I find all this really fascinating and it speaks to me across the ages. I remarked to someone in e-mail today that I feel like a double agent, gender-wise. My physiology and history anchor me to my origins and I will not deny them. Nothing contemporary in the lexicon of identities works as far as encompassing all of it, but honestly, isn't everyone a mix of paradoxes? I'm just a little more weird than others. What a feeling it is, then, to read about these long-dead folk and recognize my spiritual kin.*

Secret Selves
by Steph Russell

For some of us it isn't obvious at first, not even to ourselves. Not because it's not there, not because it's not intensely present, not because the evidence wasn't always visible, but because of internal dishonesty. We lie to ourselves first and then by extension to others, sometimes not even realizing we're doing so. The edifice we construct bit by unintentional bit eventually looms so large in our inner landscape that it becomes constricting in ways that were unforeseen. We rein ourselves in to the point of constructing a virtual prison inside our own beings. Inner revolution is never easy, but coming to terms with my gender identity is admittedly one of the hardest things I've ever had to do. What hurts is that in many respects I blame myself, and rightly so. I can be angry at the world all I want, for all its oppressive density, but I chose to hide. It's difficult to admit. I wasn't always aware I was doing it; in fact the grand majority of the time I wasn't, but in those frightened moments of realization I ran scared from my own nature and stuffed it down into the black depths of my own abyss.

Every time my truth manifested I went into denial so deep I lost track of myself, and instead lived a projection of other peoples' image of me. When I was finally forced to waking and became aware of what I was doing, that person I had made myself into died. I went through a pretty intense grieving process. I grieved for what was easier. I grieved because of the inevitable disappointments I would wreak on others. I grieved for things I thought I should have been and the worth assigned to those things. I lost my sense of self entirely and went through a full-blown identity crisis, even as I saw myself more honestly and clearly than I ever have. I grieved for that lost sense of identity, even though it wasn't real...and at the same time, I grieved for what I've missed out on and what I will never be able to be.

When Hela took me the first time, She gave me a lot of instructions, but the big over-arching one was to integrate. She talked (far more than merely talking, but I don't know how to adequately describe Her communication in a succinct manner) about the various divided aspects of myself and I mulled it over, absorbing Her instruction/revelation. The last instruction was for me to "integrate my male and female sides", or something to that effect; it wasn't so simple as only words or one word for each part of the communication. She talked about how I had stifled myself in so many ways because of my refusal to accept all parts of me. She told me how much more whole and powerful and (words fail for this part, existent in the world?) I would be— more of myself, far more present and even *real*, if that makes sense.

I heard Her and had to acknowledge that something was missing, that I had been hiding things from myself and everyone else. I acknowledged Her rightness, as there was no way for me not to, and agreed to work on things. I did, however, end up pulling from that what I wanted to and told myself later that She wanted me to integrate masculine and feminine traits in myself. That's just not adequate, but I didn't really want to face the depth of what I had been hiding. It took a serious smackdown and a removal of all of my coping mechanisms (read: escapist behaviors) to force me to action.

Even though it has been years since Hela first made Herself clearly known to me, I feel like I am still at the beginning of all this. My transformation has been painful (and of great depth) thus far, and working through my gender issues has been a large part of that. I've had to come to terms with the fact that this has always been a part of me, re-examine my life and all its bits, re-live all the painful parts, go over the points where I went into denial over and over again. I'm very aware of the fact that I'm being re-made and that I'm an active part of the process.

I've always been an outsider. Even in the depths of my denial, that part was obvious and I had embraced it. There was no other way for me to function. I moved around a lot as a child and had a terrible time trying to find a niche. I never identified with either girls or boys in any deep kind of way; girls didn't like me, and I didn't like their toys and games. Boys were sometimes more accepting on an individual level, but my strangeness went beyond mere gender issues. Most of my teachers didn't like me and found me odd, though there were exceptions. Any individual friends I had (and they were few) would quickly turn against me in a group situation. At the same time, even while being an outsider, other people were always terribly obvious to me. I could tell what they wanted, what they were up to, what their frustrations and motivations were. I could tell what bothered them and where all the lines of tension lay. It was easy to tell when differences between people were due to differences in perspective. Gender lines were easy to follow. This understanding has only deepened since starting this process.

Most of the time I feel utterly alien—neither and both, all and none. My exact point on the continuum moves around quite a bit, but my default is squarely in third, or at least I think it is. I'm keenly aware I'm not done with this part of my transformation, perhaps not even over the hump, yet one of the main aspects of my being that separates me from the vast majority of other people also gives me vital insight into theirs. It's just kind of strange realizing that it has always been this way.

Coming out from the transgender closet is doubly difficult

when you are suddenly faced with the fact that you are Owned by a Deity. Any existing intimate relationships are put through a rigorous testing, and significant others quickly become alienated, as they sense they are no longer your primary focus *and* can feel like they are with a person they don't know. Power struggles emerge between them and Deity which leave you feeling like you are in the middle, with the blame squarely placed on your shoulders, simply for being what you are. You can hardly blame the other person, as it's very unlikely they had even considered this possibility and they certainly didn't sign up for it. You might try to desperately balance everything while fighting your way through it, trying to keep your entire world from crumbling beneath you, but crumble away it will. The question is if you can build a new foundation fast enough.

A lot of my work at this point is very tied to my identity as *ergi*. The construction of my tools of power are tuned to this process of transition, so I am very aware of the fact that my being transgendered is an important part of my identity as a spirit-worker as well as a great source of personal might. A lot, though far from all, of the counseling work I have done as a spirit-worker is in relation to transgender issues, which I personally find ironic because I consider myself still only a neophyte in this realm. I can see the work piling up and fleshing out for the next year, and making use of my *ergi* nature is a big part of that.

One of the things that seems to help me most with getting through this process thus far is physically expressing my astral reality in some ways. I was born "female" (a point with which my body argues) in meat-space, but when confronted with an aroused astral form during a lesson I quickly learned that I was not entirely female. That was a bit of a shock, finding myself sitting there with an astral erection, being taught men's mysteries by a shape-shifting God. Soon I was instructed to construct an artificial soft phallus for packing, made of organic materials so as to make it good for projecting into, and something miraculous happened. I quickly learned that if my astral phallus had a place to "sit," I would experience markedly less dysphoria. I wouldn't get as frustrated as easily, and felt more myself, as it were. Soon I added men's underwear and sometimes men's pants. If I neglect to wear my phallus, things get worse again.

Over time I noticed that my energy flows were being changed, as were my sexual needs and my experience of my body, and it all feels a bit closer to "right." Having appropriate sexual outlets helps a lot, and while there is room for improvement for this in my life, I can really tell when I'm getting at least some of what I need. It makes a big, big difference. I'm still learning about what it is that I truly need, as are my partners. In my case, I happen to be a pansexually identified, fluidly third-gendered being, and as such I have a *lot* of needs. It's a tall task to get them all met, especially in meat-space, and I haven't been able to do it yet.

I still don't feel fully "clicked into place." I'm still in the middle of this thing, and n order to get back in, I've had to step completely out. Something that seems to help with this process is having an ongoing conversation with my body. I used to do this from time to time in the first person, but once the gender issues and shaman sickness started to manifest (along with a whole host of ugly internal and external struggles that often left me self-destructive) whatever productive dialogue I used to have ceased. I had to start treating my body as an entirely separate entity and giving zir credence as such.

Initially I referred to ze as she, and that was fine, because ze wasn't really talking back yet. Ze was just giving me little abstract feelings here and there, but even those were helpful. Ze was genuinely afraid of me (and rightly so) because of my inclination toward self-harm, but having a body that is in rebellion against its inhabiting being is difficult and frustrating. I had to actively work at rearranging my thought processes on a cognitive level to help combat the instinctual desire to think about offing myself (like I said, all my old coping mechanisms were forcibly removed.) Once I had done a lot of work there (and frankly, I still have those thoughts from time to time; they're just less intense and far less frequent, thankfully) ze started talking back. First thing was that ze wanted to be acknowledged as not being entirely female zirself.

Now, I am not to my knowledge medically intersexed in any way, but my body wanted that recognition all the same. Granting it to zir has helped us click together better and hopefully over time we will be even more unified. Acknowledgment of zir's needs as sometimes at odds with my wants and needs has proved rather useful, and the dialogue has helped us compromise where needed. I find that ze responds very well to understanding regardless of whether ze gets zir way as well. It might seem odd that causing a seemingly new schism (although it's not really a schism, just a method of

Acknowledgment) in oneself is a way to greater integration, but it's proving useful.

If you are just discovering gender issues in yourself, be prepared for a rough ride. My experience may or may not be typical, but in having extensive contact with others going through the same thing, there are certain similar characteristics of the process we all seem to have to deal with. There will be initially violent swings in self-perception. You may at times truly feel like you've made a mistake and that this isn't you. You will likely experience strong recoils whenever you hit upon some new and deep truth about yourself, especially if it results in some kind of extreme sexual satisfaction. Dysphoria can be devastating and can be triggered by various things—for me, the biggest trigger is an orgasm resulting from imagining myself in a sexual gender role that I can't actually achieve physically in meat-space. Realization that the actual organ isn't there can result in a morbid sense of futility. A sense of impotence and infertility can be devastating, even if you never thought it important previously, or even have any current desire to do anything active with said fertility.

The best advice I was given going into this thing was to "get a good support system." That can be easier said than done, but it's something well worth working at. Join communities and talk with other folks going through similar experiences. Don't cut yourself off from loved ones, despite the inherent danger in being open. Yes, you have to be careful, but this process cannot be stopped. You will either lose them or keep them, and that part is not in your control. Don't deprive yourself of potential support in favor of drawn-out tension and secrecy. If you are really destined to be an *ergi* spirit-worker, who you are will eventually be made entirely public anyway, and that will be part of your power. Learn to see it as power, even in the wondering eyes of others.

An Open Letter To All Transgendered Spirit-Workers

(This letter was put up on my website a long time ago, because I saw too many of us—from many different places and traditions—struggle against what we were supposed to be doing, seeing it as a curse rather than a wonderful necessity. I include it here, in its entirety, because this was the first piece of writing that spoke straight to the other shamans of my people.)

First, before I speak to you of what needs to be said, my sisters and brothers and sister-brothers and brother-sisters, please understand that I am one of you. I am no outsider. I was born female and male in one, I have lived as both, I look male now (clothed, at any rate) but I am and have always been the sacred third inside, no matter what my body was doing at the time.

Second, please understand that when the Gods and spirits took me and killed me and rebuilt me and brought me back and told me that I was a shaman now, their apprentice and tool, one thing was made clear: A shaman always serves a tribe. Without a tribe, they are nothing. And my tribe, I was told, is all of you. Transsexuals, both transwomen and transmen. Genderqueers. Cross-dressers of whatever stripe, fetishistic or otherwise. The normal-looking ones who have an inner female or male so strong that they demand part of their life, especially part of their sexual life. The intersexuals like myself who look in the mirror and know what they are, and want the freedom to be that. The ones who just know, inside, that they are both male and female—not theoretically but intimately, to know with every fiber of your body that you have walked in the world and male and female and something in between. You are all my tribe.

Even if your life path pains or annoys me, you are my tribe—the drug-addicted street queen, the autistic tranny nerd with no social skills, the FNT—fucking neurotic transsexual—who is damaged into insanity by a harsh world—you are all my tribe. Even if you hate me, even if you think that I'm a loon, you are all my tribe. I serve you all, whenever you ask, as long as you acknowledge this in yourself.

But this letter is written to a subset of a subset of a subset, a tiny number of people. I don't even know how many there are of you out there. To be a spirit-worker, to be called by the Gods and/or spirits to destroy your life and be reborn to serve others, to be ridden by spirits, to lose everything and gain this knowledge ... that's a tiny percentage of any population. I'm not talking about the folks who take a weekend class and shake a rattle, the ones who do it part-time, the ones who can say no to it. I'm talking about the ones who have no choice, for whom spirit-work has eaten our entire lives, the ones for whom saying no is impossible because we are already bound by this calling ... and, certainly, the ones who are seeing this calling come down the tracks like a high-speed freight train. I know that it can be terrifying. Believe me, I know.

But if you're transgendered, in *any* way ... and if you've been tagged by the spirits to be a spirit-worker ... you have a double load on you. Transgendered people in the rest of the population have the option of denial. They can ignore their feelings, purge their secret wardrobes, throw away those sex toys, censor their thoughts, bury half their soul in the basement. It's not a wise choice, in my book, but they have the option. We don't. When we are drafted, we give up that privilege. We must deal fully and completely with our gender issues, as quickly and as honestly as possible. It is the first thing on our training, before any drums or rattles or chanting. If we do not deal with it, nothing will go right for us until we do. Period.

If you are not dealing with—and fully living—your sacred gender, then everything that the Gods and spirits will do to you will be about forcing you to come to terms with this. If you resist, if you keep putting it off, things will just get worse and worse. This, too, I tell you from experience. I will also tell you that as soon as you start working to come to terms with it, things will improve, and they will keep improving as you being to fully live it. While this may also be true for transfolk who are not spirit-workers, please understand that when I say that things will just get worse, I mean that you are inevitably risking your life.

Understand that being a spirit-worker means that your life is fair game for meddling, if things interfere with your work. In fact, if anything interferes with your work, it will likely just go away. And since the first step for us is dealing fully with our gender issues, that means that blaming outside influences as a reason for not working with them is a bad idea. The Gods/spirits will not stand for that. What, you can't transition because your job wouldn't like it? Why, that's no problem. We can get that out of the way. There, you're laid off. See, now nothing's stopping you. What, you can't put on a skirt because of your spouse? Here, have some divorce papers. There, now you have nothing to lose. What, you can't do this because of your public reputation? How about a nice mental breakdown in public, right where everyone can see? There, now they all think you're nuts anyway, so you can do what you want.

I'm not joking. I've seen it happen, too many times. It happened to me. Any part of your life that will not support your job will go away. Clinging to it will just make it more painful when They pry it out of your fingers. If you keep resisting even in the face of all this, you will be given the final choice ... come to terms with your gender, or cease to live.

Why do we have to deal with this, first? Because it's a tool. Because it's a power. Because seeing things from both of those sides is an important part of learning to shift shape, to see from other eyes, to walk between worlds. While nontrans people can learn it in other ways, there's no question that we do have something special when it comes to gaining perspective, and I think there's even more to it than that, although that truth is elusive and arguable. But I, and other transgendered spirit-workers, have found that there are special powers and energies and techniques that only we can access. These will be your best tools, eventually.

Our situation is not modern. Any research about shamans and spirit-workers the world over will show unusual numbers of third-gender people. It's the one job where it's an advantage. It's the one area where research can't avoid finding us over and over, from Siberia to the southwest American desert. We transgendered spirit-workers have a long and very public tradition. Generally, when the oppressors wiped out shamanic cultures and tried to convert the shamans to "normal" behavior by their standards, it was us, the third-gender spirit-workers, who chose to die instead. There was no other option for us. There is no other option for us. We must be what we are.

What is it that we have to do, exactly? That depends on who you are. Certainly not all transgendered spirit-workers need to get sex changes, or alter their genitals. The trans continuum is a wide thing. There are those who are far to one end, and who may only feel the need to honor their nature occasionally with clothing and/or certain kinds of sex. There are those far at the other end who feel the need to shift their physical shape entirely. There are those in the middle who may go partway. What the Spirits want you to do is to *find your level and live it fully*. Explore your range of motion, step by step; go further until you hit the point where you get the message, "This is enough. There's no need to go further. This is who you are." You will hit that point, I promise you, wherever it might be. We all do.

So if it means that you need to change your body, then do it. Take the hormones, consider them shamanic mind-altering drugs (they are) that aid shapeshifting (they do). Get the surgeries, if that's what you need: consider them a blood sacrifice to the Spirits, like the Sanguinaria of the Roman gallae, like the Lakota Sun Dance. If you need to keep your body the same but wear certain clothing, do it. If you need to ritually put on a skirt and take it up the ass, do it. If you need to carve a sacred strap-on phallus and thrust it into a willing hole of flesh, do it. If you need to change your name, change your look, change your body, change your life, do it. Don't put it off. You don't have that privilege. Whatever point you fall on, honor it as an integral part of your life and your identity. It is who you are, and it is part of what makes you good at your job. Let no mundane reason stand in your way.

Then you have to live it, and live it publicly. The other option that you are forbidden is that of the closet. You don't have to tell every single person that you meet, but if it comes up, or they ask, you must answer truthfully. You need not make an effort to be seen, but you must make no effort to hide ... and if someone of this tribe needs you, you need to let them know who and what you are. This, too, is found in all the shamanic cultures that talk about us: we must be public about who and what we are, we must be visible, marked out, set apart, that we might be easily available to those who need us. That means that we are targets, which means that we must also be damn brave, and set an example.

One of my jobs, as a transgendered shaman who belongs to a Death Goddess, is to speak for the Dead of my tribe. And, my sister-brothers, my brother-sisters, the Dead of our tribe are angry. They rage, they weep, they cry out. They rage because we are being killed in the streets, because we are turned away when we seek food and shelter and work and health care, because we are ridiculed and often unloved, because we are exiled from our families and clans, because we are beaten down until we break and take our own lives. Because to live in our country is to live in a war zone. Our Dead are angry, and they demand this of us: that as much as we are able, we will do what has to be done to make sure that there are no more fallen in this war. In order to save each other, we must band together and take care of each other, because alone we go down. Hear their cries, if you can. If you are going down this path of serving our tribe, their cries should be audible to you. The Dead are not so hard to call up, if you dare listen. This must not happen again, they say. Hear them.

The numbers of our tribe are growing. More children are born with intersex conditions every year. More teens are evidencing transgendered behavior every year. Like the intersex frogs in the Potomac, affected by pesticide runoff, we swim in a toxic brew of poisons that is, ironically, making more of our tribe. Look for the scientific evidence; it's there. But beyond that, our tribe needs more spirit-workers, of any tradition, to serve them, to take care of our living and our dead. We are needed more than ever, and that's why we're getting drafted in such numbers.

We are needed, my sisters and brothers, my sister-brothers and brother-sisters. Don't fear this Wyrd. Embrace it.

It's not like you have any choice, anyway, so you might as well. And besides, you are so desperately needed.

For the ancestors of our tribe, for our Dead, and for those yet to be born,

Thank you.
Raven Kaldera

Jormundgand's Lessons

I was sitting at the computer, as I had been all evening and well into the night, attempting to concentrate on my work. It didn't do much good. Periodically I would twitch and start, or realize that I had drifted off into a fog and lost several minutes. I'm often one to lose time on daydreaming, but usually I have a nice imaginative full-sensory experience to remember. I don't just fall into blank-mind states; my mind is too busy for that.

Then the urge hit me, strong and hard. "I have to go to the lake," I said aloud.

"Now?" asked my assistant. "It's midnight."

"I have to go to the lake," I repeated, trancelike.

"Then let's go." He'd had too much experience with these things to argue. We drove to the lake in silence, me clad only in a ragged black cotton skirt/loincloth. There didn't seem to be any need for clothing; it was fairly warm, I was cold-hardy, and I knew that any clothing I was wearing would be shucked anyway. I was pretty sure that this was not going to involve just sitting by the water's edge. "Someone's knocking, aren't they?" my assistant said knowingly. "I can tell by the way your aura feels. Like you're full of static electricity."

"I don't know who it is," was all I could say. We parked at the lot at the bottom of the hill; I went up past the locked gate toward the town beach. He stayed in the car, waiting for me. I remember going up the hill, seeing the moonlit lake like a mirror in the gap between the trees, and moving toward it. Then nothing ...

... till I suddenly surfaced, staring at the sky. I was not in control of my body. It was neck-deep in water—I didn't remember going in!—and spinning, spinning around in a circle, fast. How could I move that fast, in the dragging water? The stars spun around and my brain felt squeezed aside, the language circuits missing. No words. Yet something was speaking, saying something, to something else. I was a telegraph pole, a medium for communication that was tongueless, languageless, communicating in images. Then I felt my body sucked down under the water and I prayed, with my last thought before I blacked out again, that whatever it was wouldn't drown me.

I came to underwater, the surface a mere inch above my open eyes. I was lying on my back under the lake's shore. My head rested on rocks; I could see the stars through the distorting water. I panicked, wrenched myself gasping for the surface, sucked air into my starving lungs. Staggering out of the water, I dragged on my ragged skirt and limped back down the hill.

I could not make head nor tail out of the incident at first, but much of that was because large pieces of my brain were still not back on line. I couldn't speak, at first, to the concerned queries of my assistant, except to croak out, "Cold. Big. Cold." In a minute, another word was added; oh, the joy of being allowed sentences! "Big. Cold. Snake."

Hours later, at home in bed, having been fed hot tea and tucked shivering under my covers, I sorted it out. The Great Serpent had moved through me, borrowed my flesh, that much was sure. Whatever I had been used for, I figured it wasn't about me and that I'd never know. Yet the Gods never do anything for only one reason. I still do not know why the Snake was using me to communicate, nor with whom ... but a trace of memory remained in my brain, like a stain on the wall that, squinted at, reveals a runic message.

Jormundgand's lesson to me, left almost as an afterthought on its way through to its unknown, mysterious purpose, was not phrased in words at all. It was entirely images, some with such depth and complexity that putting them even into the most poetic words seems clumsy and superficial. Still, this is my job, whether I like it or not, so I tried to translate it as best I could into the poem-lesson I write here.

Jormundgand's First Lesson

In
Between.

Star and sea.
Light and dark.
Water and wind.
Earth and sky.
Midgard and Not-Midgard.
Not of Midgard,
No longer of Not-Midgard.
The place between,
The point of all perspective,
The way of all clarity.

Clear and not-clear
Clear as an inch of water
Not-clear as the depths of the sea
In
Between
Clear and Clouded
Is where sight begins.

In
Between.

Male and female
The place so much both
That it is neither.
The place where two are not two
Mashed together but still visible
But are one, and have never been other.
Completion. Wholeness that needs no other
To balance it. Only itself.
The place of Third. The place
Of earliest memory, floating in the salt waters
Of birth, this place of perfect balance.
In
Between
One and Other
Is where shape begins.

In
Between.

Here and There.
This is where you start.
If you cannot find this place,
You cannot move anywhere.
This is not here, where you are,

Not there, where you want to go,
And you must know this place,
Intimately, comfortably,
And this means you must know how
Here and There look from this place,
And how you look to the
Upturned downturned faces that watch
When you live in neither.
Do their eyes widen? Do their feet retreat?
Do their lips curl? It matters not,
When you are Here you are part There,
When you are There you are part Here,
But mostly you smell of
In
Between
Touch and Faraway
Is where soul begins.

In
Between.

Beginning and ending.
The perfect circle,
Tail in the mouth,
Eternal spinning of time.
Beyond understanding spins
Sea and sky.
In
Between
The heat that birthed
And the cold that reclaims
Is where we begin.

Jormundgand's Second Lesson

This was the lesson about bindings. As a living boundary, the Snake is the keeper, the mastress, of bindings and boundaries. But there is a catch: the boundary created must be natural. In other words, it must be a boundary that feels right to be there, not one that is forced in place between two struggling parties who are not yet properly unentwined. There are ways to do those bindings, those boundaries, as well ... but they are not the Snake's magic.

I did not at first understand that the small song that was given to me had a purpose, beyond simply honoring the Snake, and the Snake did not bother to make anything clear, if indeed s/he could have done so. However, the spell that eventually dawned on me was incredibly simple. It's about tying a piece of string into a circle around some thing that symbolizes that which is to be boundaried, and singing. Getting permission from the Snake, however, is less simple than it is from most deities. Jormundgand will only deal with certain sorts of folk, and I am not quite sure what hir criteria consists of.

Jormundgand's Song

> Serpent bound, wound around,
> Holding all the world within your coils,
> Serpent bound, wound around,
> Turning through the ocean's shining waves,
> Serpent bound, wound around,
> Ring the world with power like a wall,
> Serpent bound, wound around,
> At the cost of your freedom Midgard's saved.

Blood And Fire: The Ordeal Path

There are no bindings holding her up against the ash tree, because she is here of her own free will. She had asked to be bound, to hold her against her fear and keep her from bolting off into the woods, but the one to whom her mentor had handed her over had refused her even that. "You'll stand for it under your own power, or you shouldn't be taking this on," he said. So here she is, in the dark, standing under the trees on the land of some Rökkr shaman who scares her just to look at him, her arms wrapped around the rough bark and her forehead pressed into it. She feels the tree's energy thrumming beneath her. It is a comfort.

This is only the first of nine ordeals that He has said she must endure. He needs His warriors strong and knowledgeable about the dark places, and after all, He spent nine years seeking out the Ordeal Path, culminating in His time hanging on the Tree close to death. What's a little mortal pain, to Him? The Tree ... she clings closer to the ash bark, wondering if He felt bark against His skin, when the time came.

But this is not that time. This is only the first one, the one to honor the ancestors in Hel's land, and it is Hel's shaman who initiates her, because besides Him, it is the Rökkr who understand this path the best. To learn it, she must go into their lands of darkness and learn their painful mysteries, and like Him, she will take that knowledge away and use it herself someday, perhaps on some young man ulfhednar-bound who will stand as she stands, hanging onto a tree—a Tree—for dear life, waiting for the pain.

The first touch comes, and it makes her flinch, but it is just a gloved hand between her naked shoulder blades. "Breathe," *the voice behind her says.* "Breathe in between every stroke, and out after each one. Breathe in the rune, let it come into your body, let leave what must leave." *Then the hand is gone, and she is alone in the dark, and he begins to sing in a voice that rips through the air. It is a rune song. She flinches, even before the whip falls, from the pounding of his galdr. Then the first blow falls, and she knows Pain.* Feoh, *she whispers. The rune sings into her, on the song, on the pain, green and gold and abundant, beaten into her soul by way of her body. Not just a sigil, a divinatory symbol, but a spirit ... one who will ally with her now, because it has been blown through her skin and her shields.*

Almost before she can remember to gulp breath again, the second line of the song comes and the second blow. Ur. *It comes into her like a great grey bolt, out of her like a grunt. Then the next*—Thorn—*remember to breathe! and then* Aesc, *His rune. The blows come just fast enough for her to absorb the last one, sometimes too fast. Breathe. Breathe. Weep. Sob into the rough bark. The runes she knows slam into her, inexorably, and then comes the verse with the others, the new ones whom she has not met. Hel's aett, dark and foreboding, but these too are Mysteries to be known to her. Then it is over, and her fingers slip from the trunk. Her throat is raw—had there been screaming? The man catches her with one hand, lowers her to the blanket laid next to the Tree.*

But it is not over; she hears the sound of leather gloves being exchanged for latex ones, packages being opened, her back being swabbed with pungent alcohol. It renews the pain and she groans. Then his fingers finding a spot on her lower spine that has not been touched. "Breathe," *he says, and she does, and a scalpel opens her skin. Next to her head is a pot of ashes, still warm from the burning; they are herbs gathered with prayer and intent, to take their essence into her body. Burnt to sterile ashes, they still have power humming about them, as if the burning merely made them more concentrated. Her blood flows, and a latex-gloved hand forces its way into her mouth, making her taste it. Then it dips into the pot and the ash is smeared into the wound, to heal later into a fine grey line, the first of nine bind runes cut into her. The first badge of her strength. Nine ordeals, nine worlds. When she reaches*

Asgard, the rune will bind the base of her skull, and He will be better able to enter her. She would give all the blood and pain in the world for that.

The Ordeal Path is probably the most frightening of all these Paths to the outsider looking in. It uses pain, fear, suffering, and discomfort for the purposes of achieving altered states, coming out of them, creating energy for magical work, cleansing, breaking down internal barriers, and offerings to the Spirits. From a distance, it looks horrifying, especially to people of our modern culture who see all pain as something uselessly awful to be avoided at all costs. People who inflict pain on themselves, or help someone else to create pain, are seen as sick and dangerous. But to our ancestors, it wasn't necessarily like that.

I remember being a child and seeing a film in my school about the history of Native American peoples, and it briefly mentioned the Lakota Sun Dance and included snapshots of a century-old illustration. It was dramatic and bloody, with braves hanging on hooks from the rafters of a tipi-like structure, their faces contorted with pain. I can still remember the squeals of disgust from the other kids around me. Not only could we not imagine something like that happening, we couldn't imagine anyone doing it and living. To us kids in that classroom, that kind of apparent damage might be fatal, and the idea of deliberate self-inflicted suffering was incomprehensible ... yet many of those same children went to a church every Sunday where the main figure on the altar was a crucified, suffering man.

Yet we have our own such icons in the northern tradition, the most obvious being Odin who traveled as a beggar on the roads, learned seidhr painfully in skirts, tore out one of his own eyes and threw it in Mimir's well, and ended up hanging in agony on the World Tree for nine days. There is also his counterpart and blood brother Loki, who is repeatedly imprisoned, tortured, starved, has his mouth sewn shut, and is raped by a stallion, just to name a few of his adventures. Fenris is chained and stabbed, and Tyr has his arm bitten off for the safety of his tribe. Frey walks willingly to the fields every year to be ritually sacrificed for the fertility of Vanaheim. Iduna is imprisoned, turned into a nut, and rescued by flight. Both Angrboda and Gullveig are burned three times over. Baldur is pierced with mistletoe, Loki's son Vali is turned into a ravenous wolf who then kills his brother, and there are many more tales like these. The Northern myths are full of bloody sacrifice, whichever way one turns.

Of course, just because a deity goes through a sacred mythic ordeal, willing or unwilling, does not mean that everyone who works with that deity ought to do the same. This Path is not for everyone, or even for most people, and that's as it should be. On the other hand, if an ordeal is necessary, there is greater power in linking that ordeal ritual to the paths blazed by the bloody footprints of a God in pain, if only by doing it in their honor. Linking it in this way draws divine power into it, gives it greater depth, and can take you much further than going there alone. Being suspended on hooks from a living tree has its own power, as does being cut, bound, beaten, and buried in the Earth for a time, or being bound with chains while one wrestles with one's inner wrath. However, when those rites are done in the name of Odin, or Frey, or Fenris, with attention paid to details that bring the experience closer, the rite becomes transpersonal—done not just for one's self but for the Cosmos as well. If it is done publicly, the people who choose to witness are blessed with further understanding as well.

I should disclaimer right now that the sort of applied pain and discomfort that best serves the purposes of the Ordeal Path is not that which is most injurious. In fact, serious injuries tend to put one into shock, which is not an altered state that is easily usable for magical purposes. Instead, the best sort of pain for the job is that which gives the body just enough sensation to set off the right brain chemistry, sustained over a period of time, but not enough to do any permanent damage. For purposes of this chapter, "non-injurious pain" is defined as something that does not leave any damage that can't be easily healed up over a period of days without professional medical help. A cutting or branding may leave a scar, a flogging may leave bruises and welts, a tattoo is clearly a deliberate mark, but none of these will impair the person's daily functioning in any way after they are healed, provided that the work is done skillfully on the right areas of the body.

For a concentrated look on the spirituality and techniques of the Ordeal Path that is more than this small chapter can cover, we encourage folks to get a copy of *Dark Moon Rising: Pagan BDSM and the Ordeal Path* from Asphodel Press. This is the first major text about how this path is done deliberately in a pagan-religious context, and while it is not northern-tradition per se, there are a lot of useful spiritual techniques and thought-provoking ideas from its various authors that are worth reading for anyone going into this kind of work. It also goes into much greater detail about how to create ordeal rites for people.

When it comes to actually learning how to do the physical techniques of this path—whipping, cutting, tattooing, branding, piercing, hook suspension, etc.—there is no way to learn this properly from books. Please, please find people who are skilled in these techniques and properly apprentice to them. It dishonors the techniques and those who passed them on to us to hack through them sloppily; they should be done carefully and with the proper training, and with attention to detail and to sterile procedure. The latter, too, is very important. Believe me when I say that if our ancestors had been able to procure rubbing alcohol, Technicare, and sterile packaged implements, they would have used them. Getting an infection from a poorly sanitized ordeal rite is a bad omen and does no honor to Those whom we serve. Remember that this is the Path that is second only to the Path of Sacred Plants when it comes to the ability to kill the body or put someone in the hospital, and move with respect.

It should go without saying that a spirit-worker should never do an ordeal for a client if they aren't skilled in the techniques that the client requests, even if it sounds like what is needed. If it's that important, find someone else who can do it and send the client over, or team up with the person who can do it. For example, I am not a tattoo artist, but I've run rituals for people who wanted sacred tattoos, with me directing what was happening and the actual work being done by a Pagan tattoo artist who had the equipment and the skill.

On the other hand, there are ordeals that can be done without learning physical-trauma skills. One example might be a fear/trust ordeal, where someone is blindfolded and led through a dangerous area by a guide, or just into parts unknown in order to do something unexpected. Another might be having other people embody and say aloud the things which you fear to hear, or which trigger you, in a space where you are honor-bound to stay and hear it and not lash out. Ordeals can also include simple endurance rather than pain—for example, climbing a mountain to do a rite, or standing vigil and praying for a long period of time, or trance dancing for hours. Many techniques of the other Paths, if done well past the point of comfort, become part of the Ordeal Path as well.

Spirit-workers in this tradition might use the Ordeal Path themselves for various purposes, including but not limited to:

1) Bringing the mind to a deep trance state where the soul can separate from it and do work. When noninjurious pain is applied to the body in the right manner, endorphins and other chemicals flood the brain and cause altered states of consciousness. Even for those who don't make endorphins well—perhaps because of chronic illness—adrenalin can also be used for similar purposes, although it creates a very different kind of state than the morphine-like endorphins. This kind of pain-use has been around for millennia; it's easier and safer than taking plants into your system, and it requires only your own body and a knowledge of what to do with its flesh and nerve endings. An example of this might be a seer or diviner using a pain ordeal to move through a block and force their mind out of the everyday chatter of life, in order to get better clarity on an important question.

2) Assisting in moving through shaman sickness. When one is literally spiritually dying in order to be reborn again, usually with a physical illness of some kind along with it, a pain ordeal that brings one temporarily closer to that moment of spiritual Death can hasten the period of shaman sickness. It won't make it go away entirely, and despite what some people say you can't do a series of ordeals instead of going through any shaman sickness in order to get to the same point. It is true that some would-be shamans have, in the past, subjected themselves to terrible ordeals that mimic the effects of shaman sickness in order to get the attention of the Spirits and be chosen by them, but once the Spirits have noticed them, it is assumed that they will trigger the actual shaman sickness, and these ordeals are just a preliminary. However, repeated ordeals (with the aid of the Gods and wights that one works with) during shaman sickness can move its course along more vividly, and get the suffering shaman out the other end quicker and perhaps with more of their health intact.

3) Removing psychic impurities and injuries; deep cleansing. As Galina Krasskova describes below in her experience of removing elfshot via a cutting, sometimes it takes an ordeal to get out particularly stubborn impurities. Our jobs are dangerous, and we often come in contact with astral substances that most people don't ever touch, especially when we are cleaning them out of the bodies of clients. If the "infection" spreads to the spirit-worker, it needs to be removed before it can get deeply rooted and interfere with their ability to function, and for serious problems that means drastic measures. There's also some kinds of ordeals can give the astral body a good shake back into the correct position, as it were, and flush out any number of built-up day-to-day toxins.

4) Aftercare; bringing the soul and consciousness back into the body. Spirit-workers who find trance easy and living in the body much more difficult may find it hard to come back from a dissociative state after journey-work. Pain, and especially random uneven pain—the exact opposite of the sort of pain used to create an altered state—is good for forcibly returning the consciousness to the body. When you're in that kind of pain, you have to be here, so some of us utilize that in order to keep ourselves present in our flesh after long draining travels. For this one, you really need the talents of an assistant who is trained in the particular sort of discomfort that brings you back to yourself ... and ideally one who will salve up the damage afterwards.

5) Raising a fund of energy to work with. This is similar to some of the techniques used for the Path of the Flesh, in that one is using bodily sensations to raise more energy than can be done with the body in a quiescent mode. The difference between the two is that while the energy used with the Path of the Flesh is orgasm—and orgasm can only last so long—noninjurious or mildly injurious pain can be extended for a much longer period of time than orgasm, and be even more intense. The energy raised via ordeal has a particular flavor—it is raw, strong, hot, and a bit rough for gentle purposes, so plan accordingly. Often this is the Energy Of Last Resort, the thing that you do in psychic emergencies when a great battery of power is needed immediately.

6) Making an offering to a God or wight. Many deities enjoy or at least honor pain that is given to them as an offering, especially if they are the darker members of the Rökkr pantheon, or Odin whose roads often lead down this Path. Generally, any deity involved with death or destruction will appreciate it, and some will hardly give you the time of day without it. An extreme example of this is Fenris, who is fed by being summoned into the body of a bound volunteer who is then given pain infliction, and the Great Wolf feeds on it.

7) A hunt for power. This is when ordeals are used as a rite of finding strength and courage. Even spirit-workers sometimes get to feeling despairing, helpless, and incompetent, and may need to remember their own strength and power through enduring trials or facing their fears. The old saying goes, "Where there's fear, there's power," and most people have innumerable fears around pain. Once anyone has gone through it and survived, discovered borders of their own strength that they never knew that they could endure, there is more strength and power available to them.

Even if a spirit-worker is not drawn to the ordeal path for themselves, they may be called upon to do it for clients. A client might need an ordeal for any of the above reasons plus several others, such as: A rite of passage, to prove to themselves that they are adult, or to celebrate a turning point in their lives. Facing a fear or phobia. Mourning or grieving a loss or death, especially for those who have trouble releasing such emotions. Learning trust, in other humans or in the divine. Opening their boundaries to the Gods. Shutting off the inner voices and achieving a short period of blissful silence. Celebrating the body (this last seems like a non sequitur, but the feeling of "aliveness in the flesh" that follows an effective physical ordeal is a form of celebrating to some people).

When a client comes to you and asks you to facilitate an ordeal rite for them, remember that it isn't about you. Even if you are the scariest and most impressive thing in the ritual, you have to be selfless about it. The rite is designed for their needs, not yours. On the other hand, you have to be strong enough not to break down and decide that you can't handle this—the responsibility, the pain in their eyes, seeing yourself as an inflicter of suffering. An Ordeal Master must be utterly ruthless, compassionate, and have no ego involved in the process. Even if you enjoy it, it's a service job, like everything else that we do.

That means that we have to be very careful to design an ordeal around what would really work for that person, rather than what we might like to do or see done to them, or what our favorite technique is, or what we're really in the mood for. Divination is good for this sort of thing.

Working With Ordeals
by Lydia Helasdottir

Why do it? Why do crazy painful things to your body? First, let me say this: I don't think that ordeal work is appropriate before a certain level is attained in your work. If you look at a cabalistic model—not so much accepting the entire cabalistic world-view, but just as a glyph of progression—I think ordeal stuff comes in after Paraketh, after you've got your independent solar furnace. Before that, it's too destructive. It's too easy to get yourself into a "Yes, I really must sacrifice to people who just want to beat on me" or "I just need to beat on people, so I'll pretend it's spiritual." Having said that, I've been doing vicious things to people since I was very young, and I wasn't attained at all, but I would say that the magical part of it starts after you've reached a point of having the divine indwelling to some extent. The early stuff is about learning technique—hurting without harming.

What is it for? Many things. Purification and hunting power, to name a couple. Purification includes regaining humility, offering the pain to a deity in a bhakti-yoga sense, and to recognize the illusory nature of manifestation. It's a courage-increasing activity—once you've hung from hooks, asking your boss for a pay raise is not that big a deal. That's a typical example of a power-hunting application. For me, ordeal is a measure of how far you've come, and what you can do. For those of us who have big "not good enough" complexes, the ordeal path is great for that. For those who've got big ego issues, it's good for that because you can be seriously humbled by it.

Kavadi, for instance, is an offertory rite. In Kavadi you wear a frame that carries spears that press into your flesh. The religious aspect of it is that you offer the pain to the god who is associated with the ritual. It's a devotion. From an engineering-energetic point of view, those spears act like huge antennae. First of all, you collect crud onto your energy body just from walking around in the world. With the spears, this pierces the crud, and it sort of crumbles and falls away. It's almost like you're taking a jackhammer to it, and when you come out of the ordeal you're fresh. It's the same with doing a hook suspension; you often leave the crud hanging from the hooks and you get torn out of the crud. It stays behind. It's all about breaking into pieces and being freed of the layers of crud that you get from interacting with the world.

Kavadi opens your crown chakra in a big way. The first time that I did Kavadi, I was seeing the world differently. My point of view had shifted to a place about four inches above the top of my head, and that was where I was seeing everything from. I couldn't stop it, and it lasted about two days, and it had a permanent effect of opening the crown chakra. For two days, that was where my point of view was, unless I forcibly brought it down to where my physical eyes were. It was a very strange sensation.

Hook suspensions have been around in the Tamil environment and in that of certain Native American tribes for thousands of years. It's been around to a lesser extent in the Urals where you'd have piercings and sit on top of high things, but not necessarily in the same way. How that works is that it's a huge offering of fear and lack of self-confidence, and just pushing through that. It's related to firewalking. The first time you go up on hooks, you just don't have any hope of being able to do it. It's certain failure. You put the hooks in, and you start to put tension on the string, and the moment any tension comes on it, you're saying "Whoa, no, stop!" And you think, fucking hell, I'm supposed to have my whole body weight on this? And you freak out, and you go into a pit of despair, sure that you're not going to be able to do this.

And in fact, most of the time that we do the "pre-flight briefing" with the person, we tell them that there will come a point where you will think to yourself, "There is no way in hell that I can do this." And you have to move on. We actually do this in a series of little plateaus, where you put the pressure on the hooks, and the nerves register the change and freak out. But if you then leave it there at that level, they get used to it, and after five or six breaths you can go to the next level. Some people like to get through it real quick, just "take me up and go through the whole thing at once". For me, that's a waste of the experience, especially for the first time. I want people to experience the full set of "I can't do this" to "ohmigod, I'm doing this!" The incremental process is important.

There are those who do suspensions for sport, thrill-seeking, and it does have a specific effect when you're actually up there, because then it doesn't actually hurt much any more. But people should experience the full process from just lying here with the hooks in, to "oh, they moved and I'm going to puke!" to the moment when they realize that they are getting light on the table, and they are really going to be able to take off at some point too. I have taken off and had it be unbelievable. Especially if you do it with the hooks in your back and the weight in your belly, it doesn't hurt once you get lifted up. If you compare it to, say, flying in a hang-glider harness, it is actually more comfortable, because your whole body is suspended by your skin. Your nerves, where the hooks are, are compressed and they aren't feeling anything any more. You can take about 140 pounds per hook, and you are floating in the air! It's the closest you can come to flapping your wings and taking off. It's really an amazing feeling. I'd advocate it to anyone who is drawn to the ordeal path, purely as an experience of overcoming fear and being rewarded with a marvelous thing.

A fair bit of it is endorphins, but endorphins only last about a half hour to maybe an hour, and everything that happens after that is not endorphins any more. Yes, some people, especially those who have been in chronic pain for a long time, no longer make endorphins; they've used it all up. So perhaps it might not work for some of them, but on the other hand, the guy that I know who loves this the most is someone who is in that chronic pain, and for whom endorphins don't work. He has to get given morphine shots for his pain, it's so bad. But this works great for him, because it's a distraction. The endorphin high may start you off, get you over the initial hump, but it is trivial compared to what is really going on. The reason why the hook suspension doesn't hurt is not because of endorphins but because the nerves are compressed. The nerve reacts to change, not to pure pressure, which is why gunshot wounds don't hurt that much after a while; there's no change to register.

You can distinguish the endorphin-feeling from the underlying chemistry, though. It's like when you get a big tattoo done—the first ten minutes are annoying, the next 90 minutes are kind of OK because the endorphins are there, and after that it becomes awful again. If you carry on past that point, it becomes transcendent, so sometimes the endorphins are actually getting in the way. Some people who do suspensions will actually do things to use up the endorphins beforehand, because of that.

You can certainly use the Ordeal Path as an altered state, but you have to ask: what's the purpose of this altered state? As for things that it's especially good for, there's atonement. Beyond simple purification—getting rid of the crud—if you're a person who suffers from guilt, then you can pay for things with discomfort. It's also a very great relativising force, so if you're a person that tends towards the obsessive or whiny, undergoing a proper, seriously difficult ordeal will make the things that you usually whine about seem much less onerous.

Probably its most potent use, though, is for hunting power, through going into fear and out again. Where fear is, there's power, because fear locks up a lot of power, and if you can go through a fear, or dissolve a fear, or do something despite having a fear, you can then bring that extra energy cell into your body, and you've got more juice than before because you hunted that stuff up. For me, also, it's a way of getting raw; breathing, eating, and life in general becomes quite a lot more interesting. It's a kind of anti-jading mechanism. If you get really properly frightened or really properly challenged, the very fact of being alive becomes a gift. It's the opposite of being bored or numbed-out.

I have noticed also that deities can amplify discomfort a lot. I'd modify a quote by Fakir Musafar and define pain as "an intense sensation that was either unexpected or undesired." What you're doing when you're taking an ordeal on is that you're receiving an intense sensation, but the negative connotations of the word pain frighten you. If you're in chronic pain, you expect it, but you don't desire it. Conversely, I do not like to stub my toe. This is a bad thing. I do not like to have a migraine. Gut cramps suck. But in terms of an experience of overcoming something, pain is really potent, and deities can amplify or remove it.

I had an experience where I fell while walking in the mountains and I dislocated my kneecap. Now normally I can just kind of dissociate from any kind of discomfort if I need to, but there was no dissociating from that. It was the worst thing that ever happened to me. Where the nice dome of the patella should be, there was a dip, and the patella was all the way out to the side. I didn't dare push it back, because I didn't know if there would be nerve damage by doing that. I was like that for an hour and a half while people went down the mountain and got me an ambulance. The point of it, I'm sure, was to endure the madness of really, really bad pain with no safe word, no way out. It just ripped through my whole body like a high-pitched whine; there was no escaping it. It screwed with my breathing. In fact, interestingly enough, there happened to be a midwife there, and she sat at my head and did all the breathing out and in, and that helped, but as soon as I realized that the van had come and they were going to have to lift, me, I freaked out again. And I had done years of breathing control, but this was unexpurgated madness. They picked me up and put me in the van; I was terribly afraid to scream, because I didn't want to upset people, so as they picked me up I warned them that I might have to scream. And then there was this amazing noise in the background—for a moment I thought that it was a sawmill or something—and then I realized that it was me, making this wounded-animal horrendous scream. They took me into the clinic and shot me up with morphine, but it didn't touch it at all.

The point of this is that I'm glad I had that experience, even though I don't ever want it to happen again, thank you very much, but it took me to the outer edge of a place where people in pain go. And ever since then, pain has basically been a cakewalk, including Kavadis, and terrible discomfort while running—you notice that I use the word "discomfort"; it's not really pain. Pain is what happens when your kneecap is dislocated; this is discomfort.

When I had my midriff tattoo, it was done by my teacher, and she was deliberately inflicting pain—partly because we both agreed that it would be good as an ordeal, partly because she was pissed at me—but I sang the pain out then. These are all good techniques for dealing with pain—singing it, breathing it out, or trying to distract yourself. One of the things I've found really helpful is to actually go to the inside of the pain—and I find this particularly helpful during running—and say, "OK, what is this exactly? How does it feel to be next to it? How does it feel to be next to it on the other side?" And just kind of get into what is this sensation exactly, and what is it telling me? Of course, if you're doing an ordeal where many things are happening at once, you don't have the luxury of just meditating on that one particular thing. For single things, like rope bondage or clothespins where it's pretty stable, you can have them meditate on that.

I like the courage aspect of it, I like the cleansing aspect of it. I like the worthiness aspect of it. It's an initiation, a quest, a warrior thing. Now you belong to this group of people who have done this. We sometimes say, when people have done their first suspension, "Welcome to the Club." You're now irrevocably in the special elite club of people who have done this, and in terms of the number of people on the planet, that's not that many.

We know that the Jotunfolk do violent sex—at least, those of us who work with them know that. We know that they do warrior ordeals, and coming-of-age ordeals, and the whole hunter-warrior-lord thing. Angrboda is a very strong source of inspiration for us for that stuff, because she seems to specialize in that; the whole "How good are you really?" aspect of ordeals seems to be her forte. Other deities who understand warrior ordeals might be Tyr and Odin. Hela teaches it, but in a very ritualistic sort of way. And of course Fenrir teaches it.

When I wrote the love song to Fenrir, I wrote about the fact that there's no letting it be, sometimes you have to do this to ensure that the world is enlivened. It's an anti-stagnation effect. People are generally so blunted by their daily experience that they don't get anything new and stimulating. For me to take some suburbanite and scare the shit out of them until they piss themselves with fear, or hang them by hooks, or take them on a mountaineering expedition, whatever it is, invariably at the end of it, people look at you and say, "God, I'd forgotten how good it is to be alive." Taking people to the edge of their limits is empowering. I think it's actually good for people with big egos to be shown where their limits are. From a "giving it up" point of view, it's all right to lose control in those situations, because you're in a primal state of worry for your ongoing existence, and it's OK to let go of all the usual stuff.

And if someone was saying this who hadn't actually gone out and done these ordeals, you'd say, "Romanticized crap! Why don't you actually go out and do it, then?" But I have done it for a long time, and I still feel this way about it, because it works. BDSM, for example, is just a sexually-charged way to go through ordeals assisted by someone else, whether it's a shame-confronting, or fear-confronting, or pain-confronting ordeal. Whatever the issue is, get the demon out there and fight it for real. That's where the power is. There are a hundred books on how to do it, but it's nothing to actually doing it.

There's a great book on this by Anita Phillips called A Defense of Masochism, and she argues that you deal with the overwhelmingness of the Universe by actively inviting a part of it to come and ravish and invade you, just puncture your boundaries and overwhelm you, and that's how you deal with the largeness of it all. The other thing that she was on about—which was quite interesting—was that for some people, it's hard to feel like they have any boundaries, or who they are at all, and to be invaded and ravaged means that there was a boundary to cross. You can then feel where it is, particularly for people with identity issues. "I don't know who I am." Well, put them in enough pain, and ravage them, and invade the boundary, and suddenly they know where the boundary is and they can defend it. But until they've experienced where it is, they don't know how.

It can be very therapeutic, but it's not a substitute for therapy. However, in the hands of someone who is actually a psychopomp, somebody capable, it can be very therapeutic. It can be a better therapeutic intervention, or replace many other kinds of therapeutic interventions. But to see every scene as therapy, or to foist your issues onto your top without talking about it first, or saying that "This needs to get therapeutic now," that's a bad thing, and dangerous.

If you are someone who does ordeals as a sacred service, well, first, I believe that you have to have been there. That's controversial, but for me you have to have been there. Not necessarily the technique that you're doing to them, but the particular flavor of fear and discomfort that goes with it. You're sending someone into a place that's frightening and lonely, and you need to be able to go there and pick them up. At the end of that tunnel, you need to be there with your arms open to receive them, and they have to know that you know that tunnel. I also think that is helps to be horsing a deity, either your patron or a patron of these arts, while you're doing it. It makes you more courageous than you normally would be, and more intelligent about the act.

To do this work properly, you need to be hooked up to a manifestation of the Divine, all the time. Usually underworld or death-dealing deities; that's what they do. You need a clear vision of what you're doing, why you're doing it, what the intended outcome is. Sometimes you need to be willing to take things into your own hands and go beyond what the person thinks that they can manage, so most of the time if it's ritual stuff, they don't get to say stop just because it's intense. If you're going to have this as ritual, then you can't be in control; you'll just have to trust me. If they can't let go, then they're not ready to do the ritual. If they can't trust me, then I'm not the right Ordeal Master for the job.

That's another reason to do ordeal work—it raises a whole lot of power. It's a very potent way of generating raw power. We do ordeals of just pure physical discomfort, or endurance, of fear—dealing with your agoraphobia or fear of heights, confronting the stuff. These can be warrior initiations or they can be power hunts. We do ordeals to raise power, as sacrificial offerings, purifying and atoning ordeals ... these are useful when you feel cruddy about something that happened that you didn't have the attainment to prevent, and you can't make it right with the people that were wronged because they're not there, you don't have contact with them, they're dead, and you're feeling like it's a burden that you have to pay for in the ledger, and you haven't had the opportunity to do so.

It can get addictive, if it's done without purpose. There are a lot of endorphin junkies, just going from one to the next, always seeking the next bigger high. The only way out is to improve the education of the community, because that profanes it. It's a biological thing. People have used discomfort and endurance forever for noncorporeal aims.

Wodinic Ordeals
by Galina Krasskova

I led my first Wodinic ordeal in March 2005...completely spontaneously. At the time, I was a member of a local heathen group, and they asked if I'd lead a faining to Freya for some pagan friends, one of whom was being strongly "bothered" by Woden. I agreed, and we all got a strong feeling that there should be a private Woden faining with the man in question, myself (because I belong to Woden), a friend of mine, and her husband who also claimed devotion to Woden. So we set out for the woods.

I'll preface this by saying that at this point, we were convinced that all Woden wanted was a faining. Neither of us had any inkling of what was to come, and Woden did not share His plans with me. I'll also say that though I love Woden dearly, I have never, ever experienced Him in the way that He came that night. He dampens the terror with His women, and until that night I never understood why one would flee Him. I never understood what it was Woden's men go through. I understand it now. I saw and felt and bowed to that terror myself.

But I am getting ahead of myself. We thought this would be quick and simple, but Woden had other plans. As we went into the woods, they darkened and shifted. They changed and Woden's presence, very dark, was palpable. I told them to stop at a crossroads in the woods, feeling that it was where Woden wanted us to hold the faining. The Woden's man who was with us was an ex-marine, a sniper and a shapeshifter. He (and I witnessed this later that night) is "skin swift" ... or let's just say he's very close to his wolf fetch. Woden had been courting him for some time.

We stopped at the crossroads and I filled the horn with vodka. I had brought two bottles of Jagermeister for this part of the faining, but that did not seem appropriate. They were small and I pocketed them for later, assuming each of the men could give one in offering after the horn was passed. I raised the horn and gave a verbal prayer, speaking of Woden as God of the crossroads, of the dead, hanging God, God of the hunt, etc. Then I sang the spirit song that Woden had given me years ago. Woden would not allow it to come as I wished ... and as I sang it, it changed, growing far darker than I had anticipated.

We saw Him in the woods standing by a Tree in the blackness. I offered the horn to my friend's husband, who also gave a prayer to the Old Man. I told him to pass it to Karl, for there are some things a Woden's man can only receive from another Woden's man. Woden made it very clear at that moment to both of us without forewarning that He had made us bring our wolf-shifter out there for an initiation. He wanted that man and had watched and honed and selected him very carefully. My friend's husband scribed the valknot over the horn and told the initiate exactly what it would mean (as one Woden's man to another) for him to drink. The young man paled and asked if he could have a few moments. At our nod, he went off to commune with his wolf fetch. This actually later earned him a compliment from Woden who said that unlike most of His chosen, myself included, this one actually possessed common sense (said with a fairly dry laugh).

The initiate returned after a few minutes and nodded (we had almost been hoping he'd say no), telling us that his wolf told him to do it and had never guided him wrong yet. He drank, and Woden said He wanted the valknot cut into him. I offered to do it, if this was what he wanted. I took the horn and walked towards the direction of where Woden was standing by the trees, knelt, and offered Him the rest of the horn. When we were able, our initiate led us out of that place ... only after Woden was no longer visible.

We went back to the house and our wolf went inside, then came out burning up with *wod*, even though it was a cold night. My friend wisely suggested we throw runes to see if now was a good time to do the valknot, and Gebo came up. This man, who had never met me before that night, said he trusted me to do it, wanted to get it over with and tossed a K-Bar knife down point first into the wooden porch saying, "You're doing it with this though." (I know better now, but at the time, I just shrugged and said "Ok, but you'll get a better line with a razor blade.")

I told out initiate to make himself ready, and asked my friend if she could draw a valknot freehand (she's an artist) as I did not trust myself to cut it freehand. What I didn't know, but should have assumed, is that this man was a berserker. What occurred in his initiation to Woden makes perfect sense. My friend, who had known him for years, told me later that for him, it had to have been bloody, violent and dark.

We went back out into the woods, but as soon as we hit the crossroads they changed, and I realized later that Woden had opened a gate. He'd taken us away from those woods and into a place of the dead, the place where His corpse dangled. It stole the warmth and feeling from us, and for hours after this, it was like we were the walking dead. On the way out, we had to pass by the firepit, and Woden indicated that He wanted ash from the fire smeared into the wound, so we gathered that. Woden chose a small square clearing where Hurricane Hugo had struck down a tree. Our wolf took off his shirt, sat down and wrapped his arms about the stump. Our other Woden's man sat on his legs, pinning him down, and held his arms. (If I ever do this again, we're binding the berserk in question. Had our wolf had less control, we couldn't have held him and would never have been able to fend him off. I kept a knife by my side just in case.) Our wolf gagged himself so that he couldn't bite any of us, and bade us hold him securely. The knife was doused with alcohol, the valknot drawn on his back, and my friend held the light for me. I washed his back with alcohol and Woden told me to bring Him His son. I began to cut while singing *galdr*, Woden showed me images and I translated them into the galdr bringing this *ulfhednar* to the Battle Lord. I do not remember most of the galdr, only that the son passed from the hands of Woden's bride to Woden Himself. It was the first time that Woden used me as Valkyrie, making me an extension of His will directly. Once the valknot was cut, I smeared it with ash.

We had lost our initiate by that point; part of him had begun to change, his soul had gone and he was shifting. Woden had taken him off somewhere. We called him back, which took some time, even though I utilized *galdr*. He said later that he'd never been able to come back to humanity in so short a time. The presence and energy was extremely strong. My friend, a Freyswoman, backed away and averted her eyes, knowing this was a Wodinic mystery. We wrapped our arms around our wolf, grounding him and calling him back to himself. Eventually he came back, but for the next few hours he was non-verbal, and had recurring muscle spasms throughout his body as he regained full humanity.

Once it was safe, we ungagged him and let him go. On the way out, my friend had wandered a bit ahead and Woden appeared to her—I believe to keep her from wandering farther into the place of the dead where she might be lost. She heard steps, and then the sound of a body swinging from a tree, and had the most sensible response of the night—she stopped and covered her eyes, not wanting to see. By the time I reached her, she was trembling in utter terror, too afraid to go forward or back. I wrapped my arms around her shoulders and guided her out. We took our initiate back to the firepit and got him food; my friend was wise enough to bring me food too. I was so cold inside, dead, that I didn't catch any of the signs of backlash or shock. I figured even though I didn't feel like it, I should eat and went into the kitchen. The lady of the house was an ex-paramedic, and she took one look at me and sat me down, forcing me to eat and ground. It didn't help. We sat there for hours. Folk would come in, ask what had happened and all we could manage to say was "Woden." It was a while before anyone would come near us, as the pallor of death was strong about us all. It was hard to get the sound of creaking from a body swinging in the Tree out of our minds.

I wanted to go back to Him. I did what aftercare I could (which in my state wasn't as much as should have been done) and walked back out into the woods. This is where I received my own lesson in what Woden does to His men. I needed to know this, and had asked a week or so previous that He show me why His men feared Him so. I love Woden dearly, yet I have never, ever experienced such terror as I experienced walking into those woods alone. I got halfway to the crossroads and could go no further. I sensed Him out there, dead ... a Woden bereft of even the barest hint of humanity ... a walking corpse of a God, a shade, a shadow, hunger and desire, pain and terror bound up as one. I longed for Him and I was, for the first time, shown the full measure of terror He inspires. I could not go further. I bowed my head and covered my eyes. I wanted to go in, but also knew to my bones that if I did, I wouldn't be coming out again. I'd seen Him as Lord of the Dead before, but never in that place, never after having walked between realms in a place that sucked the humanity and life from me.

I returned just as the lady of the house was about to come out to find me. She had managed to get the spasms stopped in our initiate, and he gave me *shild* for the cutting. Woden had told him he had to pay. First he offered me the bloody rags, saying that his blood was the most precious thing he had, but I refused them and told him that those belonged to Woden. Instead, at Woden's urging, I took three rounds for his rifle. If one knew him, one realized this was a powerful payment in itself, as he had ensorcelled his gun as an ally. He asked me how to honor Woden; we spoke on that for a bit and I assured him Woden would teach him what he needed to know. We all debriefed each other as best we could.

We found out the next morning that all the trees at that crossroads were felled in a circle by Woden that night.

My own first ordeal I will speak of only in brief. I had been elfshot a couple of years ago by a crazy (but gifted) ex-student with serious mother and authority issues. It was causing me ever-increasing pain and essentially crippling me. It cut off my ability to ground, damaged my back, left me constantly exhausted and often ill. It was brilliant work (I'll give credit where credit is due, the girl was one of the most talented students I ever had) and nothing I did was able to undo it. I'd get some relief, but the way it was worked on me, it spread too rapidly and in too complex a fractal-like pattern to counter. It also cut off my ability to function effectively as a spirit-worker, and blocked me off enough that it impaired my perception of my relationship with Woden, and that was worse than the physical pain.

When I attended a spirit-worker gathering last autumn, there were several ordeal masters present. Woden had indicated that if I worked four sigils into my skin, it would destroy the shot. I mentioned that I had been wanting to get them cut but didn't know anyone who did that (not knowing that two of the people I spoke with were specifically trained in cutting and ordeal work). One spirit-worker offered to cut them into me that night if I would consent to allow her to copy the sigils. She'd been told she needed protection against elfshot and would find it at the gathering. So that was a nice bit of synchronicity.

That night, around the bonfire, with at least a dozen mystics, shamans, spirit-workers, healers, God-spouses, and God-slaves present, I had the senior shaman drum while several others chanted. I bared my back, straddled a chair and allowed one of them to restrain my arms. I began to chant and pray to Woden, offering this to Him partly in cleansing and partly to reaffirm my devotion to Him. He was very present for me, waiting and watching.

I'd never been cut like that before and doubted my ability to stand the pain, but I was soon pretty tranced from the chanting and drumming and general collected *maegen* of the group. I can't say it was pleasant when the cutting began, but the sight and sense of the elfshot leaving me was palpable. Woden came into me at one point and began to laugh as He did something that sent it all back to the *nithling* that injured me in the first place. He left me, but hovered, and I remained silent until the very end when I was told to *galdr*, which I did. Once the cuttings were done, hot ash was rubbed into the wound and I was allowed to get up, though watched carefully for a time lest I pass out or get grabbed by Woden again. The physical difference was palpable, the way I moved having changed completely. While there was residual tissue damage from the shot (which, yes, appears in medical scans), the shot itself was gone and I was cleaned and free of the taint.

I've also had Woden request that I get several tattoos. He utilizes them to effect astral and spiritual modifications. While not as dramatic an ordeal as those described above, in terms of impact they were quite effective. I have a prayer to Woden, of binding, around my left wrist, a valknot on my left arm, between my breasts, other runic sigils down my back and on my right arm with more to come. In terms of sheer physical discomfort, many were more painful than the cutting. Woden has also insisted I learn to better facilitate ordeal rites and to that end has sent me for training in cutting and more recently, branding. His words on the matter were simple: I cannot take someone across a threshold I myself have not crossed.

Nine Worlds of Ordeal

Each world has People who embody the Powers of Death, and thus are the Ordeal-Givers for that world. Some spirit-workers have been called to do nine ordeals, working their way up or down the Tree and learning the wisdom therein. Generally, if they work for one of the Aesir or Vanir, they start at the bottom and work their way up (Helheim, Niflheim, Svartalfheim, Muspellheim, Midgard, Jotunheim, Vanaheim, Ljossalfheim, Asgard), while if they serve Rökkr gods they do it in the other direction, working downwards from the top.

Starting at the bottom, the Ordeal-Giver for Helheim is, of course, Hela. Her ordeals are almost always not only physically painful, but involve a good deal of fear as well. Terror is one way for her to get people opened up (Odin is not averse to using that trip either, on his end), especially if it is a sheer fear of Death. The hallmark of Hela's ordeals is the moment of "Oh, no, I'm going to be killed now," or "I can't take any more of this or I'll die." This can be achieved in any number of ways without actually seriously endangering the bodily life of the ordeal-dancer, but that moment must still be felt sincerely. If she does not choose to use Fear, another of her methods is Humiliation, which is more often used on those with too much pride or arrogance. In the face of Death, pride and arrogance have no place, and she is good at driving this point home. Generally, a Helheim ordeal will push you past your limits and bring to face to face with some aspect of your physical mortality, whatever that might be for you. Hela has no one technique that is specific to her; she is a Mistress of all of them.

For Niflheim, the Ordeal-Giver is usually Nidhogg the great dragon, but it can also be one of the frost-thurses who live in that icy, misty world. For the latter, you must have a good relationship with the frost-thurses; most people who end up with a Niflheim ordeal face the Dragon in one way or another. (For the record, while Niflheim is technically the prison of Fenrir, he does not perform ordeals there. He does not do anything there except be imprisoned; a small part of him can move between the worlds and work with people there, but there is nowhere in the Nine Worlds that he can freely go.) Niflheim ordeals are often about cold, perhaps cold water—one is reminded of the legendary Siberian shaman trick of punching six holes in the ice, jumping into the first one, coming up out of the second one, and weaving in this way down the line. While most modern shamans would not be up to such a feat, a cold ordeal can be a good test of the spirit-worker's ability to warm themselves. It might be standing naked in the snow for a time, or walking briefly into icy water. As with all such things, a balance must be struck between coddling one's self to the point of the ritual failing to be an ordeal, and lacking the common sense to avoid lethality.

Niflheim is also associated with rot, as is Nidhogg who is the Eater of Corpses. Rot can be an ordeal if, for example, the individual is made to lie next to an unattractive rotting animal corpse and meditate on it, while enduring the smell. While this may seem like a useless exercise in suffering, those who are death-phobic can sometimes benefit from this reminder that all parts of the cycle are sacred, including that little-loved part. They can also get over their phobias about ugliness and decomposition in this way.

For Svartalfheim, the Ordeal-Givers are not any of the Duergar—they are actually the creative force for that world. Instead, that lies in the hands of the Dark Alfar, and one must present one's self to one of their Queens. Svartalfheim ordeals often seem to involve broken glass of some sort, perhaps shards of broken mirrors. The Dark Alfar love to break beautiful objects, and they are equally fond of small sharp knives. One can usually guarantee that this world's ordeal is going to involve some kind of cutting, perhaps with broken glass, or if that is too dangerous, razors or scalpels. Blood should be wiped on the bark of trees, and singing out the pain is an important skill to know, as they are all about song-magic.

In Muspellheim, the Ordeal-Giver is Surt, the lord of the fire-etins and the oldest being in the Nine Worlds. Muspellheim ordeals, of course, involve heat. The classic one might be a brand, although long saunas, firewalking, or other heat rituals have been done as well. Another Muspellheim ordeal might be endurance-dancing, ideally around a fire, as fire-etins do a lot of sacred dance. (See the Path of Rhythm chapter for more information on that.)

In Jotunheim, there are several Jotunfolk whose specialty is pain, but the most respected is probably Angrboda, the Hag of the Iron Wood. She specializes in the "hunting for power" type of ordeals, where the receiver pits themselves against suffering in order to gauge their own strength and see what they can survive. Angrboda is the trainer of young warriors, especially those with animal sides or anger management issues; one of her favorite sorts of trials are "hazing"-style self-control rites which triggers rage in someone in a situation where rage will only cause them more pain, and only by mastering themselves can they win. Other sorts of Jotunheim ordeals might involve being hunted through the woods as prey, or anything involving serious mountain-climbing.

In Vanaheim, it varies depending on whether the focus is earth or sea—and all rites in Vanaheim will have one of those two focuses. Most Vanaheim rites are done with the element of Earth, and the Ordeal-Giver is Nerthus the Earth Mother of the Vanir, whose face is always veiled because to see it would be death. In ancient times, the statue of Nerthus was taken out and bathed every year, and this necessitated the deaths of several slaves who got to see her close up. Nerthus is the embodiment of the devouring Earth, and her ordeals can include being buried in the ground, or placed into a hole to keep vigil. There is also the full-on John Barleycorn-type ordeal, done in honor of Frey, where the individual is treated as the grain is—scythed down with a cutting, bound like a sheaf, beaten in a way that mimics threshing and milling, placed in a circle of fire to mimic baking, and then reburied in the earth to represent the seed that is planted anew. (The full text of an example of such a rite can be found in *Dark Moon Rising: Pagan BDSM And The Ordeal Path* by Asphodel Press.)

If the focus is the ocean, then the Ordeal-Givers are Ran and her nine daughters. (Aegir prefers to let his bloodthirsty wife do these things for him, and Njord is a life-bearer.) Their ordeals may vary depending on which undine-goddess shows up, but generally must take place in the ocean. All blood shed into the ocean's waves by one of us goes to them as an offering. One such ordeal had the individual in question tied onto a safety rope line which was held by people on the shore, and he went out and battled the undertow as long as he could, "dancing with the Sisters" as he put it.

In Ljossalfheim, the Ordeal-Givers are specific Alf-lords, but they do not advertise their nature. If you want to make an appointment with them, the person to approach is Gerda, Frey's giantess wife; if she could be said to have friends among the Alfar, it would be them, and they trust her to screen out the unworthy. One of their favorite ordeals is imprisoning someone in total isolation for a time, perhaps in the woods or field; they strongly value mental and emotional connections, so taking someone away from that is serious for them. This might start out similarly to the quiet contemplation of the Ascetic Path, but what makes it an ordeal is that it goes beyond the person's ability to handle it well, and takes them through stages of difficult emotion caused by long-term isolation. Part of this type of rite might be taking away their name, or their identity, and then giving it back when the ordeal is over. If a mark is placed on them as part of the ordeal, be sure that it will be aesthetically beautiful, or at least constructed skillfully for a particular aesthetic effect, as will the setting of the ordeal itself.

The most serious ordeal that the Alfar (or any fey-type race) might inflict on someone is to curse them with madness for a time, and see how they handle it. This might seem like setting someone up to fail—taking away their reason and expecting them to somehow come through—but madness can strip away much of a person's identity and show them parts of themselves that have been repressed. This, obviously is not an ordeal that can be inflicted for a few hours by a human agent, unless they use the Sacred Plants, and that is a very dangerous road. Instead, this kind of ordeal will likely be between the Alfar and the human in question themselves, and may or may not be announced as a specific ordeal—that may be something that the human has to figure out for themselves, which is not so easy during a bout of madness.

In Asgard, the Ordeal-Giver is, of course, Odin. Like Hela, he might select any sort of ordeals to inflict on the individual, although he is fond of suspensions and indeed anything involving hanging, and people getting runes carved or tattooed on them, and anything that honors the various parts of his nine-year ordeal. (The Rites of Odin follow in this section.) Asgard ordeals are often rites for warriors; their focus varies depending on whether they are the start or the finish of a series of ordeals, or a single one on their own. Starting in Asgard is generally an ordeal of courage, whereas finishing there is often an ordeal of honor, as it is assumed that after eight other ordeals, courage has already been adequately built up..

The one ordeal that catches most people up is Midgard. There is no one patron for the Midgard ordeal except the spirit-worker themselves, and any local spirits of earth and animal and plant who offer to aid them. The ordeal must be entirely self-designed, and usually not physical—Midgard rites deal with the demons of daily life that plague us, and that hold us back from our other work, and they are best approached with a more psychological sort of suffering. The Gods watch these ordeals as closely as they watch other ones, but they do not interfere. The test is to create a ritual for yourself that honestly triggers your deepest issues and doesn't spare you at all, nor engage in any denial. I've seen many elaborate and painful rites created by people doing this sort of thing which look terribly self-sacrificing on the surface, but don't actually touch the person's deeper problems.

To start planning for a Midgard rite, I've found that it's best to have friends who know you well tell you about what they see of your issues. As they tell you these things, watch for a particular feeling. It's a flicker of panic, an "Oh, no, not that!" after which you immediately find your attention being forcibly shoved away from it. Don't let that happen. Jump on it and look at it. If it makes you feel even more panicked—and the panic voice can disguise itself, by saying "Oh, no, I don't think that I need to do that"—that's good. It shouldn't be something that you can get comfortable with before you start the rite. You should be feeling some shadow of that "Oh, Gods, no, not this" all the way up to the starting line. That's how you know that you've gotten it right. It may actually seem silly and unglamourous, and that's good. Midgard is unglamourous. That's part of its nature. Often, it's not something that one clearly fears so much as something that one dislikes intensely, for reasons mysterious to one's self. Often that dislike, when fully unearthed, leads back to a fear.

One of the themes that I've seen in Midgard ordeals is bringing people back to an appreciation of their humanity. Working with spirits, and doing heavy magic, can change people. It can set them apart from other people, and isolate them. As discussed elsewhere in this series, sometimes this alienation is part of the package, part of the power. However, when the spirit-worker gets set too far apart, they lose touch with the very people that they are supposed to be serving. There's also that spirit-workers are not immune to loneliness, bitterness, and anger and the unfairness of their situation, and this can lead to contempt for the folk that they are bound to serve. It can also lead to contempt for the parts of them that are flawed and human just like Everybody Else. It's never possible to adequately serve people for whom you have contempt, especially when there are spiritual questions involved. Midgard ordeals often bring people face to face with those parts of them that they still share with Joe Blow sitting in front of his television set watching sitcoms, and teach them tolerance for those parts, and by extension tolerance for their Tribe, even if that Tribe is anyone who might show up at the door.

My advice for the spirit-worker who is attempting to plan a Midgard ordeal and having trouble with it is to find someone who is basically a decent human being, but who embodies everything that you associate with the short-sightedness, mundanity, and general ordinariness that you believe that your job or viewpoint has placed you above. Go to them and offer to help them with something, and in the process spend enough time with them to find something that you have in common, especially if it's something unflattering. Make that the starting-place for planning your ordeal.

The most important thing to remember with ordeal-work is that it is meant to take you beyond your ego, not simply fluff it up. While some ordeals can give you increased confidence in yourself and your power, if there wasn't a point somewhere in it that was completely humbling, you didn't do it right. Ideally, you should eventually get to the point where the part of you that is ego is irrelevant. That's one of the way that the Ordeal Path resembles the Ascetic Path (and indeed there are places where they combine). The Ascetic's Path works with small, gentle, inexorable steps, and its focus goes inward into stillness, while the Ordeal Path takes great painful ripping steps, and its focus goes outward into a scream ... after which one passes out of one's collected muck and finds a place of stillness. In the end, the Wheel of these Eight Paths all lead to the central hub, that place that we may not be able to adequately describe in words, but we all know when we've been to it.

Odin's Lesson

On The Tree
by Galina Krasskova

I have been an Odin's woman for over a decade, and during that time I have come to know Him as His God-Spouse, godatheow, devotee, horse, valkyrie and priest. He is the axis around which my world revolves. Service to Him in whatever capacity He desires is my greatest joy.

Over the years I have served Him in numerous capacities, but one of the most surprising has been that of ordeal worker, both on the side of those who give ordeals and the side of those who receive them. I've come to realize that Odin is all about the ordeal, all about delving into pain and struggle in order to hone the spirit and gain knowledge. While there is ample evidence for this in the surviving lore if one looks hard enough, the degree to which He embraces this path surprised even me.

Odin has many secrets, and contains many wisdoms. It would take an entire book to even begin speaking of all his lessons. Yet when I asked which of his lessons is most important for the spirit-worker—not the warrior, not the leader, not the wanderer, not the wordsmith, not any of the other paths which His people might take—this is the one that He gave forth to me.

It is all about ruthlessness. Mastering anything of value within any of the Nine Worlds takes a certain degree of ruthlessness. It is through struggle and a stripping away of the dross within one's being that one is readied for power, for wisdom and for magic. Such seeking is a discipline of the spirit more valuable than any wealth to be found in your world, more valuable than any candied ideology of sugar-coated iconoclasts, or any words found in weathered tomes of lore. This flesh, this spirit, this awareness ... all are tools in the process of becoming. All is expendable in the search for knowledge. Failure is often merely the price of being unable or unwilling to go far enough, deep enough, of yielding to pain before you have forced it through submission and endurance to yield its secrets to you.

Pain, you see, is the greatest of teachers. It does not lie. It does not deceive. It purifies, leaving only the rawness of a soul ready for opening. It is my favored key, for it is the purest. In its grasp, there are so few places to hide. It is a great truthbringer. Yes, the risks are great: breaking, madness, death, but these risks should only fire the soul with further hunger. Challenges such as these are to be embraced. It is how I hone my warriors.

I value darkness—for I have walked in it and mastered it—and the broken, fragmented shards of hearts and souls too scarred to find joy in Midgard. These are my people. These are the ones to whom I whisper in the lonely darkness. These are the ones who understand the singular hunger by which I found my way to the Tree. These are the ones who have known enough of pain that its further touch will not break them beyond redemption. They are the ones I have made ready.

It is this which is my darkest mystery: it is only upon the anguished body of the Tree that one may truly come to know me or taste of the power I hold. All of the paths that lead to me pass through its bloody bower. But between the pain and the breaking there is the joy of discovering worlds and how to make them, eternities and how to break them, weaving, shifting, binding, remaking, and a thousand other secrets even Gods have forgotten. All is there, waiting on the knife-edge road of Pain.

Enduring that road to the end is not about strength or weakness. It is not about devotion or hubris. It is about sheer, stubborn hunger—hunger to Know, to Know all there is to Know, to pierce the dark veil and shine a brilliant light into its depths. It is that which defines my nature, and that of those who serve Me.

The Ordeal Rites of Odin

Odin is a deity heavily associated with ordeals (and indeed his dictated lesson on ordeals is at the end of this section). He himself went through a nine-year cycle of ordeals in order to gain wisdom and power, which included at various points being homeless, wandering, cross-dressed and treated as a woman, ripping out one of his eyes, and being hanged on the World Tree for nine days. Of course, Odin is a god and can take more than we mere mortals, but ordeal initiations are a part of the gradually rediscovered Odinic cultus.

To that end, there are three separate versions below of an Odinic initiation. The first one is a description of a group ordeal ritual done over a weekend at a private gathering. The second one is a nine-day initiation for an individual wishing to honor and dedicate themselves to Odin, with the aid of their community. While it is an ordeal rite, it is suitable for most average people to handle. The third one is a description of a serious initiation rite for an Odin's Man, to be undertaken only with great care and dedication.

A Story Of The Tree:
Honoring Odin's Ordeal
by Del

Oftentimes, we learn and relearn the lesson that you can't escape something that the Gods wish to bring to fruition. A local pagan organization announced it would be holding a fall mysteries event, and immediately my soulsister had the divine inspiration of doing an Odin Ordeal. I loved the idea and thought it would be worth pursuing, but felt my calendar was too full to properly devote the time and energy to plan and execute it. Then, no less than a month later, members of my spiritual family started talking about wanting to present a track at the event, and wouldn't it be neat to combine a suspension ritual with Odin's hanging from Yggdrasil? I knew then there was no escaping this, and that it was necessary to see it through.

The following is a narrative of experiences from the first four-day event. There are some things left to mystery, as we plan on presenting this event yearly at Mythical Journeys, the fall event for which it was conceived.

One by one our new tribe arrived. Suburban housewives, mountain men, IT developers, medical professionals gathered in the same place, drawn by various aspects of our offering, but all having admitted that maybe some one-eyed Wiseman had pushed them in some way into attending. Some were just understanding their 20's, while others were ploughing right into their 60's. It sounds trite to describe us as a motley tribe, but it was definitely a crossroads for those who were called. We, the facilitators, set an altar space in our main gathering site, a large 6' table covered with food, mead, runes, tools; we also began the lengthy process of blessing our representation of Yggdrasil; a large twisty tree within eyesight of our cabin. I placed Odin statues in each of the rooms we'd be sharing as living space, as well as other Norse accoutrements.

We gathered together after dinner for our first session. Everyone introduced themselves and we discussed some of what the next three days would hold, including their last "get out of jail free" opportunity, when we explained that the piercing parts of some of the rituals were not optional, that we expected all of the participants to get pierced in some way before the weekend was over. We were pleased to see that no one left, even if some of them admitted they were frightened or challenged by the thought.

One of the three women chosen to be Norns appeared, seemingly unannounced, to tell them the story of some of Odin's sacrifices – that of his eye, and of the nine days on the Tree. Each participant, upon giving their consent for undertaking the road of Odin's Ordeal, was blessed with ash and called Odinsson or Odinsdottir. There was then a sumbel—rounds of ritual toasts—as a way to get to know each other better and share ritual space together. And did we! A lot was shared that night—silly, sacred, loving, profane.

The morning came too quickly, but we arose and took breakfast together. Every morning was a blot to Odin at the Tree. Nothing like starting off a day with good mead! The rest of the morning was spent on safety education, both about piercings and about cross-contamination. We wanted to put all fears at ease that yes, we know what we are doing, we are well trained, and also to impart tools so everyone could focus on their experience, rather than worry about their safety and the safety of others.

That afternoon there was a class on runes. Not everyone who attended had a solid background in Norse traditions, so it was important that everyone have a general understanding of the runes. You won't forget what Isa means once you've been pelted by ice cubes with someone saying "Isa! Isa!"

After all that sitting around being diligent students, we wanted to go outside and play. Part of understanding the warrior nature of Odin is to undertake ritual combat. Together, with "boffer" weapons (PVC piping covered with upholstery foam), we simulated all sorts of ritual combat. There was even a Viking raid, done in good faith and in all jestery. It was obvious some of us were feeling nervous about the mystery of the night's ritual, and this was a perfect way to work it out.

Night came. Each of us was loaned a heavy leather cloak to represent our traveling persona (as Odin frequently traveled during these stories). We met together and meditated. One by one, we gave our eyes in symbolic sacrifice to show that we were dedicated to finding wisdom through walking in Odin's shadow. Each participant was given an eyepatch and instructed to wear it for the remainder of the weekend. They had also received a personal rune to focus on for their work. Strangely enough, almost half of the participants pulled Wunjo, the rune of Joy. We took this as a blessing.

That night we shared a hunter's kill together, roasting venison over a fire, and telling more personal stories to grow closer together. Some wandered down to the communal fire circle to share space with other track's participants, and to revel in the heat of a roaring bonfire during the coldest weekend experienced at this campground in the fall … all the while adjusting to life with one eye, wearing the sign of their sacrifice proudly. The next day, we gathered together to talk about our experiences during the ritual, and to come up with a bindrune and a name to represent our Tribe. Together, we created the "One-Eyed Wunjos", and a bindrune that looked like a pair of glasses with one lens cracked.

During the day, the facilitators encouraged the participants to begin visualizing what their tree ordeal would be. Not everyone was going to be fully suspended, as it can be an overwhelming experience for someone with little to no piercing experience. We knew prior to the event that one person was fully committed to suspending; what we didn't expect was for someone who had never even had his ears pierced to feel very certain that the full suspension would be his ordeal. Others took flesh hooks or hypodermic piercings in the shape of their rune(s). One, in his wisdom, knew that he wanted to be pierced, so his ordeal was to be bound and watch the other piercings take place and overcome his jealousy.

It was time for the ritual to begin. Each took on their traveler's cloak once again, and two people symbolizing Odin's wolves Freki and Geri appeared to lead them to the tree while chanting the runes in a meditative fashion. When they arrived, they were greeted by two people symbolizing Odin's ravens Hugin and Munin, and each participant was treated as though they themselves *were* Odin. We collectively placed one final blessing upon the tree that it might stand as our Yggdrasil. Then, one by one, the travelers were pierced in the fashion of their ordeal, and in some way attached to the tree.

Odin's Steed, we come to ride;
Odin's Steed, in us confide.
Odin's Steed, we come to give;
Odin's Steed, we give to live.
   -chant by Abraham Street

I absolutely must comment here that I have participated in a great deal of ordeal rites, yet nothing to date has moved me so much as the bravery and sacrifice that these people came forward with. Each had their journey, and no one left unchanged. We were able to suspend both participants who desired it – even the one who had never been pierced before. I am continually honored and blessed that I was able to witness and facilitate such a strong and moving ritual.

Some hung for a few minutes. Some hung for over two hours. Everyone, in their own way and time, shared revelation. Wisdom was found on that tree

The rest of the night was spent in a gentle sumbel where we invited outsiders from other tracks to come and share stories of their experiences. We had stew and meat and food and mead to share, and we stayed awake to the wee hours toasting Gods and boasting of our accomplishments.

Sunday came all too quickly. We did a final ritual to thank the tree for all it had done for us. We left it offerings and filled it with our gratefulness. We gathered for a final Blot to Odin, followed by many tears and hugs. Although it was only four days, there was an intimacy and power shared by those who participated which we will all carry with us on our journeys.

Nine Days of Odin:
A Rite of Passage

This is a rite for an individual of any gender who wishes to dedicate themselves to Odin, and to honor him and his great suffering, and walk (however lightly) in his footsteps. It must be done with the aid of a community of people, for it is not something that can be accomplished alone. This is important, for although it is good to be independent, the Odin-initiate will eventually come to serve a community, even as Odin himself returned to serve the Aesir as their leader and King.

This ordeal is hard on the body, and it is important that the initiate be in reasonably good shape in order to undergo it without breaking down and quitting. If necessary, they can train for it, perhaps by doing a lot of daily walking and some strong manual labor. Some of the ordeals, of course, are rather difficult to train for, but at the least they should be able to handle the amount of walking required.

One trusted individual should be chosen as the Priest or Priestess of the rite, ideally another Odin dedicant. They must agree to meet with the Odin-initiate at sunset of each day, regardless of where they might be, and give them the instructions and blessing for the next day – the nine days of this rite being at nightfall, as days used to be counted long ago. The initiate should have a staff, a broad-brimmed hat, a simple change of clothing, and a few necessities in a bag, because for the next nine days he will not be going home again. (I will temporarily use male pronouns to refer to the initiate; mentally insert the pronoun you prefer.) For the next nine days, he will walk everywhere that he needs to go—no cars, and ideally no bicycle. This means that the event must be orchestrated in an area where the volunteering community members live close enough together for the initiate to walk from home to home, at least for a few of their homes. It is a good rite for an urban area, at least the first part. Farms—the venue of the third section—are generally further out in places that it is difficult to walk to. These final parts should be done in a private venue, and it is acceptable for the initiate to catch a car ride to those places, although they may not drive themselves anywhere. Being safe and not attracting police attention is more important than obeying the letter of the ritual law.

Day 1-2:

At sunset, the Priest/ess meets the initiate waiting on the doorstep of their home (or that of a friend whom they consider family), with whatever folk of the community wish to witness. The Priest/ess gives the initiate a bag of food which the folk have prepared themselves, and says the following invocation:

> Long, long ago, Odin the All-Father,
> The Lord of Asgard and Keeper of Valhalla,
> Stepped down from his great throne
> Came down from his heavenly place,
> Stripped off his divine raiment,
> Laid down his sword and weapons,
> And spoke unto those around him,
> "There is more than this to life.
> There is more than this day and night,
> More than this wealth and might,
> More than this poverty and hardship,
> And I will find it.
> I will seek wisdom wherever it might be,
> Even in the deepest and darkest places,
> Even if it comes hard to me,
> Even if it kills me in the end,
> I will not count this quest as wasted,
> For a great Wyrd calls me out of my life,
> And I must give up everything that I have
> To gain everything I ever wanted."
> And saying this, he put on a ragged cloak
> And walked away into the wilderness,
> And all the entreaties of his loved ones
> Were nothing to the wind in his ears

And the pull on his spirit.
For sometimes it is like this in life,
That the Spirit calls, and it will not be denied
Even when what it asks is so hard
That you fear it will be the death of you.

The Priest/ess embraces the initiate, and says, "From this moment on, you are a wanderer on the road. You have no home. You must go from place to place and work for your food, and a place on the floor to sleep. You must ask each family who grants you this hospitality to tell you of their dead, their living, and any wisdom they would pass on to you. Write this down, and go on your way." S/he hands the initiate a small blank book and a pen, and then stands back. All watch as the initiate makes their way down the road.

During the next two days, sunset to sunset, the initiate makes their way on foot from place to place. Any words spoken to them by strangers may be examined as omens. During the dark hours, they can go to the home of a willing person and offer to do work for them, some simple chores, and in exchange get a bite to eat and a place to sleep. Before they go to bed, they must ask the folk of the house for their wisdom, and it will be given, whatever those folk wish to tell them. They should write it down in the book. At dawn they must be off again, and all day they must wander, stopping only occasionally to rest, regardless of the weather. At the sunset that begins the second day, the Priest/ess should meet them at their chosen berth for the night, check in on them, and hear the wisdom they have gathered through the day.

Day 3-4:

On the sunset that begins the third day, the Priest/ess comes again with witnesses, and gives the following invocation:

> Odin the wanderer, once Lord of Asgard,
> Once Keeper of Valhalla, once All-Father of gods,
> Traveled the dusty roads of Midgard,
> Dust for his meals and dust in his eyes,
> And the folk of Midgard looked upon him
> And saw only an old beggar,
> And when he asked them for a meal,
> Many threw stones, many threw curses,
> And a few threw a crust of bread,
> And counted themselves generous.
> When he asked them for a drink,
> Many threw stones, many threw curses,
> And a few gave him a dipperful from a horse-trough,
> And counted themselves generous.
> When he asked them for a place to sleep,
> Many threw stones, many threw curses,
> And a few showed him to a pile of moldy hay,
> And counted themselves generous.
> When he asked them for work,
> Many threw stones, many threw curses,
> And a few set him to cleaning pigsties,
> And counted themselves generous.
> So was the Lord of Asgard served
> By the folk of Midgard who saw him,
> Not knowing that it was the Lord of the Aesir
> At whom their stones were aimed.
> And so Odin suffered, and made the first sacrifice:
> Understanding what it is to have no home,
> And count Midgard's folk against you.

For the next two days, the wandering will continue, only the demands of work made by the homes that he stays at will be more rigorous, and the luxuries less. A blanket on the floor in a warm place, a bowl of stew, a cup of clean water to drink, and a bowl of water with an old towel and some soap to wash with will be good enough. Again, the initiate must ask for their wisdom, and write it down. At the sunset that starts the fourth day, the Priest/ess comes again to them, checks on them, and hears what they have learned in that day.

Day 5-6:

At the sunset that begins the fifth day, the initiate is picked up by the Priest/ess and taken in the back of a vehicle to a farm (or even a large garden) whose owners are willing to aid in the ritual. If they have a barn with animals, so much the better, for the initiate will sleep there that night. Before leaving them, the Priest/ess says the following invocation to them:

> The earth breaks beneath our hoes,
> And she receives our sweat and toil
> As we work her for our survival.
> Long, long ago, Odin the All-Father,
> Lord of Asgard and Keeper of Valhalla,
> Put on the ragged cloak of a peasant,
> Wandered down the road alone,
> And worked among the peasants
> For his daily bread. Day after day,
> He who had been enthroned in the sky
> Learned the toil of the lowest on earth,
> Learned the count of the drops of sweat
> That fall like salt rain upon the soil,
> Learned the blistered hands and the aching back,
> The heat of the sun on bare skin,
> The satisfaction of a single turnip
> Pulled from the soil on an empty belly.

> He who had ordered the life and death of so many
> Learned what it was to work for his bread,
> And to fear death without it.
> On this day we honor his second sacrifice,
> The giving up of privilege,
> And we put our hands into the earth,
> Never forgetting that to be low is to close to Her,
> And therefore to be sacred.

For the next two days, the initiate will learn what it is to be a migrant agricultural worker, as Odin learned on his journeys. He should be worked hard at manual farm labor, and no job is too dirty, dull, or disgusting (although he should be given water and food and watched for such things as heatstroke, and the jobs should not be more dangerous than the farmers are willing to do themselves; cleaning out manure from barns is especially good for this ordeal). Ideally, he should sleep with a blanket on hay in the barn, and wake to work again at dawn. At sunset of the fifth day, the Priest/ess comes again to check on him, and hear what he has learned so far.

Day 7:

At the sunset that begins the seventh day, the initiate is picked up again by the Priest/ess and brought back to the area of their wanderings. However, as they are dropped off at the place they are spending the night, their clothing is stripped from them and clothing of the sex opposite to that in which they currently live is given to them to wear. They are told that for the next day, sunset to sunset, they are to live as a woman (or a man). If the individual is third gender, it should be the clothing of whichever gender is more difficult for them, and an exaggeration of that.

The Priest/ess speaks to them the following invocation:

We walk every day as man or woman,
And we think little of it,
Save for those of us who have been both,
And who never take these things for granted again.
Which fish, we ask, discuss water?
The drowning ones—that is the only answer,
And so Odin went to the goddess of love,
Great Freya of the surpassing beauty,
And asked her to teach him the art of seidhr,
The woman's magic. And Freya did agree,
But the price was that for one year
Odin the great should don the skirts
Of a woman, a mere serving maid,
And be known by all under the name of Eunuch,
And live as the lowest of women lived.
And so it was done, and Odin learned
The magic that can only be touched
By those whom the woman's energy can fill.
And he did also learn that these things
Are not static within us, and can shift,
And should never be taken for granted,
And Odin left Freya's side
Having learned much about women,
And he would never see them the same again.
And we thank him for this lesson, and his third sacrifice,
That of the smug surety of a single gender.

That night, they are to be left at the house of a spirit-worker, who will teach them whatever thing that they deem is appropriate. The next day, they will work for that spirit-worker as whatever gender they have been assigned to, doing those tasks traditional to that gender. During this time, they are referred to as some derogatory name or title that reflects their greatest difficulty with this ordeal. Ideally, their chores should not only be confined to a house, but they should be taken out in public—escorted by members of the spirit-worker's household for safety if necessary for your particular area—to run ordinary errands.

Day 8:

At the sunset that begins the eighth day, the initiate is picked up by the Priest/ess and taken to a pond or other body of water. If possible, a waterproof light should be shining under the surface, anchored just far enough out so that one must wade waist-deep to get to it. The Priest/ess says the following invocation to the initiate:

> Behold the Well of Mimir!
> Here lies the severed head of the god of wisdom
> Who would not speak what he knew,
> And here great Odin, much lessened by his travels,
> Came to seek out Mimir's wisdom.
> He saw the severed head floating deep into the well,
> And he asked Mimir to tell him all he knew,
> The secrets of the underground,
> The things unseen beneath the earth,
> Beneath the surface thoughts of men,
> Beneath his own surface.
> And Mimir laughed, and asked what price
> Great Odin would pay for this knowledge.
> And Odin said that he would pay any price.
> So Mimir asked for the price of one of his eyes,
> That he who was trapped in the well
> Might have vision in the upper world.
> And Odin agreed, and gave one of his eyes
> To Mimir in exchange for wisdom,
> Although the bargain was hard, and painful.
> Half-blind, he continued on his way,
> But two ravens settled on his shoulders,
> The gift of Mimir and the Norns,

Named Huginn and Muninn, Thought and Memory,
That he might have more eyes in the world
Who would tell him all that they saw.
And we honor Odin for his fourth sacrifice,
The giving up of worldly vision for greater sight.

The initiate must wade into the water until they come to the light, and meditate on what they must give up, what great sacrifice they must make, in order to come to this wisdom. When they come out of the water, they declare their intention to the Priest/ess, and a reading is done there on the shore to determine if this is an acceptable sacrifice as far as the Gods are concerned. If it is not acceptable, the initiate, must go back into the water and stand before the light again, and meditate until they figure out the right thing. This will be repeated until they get it right according to the divination. Then one of their eyes is taped shut with duct tape (or medical tape, if they have sensitive skin) and will remain that way for the next day, to remind them of their sacrifice and its repercussions.

They will return to the spirit-worker's house and work for them further that day, and be given shelter in their house again that night, although now they may do it in their own gender.

Day 9:

At the sunset that begins the ninth day, the initiate is picked up and taken to a private place where stands a great tree. The Priest/ess speaks to them the following invocation:

Great Odin, half-blind and limping,
Worn through by his travels,
Came before the Norns, the three Fates,
Urd the elder, grey and wrinkled as stone,
Pulling the threads of life from her long white hair
And spinning them fine and strong,

Verdandi the weaver, fair and brilliant,
On her loom of many colors,
And Skuld the dark maiden in armor
On her great black horse,
With her blade that slashes life away.
And Odin said to them, Give me magic,
That I may have understanding of all things,
That I may work great wights of power,
That my knowledge shall grow.
The Norns said unto him, What price
Shall you pay for this knowledge, O Odin,
Once King of Asgard, once keeper of Valhalla,
Once Lord of the Aesir, All-Father of the Gods,
Now a one-eyed, limping beggar on the road
With no home before you and no home behind you,
With dirt on your hands and dust in your mouth,
And the birds of ill omen flying about you,
What price will you pay for this wisdom?
Would you be wounded even unto the death?
And Odin said, I will pay any price you ask,
O givers of Fate whom all must obey.
I do surrender myself into your hands.
And so the Norns took Odin's body,
And brought it to the great World Tree,
Yggdrasil, on which lie all the Nine Worlds,
And they hung him on the great ash
And left him there to live or die.
And Odin's blood ran down the tree
In rivers, and they gathered it
Like fine red thread, and spun his Wyrd,
And wove it into tapestry, and stood ready to cut it
Should he fail in his quest.
Odin hung on that windswept tree
For nine days and nine nights,
And the worlds whirled by him

And the blood ran down him
And the hail pelted him like knives.
And in the moment before he died,
His vision cleared, and he saw before him
All the runes, their magic, their wisdom,
And he seized them, crying out,
And fell from Yggdrasil's arms
Back onto Midgard's hands,
And opened his eyes into a new dawn,
And it was Spring in the world,
And the time of renewal was upon it,
So Odin rose to his weary feet
And found that the path before him
Led him in only one direction,
And that was home.

Then the initiate is hoisted up and bound with ropes to the tree, and there he stays for some hours—ideally nine hours, so that he might watch the sun coming up. During this time he may have water passed to him, but no food—and he should have emptied himself out before going up. His job during this rope-hang, however long it takes (and the Priest/ess should use their best judgment and decide when to take the initiate down) is to sing. He should sing any power songs that he knows, the names of the runes, whatever comes into his head. He may also weep, or cry out. At the foot of the tree, the Priest/ess waits with a team of people who may drum, sing, chant, or simply keep silent vigil.

When the hang is over, he is taken down from the tree, fed, watered, cared for, and brought to his home to sleep, where he should be welcomed by folk waiting for him. The Priest/ess should make themselves available for counseling during the following week, if the initiate needs to decompress and talk about their ritual.

Ordeal Rite For A Woden's Man
by Galina Krasskova

This ritual is designed for a Woden's (Odin's) man—yes, someone born, raised, and identifying as biologically male. A woman or a third gender individual could ostensibly undergo this, but Woden treats his typical men, women, and *ergi* people very, very differently, so the rite would have to be altered in specific ways. While many of his women and ergi people are warriors, He does not temper them *first* through the same type of terror He customarily utilizes with His men. This rite is designed with that particular male psyche in mind. Men often have a dangerous habit of getting, as a priest once put it so eloquently to me, into a pissing contest with the Old Man. So He breaks them down.

Also, this is not a ritual that should be done in public. Ideally, the goal is to put the man in question through such terror, pain and extreme emotional challenge that he is forever changed. The Wodinic ordeals that I myself have overseen have involved three people in the woods, usually on the spur of the moment when Woden indicates that He wishes someone to undergo such a rite. The keystones of a Wodinic ordeal are terror, ruthlessness and pain, for He is a God of these things easily as much as He is a God of ecstasy and magic, and often His people must first endure and conquer the former before receiving the second.

The purpose of this ordeal, then, is to open the initiate to Odin. It is a type of sacred penetration, if you will, one that ruthlessly utilizes terror and pain to strip away at the blockages of ego, arrogance and humanity that men so often utilize to ward themselves from being bound to the Old Man's will. As such, what is offered here is at best an outline. Each ordeal must be customized to the initiate in question. The same tools and triggers may not work equally well for different people and that is an important fact to keep in mind.

The participants include:

1) A man willing or required by Odin to undergo such an ordeal.

2) A Woden's woman who is also His Valkyrie (warrior and ordeal priestess) to facilitate the ordeal. In ideal circumstances, this Valkyrie should have such ordeal skills as cutting, branding, suspension, and roleplaying, as well as *galdr* and rune magic. If not, other facilitators with the appropriate skills may be brought in. I, for instance, do not know how to do hook suspensions, so were I to utilize this particular ritual, I would necessarily have to bring in a team skilled in suspension work. The primary facilitator should be a Woden's woman, however. There are some things that a Woden's man cannot get from another Woden's man. The Valkyries traditionally brought warriors to their master's hall, and that is the function of the Woden's women who serve today in that capacity.

Prior to the ritual, the Valkyrie should do appropriate divination to determine what Woden wants—what ordeals are actually required, because every single thing listed here may not be required for every person, and other things might be required that aren't listed here. It's a very fluid process. Divination is a wonderful tool to use here.

3) If the Valkyrie is not a mistress of *galdr*, or prefers to have others to take that off her hands, then a team of three people of any gender can be brought in to symbolize the Nornir. They should *galdr* specific runes at specific times. I am not writing down any chants here, because the runes should speak through them, having a life of their own. Rune-*galdr* is never the same twice. The Nornir-team are chosen carefully, as they are the official witnesses to the rite, and through them the man's fate is witnessed and bound.

4) A second Woden's man present to be psychopomp to the initiate. Just as some things may only be learned from the hands of a Valkyrie, some things are best passed from Odin's man to Odin's man. His job is support and welcoming, and helping to other man to stay strong.

5) A man or three men (who can be *ergi* as long as they are "male of center" in sexual identity) representing Loki or men of the Vanir should be present for the second part of this rite.

Ideally, either the Valkyrie or the Odin's man will become ridden by Odin during this rite, but it is equally likely that some other manifestation will occur. It is also possible that the initiate may be ridden by the Old Man at some point during the final part of this ordeal. That is ideal, if the man in question is able to open to that degree. At any rate, the Valkyrie takes her orders from the Old Man and should not be afraid to deviate from the outline given should He wish it. In fact, that is a prerequisite for leading this ritual: the person in question should be ready, willing and able to throw the whole outline out the door and do precisely what Odin demands at any given point in the rite.

The location of this rite is of primary importance. The ideal place is in the middle of the woods at a crossroads, but this is not always possible. The most important factors in selecting the location are these: it must be isolated, and it must be a place where the initiate can scream without attracting attention from neighbors or police.

I am personally against the initiate knowing very much about the nature and structure of the ordeal prior to his actually undergoing it. The whole purpose of this rite is Woden removing any sense of control from the man in question, rendering him temporarily vulnerable. Knowing what is to come enables a person to guard and ward against the worst of it, and I am against giving the initiate time to ready himself like that. In fact, he should be kept off guard throughout the entire rite. Because of this, it may be wise to have him sign a legal waiver in case of injury.

Begin with a faining to the Old Man. This may be in regular ritual space, or may be held at the place of challenge. Hallow the space in whatever manner is appropriate to your practice. The Valkyrie should pour out a large horn of aquavit, vodka or whiskey and offer the following prayer:

Hail to the Lord of the battlefield.
Hail to He who hung like a corpse upon the Tree of Sacrifice.
Hail to He who ravaged Himself to conquer fear.
Hail to He who ravaged Himself to conquer pain.
Hail to He who ravaged Himself for power and understanding.
I call to the Lord of Death, Master of the ordeal.
I call to the ruthless Lord,
Bringing twin weapons of terror and ecstasy.
I call to the Master of the Tree,
Galdra-father, Sigfather, Grimnir, Yggr,
Lord of the Slain.
Come now, oh my Master,
Come now and claim this willing sacrifice
That stands awaiting the gifts
Of fear and terror, devastation and rebirth
That only You may grant.
Come now, Woden,
Grim-faced Lord of the battle dead.
To You I offer these gifts.
To You I pour out this drink.
(Raise the horn and pour some out into the ground—most but not all.)
Come now, oh my Lord,
And witness the ordeal of Your warrior this night.

Hail to the Whisperer of Secrets.
Hail to the God of the Slain.
Hail to the Ravager of Enemies.
Hail to the God of Pain.
Hail to You, Woden, All-Father,
Master of Runes, Master of the Ordeal
Who walked this road before us.
Hail, Woden.

The Valkyrie should continue praying and singing praise songs to the Old Man if she is able, until there is the palpable sense of His presence. At that point, she blesses the horn and offers it to the initiate, or may hand it to the psychopomp for him to offer. Normally a horn is never passed from man to man, but in the case of warriors during such a rite this rule is occasionally relaxed, even in orthodox heathenry. The cup is passed with the words:

"Woden wishes You to be bound to Him. If you drink of this, there is no turning back. If you drink of this, you belong to Him and He will do with you as He wills."

If the initiate asks for a few moments to consider, give it to him. He must go into the ordeal of his own free will, and with Woden, there is no turning back. He may still be snatched up later, even if he refuses to drink. It's not going to change anything if Woden wants him, but for the purposes of this ordeal rite, he must consent and drink.

The initiate drinks, and then the Valkyrie bids him to take the horn and offer it to the Old Man and pour out the remaining alcohol. The Valkyrie offers further praises to the Old Man, and then the faining is finished and it is time for the ordeal proper to begin. The initiate should at that point be stripped by the other Woden's man, and led to the appropriate place. The Woden's man says to him the following: "Woden searched for knowledge. He searched for power, for wisdom and understanding. He was ruthless in this search. Pain was no barrier; it was His ally. Anyone seeking to walk the path the Old Man has walked, to ask of His protection, His favor, His blessings must be willing to walk that same road."

First challenge:

Throw the man to the ground and bind him securely—ideally with rope, but if there's no one present who knows how to bind safely with rope, go ahead and use duct tape. The important thing is that the man cannot berserk or accidentally lash out in pain. In fact, the folks present should have some sort of weapon(s) that can non-lethally render the initiate unconscious if need be. Many of Woden's folk are berserkers and this should be taken into account.

While either doing rune-*galdr* herself or having the representatives of the Nornir doing the rune-*galdr*, the Valkyrie should take a scalpel and carefully begin to cut runes into the initiate's back or chest (whichever she feels more appropriate at the time), singing the runes into his flesh as she does so. Runes of binding to Woden, opening, initiation, and strength are appropriate. (Ansuz, Gebo, Raido, Wunjo, Algiz for example ... though do not limit it to just these runes. Feel free to cut the entire Futhark into him if need be.) The Valkyrie should, once the cutting is done, rub ash made from the nine sacred herbs into the cut, blessing each one. The blessings will vary: the Valkyrie should *galdr* whatever she thinks the man will need (or rather whatever Woden is telling her to *galdr*), singing a blessing into each rune as she rubs it with ash.

If the man is a shapechanger, *galdr* can shake his *hame* out of human form. This in itself may end up being part of the ordeal, so the Valkyrie should be prepared for that, and be prepared to sing him back into his skin and provide adequate aftercare.

Second Challenge:

Wrists still bound, the initiate is helped into a woman's skirt, very long and full. He is then taken to a private place nearby, where things can be heard but not seen. This can be a tent, or a curtained-off area, or just behind many bushes. An area has been prepared for laying down, perhaps with a mattress, futon, or sleeping bag. In this place, either a man representing Loki or three men representing Freya's cousins, men of the Vanir, are waiting.

Of the four challenges, this is the most difficult and controversial in many ways. It honors the year that Odin spent in skirts, being *ergi* and learning seidhr from Freya. During this time, He wore women's clothing and was known by the name of Jalkr (Eunuch). According to the information that many spirit-workers have gotten from Odin, it was at this time that He learned about the power of *ergi*, through being used as a woman by Freya's cousins. It was also during His nine-year wanderings, according to that same information, that He became lovers with Loki.

This ritual has nothing whatsoever to do with the sexual preference of the initiate; in fact, that preference is beside the point at best, and to be used against them at worst. Odin's sexuality has nothing to do with sexual preference; it has to do with sexual power. Is there power in this sexual act? He asks. If so, then He is willing to do it in order to gain that power. The power of this sexual act is penetration, and learning to be open to the force of the Divine.

Whether to include this part of the ritual, and how far to go with it, should be decided beforehand by those who plan it. The decision should be made with both sensitivity and ruthlessness. Discomfort, embarrassment, and shame should not be reasons for eliminating it; this is supposed to be an ordeal, remember? However, if the initiate is fragile enough around the issue that he may berserk and injure himself or others over it, then perhaps it should be skipped. Divination should be done beforehand to decide. While sexual preference, as we said, is not an issue here, the everyday realities of safe sex and monogamous love-bonds are important and not to be trifled with. Therefore, if this part of the ritual is done, there are several levels to which it can go:

1) An artificial phallus is used to penetrate the initiate's mouth, and his skirt is flung up and sexual intercourse mimed (perhaps interfemorally) by the facilitators. This is the minimum requirement.

2) An artificial phallus is used to penetrate the initiate anally, gently and with lots of lubricant. During this act, they should be encouraging him to relax, to open, to not worry about anything but opening up and letting go.

3) If it is entirely appropriate for all parties involved, and divination deems it a requirement, the initiate may be penetrated anally by the facilitators themselves, using safer sex. Again, it should be stressed that this is about letting go and opening up.

The facilitators for this part of the ritual should be chosen with care. If it is one man representing Loki, it should be done in a more caring way, although the facilitator can be as verbally sharp as he wishes. If it is to be three men representing men of the Vanir, their attitudes should be friendly, but rough. In either case, the facilitators should be in on the initial planning session, and know what the divination reads. They should be sensitive to the issues present and use their judgment as to how to proceed, or when to back off and end things.

During this part of the ritual, the Valkyrie and the Nornir stand a distance away and sing until the men return with the initiate. Afterwards, the skirt is removed and the initiate is brought naked and unbound back to the main area.

Third Challenge:

The initiate is taken to a large, sturdy tree with good outlying branches, representing Yggdrasil. At this point, the flesh of his chest is sterilized in preparation for a branding. The Valkyrie or Nornir again began to galdr as the Valkyrie brands him with a *valknot* either on chest or back. During the sterilization, the Valkyrie says:

Willingly He hung between two fires,
Willingly He allowed Himself to be seared and burned,
Willingly He ascended the Tree,
Willingly He cast off His flesh, yielding to pain
To win greater knowledge.
So must you.

I mark you now with the brand of Woden,
The *valknot* which marks His servants and warriors.
As Woden sacrificed his flesh, so must You.
As He dined on terror, so must You.
Nothing will be left of you but what He deems necessary.
All else must go to nourish the roots of the Tree.

Fourth Challenge:

At this point, nine hooks should be inserted into the man's back and he should be drawn up and suspended from the Tree. (NOTE: this should only be done by someone qualified and appropriately trained in hook suspensions.).

The Valkyrie should sing some version of the *Runatal* section of the *Havamal*, which highlights Odin's hanging on Yggdrasil. She or the Nornir may *galdr*, or after the recitation/song of the *Runatal*, they may allow the man to hang in silence and darkness. How long he stays up is completely up to Woden. The Valkyrie will know when it is time to take him down. His cries should have no bearing on this at all. Finally, the man is brought down and the hooks removed. If he is going to be possessed by the Old Man, it likely will happen while he is hanging on the Tree.

The Valkyrie and the psychopomp (and any others present) should dress his wounds, dress him, and offer him something to drink and eat. As this is happening, the Valkyrie should bless him and bring him back to his humanity. This may involve holding him, or it may involve *galdr*—it varies depending on the man in question. Once he is able to walk and is fairly coherent, the group should proceed to the ritual space. Thanks—and more alcohol—should be offered to Woden, the first of which should be offered by the initiate. The Valkyrie should be available for aftercare, and any pastoral counseling needed, for a couple of weeks after the rite.

Open To The Divine:
The Path of the Horse

The night wind is cool on his face as he sits there, emptied of himself. Hours ago, he was bathed and purified, and runes were drawn on his flesh. Now he has sat and communed, opened up the back of his head as wide as possible for the Presence to enter. In a trance, he rises and dons the clothing that is only worn occasionally: the tunic of blue and grey with the Futhark-embroidered trim, the belt with the sword, the cloak of grey with ravens embroidered on the shoulders and wolves at the hem. The spear is there too, leaning up against the tree. When this is done for the whole community, he has people to attend him, to drum the God into him, and whisper their chants, to dress him so that his hands may hang limply until the God chooses to move them. Tonight, though, it will only be a short ride, because it is just a client who wishes to speak to her Patron.

The eyepatch slips on over his head, blotting out half his sight, and the connection is made. The Presence moves into him, fills him, pushes him gently out of the way. The hands that don the wide-brimmed hat and carefully adjust it to dip low over the eyepatch are his, but it is not he who moves them.

As if from far away, he sees her approach. She bears a cup in one hand and a bottle in the other, and he senses pleasure from the Being who has borrowed his flesh. The voice that speaks through his throat is not his; it's deeper and more mellifluous, and one hand beckons the woman closer. He can't make out what the voice is saying, but that's all right; it's not his business. He's only the vehicle. As unconsciousness closes over him, he relaxes into the hands of the Divine Will, and knows that his submission here brings the Gods closer to the human beings who reach their hands out to the Powers That Be.

First, let me disclaimer right off that the word "horse" is borrowed from the Afro-Caribbean religious traditions. In those religions (Voudoun, Santeria, Candomble, Umbanda, Palo Mayombe), the person whose body is borrowed by a God or a spirit is referred to as a "horse", and the act of being spirit-possessed is referred to as being "ridden". While we who do these things in a modern northern-tradition context do unashamedly borrow this term, it seems oddly appropriate in spite of its origins. One is reminded of the runes Ehwaz and Raido, the Horse and the Ride, which are also Movement and the Path.

In northern-tradition terms, the word which comes closest to this state is possibly *wod*, which is cognate to the god Woden. It suggests becoming one with the Divine Force, although *wod* is really less about giving one's body to be borrowed by that force, and more about partaking of its energy to whatever extent we incarnate humans can manage. We don't have a surviving word for horsing, or even any clear lore on the subject. It's likely that the Christian writers who took down notes about their defeated pagan brethren were not interested in discussing the enemy Gods coming down to Earth to be among their people.

But the main reason that we spirit-workers in the Northern Tradition are horsing deities has nothing at all to do with any lore-based justification. It is the simplest reason of all: The Gods are coming back, and They want to be able to use human bodies in order to get things done. According to Them, this is the way that it was once done, regardless of what was written down (or omitted) by the enemies of their faith. We're doing it because They want us to, and that's more than enough reason for us.

In the current climate of both the overarching Neo-Pagan demographic and the smaller subset of Asatru/Heathen folk, god-possession is looked upon with suspicion and disbelief. I remember being told flatly by one rather well-known Pagan author that our group shouldn't be doing it because it was self-indulgent and dangerous. (As if those of us who had been chosen to be horses could just stop! It seemed like the most self-indulgent and dangerous thing to do in those circumstances would be to tell the Gods to go hang, and then wait for the ass-kicking that would come afterwards.) Many Neo-Pagans don't actually believe in god-possession, or are willing to believe it of Afro-Caribbean people but not of rational, modern Americans, which is a subtly racist attitude that no one has yet confronted, along with a bucketload of fear.

The main objection is that since one can't tell whether or not someone is actually horsing the deity, or just pretending to, someone manipulative could exploit the situation and take advantage of a gullible group of Pagans. My answer to this has always been that adequately trained people with the Sight can easily tell whether or not that's a God in that there body, and if there's a team of such people available to help with the horsing, not only it is a smoother experience for the horse, but any faking or delusional behavior is nipped in the bud. Ideally, there ought to be training in how to spot a real possession and a faked one, and what to do in both cases.

Certainly a spirit-worker who isn't a horse can be invaluable in this way. Experienced spirit-workers need to band together to discern what is real and what is someone's mental sock puppets. After a time, skilled spirit-workers (or even skilled psychics or witches) learn what to look for in a possession. In many indigenous shamanic practices, the beginning shamanic practitioner who claims to be able to carry spirits is tested by their peers who watch the possession and decide if it's real. This sort of peer-testing is invaluable, in my estimation, although it will only really be useful when we as spirit-workers form peer-support organizations of our own.

In the meantime, we can learn the hallmarks of real possession, rather than fakery or self-delusion. They are generally agreed to be:

1) The deity does not advocate for the horse. God X doesn't start telling the folks listening how great Joe (whose body they are borrowing) is, or why they should listen to Joe. The deity usually treats the body as

if it is their own, and doesn't refer to the horse much at all. They may have an inner dialogue going with the horse, but that's between them, and onlookers never see or hear it. In general, an over-emphasis on issues pertinent to the horse, their vendettas, etc. is a huge warning sign. If the "deity" starts lashing out over an issue personal to the horse, it's worth taking a second look.

2) If the deity does refer to the horse, they will very rarely refer to them by name; more likely they'll say "this one" or something like that. This is because being called by name can actually shake many horses out of the possession and call them back to themselves (a useful trick for helping someone ground afterwards if they're having difficulties coming all the way back). In some Afro-Caribbean religions, the Orisha or Lwa may not recognize themselves as being in a horse, although we've never had this happen with Northern-Tradition Deities.

3) Beware overstressing of the archetype of the deity: most possessions are unique. If it's nothing but a carbon copy of lore or what you'd read in a book but never gets "high", never gets personal or beyond the assumed archetype, it's worth questioning. In most possessions, the deity gets personal. It goes beyond and doesn't feel distant. They are right there with you.

4) Don't be bothered by a lack of supernatural manifestations; that doesn't mean that it's not a true possession. Not all possessions are going to involve healing or divination. Some of the most powerful do not. The Gods, after all, are not there to do parlor tricks.

5) The support staff will get better understanding with repeated possessions. If the same God or Goddess goes into the same person on more than one occasion, it becomes easier to see the pattern. Sometimes, a deity will refer to something they've said in a previous possession, even if that possession occurred in another horse.

Galina Krasskova writes: "A Lukumi friend of mine offered this advice: Take the first possession at face value…there's just not empirical evidence beyond that. Note, however, that in subsequent ones, the crisis situation of possession (by the same Deity) tends to produce the same symptoms in the horse. This is telling. The way that the individual horse reacts to that specific crisis, that particular Deity will be through certain signals, movements and gestures, which indicate that the horse is about to be possessed. The horse him or herself may not be aware of this. When I was possessed by a goddess at a public gathering recently, one of my handlers, also a horse, noted that as She was settling Herself in me, She kept making a specific hand gesture—I've no idea what it was—and he noted it's exactly the same gesture that his patron Goddess and God will make when one of Them is trying to ride him and he's resisting ... But most importantly, as a person witnessing, trust what it is you see and feel more than anything else. How do you feel about what it is you're witnessing? It should have emotional impact; you should feel something."

The Path of the Horse is the rarest of the Paths, because it isn't one that you can just set out to master via willpower. It is entirely dependent on the Gods and wights, and if They don't want to go along with the idea of you using this path, then it simply won't happen. That's another reason for the greater community to dislike it; it is (like becoming a shaman) rather an elitist situation. The Gods and wights decide who gets to do it, and we have no say over that. We can't even really understand their choices and reasoning; being nabbed as a horse doesn't seem to be contingent on any standard of intelligence, sanity, morals, or even devoutness. In the egalitarian views of the modern alternative spirituality movement(s), any spiritual experience ought to be available to anyone who works hard enough at it, and the unfairness of being chosen (or not) as the Gods' own limo driver can rankle terribly.

In ancient times, this was less of a problem because people didn't expect spiritual things to be egalitarian. They also didn't expect them to be kind, or loving, or in the immediate best interests of the humans whom they might grab. In fact, the average person in a traditional tribal society will generally avoid "spirit-ridden" sacred places as taboo; they don't want to be noticed by the spirits. They know what happens to the people who get noticed, and they'd prefer to keep living their lives with a full set of choices. This contrasts wildly to modern Pagans who desperately want to "bring more magic into their lives", without knowing what that meant to our ancestors. The Gods and wights, however, still work along the paths noted by those ancestors. They are untouched by, and immune to, our exhortations that spiritual attention be distributed fairly, by our own standards, and they will continue to work in ways that bewilder and confuse us and are mysterious to our limited understandings.

That said, one person who is grabbed as a horse may be offered a different deal from someone else. Some spirit-workers are required to horse when the Gods tell them, and their only bargaining point may be time and place. Others have greater leeway and can refuse, although if they refuse too often the gift may be withdrawn entirely. Some offer and are accepted; some offer and are refused; some refuse and are taken anyway. Some may only horse their patron deity; others might be "lent out" by their patron to horse other Gods (we call this being a rent-a-horse), and yet others may have no patron and no restrictions except for which Gods are willing to show up and use them. (This is a dangerous situation, because it's really useful to have a patron deity who will protect you, keep you from being damaged, and screen out harmful spirits. Without that, a very Open horse-type may end up becoming the equivalent of a gang-bang whore for any spirits who come along.)

There are generally five main reasons why a spirit-worker would channel a wight of whatever size and intensity. There might also be a couple of smaller reasons, but these are the main ones:

1. Training purposes. Sometimes there are skills that can't be taught to you through words, but require a wight to enter your body at least partially and "motor you through" the skill. (For example, Loki taught me pathwalking in this way.) This could also include being horsed in order to train someone else, when the wight in question needs a willing body to be their sparring partner, or to show them how a type of energy is moved, or a type of magic done.

2. Information purposes. If a client comes to you with a question and one of the Gods wants to answer that question themself, you could just take verbal dictation and relate the words, but it's useful to be able to temporarily horse them if need be. That way they can speak to the client

face to face, as it were, and you're less likely to muck things up with an unclear signal.

3. Public devotional purposes. For some people, a spirit-worker horsing a deity at a public ceremony is the only chance that they'll have to see and speak with a divine force. This is very important, both to the Gods and to the worshipers. This was driven home to me after a gathering, early on, when I horsed a deity who was special to many folk present. I remembered little or nothing about what happened during the horsing, but afterwards people were coming up and giving thanks for allowing them to speak to the Gods directly for the first time. The number of people who were genuinely moved made it clear that this was not just done because the Gods had demanded it of us. It was a real public service, and a valuable one.

4. Errands for the deity. Sometimes a God or wight will want to do something in our world that requires a cooperative human body. Most often it seems to be a one-on-one meeting with one of their dedicants. This could be just an important conversation, or something as formal and intense as a wedding with a mortal god-spouse. Occasionally it will involve an interaction with another deity which needs to happen in mortal form for some reason (usually unknown to us, as They don't necessarily give us the whole story), or even no one else at all (such as the time that a wight wanted to use me to taste meat, or gather seawater).

5. Doing work on someone that requires you as a channel. This is rather more of the "classic" shamanic work where the shaman asks his spirit-helpers to come through him and aid an individual who needs help. Most often this is simply the energy of the spirit in question coming through, which is beginning to be commonly referred to as "aspecting" (see below), but on occasion it requires full-on spirit-possession.

Levels of Deity Assumption

Some time ago, a list started circulating around the Neo-Pagan community, attributed to Willow Polson, with regard to levels of deity presence. While we found it to be useful, we also expanded it a bit to include levels-between-levels that only people who've had a lot of experience horsing deities could know. Therefore, we present the expanded list, with apologies to Ms. Polson.

1. Enhancement

This is speaking about a deity; for example, giving an invocation in the third person, or telling a story. Doing this enhances people's understanding of that deity, their immediate connection with them, and the feeling of their presence at the event. Enhancement requires only knowing about the deity, rather than having an intimate connection with them.

2. Inspiration

This is similar to enhancement, in the sense that you are giving an invocation or telling a story, but the difference is that with inspiration you speak from the perceived viewpoint of the deity. In this case, you speak for rather than speak about them. Instead of "Aphrodite did this,", it's "Aphrodite wants this." Inspiration is done by connecting on some level with the deity, picking up messages about what they want, and then relaying those messages.

3. Shadowing

This is where the deity "rides along in your head", as many folks have put it. There's a feeling of them being just behind your shoulder, and able to speak clearly to you (and some may keep up a running commentary during a shadowing experience), but they are not using your body, and you are in full control of your reactions. You may "take dictation" and relay their words, or rephrase them, or keep silent as the situation requires.

4. Integration

Integration goes one step further; here you speak as the deity in the first person. This is generally done only as the highlight of a ritual; one example of this is the classic Wiccan "drawing down the Moon", in which the high priestess steps forth and speaks as if she were the Goddess herself. "I am the beauty of the green earth and the white moon among the stars and the mystery of the waters…" Integration is done by connecting with the deity and relaying their words immediately, in the first person, as if one was an interpreter. It requires a more intimate and clear connection if it is to be done properly, rather than merely narrating the words of the Athena puppet in the priestess's head, for example.

5. Aspecting

The line between Integration and Aspecting is subtle, but basically here one is a full channel for the energy of the deity, and often their words, but the deity has not fully taken over the flesh body in order to walk around in it and treat it as their own. Some refer to this as "co-consciousness", meaning that the deity's mind and energy and their own are equally present and share command of what will be said. Aspecting is often mistaken for fully being ridden by people who have never dealt with full-on possession. Classic New Age "channeling" is one form of Aspecting, usually with dead souls or minor spirits. Many people can Aspect a deity that they cannot necessarily fully horse, and Aspecting is less exhausting and much easier on the body and the soul. Galina Krasskova comments about it: "Often at this stage, I find that I am sometimes able to (or allowed to) explain sensations, thoughts, or emotions that I pick up from the Deity to whomever the Deity is speaking to for greater clarification. There are those possessions where I am sure it's co-consciousness and later find out that while I may have thought so, large portions of time are simply blanked from my mind so that what I think is a full memory of the experience is in reality piecemeal."

6. Possession

In this situation, the strongest connection of all, the deity comes into the person's body, displacing their own personality/soul for a time, and speaks directly to the audience or client. Depending on the god and the situation, the deity may commandeer the body for other things as well. Generally the horse's consciousness at this point is either extremely distanced (horses have reported seeing and hearing things as if underwater or from a long way away, in a very dissociative manner, or the sound might be turned off entirely) or they are completely unconscious and have no memory of the experience. My Pagan group, with its wry sense of humor, often refers to the former as being "in the back seat behind the safety glass" (while the deity is "driving"), and the latter as "locked in the trunk".

Whether the horse is relegated to the back seat or the trunk will vary widely. Some deities prefer to have the body to themselves; some are fine with the horse being somewhat conscious so long as they don't interfere; some will even talk to the horse in the back seat while "driving" their body, although this is more rare. Some horses prefer to be unconscious and ask the deity to make them so, while others prefer to be at least partly present at all times, usually for reasons of assuaging personal feelings of control. We've noticed that it's common for a deity to block out the hearing of a horse while the god in question is speaking one-on-one to someone else, because it is private and not for the horse's ears. Certainly for weddings of deities with their mortal spouses, the horse is as a matter of course stuck into the trunk.

While there is no one way to "induce" a possession—it seems that the best and fullest possessions come when the spirit in question informs one ahead of time, whether a moment or days ahead, that they are coming and then just pops in—there are techniques that can help, especially when there is a public devotional possession scheduled for a particular ceremony. First, the horse should do a good deal of devotional work and develop some kind of relationship with the god or wight in question. If the horse can't carry on a meaningful conversation with them, it's unlikely that they will have enough connection to be ridden by them, and even if the wight does manage it (because many of them are bigger and more powerful than us and can push their way in, if you have the right wiring) it's better to have it be an act of devotion than violation.

Second, we've found that what we call "haunted costumes", or ceremonial clothing that belongs only to that deity, and is donned only to horse them, helps a good deal. It can be as simple as a piece of jewelry or as elaborate as a full-scale costume. Anyone who has seen the initiatory rites of Korean shamans will be impressed by the ceremonies utilizing dozens of ceremonial costumes, donned one after the other by the spirit-worker, to see which spirits enter into them and become their helpers. After a while—sometimes even after the first time—the costume gets enough magic on it to be used as a gateway for that deity to enter, which helps all but the most recalcitrant, headblind, or blocked-up horses. It should go without saying, of course, that the ceremonial costume should not be used for any other purpose, including non-possessory ceremonial use by unwitting volunteers.

Most deities like to have some sort of attendant present to get them more food, drink, or anything else that they might want brought to them. We also find it useful, at least when it comes to full group rituals, to have at least one personal attendant for each embodied Deity, whom we refer to as a "page", and also a "steward" who handles people who want to approach the Gods, making sure that they understand the proper behavior and don't approach all at once. Then we have at least one drummer, at least one staff person (in charge of general physical objects and organization), the actual Priest/ess whose job it is to read invocations and run the rest of the ritual, and of course the prep/recovery team to help the horse get into the right space and come back afterwards, who are sometimes also the pages.

Something that groups who have started to publicly horse European deities are discovering, sometimes to their dismay, is that our Gods occasionally want sex as an offering. This is in contrast to the Afro-Caribbean deities, who have been covered under a blanket of Catholicism for so long that they no longer have any kind of sex with the congregation, but our deities are still used to the ancient rites, and sometimes expect it. Before this raises hackles, I should say straight out that nearly all deities will refrain from approaching anyone in that way who isn't already interested and open to the idea. In fact, they seem to have an eye for figuring out who would be into that, and homing in on them. If there is no one present who wouldn't object, then the subject won't come up. (The sole exception to this is Loki, and other Trickster Gods; see the notes about how to handle Loki in the next chapter.) But if there are people present who are into the idea, perhaps you might want to set them up as pages, and have a private space ready in case that is wanted. This is especially important for fertility deities like Frey and Freya. I can say from experience that although the Gods are not thrilled with safe sex and fluid boundaries, they will put up with it if those boundaries are set beforehand.

As to helping the actual psychic mechanics of the horsing, being in a state of quiet, meditative Openness, however one wishes to achieve that (perhaps using one of the other seven paths) is a good way to start. Cleansing the body/vessel is important as well. For group ritual horsing, our group has a "prep team" that treats the horse as a votive object—cleansing them, dressing them, singing to them, preparing them for the spirit to enter. It also encourages an objectified feeling which helps with egotism—it reinforces to the horse that it's not about them. Afterwards, the prep team becomes the aftercare team, making sure that the horse has water, food if they want it, a warm blanket, the chance to get out of and away from ritual garb, and however much space that they need to recover from the event.

As the Afro-Caribbean folk discovered long ago, having someone drumming during the rite helps a great deal. In their case (as discussed in the Path of Rhythm section), there are special (secret and oathbound) drumbeats for each Orisha or Loa which help to call them and keep them present. I've been told that there are such drumbeats for every deity, but that the ones of the northern-tradition Gods are lost. I've recovered one of them, and I intend to discover more. However, even just a simple steady drumbeat can help the God to stay present and the horse to stay relaxed and in trance.

Some Neo-Pagan groups are starting to work with various levels of spirit-possession, but there is a disturbing trend of the occasional training group insisting that anyone can horse regardless of innate wiring (and in some cases, that anyone can horse any deity with no ill effects). In order to make this happen, some are utilizing the process of the group psychically "condensing" the individual's soul and stuffing it into a corner of their being, and then reaching through them and pulling the deity through into their body. We find this trick to be rather concerning for a variety of reasons, assuming that it even works for full possession and not merely aspecting. First, it is our experience that horsing can be a psychically strenuous activity. The individual's psychic "sphincter", for lack of a better word, is stretched wide open. Just as with physical sphincters, the best way to receive something large is to be in a state of relaxed, accepting openness. Someone else forcing the issue may or may not get the horse open enough, but even if it works, it may cause lasting damage, which can manifest as mental illness. We would rather go with the idea that if the horse can't seem to open up enough, they either don't have enough of the inborn psychic wiring for it (which is no one's fault) or they aren't ready for some internal reason of their own, which must be dealt with in its own time and way. Horsing is shock enough to the soul; having a bunch of people shoving it around is more trauma to the soul complex than is good for anyone.

We have also found that no one can be ridden by just any spirit. There has to be an element of "like calls to like", or at least some sort of compatibility. Sometimes that compatibility is subtle and not something that the horse can know until they try and succeed or fail. As the northern-tradition equivalent of a "black shaman" (that's in the Siberian sense, not the western black = evil nonsense), who is owned by Lady Death, I never thought that I would be able to horse Frey, the Golden One of the Vanir ... but he has a standing date to take me around Lammas, and it works well ... even leaving a residue of light and health in my dark insides. On the other hand, Baphomet fits well as a ride, as he is also third-gendered and is associated with the rotting-down part of the cycle, as is my Lady Hela. The old primal Hunter also rides me on a yearly basis, and my predator nature works well as a fit. But when a bride of Anubis asked for someone to horse her husband for a ceremony, I asked to see if I would be an acceptable fit and the cosmic answer came back No, even though he is associated with Death.

Sometimes the problem isn't mental fit but physical fit. Before I transitioned to a more male physiology, I had horsed Lilith. She is a fairly masculine and hairy goddess, but she is still female of center, and when I crossed the middle line she would no longer use my body. Some deities will horse bodies of a different gender, or very different physique or state of (dis)ability, than their own with no problem. Others are extremely picky—most Love Goddesses, for instance, and many of the more "macho" and physically-oriented war gods. No horse should take it personally if they aren't a good fit for a particular God or wight. (For that matter, since most people aren't "wired" to horse at all, they shouldn't take that personally either. I'll never be a pro basketball player or a genius mathematician. So what?) The Gods have their own preferences, and we just have to go with them. Some modern Pagans do hold that any trained horse ought to be able to carry any deity, but we haven't found that to be true or possible, or at least not in this particular tradition. And, frankly, if you are horsing any deity with no ill effects—or little in the way of serious aftereffects at all—we seriously doubt that you are doing full possession. It's not something that is ever done easily or lightly. On the other hand, even if it's only Aspecting, that's a good thing in and of itself ... and much easier on one's astral body.

This is probably the point where the discussion of gender comes in. When dealing with spirit-workers as a demographic, it is wise to expect that a not insignificant percentage of them will be third-gendered in some way—perhaps fully transsexual, perhaps merely very feminine men or very masculine women, perhaps anywhere on that wide and varied spectrum in between. The reasons why that happens all over the world are covered in the chapter on *Ergi*, but suffice it to say that if you are somewhere in between, it is both easier and harder to horse deities of either gender. Mostly easier, especially if you are flexible enough in your astral gender and your comfort with different gender presentations, because many Gods ask that the horse be only masculine or feminine to a certain extent (and that extent will vary from deity to deity), and do not require a factory-equipped male or female body. Occasionally it will be harder, because the minority of deities who absolutely require a factory-equipped male or female body will not take a third-gendered horse. Then again, men and women are barred from horsing at least half of that latter category anyway, so on balance it is definitely a gain.

As someone who has been both male and female, and still lives somewhere in the middle, I am more able to comfortably horse Gods of various genders, assuming that they are appropriate to the inside of my head and to my patron Goddess. Generally, they require that I be astrally shifted to their gender first, before they enter; for example, even though my body is currently "male of center", Hela can ride me with no problem if I shapeshift astrally to a female form first. If you are a single-gendered spirit-worker and you want to horse Gods and Goddesses of the opposite gender, you might want to work with a third-gender spirit-worker on the technique of astral shifting, and then shifting back afterwards so as not to walk around with vague uncomfortable feelings. If necessary, a deity of the opposite sex can come in anyway, but they may temporarily reshape things in ways that don't clear up for some time after the ride, unless you're aware and able to put them back. Considering that an unconscious wrong-fitted astral gender can affect one's sexual functioning, it's a technique worth learning.

Another reason that someone might not be able to horse a certain deity, or a type or pantheon of deities, is because their energy clashes with that of the spirit-worker's patron deity. Within the northern-tradition pantheons, this could be an issue of two deities who are enemies, or just don't get along. A Lokisman wouldn't likely be able to horse Heimdall, for instance, nor a Farbautisman horse Odin. The splits are not drawn directly across pantheon lines—I can horse a Vanir or two, and I know some Aesir-owned spirit-workers who can horse Jotnar—but in general, if one has a patron deity to watch one's back (which we recommend), that deity will have a list of who can and cannot use you, drawn up for their own reasons, and you will be expected to go along with it. That's a matter of courtesy and respect.

And as with all things spirit-related, plan for what will happen if it doesn't work, or they don't show up. We strongly discourage horses from going out and pretending that they are possessed, even if they think that the congregation won't know. Some of them will, and anyway it's disrespectful to the wight in question, and might even make them angry with you. Better to have an alternate ritual planned, or perhaps the horse can go out and tell the congregation that they are speaking as a symbol of Deity X, and what is said to them will be heard by Deity X. (Which can reasonably be said to be true, considering that it's likely that Deity X will hear them if they were to address a wooden statue of same; it's the horse becoming a votive object rather than a container.) Honesty is more important than pleasing the masses, especially when it's an issue that can come back to bite you.

Becoming a Horse
by Lydia Helasdottir

For me it started doing priestess work. One night, after a ceremony at a Gnostic church, while celebrating a Gnostic Mass there, I was laying in bed masturbating, and this identity with a huge starry span became present. I wasn't doing anything other than that; I wasn't tripping or anything, but I was taken up into this experience of existing as this starry void, which is the Egyptian goddess of the stars. So having had that experience, I spoke to my teacher, and she said that perhaps I should try being the ceremonial divine channel. It turned out that I had a natural affinity for that; it was very easy for me. With the Gnostic ceremony, as soon as you get onto the altar, one or another of the goddesses comes and possesses you, to a greater or lesser extent depending on how good you are at it. So I would have a whole variety of different goddesses looking out through my eyes at the congregation, and I would be there but not there, and my eyes would always feel funny, as if I was looking out at them secondhand. And that's how god-possession started.

Then, next, I learned how to channel, and let entities use my mouth to speak with. Then I would go into it more fully and pretty much my whole body would be beyond my control while they were there. I would hold a particular posture, something that I wouldn't usually do, like my hand would go out and just stay there in a way that would be hard to do with just muscle. Eventually Hela started to possess me pretty fully, and do things with my body.

But most of the time I'm pretty aware of what's going on, even when I'm stuck "behind the safety glass" ... although more recently less so. I don't have the luxury of amnesia, as many do. She'll possess me fully while I'm doing an ordeal ritual, or talking to someone, or if she needs to be there for any reason. I'm just her vehicle. A body is a vehicle for a disincarnate spirit which happens to be human; it can also (with a bit of difficulty) be a vehicle for a disincarnate spirit which happens to be a deity.

In terms of negotiating, Hela does whatever she wants with my body. Other deities, if they want to speak through me, have to clear it through her, and they can never go as far into possession as she does. The negotiations with me are usually about not doing anything that could send me to prison, or that would damage me. Sometimes astral spirits, lineage spirits for example, tag along to go for a ride. I don't consider that to be full-on possession; they'll just come along and sit in the body and experience what it's like to be incarnate. We'll go to the movies together, or drive a car. They'll get the sensation of being in the body, but they're not in control.

I've horsed Hela, the Enochian entity called Ebifahe, another Enochian called Narwaj, Hecate to an extent, Green Tara—she's very gentle to the body and always lets me take back control. The ones that I have horsed have been very good about my body, but I know that there are those who are not so careful. I don't mind exhaustion—I think it's part of the deal. Baphomet doesn't horse me, he just tells me what to do, but I don't know what would happen if I refused his orders, because I've never tried. Maybe I'd find out that I had much less control than I thought. Baphomet's been in the background giving direction on doing ordeal rituals sometimes, intimating movements, motoring me through them. That's how I've learned certain skills—a deity motoring me through the activity. I've learned from Arachne for certain complex bondage things. Sometimes I ask for help in doing something, sometimes they just show up and say "This needs doing, and we're doing it now. Yeah, I talked to your Boss, it's OK."

Hela's not as gentle on my body, but she sees it as a valuable possession that needs to not get broken too much. In the Gnostic priestess situation, it was such a ritually controlled space that although it is full-on horsing, the body is limited in what it's allowed to do. Their official deal is, "You get to come horse every other week when we do these Masses, but you don't get to move the body around, you have to line up and see who's going to come out, and you get to beam out energy and be present, but that's it. These are the rules." So any deity who can't live with that doesn't come. But the variety was amazing. Some of them would leave me and I'd feel really buzzed and happy; some would leave and as soon as the veil would close I'd slump over in a fit of complete exhaustion; some would leave me nauseated and I'd have to sleep for three days; sometimes I could hardly walk to get off the altar and sometimes I was fleet of foot, nimble and happy walking around. Sometimes they wouldn't even identify themselves, but because it was in such a controlled ritual context it didn't really matter. Anything that could come and be in that space had to abide by those rules; they had a pass.

Afterwards, I'd often feel run over; my back would be sore. At first I'd think that it was just from sitting in that position for a long time, and then I'd try to just do that, and it doesn't hurt a bit. It's like a massive vibration has gone through you and rattled you at a cellular level ... or like someone has ripped your spine out and put it back in again with two channels instead of one, and then afterwards they yanked the second channel out and loosely stitched it back together. It's sore. But that's also a "throughput" issue, because if you're only used to 110 volts running through your spine, and now you've got deity energy running through you—ten thousand volts and several more million amperes than you're used to—it can fry your circuits. Doing it a lot, you grow fatter wires, fatter pipes, until you can manage the deity energy easier. But then it starts to seep into everyday life; you can be in a constant state of being shadowed, a walking pair of eyes for your deity to ride along with.

I think that anyone can learn to channel, or to let something ride along with them to shadow, but not everyone can horse. Some people just can't let go of control, some people just aren't wired for it, and some spirits just won't horse a particular person. They're picky; they like a particular body type or brain type or personality. There's no judgment there; it's just not a fit with them. I think that anyone can be taught to be an energy channel, but we would never accept anyone as a divine energy channel who hasn't had some kind of experience with being touched by Deity. And just being a divine energy channel is the lowest, simplest level of horsing. I think there are cultural factors as well, so I'm undecided on the issue. I don't think everybody can naturally do it. In fact, I think some people are forbidden and precluded from doing it by their patrons. I think that you can teach people to have the channel open, but you can't force the deity through. You can teach them relaxation, mental preparation, and awe, and you can practice that, but that's not the same as Deity coming through.

Walking the Path of the Horse
by Galina Krasskova

I consider myself extremely fortunate in how I came to first learn about and experience divine possession. My first experience with a God choosing to temporarily inhabit my skin occurred in the early nineties when I was still working with Fellowship of Isis. At the time, I was serving as psychopomp for someone's initiation ritual. The woman in question was dedicating to the Kemetic Goddess Neith, and as I was guiding her through the various challenges and keeping her as grounded as possible considering the circumstances, I felt a quiet, reserved presence touching my consciousness. I had honored Anubis many times before, and I recognized the feel of that presence, so I didn't panic. He slid gently into my consciousness, and I allowed Him to take over my mental and physical reins. The possession wasn't very deep—a light shadowing, really—but it started me down the road of a horse, one who's primary spiritual "job" is allowing the Gods to speak and act directly through the medium of one's human flesh.

While possessory work is neither common nor encouraged in Fellowship of Isis, my priestess had enough experience with the Afro-Caribbean religious traditions to understand what was going on. She neither encouraged nor discouraged the practice. If it occurred, that was good and if it did not, that was good too. Thanks to her practicality in the matter, I was able to view possessory work as simply one more manifestation of my spiritual evolution. It had no particular weight attached for good or for ill, and this has served me extremely well over the years. It allowed me to approach it as an act of service from the very beginning without becoming attached to either the practice or the outcome. I never sought out possession, but when it occurred, I was able to step back and allow the God or Goddess in question to come in without too much difficulty. Some people experience possession as violating in the extreme, but I was fortunate that for myself, this was never the case.

With one exception (which I shall discuss below), the first few years involved light shadowing. It wasn't until I converted to Heathenry and got snapped up by Loki and Odin that things began to get really interesting. Even then, it wasn't always complete possession. I learned very early on that there are numerous variations, shades and depth of penetration possible by the Gods.

Once I was taken in hand by Loki and Odin, possessory work became one of the training methods that They commonly used with me. In teaching me journey work, or certain aspects of magic, *galdr*, and seidhr, Loki would often ride me lightly, enough to overlay his consciousness with mine and to guide my hands in the techniques he was attempting to teach me. Eventually, Odin gave me a spirit song and over time, used this to pattern my head and mind to Him specifically. I didn't realize precisely what He was doing at the time though, not until much later. Using the receptive state the song put me in, He would modify me slowly over a period of about a year until He could slip into me deeply and without difficulty. For that year of training, Odin became the only Deity other than Loki that I was allowed to horse, but eventually He permitted me to do so for other Gods and Goddesses.

There are certain Deities that are incompatible with me (I have been told flat out that certain Loa and Orisha will never be able to ride me, for instance) for reasons of my own emotional patterning and utter lack of compatibility, or because to horse certain Deities would inadvertently destroy too much of the patterning Odin put in place. Over the years it seems that more and more I horse primarily, if not only, the Northern pantheon. I am also not permitted to horse lesser spirits, but only certain Deities on what I like to call Odin's "approved list".

In retrospect, the manner in which Odin trained me as a horse leads me to conceive of the whole process as one of learning to welcome deeply internalized crisis. Essentially, possession is a crisis situation. One's entire ego is put aside or pushed aside so Someone/Something else can enter and take control. That is a difficult thing for many people to deal with, and the reason that some horses find the whole process very violating. I do not find it so, but I suspect my erotic/romantic attachment to Odin as well as the very organic way in which I was first introduced to the whole thing has helped me immensely there. This is also the reason why I believe a certain degree of self-knowledge and psychological stability should be a prerequisite for a horse. Of course, sometimes the Gods just don't give a damn and will utilize a person anyway, but in the ideal situation, a firm, solid sense of self is foundational toward ensuring the continued psychological health of the horse. Personally, I would not train someone as a horse unless it was patently clear from the get-go that the Gods were hellbent in using them in that capacity.

This is the reason that not only can not everyone do possessory work, but not every one *should*. It's not just a matter of having the right brain chemistry/psychic patterning for it, though that is the most important thing, but the secondary crux of the issue is the ability to get beyond that initial trauma of having one's consciousness moved aside. It's apparent from all outward appearances of the horse that the beginning manifestations of possession reveal themselves to be a crisis situation, and this is perhaps the primary reason that horses need skilled, experienced and knowledgeable attendants to minimize difficulties. Possessory work can be grueling, not just mentally, emotionally and psychologically but physically as well. Good attendants make the process before, during and after go far more smoothly than it otherwise might and can contribute greatly toward the comfort and well being of the horse, especially in the exhausting aftermath.

For many of us, coming to possessory work in traditions that lack a cohesive framework for such things, having a skilled team of handlers is a luxury. I've only had the advantage of working with an experienced team once in all the years I've been doing this work, but that experience both before and after the possession itself was markedly easier than any other. I recovered faster and had fewer aftereffects. Furthermore, good handlers are calm during the onset of the possession and know what to do to help coax and entice the Deity in, which makes the whole process far more comfortable. Having knowledgeable people in attendance helps the horse relax which goes a long way to quickly facilitating the entire process.

I've been asked many times what might be the best way to prepare a horse for possession, and I honestly think it's a very personal thing. Especially during the aftermath, when the Deity has gone, people may experience a plethora of reactions from tears to giggling laughter. Some people want to be left completely alone, whereas others may need human contact. It varies, as does what each horse will require in preparation, though the one common factor is that the experience tends to unlock emotional fetters to some degree. On a psychic level, some Deities will leave a person wide open, while Others may leave a certain muting in Their wake. I have a fairly strong gift of empathy, but after I horse Odin, that gift is blessedly muted in me for awhile. This was disturbing at first until I realized that He uses every part of my mental wiring when He's in me, and the contrast when He's gone makes the gift *seem* far more muted.

There are some commonsense preparations that one can take (and it goes without saying that these guidelines are only workable when you have been informed in advance that a Deity will be popping in, which for me until recently was rarely the case):

1) Get a good night's sleep for at least a few days prior to the possession, especially the night immediately preceding the rite.

2) Eat lots of protein the night before—I find it helps minimize energy burn out and exhaustion after, but your mileage may vary.

3) Vitamins are a good thing. Having a Deity inhabit one's flesh eats up energy reserves and can have a dramatic effect on one's health. It plays havoc with the immune system, and there can be other temporary side effects as well, depending on the level of compatibility with the Deity in question, the length of the possession, the depth of the possession. I've had emotional issues come up, my back go into spasms, migraines, dizziness and involuntary tics. Good preventive care where one's health is concerned is beneficial, not only here but in any type of spirit work.

4) Study qi gong, tai chi or a related martial art. It aids in learning to remain centered, regaining one's center and most importantly in learning to maintain and balance one's internal energies.

5) Be aware that there may be vestiges of both the Deity's energy and occasionally personality traits, likes, dislikes and even emotions that linger in the horse for some time after the possession. Be sure to eat (preferably protein, something substantial, not junk food) afterwards and to do whatever is necessary to ground and bring yourself back to yourself and to mundane time/space. It's also helpful to take cleansing baths beforehand, but most especially after.

Being opened in the way that possession does can leave one in a fairly vulnerable emotional state for some time.

6) Develop a practice of daily grounding and centering. It's boring but necessary.

7) As much as possible, take good care of yourself and your physical body and health. Horsing is grueling work in which your body and soul are used hard as a tool for the Gods. Therefore, it's advisable to keep that tool in the best condition possible (which, given how spirit-work affects the physical body, can be hard; do your best within whatever limitations you have). There are also times where horsing can help one physically. I've had Deities (particular healing Goddesses) clear away energy blockages, heal pain, etc. as They left, leaving me in better condition than before the possession. It's not all difficulties and stress.

The most important thing for any horse is to develop, nurture and maintain a strong relationship with a Goddess or God. I hate to use the dreaded word Patron, but in this case, it does seem appropriate. Many horses are also god-slaves or otherwise god-owned, so a relationship of this sort goes with the territory. I imagine it would far more difficult for a horse who lacked such a relationship to counterbalance what some find to be invasive trauma. Spiritually and emotionally, even psychologically, it helps to deeply trust the Gods and to have a strong relationship with at least one. It can mitigate many of the difficulties. In fact, I believe serving the Gods is fundamental.

So, one might ask, what makes a person a good horse? The answer is fairly simple: you're either wired that way or not. Being utilized as a horse is not a matter of being special. It's a matter of being suited by chance and genetics and a plethora of other things far out of one's own control for a job. There are other jobs just as important.

Some people have romantic notions about possessory work, or seek it out from a desire to increase their self importance. Some want to do it because they want to be the ones in this ostensibly exalted role, dispensing wise advice and performing miraculous healings, etc. This is absolutely the worst and most damaging attitude to have. Possessory work is an intensely sacred and an immensely humbling experience. To approach it as anything other than total service is to abuse both one's spiritual community and one's relationship with the Gods. Being suited to serve as a horse in and of itself is nothing special. It's a matter of having the right brain chemistry/patterning for the job. It has nothing to do with personal worth. Nothing. Those of us who horse do this work do so because we have no choice. We do it because it is of value to the Gods and to the community. It is what the Gods have asked, and at times demanded, of us as part of our service. There are those who have never and will never horse who are doing work just as sacred and just as important. I never, ever allow myself to forget that for a moment.

The horse aside, there are a few things for folks witnessing a possession to keep in mind. The most important thing to note are the wants, likes and dislikes of the Deity in question. This is especially important for those of us in traditions that lack a long-standing practice and structure for ritual possession. It's best if handlers or attendants can record what a given Deity likes for the future. Most Deities like to have some sense of continuity and continuation. Write it down. You'll get some leeway the first and second time a God or Goddess shows up, but by the fourth and fifth time, you may get a pissed-off Deity. I, for one, would not want to be there when Odin shows up, asks for a drink and there's no alcohol, for instance!

I think it's also important to remember that there are reasons the Gods choose to do this. This was driven home to me very recently at one of my first public possessions. Those of us who are taken up as god-slaves or who are otherwise owned by their Gods sometimes forget that this is not the case for the average Joe. I'm certainly guilty of this myself. I recently had the opportunity to horse Gerda at a Lammas celebration while another individual horsed Frey.

This was one of the few times where I was completely 'in the trunk', so to speak, but afterwards, people contacted me and shared how deeply that face-to-face interaction with a God and Goddess had impacted them. I got to see first hand how deeply moving for all concerned this contact was and it really struck me: for most people, this is the only time they will ever have face-to-face, in-the-flesh communication with their Gods. It's the only time they experience a Deity in the here and now, shining and speaking and moving in bodies so very much like their own. It's the only time that gap between Midgard and the worlds of the Gods is effectively (and safely) bridged for however short a time. That is why this is important. That is why it is so very sacred.

I also realized in retrospect how much the willing horse allows the Gods to experience life and flesh and each other in new ways as well. It's not just a one-sided process. It opens doors between the worlds, windows for the Gods to work. It is an incredibly humbling experience. Until that Lammas, I had never considered the impact horsing had on the human contingent. I did it because it was what the Gods asked of me and doing so pleased Them. But in the aftermath of horsing Gerda, I saw firsthand what it means to the community. It's allowed me to find a measure of commitment and peace with the whole process that I never expected.

Reconstructionist religions—in my case Heathenry—don't have a long-standing framework for possessions, and for those of us being called to do this work, this can be rather problematic. In fact, the hostility a horse may encounter in some communities can be more traumatic and difficult than the possessory experience itself! One of the immediate issues, of course, is that we have few if any references in lore to possessory work being part of elder heathen (pre-Christian) consciousness. Whether it was or wasn't, however, the fact is that the Gods are doing it now and eventually, the community is going to have to come to terms with that. Another problematic issue is that

Heathenry in particular does not seem to readily have a ritual structure—or what I like to call a 'cease and desist mechanism'—which might otherwise facilitate possession. The ritual structure overall would have to evolve, deepen and change, becoming far more fluid than it is now, and in a religion terrified of anything smacking of "neo-paganism," this is an uphill battle. When most Heathens do rituals, they follow clear-cut guidelines and a script, and they like to stick to that. Of course, if and when a God arrives, for things to go well, there has to be a cease-and-desist, and a ritual staff that is flexible and experienced enough to take appropriate action, and model that action for the community. In other words, the ritual has to stop and change to accommodate and attend the arriving God or Goddess.

Heathenry hasn't yet come to this point. As a religion, it's still occasionally debating on whether or not one needs clergy! The average Heathen ritual worker (and the average Heathen in general) doesn't want their religious experience to be expanded into unknown qualities or territory. Plus, there's a certain *ergi* quality that smacks too much of submission for the typical Heathen with their swashbuckling macho Viking psychology to accept. "Our Gods would never do that," they say. Unfortunately for them, our Gods seem to have other ideas.

Some Heathen spirit workers who are already experiencing possession eventually seek out the Afro-Caribbean diaspora religions, such as Umbanda, Lucumi, Santeria and Voudoun to learn how to safely cope with this. While this is helpful, I personally worry about the risk of transplanting African-style rituals into a Northern-Tradition context and feel that our ritual consciousness should evolve organically to accommodate possession. Of course, in the midst of ignorance and a hostile community, horses will fumble around in the dark seeking out whatever lifelines they can find so that they can better serve the Gods they love and respect, without endangering themselves or others.

It isn't just the limitations of Heathen ritual consciousness that cause problems. Most Heathens that I myself have encountered in over ten years in the community have very set ideas of what the Gods are like. This is mostly drawn from the Eddas and surviving lore. The idea that the Gods might have Their differing moods or choose not to limit Themselves to the scribblings of a Christian poet and politician from 13th century Iceland seems to be a leap of faith few can manage in a religion desperate to keep its spirituality neatly and predictably contained. One can hardly blame them, though; it's not as though divine possession is a common occurrence in the average Christian church, and the majority of Heathens are (I believe) converts from Protestant faiths. And then, of course, Gods aren't safe. Nothing truly sacred or holy can ever be made completely safe. There's always the chance They might be angry.

Yes, Gods can come angry. A Lukumi friend of mine once attended a ritual where the patron Spirit of the house showed up and angrily called for his machete, chastised a follower who had been disobeying certain spiritual taboos and behaving in general like an ass, and whipped him with said machete. My first experience with a totally amnesiac possession occurred with a very angry Goddess—in my case, the Morrigan. While it hasn't happened often—in fact, only three times have I horsed a truly enraged Goddess—it can and does occur. (Usually, when I horse, the God or Goddess in question will dispense counsel, settle disputes, teach, simply give blessings, etc.).

While experiences such as this can test the mettle of anyone involved, and while it's very difficult not to become emotionally invested, as no one wants to see the Gods they serve angry (or be the one who's used to speak harsh words), it's still important to maintain the thread of trust and respect. I have never once experienced or witnessed a position that did not have beneficial results, including the experience with the Morrigan. Even for those horses who experience possession as a violation, while they may not like the way it feels, seeing the impact it has on others makes it worthwhile and I think may help the horse find a measure of acceptance. As to why some people find it violating and others don't, I don't know. I suspect it has to do with personality quirks and where one falls on the dominance/submission spectrum within relationships.

In terms of etiquette for witnessing: do try not to interrupt a possession. It can cause damage to the horse to have the process broken off abruptly before the Deity is fully seated. This is another area where a competent team of trained handlers is incredibly helpful. It might also be useful to have a long discussion with your patron Goddess or God to negotiate what is and is not acceptable use of your body. This doesn't of course, mean that the Gods will necessarily adhere to it, but it can help to have such a "contract" in place and if the God that owns the horse agrees, terms of the contract will generally be honored. This can be important, because unlike the Afro-Caribbean religions, where the Orisha and Loa have had structure and boundaries negotiated for generations, the Gods of the North don't have a similar set of rules worked out with Their followers. For instance, in Afro-Caribbean religions the orisha will not have sex while in the horses' bodies. This doesn't necessarily hold true for the Northern Gods, who may wish to do just that. Gods may also imbibe substances that the horse is terribly allergic to, or large quantities of alcohol. It's best to negotiate that They take the effects of such substances with them when They leave! This latter point is something that most Deities will comply with. The horse is, after all, providing a necessary service. I do not believe that the Gods willingly injure Their horses. Problems arise because the act of having the tiniest drop of divine consciousness contained in human flesh is incredibly stressful simply by its very nature.

Most Deities, when They come down, like to do work. If a horse is seemingly wandering around aimlessly for too long, handlers should be cautious. Some people have a hard time getting out of possession, not just getting into it. There are techniques to help bring a person back, and it's best if the horse, early on in this work, can condition him or herself to respond to specific stimuli. For me, calling my name, touching me while calling my name (just touching or eating won't always do it because some Deities will put me extremely far under so They can eat and drink and touch while in my body), and removing ritual regalia often helps.

Once the Deity has departed, then it's best to eat—and a good handler will make sure the horse eats at this point if necessary and ground. One horse recently told me that she smokes (something she's only permitted to do on occasion) to ground herself and bring herself back to Midgard. Find out what works (unfortunately this is usually done via trial and error) and make preparations in advance. Conversely, if a horse prepares for a possession and the Deity is unable to seat Him or Herself, the only course of action is to admit this up-front. Never try to force a possession. There are a number of factors that can contribute to such difficulties and there's no shame in not being able to horse at any given time. It happens. Besides, the Gods are not toys to shove around or programs to load. They'll do what they want, and change Their minds as They like.

Those present during the possession should not be frustrated by horses' lack of ability for elaboration. After the Deity departs, many horses will have no memory of what happened, or at best only the vaguest of memories. Ask the average horse "what did Deity X mean when She said this?" and you'll likely get the answer: "Beats the hell out of me, She said it, I didn't!"

Sometimes those witnessing a possession may project certain feelings onto the horse after the possession is over. This is quite common, for it can be difficult to separate the physical person's image from the Deity that temporarily inhabited it. The horse should be aware of this possibility and make sure to be up-front about it. Attachment, romantic feelings, etc. can all be evoked by the presence of a God or Goddess. It's important to be aware of this fact because those feelings really have nothing to do with the horse him or herself, and if someone expresses such feelings to the horse after a possession, the horse should be direct and point out that it's likely transference. This is a time to set and maintain gentle but firm boundaries. I prefer not to interact with those present during a possession too much immediately after in order to counteract such perfectly natural effects.

Serving as a horse is an act of immense vulnerability and submission—you are giving over your flesh to a greater power to use as They will. It can be painful, terrifying, exhilarating, but always immensely fulfilling. It is a joy to be of use to one's Gods and for those of us who find ourselves useful in this particular capacity, it provides a unique opportunity to serve both Gods and community in an amazingly intimate way.

Negotiating with the Gods is a hard thing. As we've mentioned elsewhere in this book and in others, our Gods may be bigger, wiser, and more knowledgeable than we are, but they are not omniscient or omnipotent. They may not know, for example, that right now is not a good time for a possession, because you're sick or in charge of small children, you're having sex with a partner, you're in line at the deli, etc. You need to be able to say No, politely but firmly, and not let it overrun you. Deities in general are not particularly concerned with your daily routine, although some are better about it than others. Usually, when this happens, the normal thing to do is to mentally say *This is not a good time; I will take you on later* in the direction of the Power that wants to move in.

Of course, that means that you had better make an appointment and fulfill it, or you may get in trouble. I had a longstanding habit of putting off possessions and not coming through on them, largely for reasons of discomfort, and one night during a gathering I went to sleep and woke up four hours later by the fire wearing strange clothing, with people standing over me and saying, "Are you back?" It was an object lesson: if you want to be able to negotiate time and place, don't give Us short shrift.

If you feel a god-possession coming on and just saying No isn't working, there are things you can do to snap yourself out of that early trance state that opens you for being ridden. The idea is to change your consciousness so that it is firmly grounded in your body and the real world, and not doing anything repetitive or hypnotic. These techniques can also be used for anyone who feels that something is trying to "move in on" their consciousness, whether it is positive or negative.

1. Cold water, a lot of it, especially on the back of your neck. Step into a cold shower, as cold as you can stand it. This one has never failed me. Follow it up by eating and drinking something, which will ground you back into your body.

2. Drink a glass of cold salt water. You may not be able to get it all down; swallow as much as you can stand. You may vomit. That's all right; vomiting will bring you quickly back into your body and close off the channel. The salt is grounding, and salt water is the best way to get a lot of it down your gullet at once. Follow it up with clear cold water, and food if you haven't vomited and can stomach it.

3. Eat something extremely hot and spicy, like a swig of tabasco sauce or a spoonful of black pepper. Please have lots of water on hand to wash it down or rinse your mouth.

4. Worst case, if nothing else is working: Tell a friend to cause you abrupt physical pain—slap you, pull your hair, whack you on the rear end with a wooden spoon, whatever you think you can take. Avoid injurious things, please. The pain should be fast, sharp, random, and you shouldn't see it coming. Doing it yourself is not recommended; self-inflicted pain can actually have a hypnotic effect on some people.

5. After you've successfully slammed the door shut, do some mundane activity that requires all your concentration yet is not monotonous or repetitive. An example might be doing your taxes, or baking something from scratch with a difficult recipe. It should be complex enough to require your full attention, with many changes of

activity. Don't play music or sing while you're doing it; have a friend talk to you instead, or put on talk radio. Don't do anything rhythmic, like pace or drum or tap your fingers or jog; move around randomly. One particularly effective thing is to have someone talk to you about something that makes you angry, or at least something you feel very strongly about. The subject should have nothing to do with spirituality, god-possession, or anything ruled by that deity.

The Path of the Horse is contraindicated for:

1. People with trust issues. If you find it difficult to trust even people who love you and are reliable, you will not have the ability to hold yourself open for the god to enter. You may react instinctively, slamming the door shut instead of being responsive. Work on your trust issues, including any anger you may have towards the Powers That Be. If you are blaming the Divine Will for your problems, you won't be comfortable with letting any aspect of it run your body even more closely.

You can work on trust issues with the aid of other human beings. Ask the people who you trust the most to blindfold you and take you somewhere unknown, perhaps to do something that you have never done and have no knowledge of. If the idea makes you recoil, you're not ready to work with god-possession.

2. People with poor boundaries. You need to be able to set boundaries, or you'll just become a powerless vessel, living your life around the visitations of your patron deity. It's hard to do things like hold down a job or have relationships or care for children when you're constantly being used as a horse. If you want to take this path, you will need to work on the firm mental negative. It's difficult, because it can be an amazing feeling to share your vessel with a Power, and it's hard to turn down, but if it's getting in the way of your daily activities, it can damage your life and health and make you a less worthy vessel. This is in addition to the fact that a deity can better be served and honored if the right situation is prepared for it in advance—which is something that

most Gods can understand when you use it as a reason—"If you wait until next week, I will have a ritual set up, with your favorite foods and people to interact with! Please allow me to honor you properly!" But don't let it take over your life. If you're the ultra-sensitive type who is easily swayed by the strong emotions of others, do work on keeping your boundaries clear before opening yourself to an even stronger and more intense experience.

3. People with small children, or other full-time responsibilities that cannot be shirked. Being a horse can take up a sizeable chunk of your life. If you are needed on a moment's notice by dependents whose care hangs on you and you aren't home in your own body, it can cause problems. You might want to wait until some future date when you are no longer responsible for them and your time is your own. If the Gods are not going to let you off, you can pray to the Mother—that's the Big Mother from whom all mother goddesses draw their sacredness—and ask Her to intervene and give you space in which to raise your child, or at least never to allow horsings during times when your children will need you. I did that, and it worked, although I paid for it later.

4. People with issues of mental illness that make their grip on reality tenuous at best and easily thrown off. This includes those with multiple personality disorder, where all of the individual may not be able to consent to the horsing, and where there is a higher likelihood of one "personality" taking on the archetype of the deity that sat next to it for a time, and believing that it is indeed that deity.

5. People who are desperate for importance in their spiritual community, and think that this is a way to achieve attention and prestige. It's more like being the rock star's anonymous limo driver, actually. It's grunt work, and if you go into it with ego issues, the Gods who use you may find ways to slap you down ... perhaps leaving you to clean up their divine messes. If you can't be humble about it, don't do it ... and don't let your community give you lots of special head-pats for being the suit that the God wears, either. It encourages the wrong mindset.

Dangers of Horsing
by Lydia Helasdottir

As to the dangers of horsing ... well, I don't think that people should do it at all, not unless they're forced to. In Western magical tradition you've got this concept of "assuming a god-form", which is a mild type of horsing, where you identify with a god-form and invoke that particular kind of energy into yourself, and embody that energy. It's not the same, but the danger even from doing that is that people forget to divest themselves of the god-form, and they get stuck in that space "being" that entity—first of all, to the exclusion of all else, and secondly usually to the great annoyance of the people around them who are tired of them "being" Ra all day long. It's just not good.

The halfway stuff is actually the most dangerous, where they are only there about 40% and you attune the other 60%, and the attunement stays even when the deity leaves—as opposed to a fuller possession where the deity often takes everything with them. The obvious dangers are that they'll do something with your body that damages someone or is illegal. "Oh, cool, it's a car? Is this like chariots used to be? Yes?" and they smack you into a tree, or run a red light, or have unsafe sex, or make you ingest things you're allergic to and don't take them with them, or beat someone into a bloody hospital-ready pulp. I think there's also a psychological danger from sharing mind-space with a deity. They're so huge and you're so big. If they come forcefully, and you're not ready for them, you can tear. It can rip your soul.

It definitely causes problems with the relationships of people around you because when the God speaks through you, they may or may not accept that it's the God, because it's your mouth that is saying hurtful things to them, things that are arriving with such force that they can't defend against them. They're either going to say, "Well, this god stuff wasn't real anyway, you just made that up so that you can say these nasty things to me," or "You colluded with that nasty god, and that nasty god said these nasty things to me, and you're an asshole for letting it happen. Why didn't you stop it?" And then, there are certain truths that as a human being you don't necessarily want to know, and the god will come out and tell them to someone who needs to hear them and they'll say, "Oh, no, I didn't want to hear that!" It can be emotionally quite painful, as well as physically quite wearing.

You can get addicted to it, as well; you see that in the neo-Voudoun crowd sometimes—you get a rush when the deity comes, and you want that rush all the time, because it makes you feel important or because you love the clean, heavy deity throughput energy. It's sluicing out your whole system, and it's great, but you have to have some method for doing that yourself, not just horsing deities all the time.

Another danger is how do you know which bloody god it is? And how do you know it's even a god at all, and not some other bottom-feeding entity that can dress up as a god? That's a problem for people who just openly horse whatever comes. A patron deity can screen them out, and if you don't have one to look after you, perhaps you shouldn't be horsing. That's an unpopular, elitist view, and perhaps an overly paranoid view, but for me it's a very realistic view. Most of the horses that I know started out as divine energy channels, where they were used to it being a controlled circumstance, under certain conditions and for a particular reason—and then they go away again and give me my fucking body back. So we are used to setting boundaries. What worries me more is the kind of "Let's open up and see what wants to come in and jiggle with me" sort of people. Because that's a way into it, for sure—you can get possessed by trance-dancing, or any other kind of trancework, if you're wired for it.

Regarding the controversy of whether to put limits on the Gods: When you do public ritual, and you set rules as the price of entry for a deity, with the implication that if they don't like the rules, they shouldn't come, you aren't really setting limits on them. If they want to come and possess a person, they're going to do it anyway whether you like it or not, because human beings in general are not powerful enough to stop that from happening. But the effort involved for a deity to come and possess someone who isn't open and actively seeking it is huge, and not worth it. It's painful for them to manifest down here; that we know. It's not a walk in the park. They have to make quite an effort to get this dense.

And anyway, most Gods want to come down where they are wanted and honored, or at least where they have jobs to do. They don't come down without a purpose for all that effort, and if you can set things up so that they get the honor and ability to work that they desire, it will be worth it to them to come by appointment rather than randomly. The one exception might be trickster gods like Loki, where all bets are off, but they're a separate problem. Most Gods would rather be welcomed than fought off. Wouldn't most people, as well?

Horsing the Gods
of the Northern Tradition

The Gods and wights of the Northern Tradition have their own distinct natures, but if one had to sum up the lot of them, one could say that they are stoic, independent, warlike, earthy, bloody, pushy, practical, and passionate. While they can be terrible if they are offended, they stand less on dignity and ceremony and more on what you are willing to do for them. Unless they have decided to take an interest in you, or claim you as a god-slave, they see no reason to bother with you for no return on their part.

Some spirit-workers who work with the deities of many other pantheons as well have compared them and mentioned that northern-tradition Gods are the most likely to make strong contact before the ritual itself in order to give information on what they want, which is helpful. It was also pointed out that with the exception of Loki, who turns everything on its head, our Gods like to receive their offerings before they are asked for any aid or advice.

There are, of course, differences between them. Given that we have three separate pantheons—Aesir, Vanir, and Rökkr—with all their larger and smaller powers, we have to understand their different flavors.

The Rökkr are the oldest, and the most Neolithic in their nature. I didn't fully understand what that meant until I spoke to some Pagan spirit-workers who belonged to Neolithic Celtic deities. The Gods of hunter-gatherer Eurasia tend to be more elemental, more animal, more bloody, more shamanic, and more numerous. The Rökkr are given much more space in this series for that reason: most of these techniques go back further than the Indo-European conquest, and the coming of the other pantheons. When you are a northern-tradition spirit-worker and you move into the ancient shamanism practices, sooner or later you will run into the Rökkr, even if you are only sent to them for training by your patrons. Some of them are very difficult to horse, or are frightening when they do come.

The Vanir came with agriculture and the first coming of the ox-cart peoples. Their rites are about fertility, which is sex and death. They feed the soil with blood, and this is part of their wisdom. While they may seem tamer compared to the Rökkr, don't be fooled. They demand just as much in the way of sacrifice; they may be "lighter", but they also interface with the dark.

The Aesir came in with the conquering horse-peoples, and settled down to become the forces of civilization. While they are the most popular pantheon with the modern Nordic religions, they rarely come into the practice of northern-tradition shamanism ... except for Odin, who is the very archetype of the shaman-king. Still, he learned his stuff from the older powers, while giving it his own flavor—and in the case of some things, like the Runes, bringing new magic into the cosmos. However, since more northern-tradition folk have the Aesir as patrons than any other pantheon, they may be the ones that a spirit-worker will horse most often, both for public ceremony and for people coming to talk to their deities.

Given those differences, here is a list of some of the Gods that we have horsed, and what They have liked and disliked during Their tenures in the modern human body. As with all things, these preferences will vary depending on what They have actually come to do, so try to do some devotional work and get a feel for Their purpose in coming before the horsing begins. No, not all of them are listed here, because we've not had experience with welcoming every one ... yet. Give it time; this practice is only just beginning in our religion. This information is given largely so those whose groups decide to take up the practice of horsing (assuming that you have human horses) will not end up offending the deities that they invite. Good intentions are sometimes not enough; knowledge, common sense, and courtesy are needed as well.

Odin

First, don't invite Odin without having some good quality alcohol on hand—mead or a nice wine. That's just courtesy. (One comment was "Odin likes wine so dry that none of the rest of us will drink it!") He also loves aquavit; some say that it's his favorite. In general he will drink a lot and not be drunk, so keep the mead, wine and aquavit coming. An attendant might gently remind him to take the alcohol with him, for the sake of the horse's stomach. He likes tobacco, but prefers it in a pipe, so finding him a nice pipe and some good-smelling loose tobacco would be useful. He likes red meat, especially beef, and spearlike vegetables such as leeks, asparagus, and garlic (the latter literally means "spear-leek"). His preferred colors for clothing are blue, grey, and black—a cloak is best—and the wide-brimmed floppy hat and the eyepatch are necessary.

Odin likes to talk, to counsel, and to solve disputes. Don't mention Baldur, or Loki's chaining, or that whole political debacle—it's a sensitive subject and he's not likely to want to discuss it with you. He has a terrifying side, which can inspire utter cowering fear or complete berserk, but he won't do that side at a gathering. That's saved for initiations of his chosen ones, usually somewhere in the woods where a painful ordeal is imminent, and then you might see Odin Yggr, the Dead Man.

Make him a throne where he can sit, with furs on it if possible. He is *ergi* enough that he is completely comfortable horsing either men or women (thanks to all that work done in Vanaheim when Freya taught him seidhr). Odin's attendants can also be either male or female, and should ideally be people sworn to him—there are enough Odin's men and women around that this shouldn't be too much of a problem. If any of his mortal wives are around, they will be the obvious choice, although he may want to make off with them for an hour or so. He has also had the habit, in the past, of turning his attendants into wolves or ravens, two apiece. This tends to happen when he is given attendants who are skilled at astral shapeshifting and/or have a strong affinity to one of those creatures. He also likes to have other members of his family present, if possible; negotiate it out first if you only have room or staff for one horsing.

One thing that Odin has done while horsing is to threaten people with his spear (yes, it's politic to have a spear nearby for him, even if you're worried about him doing such a thing) by placing it against their hearts. It's a flinch test that he generally only does to warrior-types, or those who think they're really tough. So far he has not actually injured anyone, although I wouldn't push it. The right thing to do is to stand strong, neither flinching nor being arrogant and leaning into it.

Frigga

When inviting Frigga, make sure that the place is clean and neat first—and we do mean really clean. Make an effort to keep the area spotless. She prefers white, ivory, and pale blue—the colors of sky and cloud—and long flowing robes, ideally with a girdle on which hangs a bunch of keys. She is said to enjoy plum wine, or other light fruit wines, or a good white Riesling. Serve bread and pastry; it should be like a good tea party. As with Odin, it is best not to discuss Baldur or other sensitive politics with her. She prefers a female horse, preferably at least somewhat mature, and female attendants, neatly dressed and presented. If they can handspin—and if there is wool and traditional spindles about for them to sit at her feet and spin—that's a bonus. She will bless the spinning, and it can be used for serious magic.

The Handmaidens

As there are many handmaidens, and little is known about horsing most of them, only time and trial will give us all the research. However, of the few that we know of who have graced gatherings or consultations with the presence, some preferences are known. In general, they all tend to like sweet wines and fussy German pastry, so make sure that there is plenty of strudel.

Fulla wears green and wants jewelry, and perhaps precious or semiprecious stones to play with, and bless. If you can crochet her a golden snood, so much the better. She requires a female horse, preferably a young woman still able to access the Maiden archetype. Give her an unmarried female attendant with a playful sense of humor. Ideally she should come to a group made solely of women, as she is all about women's mysteries.

Eir is very centered, soft-spoken, and detached; she will generally ground and center the horse on the way out, and leave them feeling in better shape than a ride from most other Gods. She prefers utilitarian clothing, and no rings on her hands or arms, as she will likely be doing some sort of healing on people. Give her a selection of good-tasting medicinal herbal teas, which she will drink some of and pass on the rest to specific people, blessed. Give her healers of any gender as her attendants; the same goes for her horse. Ideally, anyone who horses Eir should be a vessel that is used to passing on psychic energy healing.

Var likes to wear dark colors and have a staff handy, and likes clear vodka. It is very important not to misspeak around her; watch your words carefully and weigh everything you say. Hlin also likes a staff, and she may teach women to use it. Vor wants a dark veil over her head, and some sort of divinatory things about her, which she won't use because she doesn't need them, but she may bless them. Don't call Gna unless you have a horse ready—of the biological sort, that is—because she likes to talk from horseback, and really the only reason to call her is to beg her to take a message to some Aesir deity.

Thor

"Thor Is A Guy," one spirit-worker pointed out, "and that's the first thing to remember." He doesn't mind modern clothing as long as it's a red plaid flannel shirt and jeans, or something along those lines—practical, woodsy, working-class, very masculine. He prefers his horse to be male-bodied and have a substantial beard. Ideally, he'd prefer someone not terribly small, with some muscle to them. The horse should wear a Mjollnir around his neck, as actual war-hammers are hard to find. He likes cheery colors, especially red and blue, and plenty of beer. He'll even drink the cheap stuff if there's lots of it—and if there are people to drink it with, which is the most important thing. Attendants must first and foremost be drinking and partying buddies, so pick people with the proper capacity.

The best food for Thor is a goat roast, but he has one peculiarity—don't break the long bones in the goat meat. You can separate them at the joint and serve a leg to him, but the bones should be left intact. He'll eat other sorts of meat as well, but the same applies—make sure it wasn't from an animal with broken bones, which many mean arranging to do it yourself.

Although Thor is happy to Party Down with loud music and lots of food and drink—he doesn't mind not having everyone pay attention to him as long as he has a circle of cheery drinking buddies—he is one of the least likely to hit on women, as he is mostly very monogamous with his beloved Sif. He might dance with them, but it generally won't go all the way to the bedroom, unless the woman in question is one of his mortal wives.

Tyr

Tyr wears dark red and dark grey and carries a sword slung on his right side, so that he can draw it with his left hand. He prefers a masculine-to-male horse. If the horse has long hair, it should be pulled back in a braid and not left to hang loose. Tyr is grim and stern, and tends to only show up for a short time, to speak to someone and then leave. He won't stay for merriment; he's not a party guy. He will want armed attendants, who should flank him but give him space. During the ride, the horse will be unable to move or feel their right hand—it's a kindness to provide a cloak beforehand that is slung over the right arm, but leaves the left one free—and sometimes this numbness will last a few hours after Tyr has left, so the horse will be aware that they may be missing an astral hand for a while.

Heimdall

Heimdall is almost never called into a horse, because bringing him down here means taking him away from his post. If he comes at all, it is for a short time, and he can be given beer with rams on it. He has been known to come down for the coming-of-age rituals of young men, or to answer their questions, as he seems to be a guardian of adolescent boys. He will want a male horse, and male attendants.

Freya

Freya's colors are usually green and gold, occasionally red if she is coming in her love goddess aspect (although she likes green and gold for that too) and crimson or occasionally white with armor and sword for her warrior aspect. She enjoys lovely gowns, prefers having both a cloak and a fan (for comfort), and as one spirit-worker put it, "as much jewelry as the horse can stand to wear".

Freya likes candies, especially candied fruits, honey, butterscotch, caramel, Lambec and other fruit beers, and sweet wine or brandies. If you make her a cake, mark it with a Gyfu-rune; put Fehu on bread for her. She likes pork, as do all the Vanir. She prefers a female or at least female-identified horse, but will also work with very feminine men who will do drag. Her attendants can be of either gender so long as they are willing to make themselves attractive, gaze adoringly, and accept any flirting that she may do. Both she and her brother Frey seem to be fond of gay or bisexual men when they choose male attendants. Freya is very flirtatious, and like her brother she may choose someone willing and eager, and go off with them to a bedroom. If she comes in her warrior aspect, she will be cooler and not do those behaviors, although she will still want the attractive attendants around.

When Freya comes in her Seidhkona aspect (preferring earthier tones of clothing such as brown or dark green), she is much more blunt and serious, and as one spirit-worker put it, "the thoughts that pass through the Horse's head may be vicious or frightening. It's not that She's bad, but She's totally unfazed by the prospect of doing what is necessary, magically or physically, to solve the problem in front of Her. Usually Her viciously practical solutions prove unnecessary simply because it is clear that She's not bluffing." They also comment: "We have noticed a tendency for the name "Mardoll" to signify Freya as Njord's daughter, a younger, maiden path, or the aspect of Freya who has searched the seas for Od. It is this path that Njord particularly dotes on, and gently guards."

Nerthus and Njord

Nerthus and Njord have arrived both together and separately. Nerthus likes a female horse, and she prefers "beer that drinks like a meal"—thick rich stout. She is always veiled, because anyone besides a Vanir priest/ess who sees her face must be killed. Make her attendants female. One spirit-worker commented that: "Nerthus seems to be very much a Vanaheim Farm Wife—practical, and blunt, cheerful, mothering, capable of being primal, but tends to consider that private, and not terribly fond of clothing that gets in Her way, except for the veil."

Njord prefers a masculine horse and is especially fond of rum, champagne and port wines from seacoast areas, and salmon baked in a salt dome. He likes blues and whites, sea colors. One Njordsman that I met who horses his patron wears a particular classic ivory cable-knit sweater and a blue fisherman's cap as his Njord gear. (He has been amused and pleased by being respectfully addressed as "Captain", by folk who understand that he is a Sea-King.) If he can be invoked near the seaside, that's even better. His attendants can be any gender, but they should be useful and practical, and if they know something about ships or are interested in sailing, that's even more of a bonus.

Frey

Frey is fairly easy-going, but he likes to have food present. Make it homemade food, especially with bread, and ingredients as natural and organic as possible. If you can do it, locally grown or homegrown food is best. If you serve him meat, make sure that it is organic meat, preferably humanely raised and killed at a local farm. He isn't vegetarian by any means, but he seems offended by much of modern agribusiness, especially poorly farmed animals, but also poorly farmed plants as well. As the Ing/John Barleycorn figure of the Vanir, the proper care of one's crops is important to him. Don't give him food that has been chemically poisoned, if you can help it. Serve him beer—not corporate beer, but homebrew or a local craft brew. (He will drink a goodly amount of beer, not get drunk, and take it all with him when he goes, leaving the horse no worse for wear.) Cherries are sacred to him, if you can get them in season, and any bread or grain dish will do as well. If you make homemade bread, mark it with an Ing-rune.

If you make clothing for him, Frey prefers linen (it's a plant fiber) or cotton, in shades of yellow, gold, and green. He likes having a crown of wheat/barley, or leaves. No one should approach him bearing weapons, even a belt knife, so the steward should make sure that people who come up to him are unarmed. Frey will usually sit in one place, glowing and smiling, and will motion to people and call them over, or take them as they come. Pages can be of either sex, so long as they are cheerful and happy to be there. Frey will horse men or women, so long as the latter are masculine. This is helped by them being willing to shapeshift to male astrally before he arrives, and in some cases willing to wear an enormous ritual phallus under their tunic. If you make him one (and men can do this as well; there is no natural male phallus that is big enough for him anyway) you can carve it out of wood, or—more comfortably—make it out of leather and stuff it with wool or cotton or linen.

As one of the most sexual deities in the Norse pantheon, Frey does like to have sex, and isn't picky about what gender it is. Anatomy is irrelevant; all that matters is willing enthusiasm. He will never hit on anyone who isn't willing and enthusiastic; he has no wish to make people feel uncomfortable in that way. If his wife Gerda is present (we have occasionally horsed both of them together) he has eyes only for her, and while he may smile or make a comment at someone, if he has sex it will only be with her. They have a tendency to act a bit like newlyweds together, feeding each other honey off of their fingers and such. Remember that they are always in love and are invoked for weddings, and this continual-newlywed behavior makes sense. If they are coming together, you might want to set up a bower for the two of them to retire to, if both horses are all right with that and have been prepared for it. They are both good at respecting physical boundaries and can handle safe sex (unlike some Gods who need some coaching). Even if Gerda doesn't come, you might want to set up a bower, as Frey might choose someone else. (For the record, Gerda is never jealous of this. It's part of his job, and something she loves about him. She, on the other hand, is entirely monogamous with him.)

If he is present with his sister Freya, which is another common pairing, do not be unnerved by the fact that they are extremely affectionate with each other. Yes, they do have a sexual relationship, although it is a ritual thing, done for fertility purposes to make the crops grow rather than his romantic relationship with Gerda or his share-the-wealth sexual attitude toward those who get blessed for an hour with his grand phallus. But people looking on may need to be warned.

There is one trick that Frey has been known to do to people who are in despair, and this is to gently blow on their forehead or chest, which he calls "blowing light into you". According to those who have been "blown" by Frey, this puts a little spark of light into you which can be called upon when all is dark and dismal around you, and which never fully goes out. If you concentrate on it, you can blow it up to a feeling of being a radiant light, no matter where you are. He will not do this for everyone; he's more likely to do it for people who are supposed to be light-bringers (as opposed to those who work with dark energies) and are temporarily depressed and unable to do their job.

Gerda

Gerda, Frey's etin-bride, is much quieter than her husband the Golden One. She doesn't like crowds much. Unless her husband is present, she won't come to a large gathering of people, and then she comes only to be with him. She will prefer to stay next to him, and they will generally eat off of the same plate. She is modest, preferring long gowns that cover from neck to wrists to floor, usually in dark brownish earth tones or greys or dusky purples, and likes having a veil that she can pull around her face if it is sunny. She speaks quietly and is serious and introverted. She likes having fresh-cut herbs on a table next to her, rather than flowers. She will eat anything that Frey eats, but is fond of root vegetables. Like all etins, she prefers the harder stuff when it comes to alcohol—someone once gave her Grey Goose vodka and that was enjoyed much.

The times when Gerda will show up on her own are when she is addressing a single person or a small group of people who need her aid or information. She has been called to do cleansing-rituals for women who have had abortions or miscarried, as she is their patron. If this is the situation, have the woman in question bathe first in salt water, probably with several herbs that Gerda will dictate. Have a tea of the same herbs ready for her to administer to the woman, with more salt water. Pages assigned to her should be female, and stay quietly in the background until needed.

While Gerda seems quiet and introverted, if you anger her, she will lash out verbally at you and flay you with her tongue. She is a giantess; remember that and be respectful. Don't touch her; if she chooses to touch you, allow it. (She will generally only touch women, and then only if they are in distress.) She is not interested in horsing anyone who is not female-bodied.

Heid

Heid, when riding a human body, comes across as a little old witchy woman, the sort who lives in the gingerbread house out in the forest. She prefers black, greyish-purple, and antique gold for her colors, and likes very peaty whisky—one comment was, "If it tastes like it ought to be labeled Old Bog Water, she'll like it." Heid usually only comes for a circle of seidworkers, in order to give them advice or training. She can horse men or women, but they should be older, middle-aged at the least. Her attendants should be seidworkers.

Skadi

Skadi rarely takes a mortal body, but if she does, dress the horse in furs, preferably white ones, and make sure that a bow and arrows are around. Serve her game meat, and ice wine or vodka from the freezer. Do not touch her, be very polite, and but don't grovel. She prefers people to stand strong while still be respectful and courteous. She wants a female-bodied horse; her attendants can be either gender so long as they are prepared to go haring off through the snows with her. She prefers to come during the winter, especially if you live in a cold area.

Hela

Hel or Hela, the Death Goddess, has a different sort of aura than most deities. While they glow and shine, she's more like a black hole, sucking in all the light. Live plants put next to her will wilt, and she actually seems to like feeding off of them, if they are willing to be sacrificed. If you want to give her such a gift, find a houseplant that's willing to die for her—there are many who would do this in her honor, surprisingly. She likes to be served tea—regular or herbal—or dark coffee. She will take alcohol, but seems to prefer something that's been brewed. Food is rarely important to her. She likes dried flowers, especially dried roses.

Lady Death likes to wear long, simple robes of black or shades of grey, and a black mantle around her, and usually a sheer black veil over her head. Some horses like to paint half their faces with a skull-mask in her honor. One of the things that she likes is to wear a ring on every joint of every finger of the left hand, in order to mimic the feel of hard bones. She may give her left hand to people to kiss. She never holds out her right hand to the living, only to those who have passed on, or are at the moment of dying a physical death.

Hela will horse women or third gender people or perhaps even occasionally men, but the latter two must agree to shapeshift astrally to female before she will come. She requires no pages at all, being very self-sufficient, but she has been known to appreciate them. Hela walks with a limp, slowly, is quiet, and extremely still. When she is speaking, her hands may move and gesture, but the rest of the time she is still as a statue when sitting (which she prefers to do) or standing. She especially liked my large black wicker fanback Morticia-type chair; she prefers to be enthroned. She speaks in a hoarse voice that someone characterized as "whiskey-and-cigarettes", says little, but it's very direct and to the point.

If she grips someone's hand or arm in order to say something important to them, her touch has been known to burn flesh.

One of the things that Hela often comes to do is to help with ordeal rituals. She can work with modern medical items—sutures, alcohol pads, needles, scalpels—and understands sterile procedure, probably better than most NT deities. Have everything she needs there for her in advance if she's going to do any kind of work—she will be clear about what she wants, even if she wakes you from a sound sleep at 3 a.m. in order to dictate a list. She likes things laid out neatly for her, so she won't have to hunt around for tools. She will never suddenly decide to be sexual with someone; the kind of sex that she likes to have is ordeal-oriented (meaning that she'll be causing them pain) and it is always arranged ahead of time if it's going to happen at all. Hela doesn't like surprises and is never capricious.

Loki

Loki the Trickster is a hard ride to handle. First of all, he may do things to the horse that the horse doesn't expect or like. (This is where it is important to have a horse with a patron deity to set limits and look out for their best interests, or else someone who belongs to Loki and expects this sort of thing.) Second, he may not stick to the agreed-upon rules regarding the event. Third, he tends to want to stir things up—for example, none of the other Gods would hit sexually on anyone who wasn't already open to the idea, but Loki might go hit on a straight guy while in a male body just for the entertainment value. People present at a Loki horsing should all be well aware of the situation and ready to roll with the punches, or things can go very wrong.

Loki will horse men, women, and third gender people happily, although he prefers to have sex in a body with a working natural phallus. He will eat fast food, junk food, candy, booze (especially spicy food and booze with cinnamon or red pepper in it) and likes to have a table full of weird toys that he can play with, the weirder the better. He has been known to bless whisky and tell people to add it to their bath water or pour it over themselves in the tub, which is at least kinder than the Afro-Caribbean trickster spirits who will spit rum on people.

Any page assigned to Loki has to have a wacky sense of humor, not be easily upset or offended, and willing to give him their full attention and be a sort of "chew toy", as one spirit-worker referred to the job. Make sure that they know that it's not their job to prevent him from doing ill-advised things, except as a matter of self-protection. Getting in Loki's way is the dangerous job of the priest/ess, who should be another spirit-worker with a good enough relationship with Loki to be able to make noise, or perhaps one of Hela's who can call in his daughter to ride herd on him (something that actually works sometimes).

In general, though, it's not about confrontation as much as redirection and distraction. Loki has a short attention span and this can be exploited, although don't think he doesn't know what you're doing. Nobody ever gets one over on Flame-Hair. If he goes along with it, it's because he feels generous or thinks that it's worth it to him, perhaps for the new toy, or the entertainment value of watching people jump to distract him with new toys.

Estara T'Shirai comments that: "Loki is not a great respecter of formal ritual, and if He is present during parts of that process, He will make His own ... um ... improvements. (He's fantastic at off-the-cuff doggerel, actually.) If you've actually invited Him there—this goes for all of Them, really, but Him in particular—then everyone had better be prepared to make Him the center of attention, and not foolishly avert their focus elsewhere for as long as He's present."

Angrboda

The Hag of the Iron Wood prefers to horse someone female-bodied, but not just anyone. She likes women who are tall, strong, and physically fit, or who are older and have authority regardless of their bodies. What she doesn't like is someone young and/or weak and delicate. She is very much a giantess, and moves confidently and takes large strides. She does not like clothing that is confining to her movements; if you put her in a ceremonial robe, make sure that it is easy to move in and doesn't drag on the floor. She actually tends to prefer tunics and pants, ideally made of leather, and likes things with animal skins on them. She is a warrior as well as a sorceress, so make sure that she has a sword or at least a belt knife. She'll eat with a large knife, too. If you can find them, flint knives are best for all the Rökkr, as they are more Neolithic.

Angrboda likes to be served meat, and she's not picky as to what sort, although game is the absolute best. She likes hard liquor and homebrew, even moonshine. She is forthright and loud and claps people on the shoulder and such. She has no patience for whiners, although she will be kind to the strange and deformed.

Although it is rare, Angrboda may pick out a man who is interested in her and take him off to have a roll in the bushes. She is interested in stamina, stamina, stamina, and prefers to be on top, so be warned. If she chooses a woman (even rarer) it will be not for recreation but to teach her something about Jotun women's sex magic. Her pages can be any gender so long as they are strong and armed; she especially likes people with animal-spirit natures or alliances.

Sigyn

Sigyn may come in one of two ways—as the child bride, or as the adult woman who has been through Loki's imprisonment. For the first type of horsing, dress the (female) horse in flowing dresses of lavender and pink, and lay out dolls and toys and cake. (One Sigynswoman swears that she likes macaroni and cheese.) For the latter face of Sigyn, dress her in browns and give her bread and butter, and fresh milk if you have it.

Fenris's Lesson
Extremity

I have met the Great Wolf many times, and always he brings tears to my eyes, if only for a moment. And this is good, because the next thing he does is to call to my Iron Wood blood—blood calling to blood, whether I will or no—and I have to use all my strength not to shapeshift, not to release the predator within me, who is pounding himself against the bars howling at the presence of his God. Weeping is good. Weeping keeps me human.

Fenris's lesson, like that of Nidhogg and Jormundgand, I write in poetry, but for different reasons. With the Great Snake, the lack of real language makes the poetry the best vehicle for explaining the rush of wordless imagery, and the Dragon's words came out half-word, half-image, for a naturally poetic feel. Fenris, on the other hand, I translate to poetry to buffer the raw red rush of his words, and the anger in them, from you, the reader. If you want to experience that much rage, bloodlust, and the sacred force of Nature's destruction, go speak to the Chained One yourself ... but remember that the experience probably won't be anything like what you expect.

Although I have written about my first meeting with Fenris in "Pathwalker's Guide to the Nine Worlds", I cannot count the number of times that I have come close to him since—hearing him suddenly speak to me out of nowhere, his voice rough and harsh, or seeing him horsed by chained volunteers. Why do we horse him? To feed him, as gift and offering and tribute. Especially for those of us with Jotun blood, who must keep our own wild natures in check constantly, the offering is deeply important. He feeds on the voluntarily-given pain of the horse, which we aid in creating; he feeds on blood and freshly killed meat; he feeds on our fear. We give this to him, because we care, because we understand, because we see him as that which is chained that we may go free.

There are no songs to invoke Fenris. Just howling. If he desires it, he may answer you—or not. If you come to the point of extremity where you require his aid—to help you survive some terrible torment with your soul unbroken—you will likely be in no condition to sing anyhow. In fact, if you can still form words, you should call on a different deity. Fenris is the God of Last Resort, when all is lost to your tormentors save for the last kernel of your soul.

Fenris's Lesson

What would you die for?
What would you starve for?
What would you crawl across broken glass
Rather than give up? For what would you
Suffer torture, imprisonment, pain
And never entertain the thought of giving in?
Where is that part of you,
Buried deep within the will to survive,
That cannot bend and will not break?
Where is the part of you that you cannot change
And still be yourself, still be
Anything worth being? What would you
Suffer for that final outpost of self?
Have you ever met that Self?

For if you have none, if there is
No final outpost for you that cannot be
Run over, changed, shaped, made safe
For others' comfort, then you are
Prey. Go back to your herd and huddle.
Look admiringly or fearfully at those
With that hard core of Self; you are soft
And therefore disposable. Remember that
When the dogs who guard you
From the likes of me and mine
Show that they are indeed cousins,
Not so far off; their teeth are
Very like mine, especially when bared at you.
Remember that you are their Prey as well,
That they have merely chosen not to eat
Today. What would you never give up?

FENRIS'S LESSON

If there is nothing, go home and do not
Do this work. For when you find that point,
If you have it, you find Me there,
And all that I am, teeth, slaver, claws,
Rivers of blood, lust for flesh, howls of pain,
Chains, stone walls, everything. Either I lie
At the root of your soul, or no matter what your
Fancy words and foolish bluster,
You are Prey. Go home and huddle,
For if I am not within you, I will one day be
At your window, or your door.
One or the other, you choose, or be chosen.
What would you suffer to be your Self?

The chains gall,
But there is no compromise,
Ever.
To be other than who I am …
How could I let a soulless magic
With the name of Deceiver
Win over me, my will, my magnificent
Screaming future? How could you?
I lie on my side, drooling scarlet,
And await the world's End.

Afterword: Half-Life

by Elizabeth Vongvisith
for her patron deity

In the years before you came to me,
it was all smog, the dull thud of heels
on city pavement, long store lines and
direct deposit paychecks, commercials,
magazines, the whistle of a train late
after midnight on the bad side of town.
It was all about getting the phone in time
and making calls for the boss, bouncing
checks, rain on the windshield, tires
blown out and *sorry, miss, that'll be
four hundred and eighty two dollars,*
then the rent paid a few more days late.
It was eating mini egg rolls at midnight
on weekends, drinking in bars, loading
laundry and strangers on the street ignoring
as I walked by, phone bills, TV screens
babbling impotently in store windows.
It was politics, a strangling need for love, the
uncertain feeling that maybe, if there was

more to life than all this, now wasn't going
to be the time when I found that out
for myself, for once and for all.

I led the usual half-life, tinged by the sense
that nothing was really what it seemed, but
as I reached out to prod the barrier, there was
only its soft give, then no more – like a tent
sheltering campers from the wilderness,
and me sewn inside, insulated from the world's
intractable muck and mess and danger.
I was asleep all the time while other people
nodded and said, *yes, this is what life is,
this is life: work, love, parenthood, death.
That is the beginning and the end, the
starting line-up and the final score,
the theme music and closing credits.*
I believed them, or I told myself I did,
despite that deep suspicion inside that
we were all only asleep and dreaming.

You happened in a thunderclap, wrenching me
like an abused cat from a kennel, ignoring
my hisses and howls, and you held me up
blinking in the diffused light, confused
by the tearing away of those barriers
to show me the world beyond that prison,
beyond my five senses, beyond the fear
which we use to keep the darkness away.
I saw for the first time that the mad gleam
in the eyes of a stranger was something
living inside that wasn't him, and I heard
the voices of the woods over and above
the hum of escalators, dead wood whispering

of when the forest had never been seen
with mortal men's eyes. I heard the dead giants
under concrete and asphalt, and the laugh
of a changeling lurking in the alley behind
two ordinary trash cans, pockets bulging
with the detritus of forsaken knowledge.
The *Wall Street Journal* hid the scoundrel's face,
but not until you showed me did I see the eyes
of a being older than money reckons itself.
Now I walk in two places at once, seeing
both the living reality and the dead one above,
like straddling lanes on a freeway with no exits.

Since you peeled away the world as I knew it
to show me the world as it really is, maybe I
should resent you for it, you who led me
down a path from which there's no return,
no coming back, no resettlement in that place
of self-assured human ignorance. I should cry
or scream for the loss of my real innocence
and the impulses that now make me throw
blankets over mirrors in bedrooms, or look
on the ground for lost pennies, or listen intently
to what the birds say as they hurtle from edge
to edge of the dim pollution-saturated skies.
I should feel bitterer than I do, perhaps,
because the random words of a bag lady assume
a shape and significance far beyond the tragedy
I do not know of which put her in my path.

And I should hate you because you told me
of the fair folk in lands so far away, and of
love lost and remembered, and of lingering pain.
I should hate you for that most of all,

that ruthless stripping away of forgotten things
which had hardened over my soul, the way
scar tissue marks where one was once burned.

Yet you smile, and you settle beside me
in this moving car as the mountain-edged land
whizzes by, as I drive in the dark and think
that perhaps the comfort of a half-life grows
disproportionately nostalgic like childhood
or first love or any place where one has been
both happy and woefully stupid at the same time.
For if you were to make me unremember
this place that is not a place, and everything
I have come to see beneath the stolid grime
of the everyday, and you, my love, most of all,
I know some part of me would mourn and die.
I cannot choose to deny, but I can choose
to walk this haunted land with open eyes
and reclaim the other half of my life.

Printed in Dunstable, United Kingdom